Nationalist Heroines

Puerto Rican Women History Forgot,
1930s–1950s

Nationalist Heroines

Puerto Rican Women History Forgot, 1930s–1950s

By Olga Jiménez de Wagenheim

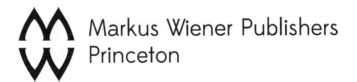

Markus Wiener Publishers
Princeton

For information, write to: Markus Wiener Publishers
231 Nassau Street, Princeton, NJ 08542
www.markuswiener.com

Photos: Centro de Investigaciones Historicas, Universidad de Puerto Rico, Coleccion Benjamin Torres, Serie: Fotografias.

Cover photo: Lolita Lebrón getting arrested in Washington, D.C. March 1, 1954.

Library of Congress Cataloging-in-Publication Data

Names: Wagenheim, Olga Jiménez de, author.
Title: Nationalist heroines : Puerto Rican women history forgot, 1930s-1950s / by Olga Jiménez de Wagenheim.
Description: Princeton : Markus Wiener Publishers, [2016]
Identifiers: LCCN 2016017723| ISBN 9781558766181 (hardcover : acid-free paper) | ISBN 9781558766198 (paperback : acid-free paper)
Subjects: LCSH: Women—Political activity—Puerto Rico—History—20th century. | Women political activists—Puerto Rico—Biography. | Nationalists—Puerto Rico—Biography. | Women heroes—Puerto Rico—Biography. | Nationalism—Puerto Rico—History—20th century. | Puerto Rico—Politics and government—20th century. | Puerto Rico—History—Autonomy and independence movements. | Puerto Rico—Colonial influence. | Puerto Rico—Relation—United States. | United States—Relations—Puerto Rico.
Classification: LCC HQ1236.5.P9 W35 2016 | DDC 320.082/097295—dc23
LC record available at https://lccn.loc.gov/2016017723

Markus Wiener Publishers books are printed in the United States of America on acid-free paper and meet the guidelines for permanence and durability of the Committee on Production Guidelines for Book Longevity of the Council on Library Resources.

Contents

For Kal, David, and María

Preface

The idea for this book emerged in the spring of 1998, shortly after I sent to press a book on Puerto Rico's colonial history under Spain. Having also written a book on the Lares uprising of 1868, I thought I would explore the topic of Puerto Rico's struggle for independence in the twentieth century. Miñi Seijo, *Claridad*'s indefatigable reporter, had written a book-length account of the Nationalist uprising of 1950, but her work focused almost exclusively on the male leadership and that gave me the idea to do a study about the women in the movement.

During a casual conversation with one of the archivists at the Puerto Rico General Archives, I learned that two of the women sentenced to prison for their roles in the uprising of 1950 were alive and might be persuaded to tell their stories. Still unsure about the direction of the project, I contacted Isabel Rosado Morales and Carmen María (Carmín) Pérez González in hopes that they might agree to be interviewed. In the meantime, I discussed the idea of studying the women involved in the Nationalist events of 1950 with historian Ivonne Acosta Lespier, whose work I admired. She was very encouraging and gave me copies of two accounts written by Doris Torresola and Carmín Pérez about "the tortures" they had witnessed or experienced during their imprisonment in San Juan's District jail in 1951.

Both Rosado and Pérez agreed to the interviews but could not see me for several months, so I spent the time doing background research in order to know what questions to ask. Having also trained as an oral historian, I decided to ask them about their lives before and after they joined the Nationalist movement. Oral histories are time consuming and are best done in peaceful, relaxed settings. This was not always possible in some cases.

For example, the day Isabel Rosado agreed to see me I was without a car and had to enlist my sister Lolin to drive me from San Juan to Ceiba, a trip that took about an hour and a half each way. Minutes after we arrived at Isabel's tiny house, a work crew, armed with a jackhammer, began drilling part of the sidewalk across from her living-room door. Undeterred by the deafening noise, Isabel signaled that we should move to the kitchen, a few feet away. I followed her with a tape recorder and other tools of the trade and just when we were getting started a rooster on the other side of the kitchen wall began to crow at precisely timed intervals.

Determined to get the job done, she suggested that we should speak louder. So, between the screeching of the jackhammer at one end and the rooster's crowing at the other we talked for several hours. Isabel was ninety-one years old at the time but showed no sign of fatigue. She was funny and full of life during the interview and even offered to make us lunch after we finished the session. Lolin and I later commented how admirable it was that Doña Isabel was still so full of love for humanity after spending so many years in prison.

In addition to Rosado and Pérez, I interviewed three other Nationalist women that spring, though not all had been arrested for the Nationalist events of 1950 or 1954. Among them were the Collazo half-sisters Lydia (Rosa Collazo's daughter) and Carmen Zoraida (Oscar Collazo's daughter). They described their parents' roles in the 1950s' Nationalist events and their contributions to the struggle for independence. Both also commented on their own involvement in the Nationalist movement at various times.

During that period, I also interviewed Juanita González Bouillerce, who had been active in the Nationalist Party chapter in Río Piedras prior to the uprising. According to her account, she was detained after the uprising but was released shortly after she was interrogated by District Attorney Angel Viera Martínez. She claimed the interrogator found no grounds to hold her. Unable to locate the text of her interrogation or any evidence to substantiate the reasons for her release, I opted to leave her out of the project because by then, I had made the decision to focus mainly on the women who had been sentenced to prison.

I returned to teaching that fall (1998) and shortly thereafter became involved in the co-creation of an archival research center at the Newark Public Library, whose purpose is to document the history of the Latino community of New Jersey. Over the next thirteen years, I helped to raise funds for the establishment of that center and also oversaw a research project that documented the history of four Latino communities in New Jersey. These activities kept me busy until the summer of 2013. Then the deaths of Carmen María Pérez, Lolita Lebrón, and Isabel Rosado, the last female survivors of the 1950s' Nationalist events, reminded me that I owed them and others the courtesy of telling at least one version of their stories.

The plaque honoring the Nationalist women is located in Mayaguez, Puerto Rico.

Acknowledgments

A book about any group of individuals is very hard to do without help from others. Mine would still be unfinished had it not been for the generous spirit of many, starting with the five women who consented to be interviewed. Their devotion to the cause of independence and their willingness to sacrifice their own freedom for their political beliefs are what ultimately motivated me to write this book.

The research work I needed to tell my version of their stories was made possible by the work of many journalists and government bureaucrats who documented the 1950s' events as they unfolded. Their accounts amount to thousands of documents, including police files, government correspondence, and prison records safely guarded at the Puerto Rico General Archives. I wish to thank the dedicated staff of the Archives for their help and guidance. I am also indebted to the archivist Miledys Sánchez at the Puerto Rico Legislative Library who made available dozens of declassified FBI files on the Puerto Rican Nationalists.

I also wish to extend my gratitude to Attorney David Noriega and his group for pressuring the Puerto Rican government, through a decade of legal suits and injunctions, to release the police files and other documents it had kept under lock and key for nearly four decades.

In addition to the individuals mentioned, I wish to thank Francis Mojica, librarian at the Centro de Estudios Avanzados de Puerto Rico y el Caribe (CEA), for his generous help in locating two graduate students, whose masters theses he thought would be of help to my work: one of them on Lolita Lebrón, written by Ivonne Marín Burgos, and the other on Doris Torresola, written by Janet Martínez González. Assistant researcher Raúl Romero Torres obtained the master thesis of Sandra Morales Blanes, another graduate student of the CEA, who traced the participation of Puerto Rican women in the Nationalist Party in Puerto Rico and New York (1941–1951). All three women also donated a copy of their work to the Puerto Rican Community Archives at the Newark Public Library. I thank them for their generosity. I also wish to thank

Gervasio Morales, director of *Claridad*, for granting me permission to make use of Miñi Seijo's 1979 interviews with Lolita Lebrón and others that she conducted over many years.

My friend Amílcar Tirado helped me to track down a few articles published in Puerto Rico following the death of Carmen María Pérez. He had earlier helped me find two research assistants, Nahomi Galindo and Raúl Romero Torres. They in turn sent me copies of dozens of newspaper articles on various topics related to women I was documenting. I am grateful to them for making my task less arduous.

Thanks also to the staff at the Archives of the Center for Puerto Rican Studies at Hunter College for making available the transcripts of Ruth Mary Reynolds' interviews conducted by Blanca Vázquez, and for xeroxing hundreds of pages from the "Ruth Reynolds Papers" and other collections I did not have time to read during the two summers I worked there. In particular, I wish to recognize the valuable guidance provided by Center archivist Pedro Juan Hernández.

Friends and acquaintances helped in many ways. Activist Margaret Randall granted me permission to use the text of an interview she conducted in Cuba (circa 1978) with the exiled Nationalist Dominga de la Cruz. Researcher and scholar Félix Ojeda Reyes helped me to contact Professor Vivian Quiles Calderín, past director of the Instituto de Estudios Hostosianos. She in turn authorized me to translate and quote extensively from Blanca Canales' testimony, which the Comité Hostosiano had published years earlier. Professors María Josefa Canino and Norma Rodríguez Roldán sent me copies of articles following the death of Isabel Rosado and a hard-to-find article by the legal scholar David Helfeld on the issue of civil rights violations in Puerto Rico during the 1950s.

Many thanks also to Professors Virginia Sánchez Korrol and Elizabeth Hull for their comments on the chapters on Leonides Díaz and Ruth Mary Reynolds. Thank you also to Professors Ivonne Acosta Lespier and Asunción Lavrin for their willingness to read and comment on various chapters. I am also very grateful to Craig Leisher for taking time from his busy schedule to copyedit the manuscript.

Lastly, I want to thank my husband, Kal Wagenheim, for reading every chapter, more than once, and for his help with the translations from Spanish to English of the five interviews that originally led me to undertake this project. I am responsible for any undetected errors.

Introduction

Nationalists Take Up Arms, 1950, 1954

On October 30, 1950, fewer than two hundred members of the Puerto Rican Nationalist Party (PRNP) rose against U.S. colonial rule in various cities and towns throughout the island of Puerto Rico, leaving behind numerous casualties.[1] The main targets of the insurgents outside the capital, San Juan, were the local police stations, the military recruitment centers, and U.S. post offices. Nearly two-dozen rebels were killed or wounded, and hundreds were captured by the National Guard, activated for the occasion. In San Juan, the rebels' target was La Fortaleza, where a commando unit of five arrived at noon on October 30, 1950, intent on killing Puerto Rico's first elected governor, Luis Muñoz Marín. Four of the five attackers were killed by the Governor's guards before they could enter the residence. The lone survivor in that group was captured alive, though riddled with bullets.[2]

One week after the uprising ended, more than one thousand persons, among them forty-one women, were detained on suspicion that they had supported the insurgency.[3] Most of the detainees, however, were released a week and a half later for lack of evidence. The culprits and some innocent individuals were indicted, tried, and sentenced to long prison terms.

Two days after the Nationalists rose up in arms in Puerto Rico, two of their comrades in New York City, Griselio Torresola and Oscar Collazo, traveled to Washington, D.C., determined to kill President Harry S. Truman, then staying at Blair House, his temporary residence. The attackers failed in their attempt and Torresola was killed by the White House guard, while Collazo was badly wounded and taken to a local hospital. He was later convicted and sentenced to death for his crime. Two years later, his death sentence was commuted to life in prison by President Truman, ostensibly in response to thousands of requests for clemency he had received from various groups.[4]

1

Then in March 1954, Dolores (Lolita) Lebrón and three male companions, all members of the New York City Nationalist Junta, led an armed attack against the House of Representatives of the U.S. Congress, wounding five congressmen. All four attackers were captured alive and unhurt and later convicted of numerous crimes and sentenced to prison terms, ranging from fifty to seventy-five years.[5]

Though no connection was found between the attackers of Congress and the Nationalists in Puerto Rico, the local authorities used the opportunity to order another wave of arrests. Thirty-eight persons were detained, including eleven Communists, on the premise that they had violated either the federal Smith Act or its local equivalent, Law #53, because they "belonged" to political groups proscribed by both statutes. Of the thirty-eight detained, eight were women, two Communists, and six Nationalists. Most of the Nationalists (including the six women) were indicted and later convicted on conspiracy charges and other crimes and sentenced to prison for many years.[6]

A Brief Historical Context

In order to understand the forces that propelled the Nationalists to take such drastic actions, and the local government to react as it did, it is necessary to provide a brief historical account of the island's colonization and the struggles for control of its destiny by various local groups.

Until the United States seized Puerto Rico in 1898 and set up its unique form of colonial rule, local political aspirants were subdivided into two camps: one which engaged in negotiation as the means to obtain concessions from the imperial power, and a minority which resorted to armed struggle in its attempt to liberate the island from colonial bondage. After the United States seized the island, the number of political factions increased and the struggle between them intensified as they sought to resolve the island's colonial status. During the first decade and half of American rule, the majority of leaders favored the idea of annexing Puerto Rico to the American Union, while a minority continued to favor independence.

Women were always active in the various political struggles. In this study I will focus on sixteen women, fifteen of whom were sentenced to prison for their participation (real or alleged) in the armed struggles unleashed by the Nationalists in their quest to liberate Puerto Rico from the United States. The Nationalists traced their liberation struggle to the nineteenth century.

Puerto Rico as a Spanish Colony

By the time the United States occupied Puerto Rico on July 25, 1898, the island had been a colony of Spain for nearly four hundred years. During the first three centuries of Spanish rule, the island remained sparsely populated (with 45,000 inhabitants in 1765) and its economy had barely been tapped. The few thousand people who inhabited the place survived primarily on subsistence farming and contraband trade with Spain's rivals. Those colonial conditions, however, began to change during the last third of the eighteenth century when a Bourbon Dynasty rose to power in Spain and began implanting a series of reforms in hopes of strengthening the Crown's control over the empire. In Latin America, the belated reforms provoked the Creoles to fight for and win their independence (1808–1825).

In Puerto Rico, on the contrary, the Bourbon reforms helped to set the stage for a "new" colonization and a belated development of an agrarian export economy. To make the island productive, influxes of people and capital were needed and the Crown offered land grants and a few tax exemptions to prospective settlers. Over the next four decades, thousands of persons from war-torn Haiti (then known as Saint Domingue) and revolutionary Latin America fled to Puerto Rico, lured by the promise of free land, economic opportunity, and a place to rebuild their lives. Thousands of slaves were also introduced during this period. In exchange for the land grants and the temporary tax breaks, the Crown required the new settlers to cultivate the soil, pledge allegiance to the king, pay tithe to the Catholic Church, and commit to stay in Puerto Rico for a minimum of five years.[7]

Though the incentives proved short lived, thousands arrived in Puerto Rico during the next sixty years, so that by 1865 the island's population had grown to more than 600,000 inhabitants, including 34,000 slaves. A significant number of the recent immigrants came from various islands in the French and British Caribbean, Spain, and Latin America. Preference was generally given to prospective planters who had experience growing sugarcane, owned slaves, or had capital and/or lines of credit which would enable them to begin cultivating their plots at once. But since food crops and manual labor were also needed to help develop the sugar plantations and feed the growing population, smaller land grants were also awarded to free blacks fleeing social unrest in the French and British Caribbean islands, where the slave trade and then slavery itself were abolished between 1807 and the mid-nineteenth century.[8]

The number of acres awarded to an incoming settler depended on various factors, including the number of workers (slave and free) to which the applicant had access. While the land grants and tax incentives lasted, they helped to encourage cultivation of large tracts along the coastal plains and to develop a relatively successful sugarcane industry. The economic prosperity produced by sugar exports lasted roughly until the 1850s, when the industry began to sag, in part because of declining prices and competition from beet sugar.

From the 1840s to the 1860s, new waves of immigrants from French Corsica, the Spanish Mediterranean, and the Canary Islands also arrived in Puerto Rico hoping to rebuild their lives, though land grants and tax exemptions were no longer promised. By the time the latter newcomers arrived, the best coastal lands had been awarded to or purchased by sugar growers and a few cattle ranchers, and that forced those interested in farming to move inland into the mountainous interior. There, they soon ran into competition with older settlers (later known as Creoles) who had moved inland either trying to escape the arm of the colonial government or the displacement caused by the expansion of the sugar farms along the coast.[9]

Over time, dozens of newcomers acquired small- and medium-sized plots and devoted their capital and energies to growing coffee for export. Those with access to the smaller plots tended to grow coffee as well as food crops and were thus not entirely dependent on wages for their survival. That situation would begin to change after 1849, when those without title to their plots were forced by a new colonial law to register as *jornaleros* "wage laborers", to carry a work document (a *libreta*) which attested to their status, and required them to work for the planters in the region plus a few days a month on public projects. The landless resisted the legal restrictions by attaching themselves to neighboring farms as sharecroppers or tenant farmers. The newly arrived Spaniards fared better than most. Those with contacts in the world of trade in Spain engaged in wholesale or retail commerce and controlled Puerto Rico's exports and imports. They also provided loans to local farmers, at usurious rates, and generally took their farms as collateral. Since they also set a low price for the crop long before it was harvested, growers had a hard time staying out of debt. A few Spaniards invested in coffee farms and hired day laborers to work them.[10]

The harsher labor policies implanted by the government in the late 1840s and the growing dependence on the Spanish merchants fueled tensions between the two groups. The Lares uprising of the 1860s and the armed attacks of the partidas sediciosas in the 1890s reflect some of the growing tensions between the two camps. Conditions were apparently more amicable between the Creoles and foreign immigrants, especially as the influx of these groups dwindled and those already there adjusted to the island's ways. In fact, within a generation or so the children of the transplanted immigrants began calling themselves *puertorriqueños*. The newfound national identity, in turn, led the most ambitious among them to feel they, too, had a right to play a role in shaping the island's destiny.[11]

For example, during the first half of the nineteenth century, while the emerging elite remained small and unsure of its strength, it resorted to petitioning the Spanish Crown for economic reforms. To that end its leading members periodically sent delegations to Spain. The first, sent in 1809, was led by Ramón Power y Giralt, the son of an immigrant sugar planter. Though Power y Giralt died in Cadiz in 1813, as a result of a plague, his delegation succeeded in extracting a few reforms from the beleaguered Spanish Cortes, which had been forced to flee Madrid in 1808 as French troops occupied Spain. During the next two and half decades, Spain was embroiled in various wars with its Latin American colonies. Hence, it is not surprising to find the Spanish ministers (and later the restored monarch, King Ferdinand VII) better disposed to granting Puerto Rico a few concessions during the period Latin America was at war.[12]

By contrast, other delegations sent by Puerto Rico over the next five decades were hardly ever successful, though the Crown always promised it would consider their petitions at a later time. When a delegation sent by Puerto Rico in 1867 again came back empty-handed, a group of disgruntled Creoles in the island's western interior took up arms in the town of Lares (September 23, 1868), calling for independence, the abolition of slavery, and the end of the *libreta* system (the coercive labor system cited earlier).[13]

The brain behind the uprising, later known as "El Grito de Lares," was Ramón Emeterio Betances, a French-trained physician who had been evicted from Puerto Rico in 1867 (along with six others) for his radical political views. By 1868 Betances, the offspring of a racially mixed immigrant family from Mayagüez, was also known for his practice of offering medical services (often free of charge) to the poor inhabitants of that city and for having raised funds among his friends to purchase the freedom of several slaves. By the time he was evicted from Puerto Rico, he had contacts among other Caribbean rebels who presumably supported his plan to liberate Puerto Rico and free its enslaved population (then totaling around 34,000 persons). (Already in 1804, Haiti had liberated itself from French colonialism and emancipated its slaves; it also had seized the neighboring Dominican Republic and liberated its slaves.) During Betances' forced thirty-year exile, he maintained close ties with Cuba's revolutionary leaders (some of them residing in New York City) and supported Cuba's struggle for independence (in hopes they would collaborate with Puerto Rico's liberation struggle). He also supported the idea of creating a Pan-Antillean Federation as a way to protect the region's independence.[14]

The Lares uprising, as I noted in an earlier study, failed to liberate Puerto Rico from Spain. The reasons for the failed attempt are many, but may be summarized as follows: the rebels were poorly armed and lacked military training; the outside help Betances had promised them (a ship, weapons, and mercenary soldiers) did not arrive when needed, in part because the colonial rulers uncovered the plot days before the rebels were due to strike, and alerted the colonial authorities in Saint Thomas to seize the rebel ship and order Betances' arrest; and most important because the rebels did not have support from the island's leading families. Though a few immigrant landowners joined the rebel cause, they failed to make a difference. In general, the majority of them and other leading families elected to protect their economic interests, which for the moment were still being served by Spain.[15]

Unaware that Betances was on the run, the rebels took to the hills to await his arrival. Within days, all but twenty of those who had stormed Lares were apprehended by the Spanish troops and locked up in various penal facilities. Since there were not enough jails to accommodate the 545 arrested, many had to be confined in makeshift prisons. Conditions in all of these places were appalling, and within months, eighty men had died, most of them before they were deposed by the lone itinerant judge assigned to investigate the case. Overcrowding, terrible sanitary conditions, yellow fever, and lack of food were blamed for their deaths. As the judge assigned to the case explained in one of his letters to the governor, the island's penal system was simply not equipped to handle the challenges of the massive incarceration.[16]

The challenges of the incarcerated, however, were swiftly resolved in January 1869 when more than 450 rebels, the majority not yet processed, were pardoned and released by the incoming governor. Two factors contributed to the unusually generous amnesty: the rise to power of a revolutionary junta in Madrid (which had just deposed the monarchy and established Spain's first republic), and mounting pleas from various local groups, including several labor-starved planters, who claimed they would lose their crops if the rebels remained in jail much longer. Fear of antagonizing the top tier of Puerto Rican society (at a time when Cuba had begun its first war of independence, 1868–1878) probably contributed to the Spanish ministers' merciful attitude toward the Lares' rebels.

The Reformists Achieve Self-Government, 1897

Though the majority of the Creole leaders rejected armed struggle as a means to achieve their goals, they were not averse to using the threat of it during their negotiations with Spain. The fact that Betances and his followers (spread out as they were among Puerto Rico, France, New York City, and Cuba) continued to support armed struggle as the most expedient means to liberate Puerto Rico, paradoxically also helped their liberal compatriots to extract important reforms from Spain. The fact that twenty or more of the Lares rebels had joined Cuba's second war of independence (1895–1898) in exchange for Cuba's help to free Puerto Rico, probably also helped to motivate the Spanish ministers to listen to the proposal being presented by the Puerto Rican delegation (1897), led by Luis Muñoz Rivera. Awareness of the island's renewed strategic importance as Cuba launched into its second war with Spain (1895–1898) emboldened the Puerto Rican delegates to ask for political concessions that would permit them to rule the colony within the framework of the Spanish government. They had evolved to this position gradually.

For example, during the early 1870s, while Spain enjoyed its first republican government, it had allowed the literate males in Puerto Rico to organize their first political parties. The leading Creoles founded the Liberal Party whose chief goal was to have Puerto Rico declared a "province" of Spain, with the same rights and duties enjoyed by peninsular Spaniards. But when the Spanish republic fell in 1874 and the monarchy was restored, that plan had to be shelved as the island was once again ruled by a series of despotic governors. But having tasted a bit of freedom during the more enlightened republican Spain, the Puerto Rican elite opted to reformulate its plan and begin its quest for self-government. To that end the leading members of this group met in Ponce (Puerto Rico's second major city) in 1887 and founded the *Partido Autonómico* "Autonomic Party". If Puerto Rico would not be accepted as a province of Spain, they reasoned, perhaps it was time to demand autonomy so they could govern the island themselves while remaining within the framework of the Spanish government. (A half century later Muñoz Rivera's son, Luis Muñoz Marín, would propose a similar plan to the U.S. Congress.)[17]

The colonial rulers on the island reacted badly to the idea and had a few of the autonomist leaders jailed in El Morro castle and several of their followers tortured. But after the United States joined Cuba in its war against Spain, the Puerto Rican reformists sent a delegation to Madrid to demand political changes. Hoping to retain at least one of its two remaining New World colonies, the Spanish ministers acquiesced and granted Puerto Rico self-government via the Autonomic Charter of 1897.

Delighted with their achievement, the delegates returned home, eager to set up the structures of self-government. At last, after a struggle of ninety years, they and other members of their class would be able to run the affairs of the island. It is hard to know what kind of rulers they would have made, given their conservative views in terms of labor, race, and gender. It is known that by the time the Americans invaded, labor had become a pressing issue and several labor organizers had been imprisoned. Santiago Iglesias, the best-known leader of the group, was released from prison by the Americans (a gesture that endeared the newcomers with the laboring classes).[18]

Puerto Rico as an American Colony

The Autonomists' long-coveted prize of self-government, extracted after years of patient negotiations, an uprising, and other forms of colonial resistance, was lost less than a year after it was secured. The local rulers had barely begun setting up the structures of government when a few thousand American troops landed in the southern port of Guánica on July 25, 1898, and rapidly occupied the island's southwestern region. The land troops had been preceded by a naval bombardment of San Juan the previous May as a form of testing the protective capacity of the Spaniards on the island. The idea of landing ground troops, according to a few expansionists in Washington, D.C., was to lay a solid claim to Puerto Rico before a truce was declared the following August. Military presence on the island, the same expansionists argued, would help to smooth the peace negotiations later.[19]

The invaders encountered little resistance in Puerto Rico, in part because the Spanish military force left to protect the island was understaffed and poorly equipped, and partly because the islanders did not come to Spain's defense as they had done multiple times in earlier centuries. The few Creoles who took up arms, according to a leading historian, did so in order to "settle old scores" with the Spaniards rather than to resist the invaders. (This point has been contested by a few advocates of independence.) Yet the Creoles' bellicose actions against the Spaniards placed the invading troops in the ironic position of having to defend their enemy from the oppressed masses they claimed they had come "to liberate." The generals in charge of the operation declared the armed Creoles "bandits" and forced them to heed military orders.[20]

Meanwhile, in Ponce and neighboring southern municipalities, several leading families outdid each other welcoming the American troops. It is suspected that some were motivated by the expectation that the Americans would bring democracy and plenty of dollars to help the stagnant sugar economy. According to several studies, the sugar industry had been negatively affected by the abolition of slavery (which deprived it of its captive labor force), by declining prices in the foreign market, and the scarcity of funds with which to undertake the modernization needed to increase production and combat the rising cost of free labor.[21]

Though the autonomists in charge of the stillborn government did not rush to welcome the invaders, they also did nothing to resist them. In reality, the Autonomists had always rejected armed struggle as an avenue to reach their goals. They were also divided in their views regarding the Americans and their intentions. The majority in their midst thought of the Americans as "bearers of democracy, modernity, and economic progress" and expected them to place Puerto Rico on the road to statehood as an equal state of the American Union. (It should be recalled that this is what they had wanted from Spain in the 1870s.) If annexation and equality were not possible, they hoped the United States would respect the autonomous government they had just obtained. (As we shall see, securing self-government from the new colonial rulers would take another fifty-four years.) Thus deluded by their views and hopes, the autonomists opted to wait and see what the end of the war would bring.[22]

Meanwhile, the advocates of independence, presumably the ones better disposed to resist the invaders, had problems of their own, as some of their leaders were still in exile and others had joined Cuba's liberation war. Of those still at the head of the Puerto Rico Section in New York, a couple were known to support the American expedition heading to Guánica (July 1898), for they believed that the United States would help to liberate Puerto Rico from Spain, as they were ostensibly doing for Cuba. Stunned by the news, their exiled leader, Ramón Emeterio Betances, warned from France "to stay away from any dealings with the North Americans." He feared that once the United States seized Puerto Rico, "it would never let her go" because her size and location made her an ideal place for the Americans to expand their naval operations and take control of the region's sea-lanes. Frustrated by his colleagues' lack of vision, he urged his compatriots in Puerto Rico to take up arms and "defend the homeland before it is too late." His pleas obviously went unheeded because the island soon passed into U.S. hands without much sign of a struggle. (This point, as indicated earlier, has been contested by several writers.)[23]

The Island under U.S. Military Rule, 1898–1900

The peace negotiations, which took place in Paris in December 1898, ended badly for Spain, as she was forced to cede Puerto Rico to the United States as a prize of war. As an American possession, the island

was to be ruled at the discretion of the U.S. Congress. For the autonomists in Puerto Rico the cession signaled not only the end of their cher-
ished government, but the beginning of a disappointing period in which
their ideas no longer mattered. Their disappointment increased when
Puerto Rico was placed under military rule. During the next two years
(1898–1900), the new rulers made it clear that they did not take kindly
to any suggestion from "unqualified" persons, especially those who, in
their view, "had done nothing to defend their homeland." They also reiterated General Miles' claim that the Americans had come as "bearers
of civilization."[24]

To that end, the military regime rapidly dissolved the embryonic autonomic government and shut down several newspapers that had begun
to criticize their actions. Editors and journalists who persisted in their
criticisms were arrested, fined, and often jailed, according to an extensive
study by the scholar Ché Paralitici. Armed Spaniards and those loyal to
them were disarmed and a new police force was established with recruits
from among the trustworthy locals. At least two willing recruits were assigned to spy and report on the disaffected. (The spying trend on one's
compatriots would grow during the twentieth century.) To get the economy back on track, new trade arrangements were sought from the U.S.
Congress in an effort to secure a guaranteed share of the protected American sugar market for the island's growers. The Spanish peso was exchanged for the American dollar, at a forty percent discount—its true
value according to the money changers. A census of the population,
lands, and other properties was conducted in order to determine the territory's worth and potential.[25]

The island's coffee, however, was of no interest to the U.S. traders
since they already had access to all the beans they needed from Brazil.
As a U.S. possession, Puerto Rico was not able to negotiate trade agree-
ments with foreign nations, and the coffee growers lost their traditional
clients. At first, due to opposition from the American sugar and tobacco
trusts, exports from Puerto Rico were required to pay fifteen percent of
the tariff required of foreign products entering the United States. Though
the tariff requirement was dropped in 1901, Puerto Rico's coffee was
never accorded the protected status the island's sugar received. The high
costs charged by the U.S. shipping system made Puerto Rico's coffee far
too expensive for any foreign client. And, as if conditions weren't hard
enough already, nature unleashed a huge hurricane in 1899 that de-

stroyed thousands of homes, wiped out the majority of the food crops, and crippled the coffee-bearing trees for years to come.[26]

Homeless and without immediate job prospects, especially in the battered coffee economy, thousands of families chose to emigrate. According to one study, within the first year of American rule, five thousand Puerto Ricans (of the near one million inhabitants) were shipped to American-owned sugar plantations in Hawaii as replacements for Asian workers who were on strike. What the recruited workers did not know when they left Puerto Rico behind was how far they were going. An estimated two thousand of the migrants became discouraged along the way and some jumped ship in Louisiana and others in California. Some eventually returned to Puerto Rico. Three thousand reportedly reached their destination, only to discover that they would be used as strikebreakers. The ill feelings created by their ill-timed arrival would take more than half a century to heal, according to some of their descendants.[27]

According to a relatively recent study, at least thirty thousand Puerto Ricans were working in the sugar plantations (most American-owned) in Oriente, Cuba, in 1930. The study, however, makes no mention of the conditions the Puerto Ricans encountered in those plantations. Many more moved to New York City, Jersey City, and Philadelphia so that by 1940 the Puerto Rican population in the United States neared seventy thousand. New York City in particular had been home to dozens of Puerto Rican families who had come fleeing political persecution after the 1860s. The thousands arriving in the twentieth century were driven by economic problems.[28]

A Civilian Government Is Established

With the island duly "pacified," the U.S. Congress, under pressure from various groups in Puerto Rico and at home, approved a new law, the Foraker Act, in 1900 in order to provide the structure for a civilian form of government. To that end, a single chamber legislature was established and new political parties were allowed to form, as avenues through which to channel the ambitions and energies of local political aspirants. A cabinet of eleven members (five of them Puerto Ricans) was appointed to serve in lieu of a Senate. Together, the cabinet and the American governor, all appointed by the U.S. president, held the reins of power and ruled the newly acquired possession for the next sixteen and a half years. These were not easy years for the colonizers, given the numerous protests and challenges posed by the Puerto Rican representatives in the House of Delegates. In 1912, for example, the members of the House refused to approve the governor's budget and then overrode his veto. He, in turn, appealed to Congress to settle the matter. Congress responded by enacting the Olmstead Act, which essentially authorized the island's governors to implement the previous year's budget whenever a similar situation occurred.[29]

A federal court system was implanted to execute the federal laws applicable to the island. The local court system and the Spanish Civil Code were retained. English was declared one of two official languages of the island, though teaching it in the public schools became a haphazard affair, as it depended on how many instructors could be imported to train the local teachers. Books and other teaching materials in English were shipped in, but their use depended on the local teachers' ability and willingness to adopt them. Many teachers resisted the imposition of having to teach in a language foreign to them and their students. American customs, heroes, and holidays were introduced in an attempt to familiarize the children with good American values, a task assigned to the schools. The number of schools was increased, and by 1917 about one third of school-age children were reportedly attending classes.[30]

Labor was permitted to organize and the number of craft unions increased. Yet labor's relationship with its employers soon soured, and by 1901 Santiago Iglesias and others fled to New York City, where they secured the support of the American Federation of Labor, led by Samuel Gompers. Though helpful in the beginning, that relationship eventually led the island's labor movement to split over political differences and a splinter group opted to join the newly formed Union Party. Others remained unaffiliated, rejecting all political alliances. Church and State were separated, though several Protestant denominations were able to preach their gospel to willing islanders. Apparently, the four major Protestant groups on the island reached an understanding whereby each would take their gospel to a different region. As a result, the residents in the northeastern vicinity of San Juan were likely to be approached by the Baptists, while those of the southern district surrounding Ponce were likely to be approached by the Methodists. (That was how Blanca Canales came to be baptized by Methodists.)[31]

Despite numerous debates, Congress ultimately declared Puerto Rico an "unincorporated territory," which "belongs to but is not part of the United States." The exotic territorial formula of "un-incorporation" meant Puerto Rico would be ruled as a "possession" (colony by another name) rather than as a traditional territory. In this, federal legislation would apply, unless Congress, which retained "plenary powers," determined otherwise. As an "unincorporated" territory, the island was not placed on the path to statehood or independence, despite arguments by a few progressives who questioned whether Congress could digress from the path stipulated by the Constitution. The U.S. Supreme Court upheld Congress's position in 1901. Given its power over the territory, Congress saw no need (at least for the moment) to extend American citizenship to its residents. Already deprived of Spanish citizenship by the act of war and not yet accepted as American citizens, the Puerto Ricans were left in limbo for the next sixteen plus years.[32]

Struggles for Local Control Resume

Until 1904, the majority of Puerto Rico's leaders wished to become American citizens and have the island become a state of the American Union. But the U.S. Congress showed no interest in either topic. In fact, the idea of granting its subjects American citizenship did not take hold until 1917, when the United States began preparing to enter World War I. Fear of German penetration of the Caribbean region seemed to have made the U.S. Congress better disposed to listen to some of the Puerto Ricans' requests for change. (It should be noted that during the war period, the United States also purchased the Danish Virgin Islands in the Caribbean and took over the receiverships of the Haitian and Dominican Republic's governments. Cuba's government had been under U.S. tutelage since the island became independent.)[33]

By the time World War I erupted, Puerto Ricans had become a nuisance for rulers in Washington. The colonial stirrings, always present, had coalesced in 1904 when a pro-independence sector of voters joined a newly founded Union Party, which had adopted independence as one of three solutions to the colonial dilemma. In reality, most of the Party leaders considered independence as "the option of last refuge." Nonetheless, the idea that the Party endorsed such a radical idea was of concern to the colonial rulers. Then in 1912 a small group left the Union Party in order to found the island's first Independence Party. And though the party disbanded less than two years later, when its leader died, it had made the point that not all the subjects were happy with the new colonial system. The pro-independence members returned to the Union Party fold, which had begun to see itself as the new guardian of Puerto Rican culture. Meanwhile, at the other end of the political spectrum were the advocates of annexation, who had organized themselves into the Republican Party. Their goal was to continue to propagate the idea that Puerto Rico should become a state of the American Union. In this they were sporadically supported by some in the colonial administration and some American investors who were taking over important sectors of the island's economy.[34]

Undecided, the laboring classes moved back and forth between the various political camps. But when promises were not kept, they opted to found a party of their own known as the Socialist Party (1915). They had four of their members elected to the House of Delegates before the Party split in the 1920s. The split was due in part to a contracting economy and partly to internal fighting among its leaders, who often settled for "sweetheart" deals, which did little to improve the lives of their members. So that by 1917 there were enough tensions afoot in the territory to merit the attention of the U.S. government.[35]

For Congress, the danger of war merely confirmed its initial decision that the best course regarding Puerto Rico was to hold on to it without becoming entangled in promises about its political future. Independence, in the congressmen's view, was simply out of the question since there was no need for the United States to relinquish a valuable piece of Caribbean real estate they already possessed and needed to protect the southern flank of the nation and the region's sea-lanes. Annexing the island as a state would also present unnecessary challenges since culturally, the islanders were foreigners who spoke a foreign tongue (Spanish) and adhered to a different (Catholic) faith. Racially, the island's inhabitants were a "mixed breed" and that would create unnecessary problems for a racially sensitive Congress. (We should recall that the U.S. Supreme Court had upheld the South's racial segregation policy in the case of *Plessey v. Ferguson*, 1896.) In economic terms, Puerto Rico was much too poor to be an asset to the Union. (That argument is still being made at present.)[36]

Given these and other considerations, the best the United States was prepared to do was to keep Puerto Rico as it was: "an unincorporated territory" and have it governed by a combination of appointed and elected officials with proper oversight from Washington. That arrangement would remain in place until the islanders "learned the arts of democratic government." If they proved themselves "capable students," officials in Washington promised they would, at some later date, consider granting reforms that could lead to self-government.

Encouraged by the dangling promise of possible self-rule, the leaders of the Union Party, led by Luis Muñoz Rivera (the same person who had wrested the Autonomic Charter from Spain in 1897), used the war as an opportunity to lobby Congress, and sometimes even the President, to reconsider and reform the island's government. The Union Party's demands led officials in Washington to grant a few changes in hopes of keeping the Puerto Ricans quiet, even if just for a while.

The Jones Act Extends American Citizenship

In 1917, the U.S. Congress approved a new law, the Jones Act, which granted Puerto Rico two significant concessions. First, it called for an elective Senate to be added to the local legislature. Second, it granted American citizenship to all island-born persons. The issue of citizenship had stopped being a priority for the leaders of the Union Party, after the Congress made known it had no intention of making Puerto Rico a state of the American Union. In fact, the Unionists now considered American citizenship to be an obstacle to independence, even if this was their option of "last refuge."

Nonetheless, Congress extended American citizenship, though with a few caveats. Since Puerto Rico was still defined as an "unincorporated territory" the inhabitants of Puerto Rico were not permitted to vote for any candidate running for office in the United States. For that, they would need to move residence to one of the states of the Union. The new citizens were also denied congressional representation, except for the lone Resident Commissioner who had been assigned a seat in the House of Representatives since 1900. His powers, however, were limited to "voice" but "no vote." (That is still the case at present.) The sting of the lack of congressional representation was mitigated by exempting the island's residents from having to pay federal taxes. But there was another kind of tax, what some have called "a blood tax." All eligible Puerto Rican males were subject to the U.S. military draft and expected to begin serving in the armed forces as early as 1918. Anyone who failed to register or sought to evade the draft risked arrest, fines, and imprisonment if convicted.[37]

The citizenship gift could be refused, so long as the person so inclined understood that he (since Puerto Rican women did not yet have the right to vote) would no longer be able to run for office or hold a job in the local government. A few refused the gift of citizenship and chose to be known as "Puerto Rican citizens." A few others refused to register for the military draft and went on to challenge the legality of the penalties prescribed. The question of military service became a moot issue for the majority of eligible draftees when the war ended in 1918 before they were called to serve. But over time thousands of Puerto Ricans came to regard military service in the U.S. armed forces as an avenue to escape poverty, and joined voluntarily.

The annexationists, known locally as *republicanos* or *estadistas*, regarded the gift of American citizenship as a stepping-stone toward eventual statehood. For the advocates of independence, who would shortly thereafter regroup around the Puerto Rican Nationalist Party (PRNP), the award of American citizenship was seen as "an imposition designed to perpetuate the island's colonial status," a status they would vow to change.[38]

Nationalist Challenges and Other Issues

During the 1920s, political conditions in Puerto Rico took a new turn when the leaders of the Union Party, discouraged by the economic downturn and pressured by the intolerance of a new governor (E. M. Reilly), dropped the plank of independence from the Union Party's platform. That action caused those who favored independence to found their own political party known as the Nationalist Party of Puerto Rico (PRNP). The expressed purpose of the new party was pursuing independence for Puerto Rico via the ballot. The departure of this faction caused the Union Party leader to seek new alliances with members of the Republican and Socialist parties. The three factions came together and founded the

Albizu Campos is speaking at the cemetery during the burial of the first two Nationalists killed by the colonial police in 1936. The two men being buried are Elias Beauchamp and Hiram Rosado.

Alianza Party, while those left behind in the Socialist and Republican parties created the Coalition Party. Thus, from 1924 until 1940 the two newly founded parties vied for control of the island's legislature since the governorship and most cabinet positions were still held by Americans appointed in Washington. (The one significant achievement of the Coalition Party was granting Puerto Rican women the right to vote, though this was done in two stages, and only after a few of the suffragists and labor leaders threatened they would take their petition all the way to Congress if the legislature failed to act. The legislature approved one bill in 1932, granting the right to vote to the "literate" women, and in 1936 granted universal suffrage to all citizens.)[39]

The changing political landscape was further complicated during the 1930s when the Nationalist Party, under the leadership of Pedro Albizu Campos, veered off the electoral path. A Harvard law graduate and Ponce native, Albizu Campos vowed to bring independence to Puerto Rico by armed struggle if necessary. By 1938, the Alianza Party had morphed into the Liberal Party only to split again after Senator Millard Tydings introduced a bill proposing that Puerto Rico be granted independence. (His bill was said to be a retaliatory measure after two Nationalists killed his friend, Francis E. Riggs, Puerto Rico's Chief of Police in 1936.) Some members of the Liberal Party seemed willing to accept Senator Tydings' proposal, but the Party's rising star, Luis Muñoz Marín, opposed it on economic grounds. He argued that the terms proposed by the Tydings bill would hurt the island's economy, as it would force it to pay the full U.S. tariff within a four-year period. Bitter debates ensued and Muñoz Marín and others were evicted from the Party. The ousted group went on to found the Popular Democratic Party (PDP), with the support of many advocates of independence, some of whom had left the Nationalist Party after Albizu Campos became its leader. The PDP would go on to win control of the island's government for the next three decades.[40]

Meanwhile, in 1932, Albizu Campos took the Nationalist Party to elections, but after a defeat at the polls, he claimed the electoral process was rigged and urged his followers to boycott it. He argued that the only way to achieve independence was via armed struggle. In this he resembled the position of the past century's leader, Ramón E. Betances. Like him, Albizu Campos had established contacts with various leaders in the Caribbean and Latin America and was apparently convinced that they would come to his aid when the time came to liberate Puerto Rico. Energized by a trip he made to various nations during the late 1920s and seemingly disgusted with the horse-trading politicians and the growing persecution by the colonial rulers, he asked his followers to reject any policy or practice designed to keep them "enslaved." After one of his fiery speeches in San Juan, he led an impromptu demonstration to the Capitol building (in Puerta de Tierra) where a Coalition Party-controlled legislature was considering a bill which, if approved, would enable the colonial government to appropriate the emblem of nationhood (now Puerto Rico's flag) as its own symbol.[41]

Unwilling to have his authority challenged, the governor dispatched a group of policemen to put a stop to the demonstration. But by the time the police arrived at the Capitol, many of the demonstrators had entered the building, determined to stop the legislators. As the crowd headed to the second floor, part of the stairwell gave way, sending Manuel Suárez Díaz, one of the demonstrators, to his death. Though arrests were swiftly made and the crowd was forced to disperse, the Nationalists had made their point. They were not going to allow the colonial government to appropriate their national emblem (designed by Puerto Rican rebels in New York City, in 1895). Having scored a point, Albizu Campos seized the opportunity to declare the dead man the "first martyr" of the (Nationalist) struggle for independence. The proposed bill was shelved for the next twenty years until a PDP-controlled legislature appropriated it for the Commonwealth government.[42]

The PDP's rise to power can be attributed in part to Luis Muñoz Marín's ability to rally the impoverished masses around his party with promises of social and economic reforms, and partly to the United States' willingness to support his plans. Faced as it was with a restless, angry people, deeply hurt by the debacle of the Great Depression, the Roosevelt administration seemed eager to find a leader who could provide an acceptable alternative to the repressive tactics employed by more than one colonial governor. Muñoz Marín and other PDP leaders were promising a "peaceful revolution," while Albizu Campos and his followers were threatening armed struggle. Already the Nationalists had been accused of inciting social unrest, as they had sided with militant labor leaders who sought to paralyze various sectors of the economy. From the rulers' perspective, any alliance between the workers and the Nationalists had to be stopped before it caused any real damage. To that end, the Roosevelt administration took a two-pronged approach: it sent thousands of dollars in "relief aid" to mitigate some of the needs of the poor, and it appointed an experienced military man, a southerner (Blanton Winship), as the next governor of Puerto Rico.[43]

Convinced that the Nationalists and other disaffected groups were to blame for the social unrest, Governor Winship took a firm stand, ordering the insular police to step up its surveillance practice and draw a list of the troublesome individuals, which in addition to the Nationalists and the militant labor leaders included university and high school students. These students were increasingly demanding the adoption of Spanish as the language of instruction and other curricular reforms. They objected to the "imposition" of English, and the policy to "Americanize" the society, which deprived them of courses that recognized the island's history and culture. For these acts, student leaders were often placed on probation and sometimes even dismissed from school. Their leaders' names (as the case of Olga Viscal indicates) were added to the police list of dissidents. Tensions took a nasty turn in October 1935 when four Nationalists were killed by a police patrol near the city of Río Piedras, after they were stopped for an alleged traffic violation. Angered by the "vicious killings," Albizu Campos promised at their funerals that their deaths would not go unpunished.[44]

Albizu's remarks, which were promptly recorded by the police stenographers on the scene, led Governor Winship to respond that "if the Nationalists want war, I am ready to wage it." Having declared the Nationalists a threat to the peace and stability of the land, he ordered the police to follow closely Albizu Campos and other dissident leaders. Yet despite the increased surveillance, in February 1936, two Nationalists (Elías Beauchamp and Hiram Rosado) made their way undetected into Old San Juan and killed the chief of police, Colonel Francis E. Riggs, as he was leaving church. The two culprits were rapidly apprehended and killed while still under police custody.[45]

Albizu Campos and seven of his aides were subsequently arrested on seditious charges and tried in San Juan's federal court. The federal jury (comprised of five Puerto Ricans and seven North Americans) could not agree on a verdict and the trial ended in a hung jury. Unhappy with the results, Governor Winship insisted on a new trial, with a more compliant jury in which the number of Puerto Ricans was reduced from five to two (both of whom were known for their sympathies to the administration). As expected, the accused were convicted as charged. They were sentenced to prison terms ranging from six to ten years to be served in the federal prison in Atlanta, Georgia.[46]

Incensed by the unfair verdict and harsh sentencing of their compatriots, a few of the remaining leaders planned to stage a demonstration in Ponce, Albizu's hometown, on March 21, 1937. The event was slated to coincide with a major Catholic holiday, Palm Sunday, and the upcoming anniversary of the island's abolition of slavery (1873). The organizers secured the required permit from the city, only to have it rescinded on questionable grounds the morning of the event. The demonstrators refused to back down and began to assemble for the scheduled march. The heavily armed police, deployed there for such an eventuality, opened fire, killing twenty-one persons (nineteen of them Nationalists) and wounding a hundred and fifty others (most of them women and children). (For more details, see the section devoted to Dominga de la Cruz in this book.)

An investigation of the Ponce event, chaired by Arthur Hayes of the American Civil Liberties Union's (ACLU), concluded in its report that what occurred in Ponce on March 21, 1937, was "a massacre." The report blamed Governor Winship for the casualties since he had ordered the police to deny the marchers the right to hold a peaceful demonstration. Ignoring Hayes' criticism, Governor Winship ordered that the upcoming commemoration of the American invasion, scheduled for July 25, 1938, be held on the very plaza where the Nationalists had been gunned down.[47]

A few Nationalists plotted to avenge their fallen comrades by killing Governor Winship during the July celebration. The attempt failed, despite the attackers' repeated shooting at the dais. A vigilant bodyguard was killed instead. An attacker who kept shooting toward Winship was captured and killed on the spot by the arresting officers. His body was never found. Seven others accused of hatching the plot were tried and sentenced to long prison terms. They were still serving time in the island's penitentiary when the last appointed American governor (Rexford Guy Tugwell) released them in 1945, as a good-will gesture.[48]

Apparently, Governor Tugwell was sent to de-escalate the growing tensions and correct some of the damage caused by four decades of colonial misconduct and investors' greed. Though a few Puerto Rican families had indeed benefited from the island's colonial relationship with the United States, the great majority had been further impoverished by an exploitative export-oriented agrarian economy supported by the colonial government. The major sectors of the economy (sugar, tobacco, and needlework, among others) were not only dependent on the American market but on American capital as well. As Albizu explained to his followers, the ongoing colonization kept the island from building the self-sustaining economy it would need to support independence.

World War II Brings Colonial Reforms

With the onset of World War II, demand for sugar and rum exports enabled the island's sugar industry to revive temporarily. Thousands of dollars generated by the excise tax collected by U.S. Customs were returned to the island's treasury to finance some of the changes proposed by the PDP leaders, starting with rebuilding part of the island's infrastructure. Urged by the PDP-controlled legislature, the governor approved the establishment of a few manufacturing plants they hoped would become sufficiently profitable to lure industrial investment capital to the island. Two of the pilot plants revolved around the rum industry, as one made bottles and the other built cardboard boxes for shipping rum. A third plant produced cement for the fabrication of houses designed to withstand the destructive winds of tropical hurricanes. The state also built a hotel (which was left to the Hilton chain to administer) as a step toward developing a tourism industry.[49]

Some of the excise tax funds were earmarked for land reform, in an effort to mitigate the abject poverty of the landless peasantry. The plan's aim, according to its supporters, was to restore some level of self-sufficiency to the impoverished residents of the countryside. The idea of a self-sufficient peasantry had been propagated by the local intelligentsia, the supporters of independence, especially the Nationalists, and now by the PDP leadership. The land reform and other economic proposals, known collectively as the, "Chardón Plan" (in honor of the plan's author, Dr. Carlos Chardón), became the basis of the PDP's "peaceful revolution," supported by the Roosevelt administration and its appointee, Governor Rexford Tugwell. Yet the same reforms were opposed by the PDP's political foes, especially the local Republicans and their counterparts in Washington who feared that Puerto Rico was "on the path to socialism."

The Second World War also produced two unexpected sources of revenue for the island. Thousands of Puerto Ricans joined the U.S. armed forces (as draftees or volunteers) and began sending part of their paychecks home to their families. Others, lured by jobs left behind in the United States by men sent to the war front also left the island and began sending remittances home. In this they were encouraged by farms and light manufacturing plants in New York, New Jersey, and Connecticut, among others, which sent recruiting agents to recruit Puerto Rican workers. Such was the lure of jobs that by 1960 approximately 800,000 Puerto Ricans resided in the United States compared to fewer than 100,000 twenty years earlier. In many cases, the employers advanced the cost of airfare as an added incentive to lure Puerto Ricans. In the early years, a large portion of the farmworkers hired during the war migrated back and forth between the United States and Puerto Rico, but as they became familiar with the areas around the farms, they searched for permanent jobs and began settling in nearby cities and towns.[50]

The departure of workers and enlisted men produced other benefits for Puerto Rico in addition to the paychecks and remittances they sent home. It eased the pressure on the labor market at a time when the agrar-

ian sector was contracting and the industrial experiment was in its in-
fancy. (The latter sector never created enough jobs for the workers who
remained behind. Even in the best of times, unemployment in Puerto
Rico did not fall below ten percent.) The thousands who joined the U.S.
armed forces helped the economy in other ways. Upon their return home
as veterans, they purchased goods and services. Many of them used their
benefits to return to school or to pay for school for their children. They
also purchased thousands of the cement houses in the suburban developments, which came to characterize modern Puerto Rico.[51]

The war also brought about political changes. Exposure to the decolonization sentiments that began spreading through much of the colo-
nized world at the end of the war re-energized the island's political leaders
to pressure the U.S. Congress to reform the existing colonial structure
and allow the islanders a more ample participation in the affairs of government. Officials in Washington had promised they would address the
Puerto Rican demands as soon as the war ended, though they also made
it clear that before any changes were made, all talks of independence had
to cease. Intent on proving his loyalty, the PDP's maximum leader, Luis
Muñoz Marín, not only renounced his own personal support for independence but in 1946 forced those who still favored it to leave the party.
The news of his turnaround was well received in Washington but caused
great bitterness among some of his followers. The ousted group went
ahead and founded the *Partido Independentista Puertorriqueño* (PIP), the
second of its kind, and promised to liberate the island via the ballot.[52]

With two independence groups on the horizon, and the local Republicans temporarily sidelined, the Truman administration chose to support
the PDP, by approving changes that helped to keep its leaders in power.

For its part, the PDP-controlled legislature, with the approval and economic support from Washington, took on the task of modernizing the
island by repairing or rebuilding its infrastructure and educating the
masses in hopes of attracting enough industrial foreign investors to trans-
form the economy. To those ends, the administration built bridges and
roads and even a modern airport to facilitate land and air transportation.
The state also built dozens of schools and deployed hundreds of teachers
to remote areas. Teachers and students were fed daily with food surpluses
donated by the federal government. Children who previously failed to
attend school because they lacked shoes were given the opportunity to
purchase a pair for the cost of fifty cents. State-produced educational

films were shown in many rural areas once a month, and reading materials were distributed through the schools and books were loaned via a bookmobile. The state also built hospitals in nearly every municipality, which provided medical services to the poor at nominal fees.[53]

But not all the programs succeeded. For example, the highly publicized land reform and government land cooperatives announced with much fanfare were eventually abandoned, in part because the cost of acquiring the land was high, as the sellers insisted on charging market price for the acreage and partly because the state planners became enthralled with the idea of developing the industrial sector with foreign capital. Also after the mid-1940s, hundreds of thousands of islanders left the rural countryside for the nearest city or moved to the United States, where jobs beckoned. Pressure from their political foes forced the government to sell its pilot manufacturing plants to private investors. The cement plant, for instance, was sold to the Ferré family, whose patriarch later became the first pro-statehood elected governor of Puerto Rico in 1968. There were other consequences to the modernization of the economy. As thousands of peasants left the farms, less food was produced for the local population, and more of it had to be imported from the United States (which, given the high cost of shipping, increased the cost of daily survival). The growing dependence on foreign-grown staples was compounded by the economy's reliance on American capital for its industrial development under the umbrella of Operation Bootstrap, which offered prospective investors tax incentives and benefits. The well-publicized Operation Bootstrap was later criticized as having deepened the island's dependence.[54] (It was to this rapidly changing world that Pedro Albizu Campos returned in December 1947, after an absence of nearly eleven years.)

Political Reforms: The Nationalists Revolt

During Albizu's absence, the United States had softened its stance, in part in response to the decolonization movement spreading around the world, which was being echoed by the island's independence movement, and partly in response to the demand for reforms put forward by the PDP leadership. Not ready to consider granting the island statehood or independence, the Truman administration chose to buy time by appointing a Puerto Rican as the island's governor. The person chosen for the job was Jesús T. Piñero, a person well known in Congress because he had been the PDP's Resident Commissioner. Next, President Truman signed into law an Elective Governor bill that permitted the Puerto Rican people to elect their own governor in November 1948. Not surprisingly, the people elected Luis Muñoz Marín, then president of the Puerto Rican Senate and the leader the islanders credited for the changes that had begun to improve their lives.[55]

Yet what was less known or ignored by his followers was the fact that before Muñoz Marín became governor he urged the legislature to approve the infamous Gag Rule, Law #53. The intent of the new Sedition Statute (like its predecessor, the U.S.' Smith Act) was to silence the independence advocates (especially the Nationalists) and other disaffected voices. With Albizu Campos back on the island, preaching "the time has come to take up arms," Muñoz Marín and other PDP leaders did not want to risk losing control just when they seemed so close to getting the United States to fulfill its promise of granting the island self-government. (In this instance, they were probably reminded of their political forefathers who had lost the autonomic government they had secured from Spain.)[56]

Before he returned to Puerto Rico in 1947, Albizu Campos had tried to enlist the help of the United Nations to resolve the island's colonial status. He had obtained the post of Observer at the General Assembly for his Party. The Observer's post, reports Sandra Morales Blanes, was occupied by Thelma Mielke, ex-member of the Harlem Ashram and a good friend of Ruth M. Reynolds. Between 1947 and 1950, Mielke represented the Nationalist Party at various international gatherings. In 1947, for instance, she presented a petition to the Ad Hoc Committee of the U.N.'s General Assembly, calling for an investigation of Puerto Rico's continued colonial status. She introduced similar petitions in September and November of 1948 in Geneva and then in Paris, respectively. Her last effort on behalf of the Puerto Rican Nationalist Party, Morales Blanes explained, was made on October 31, 1950 [the day after the Nationalists revolted in Puerto Rico and just before Oscar Collazo and Griselio Torresola attacked Blair House in their attempt to kill President Truman]. These actions reportedly led the United States to pressure the General Assembly to revoke the Nationalists' Observer post in early November.[57]

After the Observer post was revoked, the task of lobbying the General Assembly fell to Julio Pinto Gandía, the New York Junta leader who had previously served as Delegate of the Nationalist Party for the United States. His role was then assigned to Lolita Lebrón. It seems that until 1950, the Nationalists had endeavored to achieve independence via peaceful means with the support of the United Nations. But upon his return to Puerto Rico, Albizu realized that he had to find other means "to put a stop to the charade" being orchestrated between the United States and the PDP leaders.[58]

The Gag Rule (Law #53) enacted in June 1948 and the increasing arrests that followed, explained Blanca Canales, were the reasons that led Albizu to give the order to begin preparing "for armed struggle" before he, too, was arrested and sent to prison. His followers were being arrested for alleged traffic violations and other minor infractions. He knew he was followed everywhere he went by undercover agents, and his speeches were routinely recorded by police stenographers. He had recently learned that there was a plan to kill him.[59]

Meanwhile, Muñoz Marín, as the newly elected governor of Puerto Rico, continued to apply pressure on the President and the U.S. Congress to fulfill its promise to allow Puerto Rico to exercise self-government. His efforts soon partially paid off when the Congress approved, and President Truman signed, Public Law 600 on July 3, 1950. The new statute called for the creation of a Puerto Rican constitutional convention to draft a constitution for the envisioned self-government, later known abroad as the Commonwealth of Puerto Rico and locally as the *Estado Libre Asociado de Puerto Rico* (ELA). However, the constitutional convention was instructed to follow the model of the U.S.' Constitution, and make sure to insert in the Puerto Rican document the Federal Relations Act and a portion of the Foraker and Jones Acts, which described the federal powers the United States retained over Puerto Rico. Public Law 600 also stipulated that once the constitution was ratified by the Puerto Rican people in a special referendum, it needed to be sent to the U.S. Congress and the President of the United States for their approval.[60]

Incensed by the negotiations that kept Puerto Rico a colony (this time with the added injury of having the people consent to "their own enslavement"), Albizu Campos gave the order to take up arms to stop the process before the PDP administration began registering new voters for the special referendum prescribed by Public Law 600. According to what Blanca Canales said years later, Albizu Campos had started the "revolution" in order to stop "the constitution." In her view, that was what he meant when he told a Lares audience a month before the uprising, "la constitución es la revolución." (For details about the uprising and its aftermath, see the section devoted to Blanca Canales in this book.)

Despite the Nationalists' actions, the PDP achieved its political goal, for the majority of the eligible voters (some say one third did not go to the polls) approved the terms of Public Law 600, and later ratified the constitution drafted by their representatives. The ratified document was then submitted to the President and the Congress for their approval. For a moment the plan seemed endangered when several members of Congress began picking apart one of its sections. In the end, they were reminded the world was watching to see how the United States was dealing with its colony's right to "self-determination," and opted to suggest that the original drafters make the changes. To speed things up, President Truman approved the Puerto Rican Constitution on July 3, 1952, but instructed that the document could not be enforced until the changes suggested by Congress were made and a disposition was added, stating that "no future amendments can alter the relationship between the United States and Puerto Rico, as have been defined by Public Law 600, the Federal Relations Act, and the United States Constitution." In other words, the Puerto Ricans had been given a share of control over local affairs of the island but not the power they were seeking. (Postal service, military protection, regulation of the air waves, air space, currency and other areas of government continued to be regulated by federal legislation.)[61]

Whatever bitterness the PDP leaders might have felt did not deter them from the scheduled celebration of July 25, 1952, where they proclaimed to the world that Puerto Rico had become a self-governing "Free Associated State" or an *Estado Libre Asociado*. They claimed the Puerto Rican people had voluntarily entered into "an association with the United States, 'in the nature of a compact,' which could not be dissolved unilaterally by either party." Several members of Congress disagreed with that interpretation, but let it go when the case of Puerto Rico was presented to the U.N. General Assembly in 1953, in part because they knew the United States had yielded very little power. In fact, the case of Puerto Rico was brought to the United Nations by the United States, as it was looking to rid itself of the responsibility of having to submit yearly reports about Puerto Rico's political status to that body.[62]

The Muñoz Marín administration helped the United States to "save face" at the U.N. General Assembly by insisting that, according to Public

Law 600, Puerto Rico was no longer an "unincorporated territory" but had become a self-governing state, which had "freely entered into an association with the United States." The implication of their interpretation was that the island was no longer subject to Congress' "plenary powers." Apparently, the argument was not sufficiently convincing, and the United States had to do a great deal of negotiating in order to get its petition approved by the General Assembly. Though President Eisenhower also did not necessarily agree with Muñoz' interpretation, he saved the deal by sending a statement to the General Assembly through his representative, Henry Cabot Lodge, promising that, "if at any time the Legislative Assembly of Puerto Rico adopts a resolution in favor of more complete independence [he] would immediately thereafter recommend to Congress that such independence be granted."[63]

Though most delegates at the United Nations suspected this was an empty promise, the President's statement helped to resolve the impasse, and on November 27, 1953, the U.N. delegates approved the U.S. petition (26 votes in favor, 16 against, and 18 abstentions).[64]

For many in Puerto Rico, the question of what exactly was achieved in 1952 remains a topic of debate. For the Nationalist women addressed in this book the case was clear: Puerto Rico remained a colony of the United States and to change it they would continue to struggle until their dying days. For their unwavering commitment to this ideal, they were sent to prison for many years. This book seeks to rescue their names and deeds from the historical amnesia to which they have been relegated.

Distribution of the Work

In the first part of the book, I provide a biographical essay of Dominga de la Cruz, a black working-class woman from Mayagüez who became a heroine in March 1937 when she abandoned a place of safety and ran into the line of fire in order to rescue the Party's flag from a wounded comrade while the police were shooting at unarmed Nationalists in the Ponce plaza.

The second part of the book addresses the cases of seven women who were imprisoned in Puerto Rico during the 1950s for their roles (real or alleged) in the uprising of October 1950 and the Nationalist attack on the U.S. Congress in March 1954. The section begins by highlighting the actions of Blanca Canales, the Jayuyan native who led a group of rebels against the colonial government on October 30, 1950, and declared Puerto Rico a republic. It discusses the militant role of Doris Torresola, who that same afternoon took a bullet in defense of her leader Pedro Albizu Campos when the police came to arrest him. It highlights the role of Ruth Mary Reynolds, the lone North American woman, who was convicted and sent to prison in Puerto Rico on charges that she had violated Puerto Rico's Sedition Act (Law #53) by collaborating with the Nationalists up to the day of the uprising. It reviews the cases of Carmen María Pérez, Isabel Rosado, Leonides Díaz, and Olga Isabel Viscal and explores the reasons for their arrests and outcomes of their judicial processes.

A third part of the book is devoted to three Puerto Rican women who were imprisoned in the United States during the 1950s, on grounds that they had violated the Smith Act by conspiring to overthrow the U.S. government. The best known of these three women is Dolores (Lolita) Lebrón, a Lares native, who moved to New York City in 1940 in search of economic opportunities, and after six years of endless struggle, joined the Nationalist Party chapter in that city. In March 1954, she led the Nationalist attack on the U.S. Congress, for which she was sentenced to prison for fifty-six years. This section also addresses the cases of Rosa Cortés Collazo and Carmen Dolores Otero de Torresola, who were arrested twice in New York City: the first time in November 1950 on suspicion that they had aided their husbands in the plot to assassinate President Harry Truman; and the second time in March 1954 on charges that they had "conspired" with Lolita Lebrón and others in the plot to attack the United States Congress.

The fourth part of the book is devoted to five other Puerto Rican women, imprisoned in Puerto Rico following the Nationalist events described, but for whom I could not find sufficient information to write extensive biographical accounts. I include the data I found in the hopes that others might be encouraged to delve deeper into the matter. The section focuses on Juana Mills Rosa, Juanita Ojeda Maldonado, and Angelina Torresola de Platet. All three were well-known Nationalists who had police dossiers, "carpetas," and had been under police surveillance for many years before they were arrested in the 1950s.

Ramona Padilla de Negrón and Monserrate Valle de López were not listed on the surveillance records but were arrested on suspicion that they had aided their husbands (Antonio "Ñin" Negrón and Tomás López de Victoria, respectively) in their plans to attack their hometowns during the Nationalist uprising. Padilla de Negrón was released, without being charged, after spending a few horrific days in jail. Valle remained in jail nearly two years before a jury absolved her of all charges.

I am aware that the sixteen women documented here do not constitute the entire list of the Puerto Rican women who collaborated with the Nationalist Party or who struggled to free the island from colonial rule during the twentieth century. I know also that other women were arrested, though I could not locate the files to document their stories. I suspect that others escaped arrest simply because the revolt was squashed before it had a chance to spread.

This study does not address the women who struggled for Puerto Rico's independence prior to the twentieth century since I did that in my earlier study on the Lares uprising. This study focuses almost exclusively on the women who were sent to prison for their roles (real or alleged) in the Nationalist events of the 1950s and on Dominga de la Cruz, the 1930s heroine who escaped arrest in the 1950s, simply because she had moved to Mexico a few years earlier.

I am aware that other Puerto Rican women have been imprisoned for their political ideals since the 1950s and also merit an in-depth study of their deeds and contributions to the cause of Puerto Rico's independence. I regret not being that scholar.

Part I

Dominga de la Cruz Becerril (1909–1981) Rescues the Flag

Preface

Dominga de la Cruz Becerril, a black Puerto Rican woman and member of the Nationalist Party, rescued the island's flag before it hit the ground, March 21, 1937, when a comrade fell wounded during a political event later known as the Ponce Massacre. For this and other political acts, De la Cruz became a "criminal" in the eyes of the law and a "heroine" in the estimation of her comrades and other proponents of Puerto Rican

A scene from the Ponce Massacre.

independence. She was arrested and held in prison for one night in March 1937, even though she had committed no acts of violence. She was later interrogated by the District Court of Mayagüez, where the prosecutor accused her (and many others) of murdering a policeman who died as a result of the police shootout in Ponce. And though she was never convicted of any criminal charge, she became a target of the Secret Police and eventually had to leave the island. In 1945, she moved to Mexico, where she spent ten years in Mexico City and six years in Monterrey. In 1961, she moved to Havana, Cuba, at the invitation of the Castro government. She lived in Havana the next twenty years before death claimed her in 1981. She was nearly seventy-two years old when she died.[1]

Childhood and Adolescence

Dominga de la Cruz Becerril was born in barrio Buenos Aires, Ponce, Puerto Rico, on April 22, 1909. She lost her father, Domingo Clarillo de la Cruz (a Ponce native) when she was one year old and her mother, Catalina Becerril (a Fajardo native) when she was four. Without a parent to care for her, she was taken to live with her godmother, Isabel Mota de Ramery, an unusually artistic woman, who played the piano and frequently attended local cultural events. "She exposed me to the magic world of books and poetry," De la Cruz told various interviewers. She and her common-law husband owned a farm outside the city of Mayagüez, De la Cruz said, and allowed her to roam free through the countryside. She recalled spending those days "walking alone by the river bank, reciting poetry to the trees." She told Randall circa 1978 "those were the happiest times of my life."[2]

For Dominga, however, tragedy was never far behind. Her godmother died before she had finished the fourth grade. "Orphaned again," she had little choice, but to return to the family home, to share the impoverished life of her three siblings. "That life proved to be especially hard for her, she said, because she began to work alongside her sister at a garment factory in Mayagüez before she entered her teens. The pay was minimal and working conditions were horrid, she said. "Sewing for a living was a miserable existence. Some days we worked until 2:00 in the morning, by the light of an oil lamp, in overcrowded, poorly ventilated places." They had "little time to rest and hardly anything to eat," she said. (Randall, p. 20) No wonder that by the 1920s "Mayagüez had the highest rate of tuberculosis on the island," she added.[3]

Tired of the factory's appalling conditions, she and her sister opted to return home, only to find themselves "pressured by poverty" to sign up for piece work with one or more of the garment factories. "Working from home was hardly an improvement," she explained, "for we worked everyday until midnight by the light of an oil lamp, and still didn't earn enough to cover our basic needs."[4]

"Some women," she added sadly, "preferred to sell their bodies instead. But the poor souls were then doubly oppressed because the men who were supposed to protect them took their money, and often beat them as well." (Randall, p. 42)

In her own case, she confessed, she opted to marry young "because at that time a woman needed a husband just to be able to eat." Though she didn't love the man who had proposed to her, she joined him in a common-law union because she thought "he could help financially." (Randall, p. 25)

Married Life, Children and Work

Married life, however, did little to relieve her economic woes. In fact, things got a lot worse after two daughters were born. Her husband, a struggling peddler, was hardly ever home and one day simply ran off and left her alone to raise the girls. While the girls were still small she did domestic work because "at that time, we women had to wash floors or take whatever work was available in order to buy milk for our children. But when we couldn't buy enough of it, we made orange-blossoms tea, mixed it with the milk we had, and used that to fill their bellies."[5]

To supplement their meager feedings, she said, she breastfed her daughters more than two years. Yet despite her efforts, "the girls died of starvation." Her oldest daughter, Ana Luisa, "survived until age twelve," but her youngest, María Teresa, "couldn't make it that long." The adults, too, she explained, were "always hungry and would eat white rice and salted codfish," whenever they could afford the latter because "the salted cod would make us drink water and that way we would fill our own bellies." (Randall, pp. 27-28)

After her two daughters died, she took a job, as a "reader" in a tobacco workshop. During the mornings she read the newspaper the workers purchased and in the afternoons whatever book they had selected. The books that most impacted her according to what she told reporter Miñi Seijo in 1976 were those that dealt with the French and Russian revolutions. That reading job, she told Randall, exposed her to major historical events and though at first she didn't understand, she eventually learned a great deal from the workers' discussions that followed. She told Seijo "the tobacco workshop was where I woke up; where I took my first revolutionary steps because I knew nothing about politics before I went to work there as a reader." To Randall, she said, "In that tobacco workshop, I began to understand the workers' struggle." (Randall, p. 30) She added that the tobacco workshop was also the place where she also discovered Pedro Albizu Campos. She explained that one morning she read in one of the newspapers that Albizu Campos had led a demonstration against the Puerto Rican legislature in an effort to bar it from letting the colonial government appropriate the Puerto Rican flag. In the process one of his followers (Manuel Suárez Díaz) was killed and several others were wounded. Impressed by what she had read, she asked the workers, "Who is Albizu Campos?" To which a young man replied: "He is a hell of a revolutionary."[6]

Joining the Nationalist Party

Curious about this unusual leader, Dominga De la Cruz promised herself she would attend one of his speeches the next time he came to Mayagüez. She said she wanted to hear what Albizu had to say "because ever since my daughters died I had been looking for something I couldn't name." She recalled that the first time she "laid eyes on Albizu" was in 1932. He had been "sitting close to the stage, with eyes downcast" and seemed "sad, or maybe just tired from the struggle," she reasoned. But then "he came alive the minute he began to speak," she said. He started slowly and softly at first and then began "increasing his tempo, until by the end of the speech he had the audience enthralled." She liked what he said "because he told the truth, and told it in a way that his audience could understand." What she remembered best was that "he dispelled the image that the Yankees were gods." This was a man she could believe in, she said, because he was different from all the other politicians she had heard, "the ones who only toyed with the workers."[7]

Trusting he would understand the torments she had been through, she set out to look for him at the Nationalist Junta in town. She said she wanted to ask him: "Why should I live a life of hardship when I have done no harm to anyone?" But by the time she reached the Junta, he had already left. Not easily deterred, she told the men at the Junta that she wished to join the Nationalist Party. They hesitated and then one asked her: "Who are you?" She explained that she was Juan Becerril's niece. Her uncle was a well-known Republican, but was well liked among the Nationalists because he had said: "Albizu Campos is the only true Puerto Rican on this island." The strategy worked and they let her join.[8]

Unbeknownst to her, the Mayagüez Junta was about to split and she would soon have to choose sides. One of the issues driving the split was the impending visit to Puerto Rico of President Franklin Delano Roosevelt. One faction of the Mayagüez Junta wanted to welcome him "with flowers and songs," she said, while the other sided with Albizu Campos, who rejected the very notion that an oppressed people should welcome the leader of their oppressors at all. She sided with the faction that upheld Albizu's views. That group was subsequently reorganized as "the true Nationalists" and placed under the leadership of a newly elected president, Julio de Santiago. She worked well with De Santiago and he in turn appointed her to head the women's chapter of the "true Nationalists" in Mayagüez. The opposing members were evicted from the chapter and banned from ever again using the Lares' revolutionary flag or any of the Nationalist symbols, according to De la Cruz and Albizu's biographer, Marisa Rosado.[9]

Committed to her new role, De la Cruz did her best to promote the interests of the true Nationalists by submitting notices to *El Sol* (a local newspaper), and recruiting new members at poetry recitals she attended or organized. The most memorable article she wrote during that period, she said, was a tribute to Albizu Campos, which she had printed and personally distributed to passersby on the streets of Mayagüez. As her devotion to the Party and its leader became evident, she was invited to planning meetings and in 1935 she was asked to represent her group at the upcoming annual Assembly scheduled to take place in Caguas, Puerto Rico. It was on the way to the Nationalist Assembly that she finally met Albizu Campos, she said. By then he had heard a great deal about her and was eager to meet her, she said. And when he finally met her, she said, he had seemed impressed that she had traveled in the company of six men all the way from Mayagüez to Caguas, without a female escort. Yet nothing would have stopped her, she added, because she was there to represent the women of Mayagüez and bring their petition to the Assembly.[10]

Preparing for the Nationalist Assembly

She had been selected to bring "the Mayagüez women's message that they wanted to play a more active role in the Party." To fulfill that goal they were suggesting that the Nationalist Assembly "change the name of the existing women's group from 'Las Hijas de la Libertad' (Daughters of Liberty) to 'Enfermeras del Ejército Libertador' (Nurses Corps of the Liberating Army)." Since this had been her idea, she explained to the Assembly that "a change of name would encourage the women in the Party to stand on our own rather than continue to wait for men to tell us what to do." The name change, she added, would not only provide "a more defined role for the female Party members, but would encourage them to enroll in first aid courses, which should prepare them to assist the Cadets, if they were wounded." In her view, the name (Las Hijas de la Libertad) "was not specific enough" and might lead women to think that their role was limited to soliciting funds and attending poetry recitals. (Randall, pp. 38-39)

It isn't altogether clear whether the Mayagüez women wished only to rename the existing women's association, or whether they intended to replace it altogether. In her interview with Randall, De la Cruz appeared to express mixed feelings. She said that Las Hijas de la Libertad was composed of educated, middle-class women with whom she and the poorer women in the Party had little in common. (But given that debates about class, race and gender were not of primary concern of the Nationalist Party, one is left to wonder whether De la Cruz is superimposing the philosophy of class struggle she learned in revolutionary Cuba onto the Puerto Rican political struggle of the 1930s.) The question is further complicated by the fact that it was Albizu Campos, rather than De la Cruz, who introduced the Mayagüez petition to the Assembly voters. It is also not clear whether by this act he intended to help get the petition approved, or whether he as the maximum leader felt entitled to speak on behalf of the women of his Party. According to José Manuel Dávila's essay, "Metamorfosis: De las Hijas de la Libertad al Cuerpo de Enfermeras," Albizu Campos had "entertained the idea of creating a Nurses Corps for at least five years, but had failed to get it approved when it was first introduced at the Mayagüez' Assembly two years earlier."[11]

This time, however, the idea of creating a Nurses Corps was unanimously approved by a standing ovation the moment it was introduced by Albizu Campos. According to De la Cruz, she was delighted by the outcome and said "that day we women won." She was also delighted to have finally met Albizu Campos, even though the meeting had caused her "a terrible embarrassment." She explains that she was "so awe-struck when he extended his hand in greeting," that all she could mutter was: "Oh Maestro, El Maestro." Fortunately, the name was celebrated by those present and soon everyone had begun calling Albizu "El Maestro." In another part of the interview she said Albizu was also called "El Viejo." (Randall, pp. 40-41)

Attending the Caguas Assembly, she said, was "a life-changing experience," not only because she met Albizu Campos, the man who brought "clarity and purpose" to her life, but because she also met Doña Laura Meneses (Albizu's wife), who would play an important role in her life in years to come. At the moment, however, she felt happy about being at the Assembly and somewhat overwhelmed by the prospect of the decision she was about to make. She recalled standing in the huge room, telling herself: "This is no idle adventure. If I take this oath, I will have to struggle and sacrifice for the rest of my days and might even lose my life at some point." But then she thought: "While all those things are true, this is the type of struggle that brings meaning to my life." And then she recalled what Don Pedro had said that, "In order to liberate the island one has to lose the fear of death." With all those thoughts swirling in her head, she went ahead and took the Party oath, which required everyone who joined to pledge his (or her) life and fortune to the cause of Puerto Rico's liberation. From that day forward, she pledged, to live by the tenets of the Nationalist Party, as summarized in its slogan: "La Patria es valor y sacrificio." (The homeland is courage and sacrifice.)[12]

What Albizu Meant to Her

She chose to follow Albizu Campos, she said, not only because she believed in his cause but also because she admired his dignity. She explained:

> Until Albizu came [to us] we were confused. I think the greatness of Albizu Campos was that he took a people that was on its knees—because that is how we were, a people on its knees—and with his great energy he raised us to our feet. He taught us to walk, and he taught us to struggle. And after he [taught us] there was no way we would ever fall to our knees [again]. We had to move forward even though it was always hard [to fight] against such a powerful empire. Though many times we were fatigued, we kept moving forward ... because we were defending our homeland and we did it with great enthusiasm. We did not question his orders. We loved Don Pedro, not as a mythological figure, but as a father who wanted his children to have dignity; he taught us dignity. (Randall, p. 42)

They followed him, she said emphatically, because "we admired him for his decency and his moral ways, for we all knew that he lived a life deprived of comforts and never took bribes. We knew also that he had never weakened despite his desperate economic needs. That is why he was admired by friends and foes alike. We knew his qualities; we respected him because his living conditions resembled our own." (Randall, p. 44)

Rescuing the Flag in Ponce

In 1936, Albizu and seven of his closest aides were convicted and sentenced to prison for conspiracy to overthrow the United States government in Puerto Rico. Saddened by the miscarriage of justice, but powerless to stop the process, his followers organized a demonstration in his birthplace, Ponce, Puerto Rico. The activity was scheduled to take place on March 21, 1937, a date of double significance since as Catholics they would be celebrating Palm Sunday and also commemorating the anniversary of the island's abolition of slavery (March 22, 1873). De la Cruz was among the young demonstrators who traveled from Mayagüez to Ponce to join the march. She recalled boarding one of the two rented buses heading to Ponce the morning of March 21. "The buses were red," she recalled, "just like the police vans, the 'Red Fleet,' that followed us." One curious thing about that trip, she added, "was that some of the policemen [in the Red Fleet] kept staring at us and grinning, as if they already knew the fate that awaited us."[13]

They spent the two-hour ride, she recalled, "singing and joking as young people tend to do." But that happy mood changed the minute they got to Ponce and saw "the streets were lined with heavily armed policemen." Though they were used to seeing policemen at all of their events, these caused them concern "because they were everywhere and looked especially menacing," she explained. Some were even on the rooftops of the buildings facing the plaza. Seeing them reminded her that since Albizu's arrest the police had grown more belligerent, raiding homes and arresting Nationalists, without due cause. Her own home, she remembered, had been raided twice in the past few months and the last time "they had overturned the beds and cut through the bedding on the pretext that I might be hiding weapons." Thankfully, she added, she had never owned any weapons. (Randall, p. 50)

Deep in thought, she followed her fellow travelers to the Junta office, where they were supposed to be given instructions regarding the path of the march. Hours passed, before the organizers returned to the Junta to explain that their permit to march had been revoked by the Mayor earlier that morning. Their appeals had been fruitless, they said, because the order to stop the march had come directly from the Governor (Blanton Winship). And now there was no one with whom to negotiate because the Ponce Chief of Police had left town and left no one in charge.[14]

After some deliberations between the organizers and their followers, it was agreed that they had the right to march, and besides, it was "too late to cancel the event." Concerned for the safety of the group, the organizers reluctantly agreed to allow the men to participate, but not the women and children. The women protested vehemently, De la Cruz said, and the leaders acquiesced, provided the women and children marched behind the men. "Imagine," she said indignantly, "our women having to fight for the right to participate in the struggle!" Finally, around 2:00 in the afternoon the marchers began lining up "and the policemen got ready for action," she said. As they moved forward she overheard a young woman next to her comment: "Look Doña Dominga how many firearms there are!" She had noticed and was also afraid, but hoping to give the young woman courage, she said: "I see them but we have to go on." What helped her find her own courage that day, she recalled, "was that my fear was mixed with a huge rage." (Randall, p. 51)

The marchers lined up, in formation: "The Ponce Cadets in front and the Mayagüez Cadets right behind them ... all of them, waving their flags," De la Cruz recalled. "Then the band began playing 'La Borinqueña' [now Puerto Rico's national anthem] and we all stood still, stood tall; it was very beautiful," she explained. And then the marchers saluted the Cadets, and [Tomás] López de Victoria gave the order: "Forward, March!"[15]

They stepped forward, and as they did, the police opened fire. She could not recall "what happened next," or why she wasn't killed that day. "The policemen were so close," she said, "I could hear when they unlocked the safety pins on their machine guns." Then, she saw comrades in front of her "fall to the ground, some badly wounded; others struggling to escape the tear gas bombs the police were throwing." Short of breath herself, she began running towards a house across the street. (The house she later learned belonged to Don Mario Mercado, a sugar baron.)[16]

But as she was running, she saw one of the flags headed for the ground, as the woman carrying it [Carmen Fernández] had been wounded. "This could not be," Don Pedro had said, "the flag must never touch the ground." So she ran towards the wounded comrade and lifted the blood-splattered flag. The flag was heavy and she lost her footing, but then another woman stepped in and helped her regain her balance. Then she and that woman walked to the house across the street in search of cover. There were others there trying to get in, but the door was locked. Not sure what else to do, she and a few others "locked arms and pressed their bodies against the wall and "waited to be shot." Then one young man climbed on the shoulders of another and jumped onto the porch and opened the door. They all rushed in and "the women immediately got to work, making bandages from sheets they found in a laundry basket for the two who were wounded." In her interview with Miñi Seijo, she said, they laid the two wounded comrades in one of the bedrooms.[17]

The baron's wife (Sra Mercado), De la Cruz said, came and asked them to leave, saying she had called her lawyer and he was calling the police. They pleaded with her to no avail, she said, and within an hour the police came and took them away: the wounded (presumably) to the hospital and the rest to the police station for questioning. She was among the latter. She was so irate, she said, she would have shot that woman right in her own home had she owned a gun. In retrospect, she said she was glad she had never owned a firearm.[18]

News of their arrests, De la Cruz recalled, brought several lawyers to their defense, and thanks to them she was released the following morning and later won the case against her. Among the well-wishers who came that night was Julio Pinto Gandía, who had become Acting President of the Nationalist Party after Albizu Campos was incarcerated. With him also was the Party's Secretary General, Lorenzo Piñeiro. That night also she and her comrades were helped by the townspeople who came by the station to bring them food and drink. She was released the following morning and returned to Mayagüez. When she arrived home relatives came to warn her that the police had come twice looking for her. Not wishing to embarrass her family any further, she turned around and went to the Mayagüez station to answer questions. There, she said, the prosecutor was more belligerent (than the one in Ponce) and tried his best to intimidate her, accusing her of crimes she had not committed. Convinced that she had "done nothing wrong," she said, she "waited until he grew tired of his game" and let her go.[19]

The Hays Commission Investigates "the Ponce Incident"

Seven weeks after the March "events," De la Cruz said she was summoned by the Hays Commission and asked to recount what she had witnessed in Ponce on March 21, 1937. The Commission, established at the insistence of various Puerto Rican leaders, was chaired by Arthur Garfield Hays, a leading member of the American Civil Liberties Union (ACLU). The commissioners' mandate, according to Mr. Hays, was to investigate "the facts" of the Ponce "incident" and render a report. When it was her turn to testify, De la Cruz said, she told the investigators what she "had witnessed, without embellishment." And then Mr. Hays had asked her: "Why did you pick up the flag instead of running for cover if you were in danger of being wounded?" And she had replied, "because El Maestro taught us that the flag must never touch the ground." After that exchange, she said proudly, "Mr. Hays would always rise from his seat every time I walked by."[20]

After many weeks of work and dozens of depositions, the Hays Commissioners concluded that what occurred in Ponce, March 21, 1937, was "a massacre" in which nineteen unarmed Nationalists were killed, most of them women and children, and more than 150 others were wounded. A policeman and an off-duty National Guardsman had also lost their lives in the shootout. The report laid responsibility for the massacre on the shoulders of the Governor and the island's new Chief of Police, Colonel Orbeta. (The latter had been appointed to replace the late Colonel Riggs.) The Governor was blamed for seeking to deny the Nationalists the right to carry out a peaceful demonstration and Colonel Orbeta for deploying heavily armed policemen to the site and then leaving them without instructions about how to protect the demonstrators. The report concluded that "the presence of 150 policemen, armed with revolvers, shotguns and tear gas bombs had set the stage for the bloody incident." It added that the Nationalists had no way to escape because they were "trapped between eighteen policemen in front of the line and twenty at the rear ... armed with Thompson machine guns."[21]

Though the Hays Commission established that the Nationalists weren't armed, Winship's government insisted "the police had fired in self defense" because the Nationalists "had fired first." The fact that one policeman was dead was hard to explain unless the Nationalists were blamed. In time, De la Cruz said, the Nationalists, too, came up with their own tale, which claimed that the policeman was killed by a fellow officer who "saw him saluting the Puerto Rican flag." Based on what she told Miñi Seijo (1976) she seemed to accept the Nationalists' version. But in her interview with Randall two years later, she was no longer sure. (Randall, p. 54)

Life after the Ponce Massacre

After the Ponce Massacre, De la Cruz said, she felt "too distraught" to do any political work for a while. She said she had developed "a bad case of nerves" and had to go and see a doctor. He suggested that she take time off to let herself heal, doing things that brought her pleasure, such as listening to soothing music and reading poetry. She followed his advice and stayed home as long as she could but then had to go to work. One day, she recalled, she heard on the radio that WPRA, a local (Mayagüez) station, was looking for new talent and she went to audition. She was hired, part time, to do poetry recitals. She began performing the poetry of Luis Palés Matos, she said, because his poems spoke to her about "the pain and suffering of black people." She loved her job because it brought her "peace of mind, and even minor popularity." But she had to leave it, she said, because it did not pay enough to cover the bills. (Randall, p. 62)

In 1940, she moved to San Juan in search of new opportunities, only to find that good jobs in the capital were just as elusive and the cost of living was much higher. She muddled through for about two years, doing occasional poetry recitals (at The Puerto Rican Atheneum) and at some public schools Doña Laura Meneses and others booked for her. One individual who helped her during this period, she said, was Jorge Font Saldaña, who helped her book a poetry recital and then introduced to her a few members of the press "as the best interpreter of black poetry." For reasons that are unclear, he recommended that she adopt part of her father's surname (De la Cruz) as her stage name. She took his advice, but does not explain why she did it or why this was important. In the account she wrote for *Correo de la Quincena* in March 1976, she said that she met Font Saldaña through her landlady. Yet in her interview with Randall two years later, she said money had been so tight she hadn't been able to rent a place and had stayed with friends whenever she couldn't get back to Mayagüez. It is possible, however, that she could not stay in any place very long because after the Ponce Massacre she became a target of the island's Secret Police. She described that period in San Juan as "very exhausting."[22]

Tired of the economic problems, and hoping to improve her diction and declamatory skills, she went to Havana Cuba in 1942. Apparently, she was helped by Doña Laura (Albizu's wife) who wrote letters of introduction on her behalf. Life in Havana, she said, also proved hard and she often had to do domestic work in order "to eat and pay for the speech classes." Occasionally, she was invited to participate in poetry recitals, thanks to her teacher and other friends of Doña Laura. After two years of that struggle she returned to Puerto Rico hoping for a better life. (Randall, p. 66)

She landed in San Juan in 1944 but remained there less than a year before she had to set out again because of the lack of jobs and constant police harassment. This time she moved to Mexico City with the help of the Communist Party president in Puerto Rico, who wrote a letter of recommendation on her behalf. She landed in Mexico City on June 3, 1945, where she was soon greeted by many Latin American exiles. Among the persons who proved helpful to her was Ana María Senadel (Pedro Albizu Campos ex-girlfriend from his days at Harvard), whose home (Casa Lucha) was a place of refuge and intellectual activity for many revolutionaries in the making. Senadel, she said, often invited her and other exiles to Sunday lunch. It was in that home, she told Miñi Seijo where she first met Fidel Castro and Ernesto (Ché) Guevara. Always eager to learn, she said, she once asked Ché Guevara to recommend a few books she should read on Marxism. He suggested she start by reading world history. After a while, she recalled, Fidel was arrested and left Mexico. She later learned that he and Ché had gone to Sierra Maestra to begin the revolution. After ten years in Mexico City, she also left, she said, because the CIA was on her trail. With the help of friends, she moved to Monterrey, Mexico and stayed there another six years. She survived financially thanks to her Mexican friends who gave her a place to live and booked poetry recitals for her. She makes no mention of having to do domestic work during the sixteen years she lived in Mexico.[23]

She explained that after Doña Laura moved to Mexico City [circa 1948] she would regularly accompany her to meetings at "the Workers' University." The meetings, which often lasted from 9:00 in the evening until 2:00 in the morning, she said were always educational and helped to shape her thinking. The most memorable of the lectures she attended at the Workers' University were those offered by Fidel Castro and Ernesto Ché Guevara, she added. But though she had been very attentive, she hadn't always understood everything they said, perhaps because she was "not a theorist." (Randall, p. 77)

Visiting Albizu Campos in New York City

In 1945, she traveled from Mexico to New York City in order to visit Albizu Campos who had recently been released from Columbus Hospital. She went to New York City, she said, at the invitation of Ruth Mary

Reynolds, the well-known Pacifist from South Dakota who had become a good friend of Albizu Campos and other Nationalist leaders. She stayed in Manhattan for about four months, she recalled, thanks to the generosity of Ruth Reynolds and others who helped her to book a few poetry recitals. The most memorable of these recitals, she explained, was the one she performed at La Casa Hispánica at Columbia University. (Randall, p. 71) She told Miñi Seijo in 1976 that during that visit to New York City she had been offered an opportunity to perform at Carnegie Hall, but had not taken it because Albizu Campos had dissuaded her. He had said, "you already earned your place in history by your action in Ponce and don't need ephemeral fame." He had suggested that she return to Mexico where she was needed. She heeded his advice, she said, and returned to Mexico. She remained there until 1961, when she moved to Cuba at the invitation of the Castro government.[24]

Settling in Cuba: Visiting Moscow

In 1960, De la Cruz said she participated in a conference of Mexican, Central American, and Caribbean women held in Mexico City in support of the Cuban Revolution. At the end of her presentation she introduced a resolution calling for support for Puerto Rico's independence. The motion was seconded by Violeta Casals, the radio personality who had transmitted the rebels' revolutionary messages from Sierra Maestra, she explained. As a result of that fortuitous meeting, she was invited to go to Cuba by the director of the Instituto Cubano de la Amistad con los Pueblos (ICAP). She accepted the invitation and landed in Havana, Cuba in 1961. During the first fifteen days of her stay, she was housed at the Hotel Habana Libre. After that, she was moved to the ICAP's headquarters, which had already been renamed Hotel Sierra Maestra. She lived in that hotel for the next two years until she was given her own apartment, she explained. By then she already had a steady job, teaching revolutionary poetry to Cuban workers.[25]

Grateful for the opportunity to be earning a living while doing what she liked, she volunteered to join one of the cane-cutting brigades. "Volunteering to cut cane was then a common practice among revolutionary Cubans," she added. But the strain of the cane field proved too hard for her fifty-four year old body and she collapsed from fatigue. The Cuban doctors who cared for her explained that she collapsed because she had "a sick heart." They told her they had done all they could but then one of them suggested that she appeal to the Soviet Women's Committee to see if they could take her to Moscow for the medical treatment she needed. That doctor, she said, "even helped me to fill the application I needed." To her surprise, the Soviet Women's Committee agreed to sponsor her and in July 1963 she flew to Moscow. (Randall, p. 85)

She was surprised also by how "warmly" she was received at the Moscow Airport by a Soviet Minister's wife. From the airport she was driven directly to an International Women's Council, which was meeting at the Kremlin. She told Randall that she had been grateful for the honor of meeting so many women from different regions of the world, who, like her, had "suffered and struggled." (Randall, p. 85) She told others that when her time came to speak, she had denounced the colonial situation in her homeland, the forced military conscription imposed by the United States and "forced sterilization of Puerto Rican women practiced by the island's government."[26]

At the end of the conference, her hosts took her to see various monuments, the most memorable of which, in her view, was Lenin's tomb. She was impressed, she said, to be standing before the tomb of "the great man, who looked as if he had just had lunch and was sleeping the siesta." (Randall, p. 85)

But after a week of touring, she said, her legs became terribly swollen and her hosts took her to the hospital where "caring doctors" explained that she had "a sick heart, from a life of struggle and needed to rest." She remained in Moscow for about three months before she was permitted to travel to Prague, Czechoslovakia, where she was also advised to rest for another month before she was permitted to fly back to Cuba. She flew to Cuba via Mexico, she said, in order to attend the conference of Central American and Caribbean Women, already in progress. She used time there, "to cement relations" between the conference attendees and Cuba's women. (Randall, pp. 86-90)

Once back in Havana, she returned to work for a few more years, but then she fell ill again and was permitted to retire, with a pension from the Cuban government. The sum assigned, she said, allowed her "to live comfortably." (Randall, p. 95) In retirement, she had time to attend many cultural activities and often went to Lenin Park in Havana, where poets and writers tended to congregate. She was particularly fond of a spot called "La Peña Literaria," she said, "because its stones, trees and plants," reminded her of the farm where she had roamed as a child. "That place," she explained, "makes me feel as if I am in a dream; I feel peaceful in that place."[27]

Occasionally she was invited to political rallies where she was almost always asked to speak about the Ponce Massacre. These were her least favorite times, she said, because recounting that story stirred many sad memories about the young men and women who were killed or wounded that day. "We lost our innocence in Ponce and since then I have never felt that youthful happiness again," she added. More recently, she recalled, she had been invited to an activity for mothers who had lost children to the revolution and that had been emotionally very difficult. She explained, "At those rallies it is common for the audience to throw flowers on the stage in honor of the mothers." On that occasion, a twelve-year old boy took some of the flowers from the stage and handed them to her, saying, "here Dominga these are for you because your children were killed in Ponce." She was so overwhelmed by his gesture, she recalled, that she had to be escorted off the stage. (Randall, pp. 102, 107)

One Last Visit to Puerto Rico

At long last, in 1976, at age sixty-seven, she traveled to Puerto Rico, to visit family and friends and see her homeland, perhaps for the last time. The Cuban government, she said, not only facilitated the trip but told her that Cuba would always be her home. She had considered staying in Puerto Rico to live out the rest of her life, but when she got there she saw the island had changed. In her view, the island "had become too Americanized" and she could not adapt to its new rhythm, crime, drugs, and rampant consumerism. She had been warned, she said, by her Cuban friends who feared she would no longer fit in. So after four months she said good-bye to her friends and relatives and returned to Cuba. She left with a "heavy heart," according to a letter she wrote to her friend and comrade Juan Antonio Corretjer from Havana, Cuba on October 4, 1976. In that letter she recounted that she was "well received in Cuba" and was in temporary housing until a new apartment was found for her. She gave him the new address in hopes that his wife and daughter would write soon because she already "felt a great nostalgia" for the people and place she had left behind.

But before she left Puerto Rico for the last time, she wrote an account of what she had witnessed during that fateful day in March 1937. She gave the article to Corretjer, who published it the following March (1977) in *Correo de la Quincena*. Three months later (July 1976) she also sat for a long interview about the same topic with reporter Miñi Seijo. That account was reprinted by *Claridad* in March 1997.

Dominga de la Cruz died in Havana, Cuba, on November 25, 1981, barely five years after she left Puerto Rico and nearly three years after Margaret Randall interviewed her in Havana. She was seventy-two years old when she died. To my knowledge, very little was published in Puerto Rico about her death, perhaps because she had lived most of her adult life abroad. The only eulogy I obtained was a flier written by the President of the Nationalist Party, Jacinto Rivera Pérez, titled: "Muere Heroina Puertorriqueña: Dominga de la Cruz Becerril." In this, he recounts the deeds for which she had become known and he declared her a heroine in the struggle for Puerto Rico's independence.[28]

Part II

Nationalist Women Imprisoned in Puerto Rico, 1950, 1954

1. Blanca Canales Torresola (1906–1996)

Preface

Blanca Canales Torresola was born on February 17, 1906. Forty-four years later (October 30, 1950) she declared Puerto Rico a republic, without firing a single shot. Accused of killing a policeman and wounding three others, she was tried and convicted by a jury at the District Court of Arecibo, Puerto Rico and sentenced by Judge Rafael Padró Parés to life in prison plus three terms of six to fourteen years. Convicted also of having destroyed U.S. federal property in her hometown, Jayuya, she was sentenced to ten years imprisonment by the U.S. Federal Court in San Juan, and sent to serve that term at the Women's Reformatory in Alderson, West Virginia.[1]

Canales' participation in the Nationalist uprising is based in part on a testimony she wrote during the late 1960s while she was still incarcerated in the Escuela Industrial Para Mujeres (a women's prison) in Vega Alta, Puerto Rico, which she titled, "La Constitución es la Revolución."[2]

According to that testimony, she was one of three Jayuyan leaders, and the only woman, to lead a small group of rebels from her farm in Coabey, on Monday, October 30, to seize the town of Jayuya and declare Puerto

Blanca Canales being escorted to the Federal Court in San Juan. February, 1951.

Rico a republic. Her own decision to take up arms, she explains, was in part influenced by the idealized stories of women warriors she had read in her youth, and by her own conviction that she was "destined" to take part in the liberation of her homeland. The decision to take up arms, she declared, was also influenced by the teachings of the Nationalist Party to which she had belonged for nineteen years prior to the insurrection. The Party oath, which she took in 1931, demanded that she stand ready "to pledge life and fortune" for the liberation of Puerto Rico.[3]

Though she knew that the rebel forces were "inadequately prepared to wage war and win against the powerful American empire," she set out before noon on Monday, October 30, 1950 with other determined Jayuyans to carry out Pedro Albizu Campos' order: to implement the revolutionary plan he and other Party leaders had devised less than two years earlier. For more than a year, she and her younger cousin Elio Torresola, the military commander the Nationalists in Jayuya, had secured a small cache of firearms and hidden them in her farm. They had also done their best to train themselves and others in the use of firearms, in

preparation for a military confrontation with the colonial regime scheduled for a future time. But during the last weekend of October 1950 she
learned that the time for the confrontation had come. In the section that
follows, she explains the developments that precipitated the uprising.[4]

Events Leading to the Nationalist Insurrection

On Friday October 27, 1950, as she drove home from San Juan, she
stopped briefly at a friend's house in the town of Manatí, where she
learned that several of Don Pedro's escorts had been arrested the previous
evening. That Thursday (October 26) Don Pedro had gone to Fajardo
[in northeastern Puerto Rico] to commemorate the birth date of General
Antonio Valero Bernabé, and near dawn, three of his escorts and a
woman passenger had been detained, as they were approaching San Juan.
(Canales, pp. 19-20)

Albizu's car, she learned later, had managed to evade the police trap,
thanks in part to the advanced warning he had received from Ruth Mary
Reynolds, who claimed she had overheard a conversation at a restaurant
about government plans to kill Albizu during or after the Fajardo activity.
According to Reynolds' account, she attended the Fajardo event and was
one of the four detained by the police the evening of October 26 as they
drove back to San Juan around one in the morning.[5]

Canales said that she had not heard the news about the escorts' arrests
because she "had been in the dentist's chair all morning" and had not
listened to the radio during her drive back to Jayuya. Concerned for her
wellbeing, her friends begged her to stay the night in Manatí, but she
declined, explaining: "I need to get home, my base of operations, in case
there needs to be a confrontation with the puppet government."
(Canales, p. 20)

She reached her farm by nightfall, she wrote, after talking to her
cousin Elio [Torresola], whom she found at a store not far from her
home. She told him what she had heard and suggested that they "begin
preparations in case the authorities decide to arrest Don Pedro"—as they
had in 1936. "Except that, this time," they both agreed, "Such a feat
would cost them dearly because ... this time we would not ... remain
calm while he is sent to jail." (Canales, p. 20)

During her ride home, she recalled, she had worried about Albizu, whose life had been threatened many times by "the imperial forces." What had foiled "all those attempts to kill him" she reassured herself, "was his valor" and the care with which his guard had protected him day and night. It was "the need to protect Don Pedro," she remembered, "which had led the Nationalist leaders to arm themselves ... and later to create the military branch of the Party." Even she had found it necessary to arm a few men at her farm in order to protect Albizu and his family whenever they visited her. She had entrusted that mission to her cousins Elio and Griselio Torresola, and they in turn had enlisted their trusted friends and neighbors: Carlos Irizarry, his cousins Fidel and Mario (Irizarry), the Morales brothers (Luis and Reinaldo), known as "Los Mencha" and Heriberto Marín, among others. The guard, which had operated out of her basement, she said, had been quite busy the summer of 1948 when Albizu remained in her home for nearly three months. A few of the youths, she recalled, had taken turns watching over Albizu during his daily walks while others guarded her home in the evenings. (Canales, pp. 21-22)

She spent much of that weekend, she wrote, reminiscing about her past role and wondering about the consequences of her actions when the armed attack was launched. She remembered being attracted to the struggle of independence after listening to one of Albizu's speeches at the University of Puerto Rico in the early 1930s. She was then a graduate student, enrolled in courses in Social Work. She left that speech, she recalled, utterly convinced that Albizu was "no ordinary politician," for he not only understood Puerto Rico's problems better than any other, but he seemed totally committed to liberating Puerto Rico from its colonial yoke. (Canales, pp. 21- 22)

To be sure he was the leader she would follow she decided to pay him a visit at home one evening. She was surprised, she wrote, "to find the great man sitting in his living room with a child on his lap trying to put him to sleep." He greeted her warmly, she noted, and gradually eased into a discussion about the island's problems and the solutions he envisioned. She was greatly impressed not only by his knowledge, but "by the tenderness with which he dealt with his wife and children that evening." Thus, by the time she returned to her dorm she was completely convinced that "Albizu was not only an unusual man, but the leader Puerto Rico needed." She joined the Nationalist Party and shortly thereafter became one of Albizu's most trusted supporters. Apparently, part of her commitment also involved supporting the women's groups of the Party: "Las Hijas de la Libertad" (Daughters of Liberty) and "El Cuerpo de Enfermeras" (Nurses Corps), both founded in the 1930s.

Though Canales does not offer any details about either of the women's groups, she did mention having used "her nursing skills" one time when Reinaldo Morales (one of the young men who guarded Albizu) accidentally shot himself while he was cleaning a firearm. (Canales, pp. 30-31)

She opted instead to provide a few details about the Party chapters, which operated in smaller towns outside San Juan. According to her description, the Party chapter of Jayuya was subdivided into two camps: a civilian junta or board and a military camp. The leader of the civilian junta in Jayuya, she said, "was Ramón Robles, a cabinet-maker, later known as 'hero of the uprising,' while the head of the military camp was (her) cousin Elio [Torresola.]" The municipal juntas, reported the Puerto Rican Secret Police, generally scheduled meetings, recruited members, organized fundraising activities, and sponsored out of town speakers. The military camp apparently recruited youths and trained them as Cadets of the Republic. (Canales, pp. 21-23)

The Cadets, according to various others, attended major Party events in uniforms (white pants, black shirts, and black berets), carrying the flag (now the official flag of Puerto Rico) and "wooden rifles." (The few rifles they owned could not be shown in public for fear of arrest.) In Jayuya, Canales added, the military branch had the additional problem of "finding safe places to train the youth" with the firearms they had available. Generally, they were "forced to train by the river's edge, on the pretext of hunting birds," she added. Training in Coabey "was particularly difficult because the area is a valley surrounded by mountains and shots echo and alert the neighbors." Yet despite these risks, she practiced "shooting with a .38 caliber revolver Don Pedro had given me." In the fall of 1948, she explained, "Elio's younger brother, Griselio, 'later known as hero and martyr' [of the attack on Blair House in Washington] was sent to New York on a special mission that probably included buying firearms." And while the military camps "had been in place since the 1930s," she said, "they were not activated by Don Pedro until after the Gag Rule (Law #53) was enacted in June [1948]." (Canales, pp. 21-23)

Had plans for a revolution been hatched prior to June 1948? Quite possibly, but she apparently had not heard about them until Albizu chose to tell her during his visit that summer. She explains: "One day Don

Pedro was pacing back and forth in the living room of my house … with his head down, as if in meditation … [and] suddenly [he] stopped and said: 'I am thinking that it is necessary to prepare for the revolution because the government is bound to arrest me at any moment. I am also getting old and that is what they are waiting for, my old age, and my death. It is time to speed up the preparations.'" (Canales, p. 24)

He either did not tell her, or she forgot to mention, the date the armed strike was supposed to start. But others in the Party later claimed that the armed attack was supposed to coincide with the establishment of the "new form of government" being discussed between the newly elected Puerto Rican leaders and top Washington officials (1948-1950). The armed strike would be "in response to any attempt by the United States to impose a new colonial regime under the guise of self-government."

Canales does not disagree with that explanation, but chooses instead to focus on the forces that pressured Albizu to order "a premature attack" in October 1950. The most important event, which forced Albizu's hand, she said, was "the approval of Public Law 600 by the United States Congress" (the statute which authorized Puerto Rico's legislature to convene a constitutional convention in order to draft a constitution which could be used as the legal basis for the new government). Another troublesome event, she said, was the renewal of the U.S. military draft (1948), which continued to conscript Puerto Rican males to fight in U.S. military conflicts such as the Korean War. But though military conscription of Puerto Ricans had always been unacceptable, she argued, for the moment the most pressing issue was to reject the proposed constitution because letting it to move forward, without a fight, meant the islanders were consenting to the new colonial formula. That was what Albizu had meant when he told a Lares audience, September 23, 1950, "La constitución es la revolución," she added. (Canales, p. 24)

She noted that Albizu had been "pressured" to take action during the last weekend of October because the colonial authorities attempted to blame the Nationalists for the outbreak at the Río Piedras penitentiary (Saturday 28, 1950). Calling the prison outbreak part of a "Nationalist plot to unseat the government," the police had raided numerous homes of Ponce Nationalists, in hopes of finding evidence they could use to justify their arrests. Fearing that his own arrest was imminent, Albizu had called his top military advisors and ordered the attack to begin the following Monday, October 30, 1950. (Canales, p. 24)

In another section of her testimony, she describes the manner in which she and Elio Torresola were notified of Albizu's decision. "On Saturday (October) 28, I went down to the town of Jayuya to run some errands and buy the newspaper. As I drove into town, I saw Mr. Juan Jaca [a well-known Nationalist leader from Arecibo] on the bridge that connects [barrio] Coabey to Jayuya." She stopped the car, and as he got in, he told her that he had "a message for Elio." Aware that "in military matters Jayuyans answered to their commander in Arecibo" she drove Jaca to Coabey "and sent word to Elio." (Canales, p. 25)

When Elio arrived, she recalled, Jaca repeated Albizu's orders: to take control of Jayuya at noon on Monday. He told them "the noon hour was deemed appropriate for a surprise attack." But either he did not explain why, or she forgot to tell us, leaving the reader to wonder: "What message was Albizu trying to convey by attacking at mid-day?" Was it meant as a signal that the rebels had nothing to fear? Or did it imply that a new revolutionary government would be transparent? She reveals only that she invited Jaca to stay for lunch, but that he declined because he was pressed for time. (Canales, p. 25)

She said also that after the meeting with Elio, she drove Jaca back to the bridge where she had collected him earlier, and that along the way they "talked about the importance of the step we were about to take." She admitted that she was "pleased the decision to act had been made," because she had "been waiting a year and a half … and was tired of waiting." She conceded that, though they didn't have enough firearms, they "must act without delay." She explained that her impatience stemmed from two sources: "the fact that every revolutionary or conspirator lives on two planes: the secret one in which he plots and prepares; and the public one in which he deals with daily challenges." In her own case, she confided, she was faced with the decision "of having to start a gardening business, in order to generate some income," because she was on "an unpaid medical leave, due to health issues." (Canales, p. 26)

After she dropped Jaca off at the bridge (with instructions where he could find the transportation he needed), she drove to the gas station in town, "filled up the tank and returned home." She found Elio at the house, she said, "hurriedly making preparations because as the military man, it was his job to locate the firearms, hidden in her farm, and notify the men needed for the assault on Monday." By early Sunday, Elio had located Carlitos (Carlos) Irizarry and had asked him to stay around instead of returning to the University of Puerto Rico, where he studied. Carlitos was needed, she said, because "he had military experience, [for he had served in the American military forces, in Germany, during the Second World War]. (Canales, pp. 26-28)

She stayed home that weekend, she noted, "preparing remedies because (she) hadn't yet recovered from the oral surgery of the previous Friday." She also needed time, she explained, "to burn documents" she wanted to keep out of enemy hands. All weekend long she worried about having to entertain unexpected visitors since friends and relatives tended to show up at the farm "unannounced." If anyone came at all, she hoped it would be her cousin Gladys Torresola "who shares our ideals." Otherwise, she would rather be alone (though her uncle Raúl was around since he had recently moved to the farm). Yet being alone also had its drawbacks because it meant "she had no one to help her in the kitchen." The two sisters who had worked for her until recently had left suddenly, on the pretext that their family was moving to Ponce. As one thought fed on another, she began to wonder: Why the sudden move? Had the sisters become police informants? And if so, "Had any of them seen the bayonet cousin Griselio had carelessly left in one of the bedrooms when he last visited?" (Canales, p. 30)

What about Elio? What was he thinking? Why had he decided to postpone notifying his men until Monday morning? Other than Carlitos [Carlos Irizarry] and the "lad in the basement" [Reynaldo Morales], he had not contacted anyone else. Irizarry, she reasoned, was crucial to the operation because of his military training. But Morales seemed a bit "too young," though he had been totally devoted to Don Pedro since 1948. He also "acted grateful" in her presence, perhaps because she had taken him to Dr. Peregrina when he shot himself accidentally and then allowed him to stay on the farm while he healed. The thoughts about Morales reminded her that the good doctor (Peregrina) treated "the lad" but never reported the accident to the police. Perhaps, she told herself, the best thing to do was to keep busy and hope the weekend "passed without incident." (Canales, pp. 30-31)

Aware that she "would either be killed, or at the very least have to spend the rest of (her) life in jail," she said, she remained determined that "this is time to confront the enemy," an enemy, "which in the best of times opts to persecute even those who pursue independence through peaceful means." She was convinced, she said, "this is the moment to rise and let the world know we are a people who want to be free." And if victory eluded them, as it probably would, she hoped that they could keep the struggle going for a while, "because the longer the struggle lasts, the better the chances that the world will take notice." (Canales, p. 31)

Conscious of the fact that she might "never again set foot in the house of my childhood ... the family's favorite summer home," she visited each of its rooms for what could be the last time. First, she sat "on a rocking chair in the living room and stared at the Puerto Rican flag hanging on the foyer wall." Then she went from room to room, and when she reached the bedroom where Don Pedro slept when he visited, she "stood at the window, looked at the trees outside ... and the mountains beyond and thought of Lares." (A reference to Puerto Rico's 1868 uprising against Spain.)

At last, on Sunday evening, she approached Elio and Carlos, who were sitting on the porch, and asked them: "What has been done?" Elio told her that he and Carlos had "brought in the firearms and stored them in the basement where Reinaldo Morales was guarding them. Elio then said that there weren't enough firearms and he would need to make a few incendiary bombs ("Molotov cocktails") with some gas from her car. The bombs, he reassured her, would be stored in the empty pigeon coop, northeast of the house. She then asked: "What about the plans to cut the telephone wires and destroy the bridge?" 'Unfortunately,' he had replied, 'the bridge cannot be blown because the dynamite we had was sent to Mayagüez and we no longer have it.' They agreed "that weekends were never a good time to go buying dynamite, without arousing suspicion." It would be best to remember what Don Pedro had said: "to keep all preparations secret until it is time to strike." (Canales, pp. 28-29)

Before retiring for the evening, the three reviewed their assignments for the following day. Her tasks were to cut the telephone wires and silence the calling center in town and then proceed to the River Palace Hotel and proclaim the republic from its second floor balcony. Carlitos [Irizarry], because of his military training, would lead the assault on the Jayuya police station, while Elio and his men would bring up the rear. Once the police station had been captured, the two men would regroup their troops at City Hall, and after that site was captured, Canales would join them, to jointly proclaim the republic. (Canales, p. 29)

Convinced that she "was about to take an important ... necessary step in the history of Puerto Rico," she said, "I went to bed and slept soundly

... until six the next morning," [the day destiny had assigned her to rise and defend her homeland, just as her idol, Joan of Arc, had done in France so many centuries earlier]. (Canales, pp. 32-33)

The Attack on Jayuya

Monday morning, October 30 she stayed in her bedroom, listening to the news on the radio, while men began assembling in the front yard, she said. The first to arrive was Carmelo Maldonado (alias El Cano), a "público" driver they often hired to drive Don Pedro from San Juan to Coabey or to other destinations out on the island. As the men gathered outside, she found herself wondering how she was going to feed them since she no longer had help. "With so much to worry about this weekend," she wrote, "there hadn't been any time to think about meals." (Was this merely a sign of her generosity, or was she thinking about Manuel Rojas, the Lares military commander who served dinner to his troops before he led them into battle?) She makes no further mention of Lares at this point, so it is hard to know what elicited that preoccupation.) She finally resolved the matter around 9:30 in the morning, by asking her uncle Raúl "to serve coffee and crackers to the men outside." She added that, "the men drank the coffee and ate the crackers still standing, as soldiers do when they are in a great hurry." (Canales, pp. 34-35)

At 10:30 in the morning, she heard the first troubling news: at dawn that morning there had been a shootout between Ponce Nationalists and the police, in barrio Macaná, Peñuelas. According to a police report, one of their patrols had discovered a group of Nationalists "transporting firearms from Ponce to a farm in Peñuelas." Ostensibly, their officers "had been alerted by a shot from one of the Nationalists" and when the officers "went to investigate ... they were received with bullets." In the shootout that ensued, the news bulletin said, "the well-known Nationalist Guillermo González Ubides had lost his life." (Canales, p. 36)

Worried that the Peñuelas incident would blow their cover, if they tarried, she called down to Elio to report the news. He apparently told her to keep listening for details while he finished what he was doing. A half hour later there was a more troubling bulletin: the Nationalists of Arecibo had attacked the police station, killing four officers and injuring six others. The Arecibo Nationalists, she reasoned, had heard the news about Peñuelas and had decided to act at once. Fearing that this time the road to Jayuya might be blocked by the police if they delayed much longer, she called Elio up to her bedroom to revise their plan. He agreed they had to move out quickly, and asked her to speak to the men in the basement "because at times like this, a woman's words help to infuse men with valor." (Canales, p. 36)

Not sure what she could say "to arm the men with valor," she rushed to the foyer, removed the flag from the wall, and walked with it downstairs. "This flag," she improvised as she walked, "has a long history, for it was flown at the San Juan gate ... the day Don Pedro returned home (December 15, 1947) ... and in Manatí (June 1948) and Lares (September 1949) during the last two years." She walked into the basement, where Carlos had gathered a group of men and told them the news she had heard three days earlier about "the arrest of Don Pedro's escorts." Then, "while waving the flag," she told them: 'This is the moment to act. We will go and seize the town.' Then she ordered them: 'Kneel and swear to defend Don Pedro, this flag and the liberty of Puerto Rico.' She saw Carlos kneel and signal the others to do the same. Then in his booming voice, she heard Carlos say: 'I swear,' an oath and the others repeated in unison." With that done, they left the basement, ready for battle. (Canales, pp. 36-37)

She found Elio outside and told him they were moving out. He told her he would follow because he only had "fifteen men and needed more." Next, she saw Carlos and another man (a witness later said was Luis Morales) "pistol in hand" commandeering a van, for they were short one vehicle in which to take the men to the center of town, a distance of four kilometers. The driver of the van, she said, appeared reluctant at first, "but after Carlos threatened him with the pistol, he dropped off the passengers and handed over the van." Out of the vehicle came a woman, she said, "screaming hysterically." She took her up to her porch and tried to reassure her, saying: "Look, there is nothing to fear. This is a revolution we are doing for you, for the good of the people. As you can see, I am economically well-off, but I am risking all this for the liberty of the homeland." (Canales, pp. 37-38)

But since she was in a hurry, she left the woman on the porch and boarded El Cano's car, which was leaving for Jayuya. Hers had been taken by Carlos to transport his men to the police station. (The fact that Canales' car was seen in town that morning led several eyewitnesses to claim, during one of her trials, that she had been among the rebels who set fire to the police station, where a policeman lost his life and three others were injured.) She, on the other hand, always maintained that after El Cano left her in Jayuya she went directly to the telephone office, to cut the wires. That mission, however, had not been completed because the tool she brought with her proved inadequate. What saved the day, in her view, was that, "the bag where I had my revolver flew open, and the telephone operator became frightened and promised to lock up the place and go into hiding." Unable to find any of her comrades to watch the telephone operator, she left for her next assignment, "hoping the woman had been sufficiently frightened to stay in hiding." (Canales, p. 39)

She climbed the stairs to the balcony of the River Palace Hotel (located above Guillermo Hernandez pharmacy), and from there saw "smoke coming out of the police station." The sight of the burning station, she noted, reassured her that Carlos and his men had carried out their assignment." Determined to do her part, she "unfolded the flag (now the official flag of Puerto Rico), and holding it by the blue triangle let the rest of it fall downward." She waved the flag many times, she wrote, and cried out: 'Long Live Free Puerto Rico!' and invited the people gathering below (the balcony) to join the revolution." (Canales, pp. 39-40)

The River Palace Hotel, she said, was located on a heavily trafficked cross street and there were many people about, some of whom actually "stopped to cheer and give their tacit assent to the cry: 'Long Live Free Puerto Rico! Others passed by hurriedly." (Canales, p. 40)

With that assignment completed, she waited for Elio to join her, so they could proceed to City Hall to find Carlos and "proclaim Puerto Rico's independence." But when Elio reached her, around 1:00 in the afternoon, he said, he was tracking several policemen who had fled the station and had gone into hiding. Before she had time to react to the change of plans, a young man came to tell her that Carlitos had been injured and was lying in front of the Jayuya Hospital, where he had been denied treatment. Not sure where Carlitos had parked her car she asked the messenger to help her, and once she found it, she went to rescue her wounded comrade so she could take him to Dr. Peregrina's clinic in neighboring Utuado. (Canales, p. 41)

She found Carlos lying on a patch of grass in front of the Jayuya Hospital, with his cousin Mario Irizarry watching over him. As she approached, she realized that "though Carlitos had a chest wound he was not visibly bleeding or had yet lost consciousness." But when he saw her, "the gallant warrior" had said: "Don't take me to Utuado. Leave me here and go on with the struggle." To which she had replied reassuringly: "Comrade, the town has been taken and other men have joined the struggle, so we will take you to Dr. Peregrina's clinic … and then will come back here." (Canales, p. 41)

Thinking that she was on "a Red Cross mission" and that "in war rescuers of the wounded are respected," she gave her revolver to a comrade and left the flag with another, "so that it could be flown at City Hall when the republic was 'formally' proclaimed." After Mario moved Carlos to the back seat of her car, she drove him to Hernández's pharmacy, so that he could be given an injection to slow the bleeding. With that done, she set out for Utuado. The exit out of Jayuya was blocked because of the fires set by the rebels, forcing her to detour. So, by the time they reached Utuado, forty-five minutes later, Carlos "was fading and asking for water." (Canales, p. 42)

She stopped for water at the entrance of Utuado and after Carlos had his fill, she heard him cry out: 'Viva Puerto Rico Libre!' "Those words," she recalled, still teary-eyed seventeen years later, "would be the last the gallant warrior would utter. He probably knew he was dying," she said, "and as any good revolutionary wished to leave [this earth] with the word of liberty [on his lips]." She vowed never to forget him because he had made her "proud to belong to a group of brave Jayuyans, who inspired by Don Pedro Albizu Campos, had declared Puerto Rico a republic." (Canales, pp. 42-43)

Utuado's streets were also blocked due to an ongoing shootout between the Nationalists and the police. A few passersby explained she would not be able to reach Dr. Peregrina's clinic and suggested that she take Carlos to a Veterans' Hospital in the vicinity. The fact that Carlos was a veteran, she reasoned, meant the hospital would have to admit him and provide the treatment he needed. She drove him there and waited until he was admitted, before she and Mario set out again, intent on rejoining the rebels. (Canales, pp. 43-44)

They never got to Jayuya, for they were arrested a few minutes later. She explains: "as we approached the small bridge in Jayuya Abajo a man driving a van [in the opposite direction] yelled something we couldn't hear." "We, thinking … the rebels had occupied the area, smiled at each other. A few kilometers later, as we approached the now defunct sugar mill Santa Barbara, we saw a police patrol, but there was no time to ... get away." (Canales, p. 45)

"Two patrolmen motioned us to stop and I, thinking they couldn't arrest us because we were unarmed ... stopped the car." They approached, "with guns drawn, and ordered us out of the car." The one on her right, she recalled, searched her roughly and took away her purse, which contained money and other valuables, which were never returned. The other officer parked her car near the sugar mill while the first escorted her and Mario to the back seat of the patrol van. Then he called San Juan to report the news that the "Nationalist leader Blanca Canales and her companion Mario Irizarry have just been arrested." She was amused, she said, to hear the policeman call her a leader because she only thought of herself "as a rank and file soldier." (Canales, pp. 45-46)

It was about 2:30 in the afternoon of a very hot day, she recalled. The police van was "stifling hot due to the enclosed space" and the lack of ventilation made her "nauseous." She "hadn't felt well all day probably due to (her) thyroid condition." But rather than "make a spectacle, which the officers would surely interpret as lack of courage," she decided to pray and then pushed herself closer to the front section of the van, where two windows had been left open. To distract herself, she played mental games, asking herself at one point: "Why would anyone want to be a policeman ... and ... persecute those who struggle to free them?" Hours passed before one of the patrolmen returned, with the suggestion: "let's take these two into town and use them as shields against their comrades' bullets." They were not intimidated, she wrote, nor did they say anything, "so as not to provoke the furious beasts," but inwardly she thought: "The cowards won't dare enter the town, even after their reinforcements arrive." (Canales, p. 46)

At 4:00 in the afternoon, one of the policemen moved them from the patrol van to her own car, which was being guarded by another armed officer. That policeman, she suspected, was probably afraid, "because he kept pacing around the car while stealing looks at the cane field behind the mill, as if he expected the rebels to be hiding there." Then he suddenly stopped pacing and looking at her yelled: "I feel like killing this old hag," a threat which did not frighten her, she explained. (Canales, pp. 46-47)

Sitting in her car, she said, was not only more comfortable, but allowed them to hear what passersby were saying. She overheard a townsman say that: "City Hall has been torched and there are more than two hundred rebels in control of the town." She was glad to hear the news because this "meant that Elio and his men had kept up the struggle even without Carlos and Mario's help." (Canales, p. 47)

At dusk "a police captain took over the wheel and drove us away," she explained. At first, she and Mario thought they would be taken to the District Court of Arecibo, but soon realized they were on their way to Ponce. (Canales, p. 48) The mystery of their destination was cleared up a few days later when a journalist reported that Blanca Canales and Mario Irizarry were taken to the District Court of Ponce "because they were arrested in the outskirts of Adjuntas, which falls under Ponce's jurisdiction."[6]

Canales concludes her testimony by recounting bits of information she gathered from Jayuya comrades, arrested a few days later. They told her that portions of Jayuya had remained "under rebel control for three days, before the National Guard bombed the town from the air and then dispatched ground troops to hunt them. They assured her that Elio's forces had proclaimed the Republic of Puerto Rico after she left for Utuado and had hoisted the flag on the very spot where she had displayed it earlier. They told her that Elio and his men had set fire to the police station and the post office. His men had also destroyed postal material and the records of the U.S. Selective Service Center. In the end, they had even set fire to homes and businesses "of those who spied on us." But that as the National Guard began bombing the town Elio had retreated with his troops to Coabey and continued the struggle from there until November 2 (1950) when they "had been forced to surrender to the ground troops." (Canales, pp. 48-49) (Elio told reporter Miñi Seijo years later that he surrendered after he learned that his brother Griselio had been killed in the attack on Blair House in Washington, D.C.)[7]

What Canales' comrades apparently didn't tell her was that some of the terrified townspeople had agreed to collaborate with the authorities. Some, according to one press account, were overheard "shouting at the rebels as they were brought to the District Court of Arecibo for questioning." A follow-up article the following day reported that, the U.S. Marshals escorting Elio Torresola and other Jayuyan rebels had been "hard-pressed to protect them from the wrath of the Jayuya townspeople."[8]

Detention, Trials and Sentencing

According to the widespread press coverage of the 1950 Nationalist uprising and its aftermath, Canales was first interrogated at the Ponce District Court before she was transferred to the District Court of Arecibo,
where she was charged and then sent to the Women's Wing of its District
Jail. The charges brought against her in Arecibo were: murder in the first
degree; three attempts of murder; setting fire to Jayuya's police station;
and destruction of various town properties. Though Canales and various
eyewitnesses said that she had nothing to do with the fires because she
had left town long before, the district attorneys insisted that she was to
blame for the casualties and destruction of property because she was "the
brain behind the events that led to those atrocities."[9]

She was next charged by San Juan's District Court of conspiring to
overthrow the island's government by force and violence, an open violation of Puerto Rico's Sedition Act, Law #53. She was also charged with
possession of an unregistered firearm (a charge she never denied), a
violation of Puerto Rico's Arms Statute. On the basis of these crimes (real
and alleged), she was sent to San Juan's District Jail, known as La
Princesa, where she was to be held, without bail, until her various cases
came to trial. At La Princesa she was housed in a tiny cubicle (other inmates called "la alacena"). That cubicle was adjacent to a larger room
where her comrades: Doris Torresola, Ruth Reynolds, Olga Isabel Viscal,
and Carmen María Pérez were being held.[10]

Lastly, on November 28 Canales and seven Jayuyan comrades were
also charged by the U.S. Federal Court in San Juan for the following:
"conspiring to destroy U.S. federal property; forced entry of the U.S. Post
Office of Jayuya; destruction of postal material; setting fire to the post
office and damage to other federal property." The federal judge, Thomas
H. Roberts, set bail of $25,000 for each of the accused, only to discover
that none could be freed because the Puerto Rican authorities had denied
them the right to bail (for the alleged crimes listed earlier).[11]

The group pled innocent to the federal charges, and then Canales'
principal attorney, Charles H. Juliá, requested a reduction of bail for his
client. Judge Roberts instructed the counsel to submit his motion in writing. Next, Gaspar Encarnación Santana, another member of the defense,
asked Judge Roberts to consider the fact that he and his colleagues had
restricted access to their clients at La Princesa because the Puerto Rican

Department of Justice insisted that they must submit their requests, in writing, twenty-four hours prior to the intended visit. Judge Roberts replied that the Federal Court "does not permit restrictions of a defendant's constitutional rights," but cautioned that since he was "unfamiliar with the island's statutes," the counsel should attach a copy of the island's legal code to his petition. That exchange led Federal Prosecutor Francisco Ponsa Feliú to remind Judge Roberts that, "since the accused are held in a Puerto Rican jail, they are bound to obey the rules and regulations set by the local Department of Justice, which are amply supported by the island's statutes." With that impasse unresolved, the eight were sent back to jail to await trial.[12]

In the meantime (November 30, 1950), the Attorney General of Puerto Rico, Vicente Géigel Polanco, ordered that Blanca Canales be dismissed from the job she had held at the Department of Health since 1943. At first, a reporter said, she had worked at the Department's San Juan office, but since July 1, 1946 had been the Director of Social Relief Services in Jayuya. It was from that position, the head of personnel, Manuel A. Pérez explained, that she had taken a "six-month unpaid medical leave, which would end in December (1950). He said she had requested the transfer to Jayuya, even though the move did not represent a promotion or a raise in salary. In fact, he added, the transfer had cost her nearly three hundred dollars cut in salary, [from $2,100.00 to $1,800.00 a year]. But due to gradual pay increases she was earning $2,040.00 a year at the time she was granted the medical leave, July 1, 1950. But given her present situation, she "no longer qualified to hold a government job," and would be dismissed.[13]

Canales' economic and legal problems mounted at the end of the year, when Jayuya merchant Domingo Rodríguez Roldán sued her for damages in the sum of $31,000. According to the plaintiff, she was responsible for the destruction of his store (on October 30) "because she had conspired with others to set the fire which resulted in the destruction of so many town properties." According to the municipal authorities, the estimated damages caused by the fires, set by the Nationalists on October 30 exceeded $700,000. It is not clear how Rodríguez Roldán's suit was resolved, but the Jayuya case took a couple of interesting twists. First, according to a "confidential, unofficial letter" sent by the Secretary of Justice to the Office of the Governor, the insurers of the municipal properties were "balking at having to reimburse the town for the damages caused by the Nationalists." According to what he had been told, the insurers were claiming that, "they could not be held responsible for damages caused by armed revolts, revolutions, rebellions or other politically motivated acts." But a friend in the field had advised that, "the insurers might consider paying half of the municipality's claims "if it were proven that the destruction had been the result of "criminal" rather than "political" acts.[14]

Apparently his friend's suggestion had the intended effect because from the start the prosecutors and the courts, where Canales and other Jayuyans were tried, rejected any allegation or implication that the deaths and destruction of public property were anything other than "criminally motivated acts." Apparently, the insurers were satisfied because the Jayuya government was subsequently paid half of its claims by the insurers.[15]

The other interesting twist in the Jayuya story was that it forced the Puerto Rican government to come to terms quickly with the issue of the language it should employ to describe the Nationalist attacks of October 30. Eager to downplay the importance of the uprising, which occurred so soon after they took office, the newly elected administration dismissed the terms "revolt, rebellion and revolution," when either was introduced by the defense, in favor of the neutral word "sucesos" (events). The District Courts led the way by rejecting the use of any of the politically charged terms, or their implications, by declaring that these had been "criminal acts." One interesting exchange occurred during Canales's second trial, in May 1951, when Juan Hernández Vallé, a member of the defense team, repeated the statement: "this Court lacks jurisdiction to try the case before it because the charges for which the defendants are being tried are political and not criminal acts." Annoyed with the implication of the counsel's argument, Judge Rafael Padró Parés warned him that if he persisted in his allegations, he would have him cited for contempt and removed from Court.[16]

The first of Canales' trials, however, took place in the U.S. Federal Court, in San Juan, in February 1951. She was one of the eight defendants and the only woman being tried for the damages caused to federal property in Jayuya. Tried along with her were Elio Torresola and the brothers Fidel and Mario Irizarry and four others. The prosecutor in that case, Francisco Ponsa Feliú, was aided by a few policemen and several eyewitnesses, including the passenger of the van Canales had left on her porch the morning of October 30. The star witness for the prosecution was the policeman Modesto Estrada, who testified that he had been on duty at the Jayuya police station when the attackers arrived. He identified Blanca Canales as one of them. He said that she was carrying a flag, which she "waved twice, before Elio Torresola began shooting and throwing [fire] bombs at the place." In the attack, he added, officer "Virgilio Camacho received a gunshot to the head," and he and Miguel Figueroa (another policeman) were also injured. He explained that he jumped out of the police station into the patio of the parish home next door when the fire started. "No, Virgilio did not jump," he said, "because he was badly wounded and that's why he perished in the fire." He claimed he "saw eighteen attackers" storming the police station, and suggested that they were same people who set fire to the U.S. Post Office, the Selective Service, the theater, and other town properties.[17]

The owner of the town's hardware store, Ricardo Abruña, testified that his business had perished in the fire, set by the persons who attacked the police station, among whom he identified Blanca Canales. Yet the next merchant called to the stand, Carmelo Andújar, said, "the fire [at the police station] was set by Elio Torresola." He made no mention of seeing Canales in the group of arsonists. Later, the manager of Jayuya's Post Office, Armando Rivera, said that he had closed the place (and a business he owned in town) as soon as he heard "gun shots." He recalled "seeing Blanca Canales on the porch of the River Palace Hotel, waving a flag and shouting, 'Viva la República,' 'Viva Jayuya, el Primer Pueblo Libre de Puerto Rico.' He added that a little later he came upon Elio Torresola, and the Irizarry brothers, Fidel and Mario, who were "all well armed." After that encounter, he said, he went home and locked himself and his family in the bathroom, where they would "have surely perished had it not been for two neighbors who rescued us when the fire at the station started."[18]

Lastly, the passenger of the van testified that she saw Carlos Irizarry and Luis Morales Negrón (one of the Menchas) threaten the driver and force him to drop off his passengers and hand over his vehicle. Then, she said, "Blanca Canales came and took me up to her porch, and told me I would not be hurt; that they just needed the van to go to town to fulfill (their) duty."[19]

During cross-examination the defense challenged many of the witnesses' statements. For example, Attorney Hernández Vallé asked Officer Estrada: "How can you be sure there were eighteen attackers at the police station, if by your own admission, you fled shortly after the fire began?" Adding: "When did you have time to count them?" Next, Attorney Charles H. Juliá challenged Ricardo Abruña's assertion that he had seen Canales among the rebels who stormed the police station. "How can that be," he asked, "when others in this Court have clearly stated that she was on the balcony of the River Palace Hotel, waving a flag and proclaiming Puerto Rico's independence?" He also challenged Estrada's claim that Canales had been among those who set fire at the U.S. Post Office. "How could she possibly be where you say she was, when others here have testified seeing her leave town an hour before the post office fire began?" (The three witnesses who claimed to have seen her leave town before the fire at the post office started were: the owner of the gas station in town, Ariel Dávila, the Pharmacist Guillermo Hernández, who had given Carlos an injection to stop the bleeding, and homeowner Cecilio Díaz, who claimed he "had spent the entire day watching (his) home while the post office was burning."[20]

Despite the fact that much of the evidence presented by the prosecution focused on the fire at the police station and on the destruction of municipal property, the jury at the Federal Court rendered a guilty verdict on all counts against all eight defendants on February 26, 1951. Perhaps because the verdict was rendered at 11:40 in the evening, stated a reporter on the scene, Judge Roberts chose to adjourn the Court without setting the date for sentencing. The lack of concrete facts to report on that topic led a journalist for El Imparcial to predict that Judge Roberts was likely to hand down a sentence of twenty-five years (ten years for the crime of conspiracy to destroy U.S. property; and five years each for the other three offenses (forced entry of the post office; destruction of postal material; and setting malicious fires). His counterpart for El Mundo forecast a longer sentence of thirty-five years. What both accurately reported to their readers was that the trial that had just ended was only the beginning of the legal ordeals for the eight, who would soon have to face two other trials in the local courts.[21]

The sentences handed down by Judge Roberts on April 9, 1951, were a few years shorter (ten to seventeen years) than the ones the journalists had predicted. In Canales' case, for instance, she was given three prison sentences, totaling ten years (five for the count of "conspiracy" to destroy federal property, three years for "destruction" of the U.S. Post Office, and two years for "damages to other federal property"). Arguing that the charge of destruction of the U.S. Post Office had not been proven, Charles H, Juliá appealed the three-year prison sentence for that count. Since the sentences were to run concurrently, the journalists again speculated that Canales might not have to serve more than eight years at a federal penitentiary, even if her attorney failed to win the appeal. They had reason to suspect the appeal might be lost since it was already being challenged by the Federal Prosecutor Francisco Ponsa Feliú, who argued that even if Canales "did not set the fire that destroyed the U.S. Post Office, she is the brain behind the attack that caused its destruction." Eager to extricate himself from the ongoing political bickering surrounding the case, Judge Roberts explained his reasoning for his sentencing, saying he "had not viewed the attacks on the U.S. Post Office and other federal property as anything other than violations of federal statutes" and since "the culprits had been convicted based on the evidence," his sentencing was "not done out of vengeance, but in accordance with what the law prescribed in such cases."[22]

Canales' federal appeal was reviewed on April 20, 1951, but failed to be resolved because of repeated objections by Prosecutor Ponsa Feliú. In a letter she wrote to Juan Hernández Vallé, on June 29, 1951, from the Women's Reformatory in West Virginia, she makes it clear that her appeal was still pending. Yet the fact that she served only five-and-half years of the original ten-year sentence in Alderson suggests that the appeal was resolved in her favor at a later time.[23]

But before Canales was sent to West Virginia, she had to be tried by Puerto Rico's courts for the various alleged crimes described earlier (the death of Virgilio Camacho, the injuries of three other police officers, the destruction of Jayuya properties, violations of Law #53 and the illegal possession of a firearm). The trial, for the alleged crimes committed in Jayuya, began with a review of the charges at the District Court of Arecibo, on April 30, 1951. The prosecution assigned to the case included two district attorneys from Arecibo and four from San Juan. Leading the San Juan group was Chief Prosecutor, José C. Aponte. On the side of the accused were several public defenders and a few privately engaged lawyers from San Juan. In Canales' case, the principal counsel was Charles H. Juliá, the same San Juan attorney who had defended her in the federal case. Ostensibly, he had been hired by her brother, House Representative Mario Canales.[24]

The first action Juliá took on her behalf in this case, according to one press account, was to seek a reduction of her charges by petitioning the Court to grant her a separate trial. Apparently, he had not consulted her because she immediately asked him to drop the petition, and then addressed the Court, saying: "I wish to run the same fate as my comrades from Jayuya. History shall take care of putting these events in their rightful place. I'd rather be judged by history and thus want to be tried together with my comrades and not separately."[25]

After her motion was withdrawn, two other members of the defense (Juan Hernández Vallé and Juan Hernández Vargas) requested that Juliá be allowed to join their team and that Blanca Canales be added to their list of clients. The Court agreed to both requests. But then other attorneys submitted motions for "separate trials" for eight of their clients, arguing that "a joint trial" deprived their clients of "substantial constitutional rights and the opportunity for a fair and impartial trial." The prosecution objected in each instance, arguing that "joint processes are perfectly legal and in no way deprive the defendants of substantial rights." The question was left to the discretion of the Judge (Padró Parés), who took another two days to study the matter before rendering a decision. In the meantime, the prosecution continued to amass witnesses, and by the time the trial began, it had more than one hundred persons (most of them members of the police force) spread out through various Court chambers.[26]

Finally, on May 4, 1951, Judge Padró Parés notified the defense that, he was allowing separate trials for the eight. To simplify the process, he then divided the accused into two sub-groups: one consisting of the eight who were to be tried separately, and the twenty-one others (twenty men and one woman) who were to be tried jointly. A jury for the joint trial was then selected and the following day the prosecution was allowed to begin opening argument. Special District Attorney José C. Aponte, aided by his five colleagues, spoke for hours, promising to prove the accused were guilty as charged. They also expressed hopes that once convicted, the culprits would receive the maximum penalty prescribed by law.[27]

After the first day of argument, a journalist reported a rumor he had overheard, which claimed that Blanca Canales might be contemplating suicide. The story, according to the defense "lacked basis in fact." He explained that Canales had merely asked the Court for permission to have a medication she needed brought in. Her request was presented to Chief Prosecutor José C. Aponte, who in turn submitted it to Judge Padró Parés for approval. The Judge chose to turn it down, saying he could not approve it "for fear that the pills might cause her death." In the defense's view, there was no need to worry about Canales, for she was perfectly calm and had no intention of ending her life. The press account led the Secretary of Justice, to call the journalist to his office to explain the source of his story.[28]

The trial resumed on May 6 and the prosecution called Canales' uncle, Raúl Torresola to the stand. The uncle (as indicated earlier) had been living on Canales's farm when the uprising began. (Since he had also lived in Albizu Campos' home in late 1940s, the prosecution viewed him as a valuable witness.) In Canales' case, he testified that around 9:00 in the morning, October 30, 1950, he went to her bedroom "to bring her coffee, and found her listening to the radio." He said, "After she drank her coffee, she asked me to serve milk and crackers to the lads in the basement." He did as she instructed and in the basement "found Elio Torresola, Luis Morales Negrón and many others (he identified for the Court) armed with pistols and revolvers." In the basement, he also "saw rifles, carbines and bottles filled with gasoline, and stuffed with rags" (Molotov cocktails). He added that, he returned to his niece's bedroom, and this time she had given him "a $10.00 bill, saying: "Take this because I don't know if I'm going to jail or the cemetery" and then handed him "a small briefcase, saying take this to Arquelio Torre's house." After that exchange, he recalled, he "saw her walk down the stairs, with the flag from the foyer on her arm, and got into a car that was leaving for Jayuya."[29]

Then thirteen-year-old Luis Quiles, a self-proclaimed participant in the attack of Jayuya, testified that he had been in Canales' basement the morning of October 30, and had "sworn to defend the flag, Don Pedro and the homeland with my life, if necessary." He knew Miss Canales, he explained, "Because she is a social worker in town who helped me get a pair of special shoes because I am handicapped." In his estimate, he was one of about "thirty men who left for Jayuya that morning." He said he rode in one of the cars, "holding two boxes of bullets and explosives on my lap." He added that after the shooting at the police station ended, a few of the men had set fire to the building."[30]

Next, town merchant Carmelo Andújar testified that several of the defendants present (whom he identified) "entered my furniture store (located on the ground floor of the police station) took a mattress, doused it with gasoline, and set it on fire," even though he had begged them not to do it. The fire spread quickly, he explained, and "within minutes the entire building was engulfed in flames." Since one of the charges levied against Canales and her codefendants was the death of Virgilio Camacho, who presumably had died as a result of the fire, a pathologist was then called to describe his findings. He remarked only: "All I can say with any degree of certainty is that the remains I examined belong to a human between the ages of twenty-three and twenty-five, but can't tell you whether they belong to a man or a woman." The defense, a reporter wrote, was pleased with the pathologist's "unadorned professional opinion," because they were tired of "seeing the prosecution parading around with a box, claiming it contained the bones and ashes of the dead policeman." A firefighter called to the stand next also stuck to the facts, saying he had found in the ashes: "a police badge, with an illegible number, a black jack, a dental bridge, and a "Sam Brown" belt buckle," the kind policemen sometimes wear." So, "no concrete evidence that any of it belonged to Camacho," said a member of the defense team.[31]

During cross-examination the defense challenged many of the witnesses' statements (some obviously contradictory). On several occasions it also had to remind the Court that the defendants (especially Canales) were not on trial for the events at the U.S. Post Office and other federal sites "because that case has already been tried in the U.S. Federal Court." In his closing argument, Charles H. Juliá made the case that the prosecution had failed to prove that Canales had taken part in any of the events at the Jayuya police station. Judge Padró Parés ignored the defense's arguments and allowed the jury to proceed on the basis of the evidence presented by the prosecution. As indicated earlier, he also dismissed Hernández Vallé's claims that the defendants were "revolutionaries," or that their acts were motivated by political aims. In the Judge's view, the defendants "were criminals as the evidence had shown."[32]

On May 12, 1951, after nearly two weeks of depositions, interrogations, counter interrogations, and more than two days of deliberations, the Jury rendered a guilty verdict on all counts for all the twenty-one defendants. The Judge then set May 21 as the day for sentencing. This time the journalists made no predictions, but merely commented that the convicted "appeared calm and serene" despite the guilty verdict.[33]

The sentences handed down by Judge Padró Parés on May 21 (1951) were as follows: life in prison for the crime of murder in the first degree; three prison terms of six-to-fourteen years each for the three attempts of murder; plus a variety of other penalties for the crimes of destruction of the police station and other public properties. In other words, all twenty-one were condemned to spend the rest of their lives in prison. But before the Judge passed sentence, Canales and several others were summoned to a new trial (her third) by the District Court of San Juan. This case focused on the alleged crimes against the state, the so-called violations of Law #53 and the violations of the Arms Statute. If convicted of those charges (as she was), she could expect an additional sentence of six-to-ten years.[34]

Prison Life at Alderson, 1951-1956

Once the trials in Puerto Rico ended, Canales was sent to the Federal Reformatory for Women in Alderson, West Virginia, to serve the federal sentences handed down in San Juan by Judge Roberts. She arrived at the Reformatory in early June 1951 (possibly June 10th), according to the letter she wrote to Juan Hernández Vallé. In that letter, she reported, conditions at the Reformatory were "surprisingly humane because though I am still under 'quarantine' I am permitted to write to you, Charles H. Juliá, and Guarina" [her sister]. "This prison," she explained, "has no bars, yet discipline is good." She said she felt well, though already "feeling nostalgic for Puerto Rico." She attributed the nostalgia to "the beauty of the ... mountains, trees, and flowers here," which reminded her "of the grounds of the Instituto Politécnico of San Germán" (now Inter-American University). In closing, she instructed Hernández Vallé to use her two surnames in any correspondence he might send her, "because here I am known by my mother's surname [Torresola], a curious detail that will surely amuse my cousins."[35]

The Reformatory, where Canales spent the next five-and-half years, explained jail mate Elizabeth Gurley Flynn, was built in 1928, as the 'first federal penal facility for women established in the United States." At first, she wrote, "the institution was known as the Federal Institute for Women and its focus was on reforming first-term offenders." For that reason, it did not accept recidivists or parole violators in its population. During the 1930s, she added, the Reformatory had lived up to its mission as it provided "a variety of educational programs in a safe, humane environment." The location of the Reformatory, she explained, was chosen in part for its natural beauty and moderate climate, (except for a short winter), and partly because the county government had donated two hundred of the five hundred acres needed. Conceived as an experiment in self-sufficiency for about five hundred women, it included a farm, dairy, greenhouse, bakery, kitchens, infirmary, library, auditorium, chapel, garment shop, and laundry.[36]

In keeping with the idea of reforming its residents, the buildings that housed the inmates were called "cottages" and were built around two concentric quadrangles called "campuses." The cottages, except for numbers 26 and 27 (used to quarantine newcomers and house the mentally ill) did not have bars (a detail Canales reported in her letter to Hernández Vallé). By the 1950s, when Canales arrived, the various educational programs offered initially had been suspended, and the population was no longer limited to "first-termers." As a result, the number of inmates had grown to six hundred, said Gurley Flynn. By the 1950s, all organized sports had also been abandoned, though inmates were still "permitted to play ball directly in front of their cottages." Previously, the prison had allowed a "religious worker to visit inmates in their rooms," but that practice had been suspended in the 1950s on the pretext that the religious worker had become "too friendly with the Puerto Rican nationalists," noted Gurley Flynn.[37]

In earlier days, she continued, "inmates had been allowed to buy flower seeds and grow individual gardens and some of the "long termers had planted beautiful gardens, a joy to all." But that practice was dropped in 1957 "when official landscaping became the rule." The women were so upset, she added, that "they tore up the gardens." Previously when an inmate was ill, or chose to stay "locked-in" she could expect a tray of food delivered to her room. But that too had changed and inmates who were "locked-in" would not be allowed out "even to shower." For food, they could expect "black coffee, without sugar, for breakfast; bread and vegetables for lunch; and peanut butter sandwiches for dinner." And though the Reformatory had undergone many changes since the 1930s, she added, it still operated under the illusion of its past, in part because of "the natural beauty of the place."[38]

The optimism expressed by Blanca Canales in her June letter apparently vanished the minute she was faced with winter. According to a description offered by Gurley Flynn: "Blanca had never been to the United States before coming to prison, and she suffered a great deal from the cold in winter. She wore blue slacks and tied them at the ankles over heavy socks. She wore a heavy overcoat, much too large for her, which came to her shoe tops, and a knitted stocking cap with a muffler. But even in this quaint attire there was a certain dash to this little woman."[39]

She recalled meeting Blanca Canales when she went to visit her comrade, Claudia Jones who was ill: "On one of my visits to the clinic ... I saw a stout little, white-haired woman, who spoke [English] with a Spanish accent. She smiled at me with such cordiality that I felt she must be someone special."[40]

When she mentioned the encounter to Claudia Jones, she had said: "That's Blanca, one of the Puerto Rican Nationalists." She recalled later that Claudia had often spoken of this woman for whom she had written a poem, titled "My Anti-Fascist Friend." (Jones later re-titled the poem: "For Consuela—Anti-Fascista," according to her biographer, Carol Boyce Davies.)[41]

In Alderson, Gurley Flynn recalled also meeting Lolita Lebrón, Rosa Collazo, and Carmen [Dolores Otero] Torresola. "The Nationalists," she said, "were known for their unquestioned honesty and one had been placed in charge of the garments of women about to be released." She recalled that, before they got to know each other, the Puerto Rican women had been "puzzled by my friendship with the priest since they knew I was a Communist who never went to church." She told them that this was possible "because we are both Irish." To which they had replied: "Oh, nationalism!" That they understood, Gurley Flynn said, "Because nationalism was their second religion."[42]

In another section of her book, titled "The Politicals in Alderson," Gurley Flynn described what she had learned about Blanca Canales in that prison:

> In her country she was a well-known social worker, who belonged to a leading family. I heard that her brother was a member of the Puerto Rican House of Representatives. She had been a member of the revolutionary Nationalist Party and a great admirer of their revered leader, Dr. Pedro Albizu Campos, who is now in prison for life, in his country. When I told her that I visited him years ago in the Columbus Hospital in

New York, her eyes sparkled with excitement. A woman who
knows her at home told me she was one of the best-dressed
women there, had her own car, and was extremely competent.
Later, when I knew Blanca better, I told her this. She laughed
merrily and said, 'My friends should see me now!'[43]

"At Alderson," Gurley Flynn added, "Blanca worked on a small hand-
loom because she had a heart condition [and was not] strong enough to
operate a wide loom." Yet she was "one of the best weavers ... and wove
place mats in lovely contrasting colors." Blanca, she added, "was a devout Catholic and made altar pieces for the chapel." Though they "differed on matters of politics and religion," she wrote, she had been happy
"to be able to discuss a wide range of topics with such an intelligent
woman." She also told a story about the time Blanca led a protest because
a guard had ordered one of her compatriots to speak English. "Blanca
was so incensed," she said, "that she marched her comrades out of the
cottage and led them in singing the Puerto Rican freedom hymn [La Bor-
inqueña]. And when the guard heard the "hubbub," Blanca had said,
laughing triumphantly, 'she came outside and retracted her silly order.'"[44]

Correspondence and Censorship

West Virginia was much too far for friends and relatives from Puerto Rico
to visit Blanca. They wrote letters instead to keep her abreast of family
matters, Don Pedro's health, and the fate of other imprisoned comrades.
Though most letters (incoming and outgoing) eventually reached the
intended party, the process generally took a month because it first had
to clear the censors at the FBI's Division of Correspondence in Pittsburgh, Pennsylvania. The person intercepting Canales' letters at Alderson
was the warden, Nina Kinsella. A review of several FBI files suggests that
the person who wrote most often to Blanca was her cousin and comrade,
Angelina Torresola. From the censor's perspective, Angelina's letters were
important "because she is in an ideal position to report on all members
of the Torresola family since she is in regular contact with her siblings
[Doris and Elio] and other imprisoned Nationalists." Her home, they
wrote, "is where relatives congregate and Nationalists visit." Hoping the
letters might yield information they could use, the censors photocopied

and translated (from Spanish to English) each piece of correspondence and forwarded copies of it to FBI headquarters in Washington, D.C. and to the regional offices in San Juan, New York, and Chicago.[45]

Among the pieces of mail Warden Kinsella forwarded to the censors in Pittsburgh was a short note sent to Blanca by her godchild, five-year-old Ana María Platet (Angelina's and Alfredo's daughter). In the photocopy I examined, dated December 7, 1952, the child merely wished her godmother joy and peace for the upcoming holidays.[46]

In one of Angelina's letter, dated October 14, 1953, she told Blanca, she had only visited Albizu "twice" since his release from prison two weeks earlier. She said she felt badly, but couldn't do any better because she had too "many obligations at present." At the time she was caring for her elderly mother Doña Rosalina Roura. In addition to her husband and their child, there were other relatives living with them in their small house in Puerto Nuevo (Hato Rey). Among them were Elio's wife Delia Rivera and her son Elio Ariel. Her sister Doris had lived there for a while after she was released from prison but was at the moment in Albizu's apartment helping to care for him because he was very ill.[47]

In a letter of January 21, 1954, Angelina expressed her joy about having met Rosa Collazo at Albizu's place. She wrote, "Rosa came directly from the airport to share the news that she had just visited her husband [Oscar] and found him well and in good spirits." After they were introduced, Rosa had said that "she is interested in meeting my mother" and that she would be visiting Lolita's children in Mayagüez because she "is anxious for news about them." (The Lolita mentioned here is Carmen Dolores Otero de Torresola, Griselio Torresola's widow, known in Puerto Rico as Lolita Otero, and in New York as Carmen Torresola.) "The poor thing," Angelina added, "It must be terrible for her to be separated from her children when they are so young."[48]

In another letter six days later (January 27, 1954), she offered the names of the persons who had met Doris when she left prison the previous August. She explained that in addition to herself and her husband Alfredo [Platet] there were six others who went to receive her in Arecibo: Juanita Ojeda Maldonado, Isabel Rosado Morales, Carmen María Pérez González, José Rivera Sotomayor, Enrique Ayoroa Abreu, and Doris' lawyer, Juan Hernández Vallé. Though all these names were known to the FBI, the Pittsburgh censors recorded them and filed the letter.[49]

On February 14, 1954, Angelina wrote again, obviously saddened by

Albizu's declining health. "He is so ill," she declared, "that his poor care-
givers ... work day and night without rest or sleep." She despaired, she
said, "Because I am unable to help when I visit." The only ones who "relieve them from time to time when they visit are Juanita Ojeda and Isabel
Rosado." But rather than end the letter on a sad note, she added, "I am
happy that we left Jayuya, where men go dancing without their wives, a
conduct that has ended here. And, with God's help, we will soon be buying a house in a new development here (Hato Rey), which can be paid
for in twenty years." In closing, she conveyed greetings from Heriberto
Marín (one of the Jayuyans imprisoned for his role in the town's uprising). By late February 1954, the censors had "grown bored" with the
cousins' letters because of the "meager yield" they provided. But the file
was kept open just in case.[50]

La Escuela Industrial Para Mujeres

According to official records, the Escuela Industrial Para Mujeres was
Puerto Rico's first female prison, built in 1954, in an attempt to "reha-
bilitate its inmates in a more humane environment." Previously, women
had been housed in designated areas of prisons built for men. But unlike
the facility in West Virginia, where Canales had spent more than five
years, the Vega Alta prison did not restrict its population to any particular group of inmates. In her December 1957 report, explained the
prison's second director, Lydia Peña de Planas, the facility had 393 inmates, including a few minors. She wrote that during the last trimester
of 1957, ninety-one prisoners had been released: some on parole and
others after completing their terms and during the same period, ninety-
five new prisoners had been admitted, thirty-four of which hadn't yet
been sentenced. Of the sixty-one who came already sentenced, she
added, forty-eight were due to serve six months or less, nine had "inde-
terminate sentences," and three were due to serve from six months to a
year. Included in the December 1957 population, she said, were four Nationalists: Blanca Canales, Carmen María Pérez, Isabel Rosado, and Doris
Torresola. (It should be noted that by December 1957 Leonides Díaz,
Juana Mills, Juanita Ojeda, Angelina Torresola de Platet, and Olga Isabel
Viscal had come and gone and that Monserrate Valle and Ruth Mary
Reynolds, who had served time in the Women's wing of the Arecibo Jail,

had been released before the Vega Alta prison was even built.)[51]

The two Director's reports I examined suggest that though she was not consulted about the type of inmates the prison received, she was apparently free to decide the manner in which the institution functioned. According to a report she submitted to the Superintendent of Prisons in 1954 (shortly after she was appointed to the post), the first problem she addressed was "to remove the few minors from the institution." She said she sent them to an "age appropriate facility, the Escuela de Niñas de Ponce," where she had worked previously. Then she relocated the Admissions Office next to the Infirmary in the area of Maximum Security in another building. She explained that, relocating the Admissions Office made the "in-take" process more efficient, "since that is the first place where newcomers are sent for their routine medical examinations before they are admitted." To simplify the registration process further, she said, she reassigned the "in-take" task to the nurse on duty at the Infirmary (Sra. Eugenia Molina), "who is a trained professional, who deals wisely with the new arrivals." Once the admissions process was completed Sra. Molina was instructed to forward the paperwork to the Classification Office, where "Sra. Micheo is in charge of assigning housing (according to the inmates' type of sentence, length of stay, behavior and mental health) and registering the new arrivals for classes, workshops and jobs." Both processes, she added, were overseen by her assistant, Srta. Crucita Arzuaga.[52]

She added that she had also reassigned the staff, according to training and prison requirements during each of its three daily shifts. Each guard had been required to submit a written report at the end of her day in which she listed what issues had surfaced during her shift and whether these had been resolved or left pending. A few of those reports suggest that the prison faced a variety of challenges, not all easily solved. For example, a guard assigned to the morning shift (6:00 a.m. to 2:00 p.m.) in Maximum Security reported that there were days when the mentally ill inmates refused to leave their beds, shower, or clean their rooms before she could escort them to breakfast. On more than one occasion a guard assigned to the night shift (10 p.m. to 6 a.m.) also in Maximum Security (where the Nationalists were housed) reported that two mentally ill inmates would not go to sleep unless she gave them sleeping pills, otherwise they would stay awake all night "and keep everyone else from getting their needed rest." On another occasion, the guard on the morning shift discovered the entire cellblock of Maximum Security had flooded. According to what she reported, one of the mentally ill inmates had stuffed the toilet with paper during the night because she was "angry." She was angry, she said, because her cellmate (another mentally ill woman) "had spent the whole night singing" and didn't let her sleep. The same two inmates were later caught fighting, and a male guard was called in "to separate them." The two were then sent to solitary confinement "until they settled down," according to the guard's report.[53]

The mornings the guards encountered problems, they kept everyone "locked down" until the culprits were removed. The mornings everyone followed the rules: rising at 6:00 a.m., washing up and cleaning their rooms before 7:00 a.m., they were taken to breakfast on time, and after the "morning recount" were escorted to their jobs, classes or workshops without delay. The goal of the institution was to keep the inmates (except those who were ill or in isolation) busy at all times, doing "useful work," such as sewing, knitting, cooking, cleaning, or gardening.[54]

Within the environment described, the Nationalists, the best educated of the group (two were social workers and the two youngest had high school diplomas), became assets to the administration. According to several guards' reports, they taught the literacy classes, worked in the library and often oversaw the sewing and knitting workshops. Blanca Canales, who was also proficient in English, was occasionally asked to translate documents for the administration.[55]

Yet despite the Director's plans and voiced optimism, the Vega Alta prison, like the Alderson Reformatory, failed to achieve its goal of rehabilitating its population. In one of her reports the Director suggested that implementing the programs was a problem because of the constant shift in population. According to Isabel Rosado and Carmen María Pérez, who spent many years in that prison, the reason the programs failed was because they didn't offer "anything of value to the inmates." They said the women came to prison "already knowing how to sew, knit, cook, clean and garden and didn't learn anything in those workshops." The literacy classes could have worked, Rosado said, because many of the inmates were illiterate, but the prison lacked the teaching materials and the classes were taught irregularly. According to the Director's reports, the skilled sewers and knitters in the group "sewed uniforms, aprons and other items the prison needed." The recreational sports, prescribed as a fundamental part of the rehabilitation program, never got off the ground, according to the guards' own reports. As a result, "boredom" was one of the biggest problems of prison life, according to Carmen María Pérez and Isabel Rosado. To combat it, they and their comrades had decided to work everyday, even if the task they performed was not always meaningful.[56]

The mornings when there were "no chores," or the inmates finished what they were assigned ahead of time, wrote one guard, she would "take them outside for one hour of passive recreation, so they could breathe fresh air and enjoy the sunshine." Regrettably, she added, this was only possible if there was enough time left to get them back inside for the late morning recount, before they had to report to lunch, which was served at 11:30 in the morning.[57]

Though the Vega Alta prison was much newer than the other prisons where she had been, Rosado said, in some ways it was much worse, for it promised what it couldn't deliver. "The reality of the place," she said, "was a far cry from the idyllic picture portrayed in the official literature." She explained: "The main difference between "the 'famous Escuela' and the older prisons was that it was built in a rural area. But don't be fooled by the name Escuela," she admonished, "It was just a prison pure and simple, with bars everywhere." Other than "the alphabetization classes [she often taught] there was no rehabilitation program as such," she added.[58]

What she remembered best about the 'so-called Escuela,' she said, were the injustices that were committed. She recounted the story of Genoveva Flores, who after several days in solitary confinement began screaming one night that she wanted water. The guard on duty, she added, continued to ignore her, which meant that no one in the cellblock would be able to sleep that night. To put an end to the ordeal, Rosado offered the guard a paper cup in which to bring "the poor woman the water." The reason for the paper cup, she explained, was that many times "the women in solitary confinement used the empty cups to bang on the metal bars." The guard took the paper cup, Rosado said, and brought the water, but when she opened the gate she "found Genoveva in the midst of giving birth, with the child's head already showing between her legs." So at that hour, she said laughing merrily, "She had to rush woman and child to the hospital."[59]

The story of Genoveva's childbirth led me to ask Carmen María Pérez whether any of the Nationalists had ever been sexually molested in any of the prisons they were held. Surprised by the question, she asked me to turn off the tape recorder before responding: "It happened," she said, "but not to us" (meaning the Nationalist inmates). "No one dared to mess with us. But there were cases of common prisoners who were taken from their cells at night by the male guards who wanted to sleep with them."[60]

Were the Nationalists ever disciplined? According to the prison logs I examined, the Nationalists were rarely reported to the Disciplinary Board of the Vega Alta prison. When asked about this, Rosado said, "That's because we knew our rights and we also didn't bother much with the guards, so they left us alone." Yet there was one instance in which Pérez and Canales were reported by one guard for disobeying her orders. But rather than send them before the Disciplinary Board, the Director, Peña de Planas, visited them in their cell, "to hear their side of the story." Both readily admitted they had disobeyed the guard's orders, but explained that they had done so "because she addressed us in a rude and disrespectful manner." Since the guard in question was known for "her brusque treatment of inmates," the Director chose to drop the matter after admonishing both parties. Apparently neither Pérez nor Canales suffered any reprisals, as often happened with the common prisoners.[61]

According to a brief sampling of the Visitors' Logs, relatives visited Canales regularly at the Vega Alta prison. Among those who came on November 26, 1956, when she first arrived, were: her brother Mario Canales and his wife Mary Vélez de Canales, who came directly from Jayuya. Also present during that visit were her sister, Guarina Canales de Culpepper (then residing in Hato Rey) and two nieces (Paulita and Alicia Platet, residents of Santurce and Hato Rey respectively). Most of the same visitors came every week during the month of December. On December 29, 1956, for example, Guarina's husband, Samuel Culpepper and their daughter, Carmen Culpepper also visited. Though the number of visitors dwindled a bit over time, Canales was never alone during visiting days, as was the case for a few others.[62]

Other prison logs indicate that Canales received a larger supply of allowable foods from her relatives than did her comrades. Her brother Mario and his wife Mary, for example, brought her fresh fruits, vegetables and eggs from their farm in Lares, while other family members, living in San Juan, brought her packaged foods, such as canned meats, fruits in syrup, powdered milk, cocoa powder, crackers, hard candies, and other sweets. Guarina and her daughter Carmen Culpepper often brought

Blanca books, magazines, writing paper, ink, stamps, tissues, sanitary napkins, soap, tooth paste and other toiletries she had either had requested or they thought she needed. Occasionally, Guarina also left her a money order or check with which she could purchase items she wanted or needed from the commissary. A few friends and comrades (who had been released) also came to visit and brought her news about Don Pedro and others still incarcerated. Some of them also updated her on the island's politics.[63]

Though visiting Blanca was now easier for Angelina, she still wrote to her. As in the past, the letters between the two were detoured, this time to the censors at the Department of Justice headquarters in San Juan. Receipt of their correspondence was delayed from three weeks to a month, even when what they wrote was "deemed safe enough to be allowed through." In a letter Blanca wrote to Angelina, on February 11, 1966, she said, that she was "on a spiritual retreat," which would end on Sunday, "the day of my sixtieth birthday." She had taken a break, she said, "to let you and Isabel [Rosado] know that, I took communion at six this morning and prayed for the liberty of Puerto Rico." She closed by saying that as of that day she had been in jail "fifteen years, three months."[64]

She had no way of knowing then that she would be freed within a year and half, thanks to a pardon she would receive from the newly elected governor, Roberto Sánchez Vilella. Nor did she suspect that over the next four years, the new Governor would pardon other Nationalist convicted for similar violations of Law #53. (It should be noted that Law #53 had been abolished ten years prior.) It is hard to know exactly what motivated Governor Sánchez to free them, while he continued to support the arrests of other independence advocates. Some have argued that he was merely responding to pressure from local and international groups, which were clamoring for the release of the political prisoners from Puerto Rican and United States prisons. By the time Canales was released (late August 1967), she had served nearly eleven years of a life sentence in the women's prison in Vega Alta, Puerto Rico and five-and-a half years in the federal prison of Alderson, West Virginia. Prior to that, she had spent six months in pre-trial detention in three of Puerto Rico's jails. Asked by an eager reporter how she felt about being pardoned by the Governor, she replied, "I was released because I am too old to do any harm."[65]

Life as a Free Woman

Though Canales lived another twenty-nine years after she was released from prison, she never again inhabited her family home in Coabey, just as she had feared that last weekend of October 1950. At the time of her release, she was sixty-one years old and plagued with various illnesses: thyroid problems, a heart condition, and arthritis, among others. Unable to return to the Coabey home, which had fallen into disrepair during her imprisonment, she moved in with her sister Guarina until she could find a place of her own. According to reporter Peggy Ann Bliss, who interviewed her in 1993, Canales (then eighty-seven years old) was living in a government-subsidized apartment complex in Hato Rey, Puerto Rico, called the Leopoldo Figueroa Residences for the Aging. Apparently, she was unwell and was being cared for by the nurse Conchita Crespo.[66]

According to what she told Bliss, she had been unable to work since her release from prison, in part because of her ill health. Fortunately, she had not had to work, she said, because her sister Guarina had sold her share of the family farm and given her the proceeds to cover expenses. She made no mention whether she was also receiving Social Security, a benefit she had paid for and to which she was entitled. Asked by Bliss whether she had ever married, Canales replied, "No, but there were suitors who wrote me letters." Adding: "They were men without spirit ... I loved them all but could never feel [for them] the admiration I felt for Don Pedro."[67]

Bliss reported that Canales' handbag (the one the police took from her during her arrest in 1950) had been found a few months earlier at the Ponce Court as it was undergoing renovation. According to the police, "the handbag contained a picture of Joan of Arc, with a message scribbled below that said: Help us gain the independence of Puerto Rico." When asked about her experience in the Alderson prison, Canales reportedly recounted the story (described earlier by Gurley Flynn) of her having led a protest when one of her compatriots "was ordered to speak English." And then added proudly: "My Puerto Rican jail mates learned many things from me." She told Bliss also that her brother Mario Canales had visited her three times at Alderson. She added: "My family supported me because I acted for the country."[68]

In a follow-up article Bliss wrote after her visit, she described the transformation of the Canales' family home into a museum. She explained that various figures had wished to recognize "the importance of the Canales family in the town's development." They explained that the "family patriarch, Don Rosario, who died in 1924, had been not only one of the town's founders, but its first mayor." His oldest son, Nemesio Canales, "was a celebrated journalist, poet, playwright and novelist." His other son Mario (from a second marriage) "became a well-known political figure within the Popular Democratic Party and served for more than twenty years in the island's House of Representatives before he was appointed Secretary of the Department of Agriculture." While his younger sister Blanca, though best known for her revolutionary actions, had "worked as a teacher and social worker in town for many years."[69]

Transforming the Canales' home into a museum was considered an important step in the town's history, according to José (Pepito) Reyes, head of the Círculo Canalino, the organization that spearheaded the project. Converting the house into a museum, he told Bliss, took nearly two decades, in part because the house had to be rebuilt after so many years of neglect. He said he had grown up in the area because his father had managed the Canales farm for years. He recalled that he was a teenager when the Nationalists attacked Jayuya and had seen many townspeople hide in the cemetery the next day when the National Guard began bombing the town from the air. Thus, he felt it was important to preserve the Canales home as part of the town's legacy. The cost of transforming the home into a museum, he explained, was nearly $60,000, but fortunately most of the funds had been donated by Héctor Ramos Mimoso, past member of the House of Representatives (1952-1956) and supporter of Puerto Rican independence.[70]

According to Bliss, Blanca attended the opening ceremony of the "house-museum." Though the place was still a "work in progress," it already had several items of interest on display. The Canales library, for example, exhibited part of Nemesio's collection, such as copies of his writings: a novel, plays and clippings of his columns "Paliques." It displayed also a few family photographs as well as a small sampling of weapons and artifacts from the assault on the town on October 30, 1950. The founders were enthusiastic because they were in the process of recreating the room where Albizu Campos had slept when he visited. Apparently, 1993 was the last time Blanca Canales visited the place she had called home until she was arrested four decades earlier.[71]

What became of Blanca Canales during the last decades of her life remains a bit of a mystery. Except for a few details culled from newspaper articles, there is little to go on. In an interview I conducted with Lydia Collazo (Rosa Collazo's daughter), she mentioned that after Canales was released from prison in 1967, she used to visit her mother (whom she had met in Alderson, West Virginia years earlier) and "take her to meetings and Nationalist activities." Assuming that Canales still drove a car at this point, it is possible that she remained politically active through the 1980s, as Rosa Collazo did. Yet one wonders: Why would she abandon her earlier pattern of avoiding public appearances?[72]

There is some evidence to suggest that she didn't totally abandon her earlier ways. In a letter she wrote to Rosa Collazo in December 1984, she excuses herself for having missed the celebration in Rosa's honor, held at the Puerto Rican Bar Association in Miramar, Santurce. Also, in an article published in *Claridad* in June 1985, the reporter comments on Canales' absence from an activity where she was one of the six women being honored. The event, which took place in barrio Santana, Arecibo, was dedicated to the late Leonides Díaz, a Nationalist who, like Canales, spent many years in the women's prison in Vega Alta, Puerto Rico. It is not as if Canales didn't know the other women being honored, for they had all spent time together in the same cellblock in the Vega Alta prison.[73]

For the most part the reporters who interviewed Canales between the 1970s and 1990s did so during the month of October, as the anniversary of the uprising drew near. Curiously, they tended to interview her about the male leaders she had known. For example, in October 1975, reporter Miñi Seijo interviewed her for an article she was writing about Carlos Irizarry, the Coabey leader who lost his life in the attack of Jayuya's police station. Asked when and how she met Irizarry, she replied: "I first took notice of Carlitos after a coworker at the Office of Public Welfare in Jayuya told me about his fiery defense of Puerto Rico's independence." Before that, she added, "we merely greeted each other in passing because we were neighbors." She reiterated, "After I heard that story, I went home and asked Elio to invite Carlitos to join our group. By then Carlitos was a student at the University of Puerto Rico and was attending Nationalist Party meetings in Río Piedras with Raimundo" [Díaz Pacheco], she explained.[74]

Five years later (October 1980) Miñi Seijo again interviewed Canales, this time for an article about Raimundo Díaz Pacheco, the Nationalist Party military commander, who lost his life during the attack on the Governor's mansion (La Fortaleza) in 1950. She said she "met Díaz Pacheco in 1932" and thought he was "an upright, courageous man, a devoted member of Don Pedro's guard." She explained that his family had lost a farm they owned in Trujillo Alto during the Great Depression and that "had forced Raimundo to work as a laborer for the San José Sugar Mill" in Río Piedras. "While he was working there," she added, "the fields went up in flames and Raimundo was accused because he was a Nationalist." But "nothing was ever proven, so he was released," she said.[75]

In 1990, as the fortieth anniversary of the Nationalist uprising approached, *El Mundo* sent a reporter to interview Blanca Canales. He asked her: "When was the revolution supposed to take place, if not in 1950?" She told him what she had said twenty-three years earlier that, the armed attack had been planned for 1952, in response to the United States plans to establish the commonwealth government. "What was their goal?" he asked. "The goal," she replied, "was to pressure the United Nations to address the case of Puerto Rico's colonialism." No, she replied, she hadn't known about the change of plans for the attack until the last weekend of October.[76]

Then in the early 1990s, Jean Zwickel, a close friend of the late Ruth Reynolds (from their days at the Harlem Ashram), visited Puerto Rico in order to interview Canales and other Nationalist women. According to what she wrote, she had been "surprised to find that though [Canales] lives a quiet life in a government housing project, she is still kept under surveillance, phone tapped, and her every move checked by a woman undercover agent." She stated that, "Though [Canales] is still a devout Catholic, she remains unafraid and rooted in the revolution." (Zwickel, like Reynolds, was a Pacifist.) In her earlier interview with reporter Bliss, Canales had explained that she had been "baptized a Methodist because my father had donated land for a Methodist chapel and the grateful fathers baptized me." She added that she had later "converted, and the Catholic Church with its mystical heritage won over." She showed Bliss the religious items she kept in her room, saying: "Converts are more devoted."[77]

Canales died on July 25, 1996, at the San Francisco Hospital in Río Piedras, Puerto Rico. She was ninety years old. In a biographical essay Marisa Rosado wrote a few days after her death, she recounted two anecdotes for which Canales is generally remembered: 1) her refusal to be tried separately from her from her comrades in Arecibo in May 1951;

and 2) her request to one of the defense lawyers to "stop trying to wrap me in the American flag in order to defend me." (Apparently the counsel in question had been trying to appease Judge Padró Parés by speaking glowingly about the American flag.) "I admire the American flag," she said, "as I do the flag of any other nation, but I prefer mine, the Puerto Rican flag."[78]

For her actions and her courage, she is still honored by select groups of admirers throughout Puerto Rico, New York, and Chicago.

2. Leonides Díaz Díaz (1900–1967)

Preface

Leonides Díaz Díaz was a fifty-year old woman when she was convicted of eleven crimes she had not committed. Ironically, the Justice Department that sentenced her to nearly five hundred years in prison was a recent creation of the first elected government in Puerto Rico's history. She would have probably died in prison had it not been for the dogged efforts of her counsel Santos P. Amadeo, and for the opportune ruling of the United States Supreme Court, April 2, 1956, in the case of Pennsylvania vs. Nelson. For though Puerto Rico's colonial government had been reformed in 1952, the United States federal laws still applied, unless the United States Congress determined otherwise. In the following account I will strive to outline the events that sent Leonides Díaz to prison and those which helped to gain her release seven years later.

Family Life in Rural Puerto Rico

Leonides Díaz Díaz was born in barrio Santana, Arecibo, Puerto Rico, June 21, 1900. She grew up on a farm, surrounded by five siblings, and a loving extended family. Her parents Isabelino Díaz Díaz and María Díaz Cintrón agreed to send her to school, but the facility she attended was far from home and she opted to leave it before completing the third grade. Like most women of rural Puerto Rico of that time, Leonides then stayed home to help her mother raise her younger children. During her teens she was taught to sew, knit, and embroider: skills that would serve her well in her adult life.[1]

According to various stories told about Leonides' mother, Doña María Díaz, she had been an ardent supporter of Puerto Rico's right to independence. She reportedly told Isabel Rosado, whom she met through her daughter Leonides, that in 1898 she "had seen American soldiers on her

91

parents' farm "appropriating the corn the family had sown and feeding it to their mules. They neither asked nor paid for it but simply took it," she said, still in disbelief. She also told Rosado that by the time the soldiers arrived at her parents' farm, she had overheard many stories of their 'unspeakable acts.' "No woman," she had been forewarned, "would be safe in the path of these barbarous men." Thus when she first saw the soldiers enter the shed where the family dried the corn, she locked herself up "in the house, with a sharp machete on hand." Her grandsons Ricardo, Jr. and Angel Ramón Díaz would tell the newsweekly *Claridad* years later that, in 1936, when Doña María learned that Nationalists Hiram Rosado and Elías Beauchamp had been killed in San Juan while in police custody, she had summoned her young sons and asked them, "Why aren't you in San Juan fighting for justice for our homeland?"[2]

Thus, it appears that young Leonides Díaz grew up hearing stories about the abuses committed by the invading troops and the injustices later perpetrated by the new colonial rulers. Then at age twenty-two, she married Ricardo Díaz Díaz, who later became a devoted member of the Puerto Rican Nationalist Party and ardent follower of Pedro Albizu Campos. Together, she and Ricardo raised six children: four boys and two girls. One of the couple's sons, according to her prison data, died young, while the two oldest, Ricardo, Jr. and Angel Ramón, became active members of the Nationalist Party and joined their father in the assault against Arecibo's police station during the uprising of October 30, 1950. Only one of their adult sons, Andrés, and daughters Jovita and Ana Clotilde remained free to visit their parents and siblings after they were sent to prison.[3]

Arrest, Trials and Incarceration

The day Leonides Díaz was arrested (November 2, 1950) she was at home, where she had always been. But since her home was the place where the plot to attack the Arecibo police station was finalized, according to ex-Nationalist Guillermo Hernández Vega, she was detained by members of the National Guard and brought to Arecibo's District Court for interrogation. Following the interrogation she was indicted on eleven felony counts and sent to the Women's Wing of Arecibo's District Jail. The basis for her arrest, explained her sons, Ricardo, Jr. and Angel

Ramón, many years later, was a statement made by the National Guards-men, who questioned her. They claimed that when they went to the Díaz' farm to inquire the whereabouts of Ricardo, Sr. and his sons, Leonides had told them: "Gentlemen it is unbelievable that you should be looking for them here on a day like today when you should be out there fighting for the independence of our homeland." This statement, according to her sons, "was all the evidence the authorities needed to indict her on charges of conspiracy in the attack of the Arecibo police station." The attack left four policemen dead and six wounded. Her support for her husband and sons also caused her to be charged with one violation of Puerto Rico's Sedition Act (Law #53).[4]

Denied bail by Arecibo's District Court, she was sent to the Women's Wing of the Arecibo jail, where she would remain until her cases came up for review. The first trial against her and twelve others accused of the attack on the police station began in mid-April 1951. Ideally, colonial law stipulated that the accused should expect "a speedy trial," no later than six months from the date he or she was officially charged. Failing that timeline, the defense could request the client's temporary release until the case came up for review. In Leonides Díaz' case, the trial came up within the term stipulated by law. The problem, according to her defense, was not a violation of the time frame in which her case was reviewed, but the many unfair practices the legal system inflicted along the way. First, she had been detained by members of the National Guard, persons not authorized by law to make citizens' arrests. Next, she had been denied bail, which caused her to be deprived of her freedom before she had been convicted of any crime. Then, when the cases against her were finally brought to trial, she had been ill served by a legal system, which "per-mitted the presiding judge to commit numerous irregularities."[5]

Articles in the local press described how during the proceedings against Leonides Díaz and her co-defendants, Judge Rafael Padró Parés had been "exceedingly partial," allowing the prosecution, "to drag the case" by summoning more than fifty witnesses to the stand, most of them detectives and undercover policemen, simply to make the point that they had seen many of the defendants at numerous Nationalist Party activities. Since most of the defendants also had been photographed without their permission or knowledge by the detectives or undercover agents, "a lot of time was wasted by the District Court in identifying the photographs and placing them in evidence, despite repeated objections from the defense." Judge Padró Parés apparently ignored the fact that the surveillance records he admitted as evidence were in themselves gross violations of the defendants' constitutional rights. Throughout the proceedings, the press contends, the Judge did little to hide his antipathy toward the accused or his tendency to disregard the attorneys appointed to defend them. As a result, many confrontations erupted between the two parties. Another problem, the press noted, was that the defense attorneys, most of them public defenders, were either appointed late in the game by Judge Padró's Court, or given incomplete files. Thus, in some instances the defense was seen leafing through their client's files as the proceedings were underway. When Francisco Colón Gordiani, one of the public defenders in that case, protested the conditions in which he was expected to work, Judge Padró threatened to cite him for contempt and have him removed from court. Not easily intimidated, the veteran counsel continued to press his case, arguing that he had been unable to interview two clients assigned to him that morning. He added that one of the files was also missing important documents. When other counsels made similar claims, the Judge reluctantly acquiesced, and ordered the Court's Secretary to furnish the documents requested, in order to proceed with the case.[6]

In this rather unlevel playing field, the prosecution began by calling upon the two pathologists who had conducted the autopsies on the four policemen killed in the assault, the crime for which all thirteen defendants stood accused. Leonides Díaz, the only female in the group, though nowhere near the scene of the assault, also stood accused of the same crimes. The defense, one journalist said, posed no questions to the physicians and that allowed the prosecution to proceed to call to the stand its star witness, Guillermo Hernández Vega. A Nationalist until quite recently, Hernández Vega had opted to collaborate with the prosecution in hopes of escaping many years of imprisonment. To that end, he remained on the witness stand for more than four hours at a time, detailing all he knew about his former friends and comrades. Since he had been a trusted member of the Arecibo Nationalists until the day of the uprising, he was in a good position to offer details about the Party, its plans, and its major leaders. Those details would later be useful to the prosecutors in the proceedings that followed. For example, Hernández Vega explained that the attacks on the island's police stations were integral parts of the overall plan for the insurrection, while the plan itself had been designed and approved by Pedro Albizu Campos and the Party's military commander,

Raimundo Díaz Pacheco. The assault on the Arecibo police station, he said, had been approved and led by Tomás López de Victoria, the region's military man, and Juan Jaca Hernández. He also disclosed that the Arecibo plotters had accumulated a variety of weapons, which they kept hidden in Ricardo Díaz Sr.'s farm. The weapons, he explained, consisted of "rifles, pistols, a sub-machine gun and other firearms." Díaz's home, he revealed, was also the place where the plotters had met to review the plan of attack a few days prior to the event.[7]

He revealed also that he and his comrades were instructed to use "secret words" to safeguard their plans in the presence of strangers. He recalled that one day when he was assigned to patrol Ricardo Díaz' home he had been given a rifle and instructions to keep strangers from venturing near the house. He was told to greet the stranger with the word "sol" (sun) and wait for him to respond "luna" (moon). If he didn't utter the correct word, he should not let him pass, no matter what reasons the intruder gave. We might recall that nearly a century earlier the Lares's rebels also used secret words and symbols to communicate amongst themselves. At some point during Hernández Vega's testimony, Jaca Hernández, one of the defendants, was so enraged that he gestured, threatening the witness' life. According to another press report, the Judge noticed Jaca's gesture and issued him a stern rebuke. Obviously, the witness was in a difficult place. Having been offered immunity, he had to be candid with the authorities regarding what he knew, but betraying his comrades could mean losing his life at the hands of a fellow Nationalist.[8]

Curiously, three years after the Arecibo trials concluded, the same witness, Hernández Vega, was brought to the Southern District Court of New York, to testify against Dolores (Lolita) Lebrón and sixteen other Puerto Rican stateside residents then on trial for conspiracy in the March 1954 shooting of the United States Congress. Intrigued by the witness' new role, FBI agents in New York asked him whether he was receiving monetary compensation from the Puerto Rican authorities. He replied that in 1951 he had been "paid the standard witness fee of $1.50 a day," and given police protection (which continued in 1954) because his life "had been threatened by various members of the Nationalist Party." The FBI agents asked next whether he had been arrested after the attack on Arecibo in 1951. He replied that he had not, a detail they found hard to understand, given the witness' previous record as a Nationalist. Until October 1950 he had been a member of the Nationalist Cadets, and one who enjoyed parading in full uniform at Party activities. Yet this individual, a self-admitted member of the Arecibo conspirators, was not only allowed to go free after the attack on the Arecibo police station, but remained under police protection, while Leonides Díaz, one of the many he had accused, was convicted and sentenced to spend the rest of her life in prison.[9]

Following the April 1951 trial, which lasted nearly two weeks, Leonides and her co-defendants were convicted on all four counts of "assassination in the first degree" and six counts of "attempted murder." The males in the group were also convicted of several arms violations. Leonides escaped that charge. All of them were also tried more than a year later (August 1952) for alleged violations of Law #53. At the conclusion of the various trials, including those related to Law #53 all thirteen were convicted and sentenced to more than 480 years in prison. Leonides Díaz, for example, was convicted of eleven crimes and sentenced by Judge Padró Parés as follows: four life terms (one per each of the dead policemen) and six terms of six-to-fourteen years (one per each of the wounded officers) plus a term of two-to-ten years for the one violation of Law #53. All told, by September of 1952 Leonides Díaz had been convicted of all eleven crimes set against her and sentenced to 495 years. The sentences did not take into account the nine months she had spent in prison before she was brought to trial.[10]

The case of Leonides Díaz is significant because she was sentenced to multiple prison terms on scant and questionable evidence. Prior to her arrest, November 2, 1950, there were no records to suggest that she had been an active member of the Nationalist Party. Her name did not appear in the surveillance records gathered by the Division of Internal Security or in those submitted by the San Juan FBI office to its headquarters in Washington. Her name does not figure on the list of members or affiliates who attended Nationalist Party rallies or meetings or who visited Albizu Campos at the Nationalist headquarters. She was also not listed among those who contributed or raised funds for the Party coffers. According to the appeals filed later on her behalf by attorney Santos P. Amadeo (1954, 1956) she was "arrested, tried and convicted on hearsay and guilt by association." At one point, he said, "The most she could have been accused of was being a loyal wife and mother." Yet as he also acknowledged, she was arrested, convicted and deprived of her freedom because the first elected Puerto Rican government had created its own version of the McCarthy era.[11]

Life in Prison for Leonides

After her sentencing in August 1952, Leonides Díaz was returned to the Arecibo prison where she had been held all along because at the time Puerto Rico did not have a penal facility just for women. Her husband Ricardo Sr. and her sons, Ricardo, Jr. and Angel Ramón, along with the other nine males similarly sentenced, were transferred to the state penitentiary, the infamous "Oso Blanco," in Río Piedras, Puerto Rico. The transfer from Arecibo to other penal facilities created an added burden for the Díaz children, who visited their parents and siblings regularly. Since few in Puerto Rico then owned their own cars, and public transportation was practically non-existent, the Díaz siblings had to hire a public car service every time they needed to travel between Arecibo and San Juan. Yet despite the expense and the inconvenience those trips entailed for the family, Andrés and his sisters Jovita and Ana Clotilde visited their parents and siblings as often as twice a month for many years.[12]

During the first four years of her imprisonment, Leonides Díaz came into contact with six other women who, like her, had been arrested for alleged crimes against the state, the so-called violations of Law #53. Among them were: Carmen María (Carmín) Pérez González, Doris Torresola Roura, Isabel Rosado Morales, Olga Isabel Viscal Garriga, and Ruth Mary Reynolds. The first two on the list were arrested at the Nationalist headquarters in San Juan, where they had been caring for Albizu Campos when the police came to arrest him on October 30, 1950. Of the two, only Doris Torresola had the distinction of having been wounded in defense of her leader. Viscal had been subpoenaed as a witness prior to her arrest.[13]

The practice of subpoenaing witnesses on the basis of their political beliefs, reported a Civil Rights Committee established several years later, was a gross violation of Puerto Ricans' civil and human rights. More than eight hundred Puerto Ricans had been summoned "as witnesses" during the first week of November 1950 and held in police custody, without just cause, for a week or more. Though most were released, their detention records were never cleared, and that caused several to lose their jobs and others to be kept under police surveillance. That miscarriage of justice has led some scholars to suggest that the Puerto Rican government used the uprising of October 30 as a ruse to lock up its critics in order to pave the way for the registration of new voters, slated for the first week of November 1950. It was hoped that by this measure the PDP administration could secure approval of Public Law 600, the statute that would enable the island to change (disguise, the Nationalists said) Puerto Rico's colonial status. Public Law 600 was approved by a majority of Puerto Rican voters and the United States kept its promised and permitted the establishment of the Commonwealth of Puerto Rico in 1952). It was against this political backdrop that Leonides Díaz and her comrades were incarcerated with the consent of a compliant Justice Department.[14]

Pérez and Rosado said during their interviews that they had become close friends of Leonides Díaz during their time in prison, and had often gone to visit her at the family farm in Arecibo after they were all released. Although Reynolds and Viscal also interacted with Leonides Díaz in the Arecibo prison, there is no record to suggest that they ever became friends. According to some of the prison staff, Viscal might not have been welcomed by the "quiet, sweet-natured" Leonides Díaz. For her part, Reynolds indicated during one of the many interviews, that she had not cared much for Leonides' spiritualist beliefs or practices. Apparently, Leonides held séances in jail.[15]

Pérez and Rosado also said that they admired Leonides Díaz, "because she was a devoted wife and mother." They described how she had spent "most of her spare time in (the Arecibo) jail knitting and sewing in order to earn money she would then send to her husband and sons." All her family, Rosado explained, had initially been held in the same Arecibo prison but then the males had been sent to the state penitentiary in Río Piedras. Rosado lovingly described what "Doña Leonides" did for her and her comrades to "mitigate our hunger." She recalled that since dinner in jail was served at 4:30 in the afternoon, they were generally very hungry by eight at night. "But fortunately for us," she said, "Doña Leonides worked in the kitchen, so she collected the leftovers from dinner and used them to make a delicious soup for us." Smiling, she added, "that soup calmed many a hunger pang."[16]

Leonides in Vega Alta Women's Prison

According to the records kept by the Vega Alta prison staff, Leonides continued her sewing and knitting work after she was transferred there in September 1954. "She is so busy knitting and sewing every spare hour of the day," reported one of the guards, "that she is considered a model prisoner." Another called her "a devoted wife and mother," a distinction she would not bestow on any of the other inmates. A third called her "an honorable woman," who not only "follows the institution's rules and regulations, but does it without complaint." The guards apparently liked her "because of her respectful manner and kind disposition toward others."[17]

Yet the same kindness that made her stand out from the rest of the population nearly got her into trouble once when inmates Elena Ramos and Marina Torres asked her to deliver a package to María Andino, a friend locked up in another section. Watchful Mrs. Soto, the guard on call, interrupted the transaction before it was completed, confiscated the package and reported the trio to her supervisor, Mrs. Bermúdez. The latter could have easily taken the matter to the Disciplinary Board, but upon hearing that Leonides Díaz was involved, she decided to discuss the matter informally with the director, Mrs. Peña de Planas. Two days later, December 29, 1956, the matter had been resolved and Mrs. Bermúdez let off the trio "with only a stiff warning." She reported that, after hearing what the inmates had to say, she had been convinced that the trio acted "out ignorance rather than out of malice." Satisfied also with the "respectful manner in which the three had behaved" when she admonished them, she decided to let the matter rest. She added that to her knowledge, "Leonides Díaz has always observed an exemplary conduct in this institution and most likely acted out of concern for the others, as she claimed."[18]

A review of the prison's visiting logs makes it evident that Leonides Díaz was also well liked by many members of her extended family. Among those who often visited, in addition to her son and two daughters, was her sister-in-law Alicia Solaberrios. On holidays and other special occasions other relatives came as well, occasionally all at once. The latter was certainly the case on October 18, 1956 when ten members of her family, including her married children, their spouses and their kids paid a visit. That day even a young nephew came along. Generally, during such visits inmates were likely to receive packages of foods, items of clothing and occasionally small sums of money (in the form of checks or money orders) with which they might buy items they needed from the commissary. But in Leonides' case, according to other prison logs, it was not uncommon for her to be the one sending out packages, letters or money orders to her husband and sons while they remained in the state penitentiary in Río Piedras. Sending them care packages, she told Isabel Rosado, was the least she could do for her imprisoned husband and sons.[19]

Appeals and Release from Prison

In November 1954, the Puerto Rican Supreme Court reviewed an appeal introduced by Attorney Santos P. Amadeo on behalf of his client Leonides Díaz. The goal in that case was to get the Supreme Court to dismiss the ten sentences for murder and attempted murder that had been handed down by Judge Padró Parés at Arecibo's District Court in 1951. The counsel argued that Díaz had been unjustly convicted and sentenced for crimes she had not committed. The Supreme Court accepted the arguments and dismissed all ten sentences against her. Yet she would have to remain in prison, possibly for another six years, unless her lawyer succeeded in a new appeal he filed in 1956, requesting that she be released on bail until her case was resolved at the Puerto Rican Supreme Court. For reasons that are not altogether clear, the Supreme Court did not move on this appeal and Díaz remained in prison for another year before she was pardoned by the Governor.[20]

In the meantime, Attorney Santos P. Amadeo had been endeavoring to encourage the American Civil Liberties Union (ACLU) to undertake an investigation of the civil rights violations, which had been committed by the Puerto Rican government against a sector of its citizenry. In addition, he was preparing to bring a "test case" before the Puerto Rican Supreme Court in which he hoped to challenge the constitutionality of the statute (Law #53), which had led to the incarceration of eleven of his clients. His hopes, however, were dashed in November 1954 when the ACLU reluctantly agreed to intercede, but only "as a friend of the court" in the Appeals Case of Ruth Reynolds, which had already been submitted to the Puerto Rican Supreme Court by her New York counsel, Conrad Lynn. Lynn also had been asking the ACLU to undertake an investigation of "the multiple violations," he believed had been committed by Puerto Rico's judicial system against his client and other Nationalists. After much pressure on his part, the ACLU had finally agreed to let Santos P. Amadeo represent them in the Reynolds case in Puerto Rico but insisted that their lawyers (not Amadeo) should write the brief.[21]

Disheartened by the ACLU's apparent reluctance to investigate the Nationalists' case, Amadeo announced in the local press that he and some of his colleagues were planning to establish a Puerto Rican Civil Liberties Union, in order to investigate "the egregious violations of civil and human rights which had been committed in Puerto Rico." He also announced that he and a few colleagues were preparing to appeal the cases of Leonides Díaz and ten other Nationalists who had been convicted and sent to prison for their political beliefs.[22]

To their surprise, help arrived from an unexpected source. On April 2, 1956, the United States Supreme Court, in the case "Pennsylvania vs. Nelson" upheld a ruling of the Pennsylvania Supreme Court, which had revoked the sentences imposed on Steve Nelson by the Court of Quarter Sessions of Allegheny County for alleged violations of the state's Sedition Act. In its review of the case, Pennsylvania's Supreme Court had ruled "that The Smith Act, as amended, 18 U.S.C. 2385, which prohibits the knowing advocacy of the overthrow of the Government of the United States by force and violence, supersedes the enforceability of the Pennsylvania Sedition Act, which proscribes the same conduct."[23] The obvious question for Amadeo and his colleagues was, "Could a similar argument be made in Puerto Rico's Supreme Court regarding the Nationalists who had been convicted of violations of the local Sedition Act, Law #53?"

The fact that Puerto Rico at the time was neither a state nor an outright colony complicated matters a great deal. Did Puerto Rico's new commonwealth status mean that Law #53 was (or not) 'superseded' by the Smith Act?" Probably the one way to find out was to bring a 'test case' to the island's Supreme Court. Naturally, there were immediate political reverberations, as local rulers and their counterparts in Washington, D.C. rushed to restate the official line that Puerto Rico was a "self-governing," territory, which according to the Popular Democrats who engineered it, had the authority to enact its own laws to protect the government from internal threats. But there was also the unexplored reality that in 1950 the United States Congress, convinced that it had not yielded any of its "plenary powers" when it approved Public Law 600, had insisted that the federal powers prescribed in the old Foraker and Jones Acts be part of the Estado Libre Asociado's (ELA) constitution. If federal laws still applied in Puerto Rico, except those the Congress deemed inapplicable, and if the United States was still responsible for the safety of the island's government, did the Smith Act apply (or not) in the case at hand?[24]

As Amadeo and his colleagues would discover, the answer would be both "yes and no." For example, in March 1954, after four Puerto Rican Nationalists attacked the United States Congress, the Smith Act was applied, and nearly a dozen well-known Communists on the island were arrested under the jurisdiction of the Federal Court in San Juan, while the local Justice Department applied Law #53 to more than two dozen Nationalists. Two years later (May 1956) after the island's District Courts sentenced many of the new suspects to prison, and Amadeo and others prepared to appeal their cases in the island's Supreme Court, the FBI office in San Juan reported that Chief prosecutor, José C. Aponte, was "preparing to argue in Court that the Smith Act has no bearing in the Nationalists' case because [they are not] Communists." In other words, the island's judicial branch was not willing to let go of the power it had secured four years earlier when the island was officially declared a commonwealth by the United States. The local Justice Department was apparently preparing to argue that the "Nationalist problem was an internal affair" which could only be resolved by the island's courts.[25]

But rather than let his administration become entangled in prickly political questions that might challenge the constitutionality of Law #53, Governor Luis Muñoz Marín opted (apparently on the advice of Roger Baldwin, ex-director of the ACLU and later advisor to the United Nations) to bypass the matter, by establishing a Civil Rights Committee of his own. As he explained to the legislature in his January 1956 State of the Island Address, his decision to create a Civil Right Committee had been motivated by a recent United Nations' declaration, which sought to protect human rights around the world. His government, he proudly told his people, was "the first democracy to undertake such a challenge." To that end, he would ask the Committee, which he established in February 1956, "to conduct a thorough investigation of the state of the island's civil and human rights, and make its recommendations." To head this "pioneering mission" he named the newly appointed Secretary of Justice Juan Hernández Badillo and ostensibly "persuaded" his good friend Roger Baldwin to oversee the Committee's work.[26]

In April 1957, after fourteen months of investigation and countless reviews of oral testimonies, the Governor's Civil Rights Committee rendered a lengthy report, along with several major recommendations. One of these urged the Office of the Governor as well as the Departments of Justice and Police "to review the Government's past actions in relation to the Nationalists and the uprising of 1950, and establish guidelines to ensure protection of the fundamental rights of the island's citizens in the future." Another suggested that the Puerto Rican legislature "provide compensation to the individuals whose rights had been violated in connection to the Nationalist uprising." A third called for an end to the "police practices of targeting citizens (photographing, tailing, and keeping dossiers) because of political beliefs." Another specifically suggested "eliminating the Division of Internal Security." The last recommendation urged the government "to explore the applicability of the federal laws which seek to protect and promote the civil rights of citizens."[27]

Claiming he had been pressed for time when the Committee's report arrived at his desk, the Governor called for an extraordinary session of the island's legislature in July 1957 in order to request the repeal of Law #53 at the earliest date possible. The Legislature abided by his request and less than two weeks later abolished Law #53. Thus, in one magnanimous sweep, the law that had created much fear and sent hundreds of Puerto Ricans to prison for their political beliefs came to a swift end on August 7, 1957. For Leonides Díaz, whose appeals case had been held up in the island's Supreme Court for more than one year, the Governor's request for the abolition of Law #53 was seven years too late. Nonetheless, the Governor also made it possible for her to be released from prison before the legislators finished their work. On July 19, 1957, Governor Luis Muñoz Marín pardoned Leonides Díaz. Coincidentally, the pardon was granted one day before her case was to be heard by the island's Supreme Court. Ten others similarly convicted of violations of Law #53 were gradually pardoned as well.[28]

From a personal standpoint, the derogation of Law #53 and the Governor's pardons that followed represented good news for the unjustly incarcerated. But from the standpoint of Amadeo and his colleagues, who had endeavored to challenge the constitutionality of Puerto Rico's Sedition Statute, it was a disappointment. According to historian Ivonne Acosta, they worried that robbing the Justice Department of the chance to decide the case of Law #53 left unanswered the question, "Does the Puerto Rican legislature have the authority to enact similar laws in the future?"[29]

Two days after her release, Leonides Díaz did what she had wanted to do for the last seven years. She went to the state penitentiary in Río Piedras to visit her husband and sons. Yet her wish was only partially fulfilled because the guards at the penitentiary allowed her only to see her husband, but not her sons. According to Heriberto Marín, then an inmate in that facility for his role in the uprising of 1950, he and the 'Díaz boys' had "watched Leonides as she walked past their cells." He recalled that when Ricardo, Jr. saw her, he exclaimed, "Look how young she looks. They (her jailers) could not destroy her," while Angel Ramón (her other son) simply cried out, "Adiós mamá." Her visit, Heriberto Marín said, "Was difficult for us because we knew that Don Ricardo (Leonides' husband) was quite ill and had been confined to his cell due to a nervous breakdown." He explained that Don Ricardo had become ill after he discovered that one of his sons "had become despondent." Yet in time, the son recovered his mental health, but his father did not, according to Marín. (It should be noted that a significant number of Nationalists suffered bouts of mental illness while they were in jail.)[30]

In 1960, as Don Ricardo's mental and physical conditions worsened, Governor Muñoz opted to pardon and let him go home. He died there shortly thereafter.[31]

Leonides, the kind and ever devoted-wife, took care of her sick husband until the end of his life. She survived him by another seven years in their beloved farm in barrio Santana, Arecibo. She also continued to visit her sons at the state penitentiary until death claimed her on May 5, 1967. Sadly, she died one year before her two sons were pardoned and released from prison by the next elected governor, Roberto Sánchez Vilella. At the time of their release (1968), the Díaz brothers had served eighteen of the four hundred plus years to which they had been sentenced.[32]

3. Carmen María Pérez González
(1929-2003)

Preface

Carmen María Pérez González, better known as Carmín Pérez, was arrested twice during the 1950s for her political acts and ideals. In October 1950 she was indicted on alleged violations of Puerto Rico's Gag Rule, Law #53. She remained in jail for nearly two years before she was absolved of those charges by a jury. She was arrested again in March 1954 for engaging in a shootout with the San Juan police when they came to arrest Pedro Albizu Campos. This time she was convicted of several felony charges and sentenced to prison for many years. She was released in 1965, in part thanks to a habeas corpus filed by her comrade Isabel Rosado, and partly because the Gag Rule (Law #53) for which she had been sentenced to prison had been abolished eight years before. After Albizu's death (April 21, 1965), she joined the Socialist League (founded by Juan Antonio Corretjer) and other activist groups, including those pressuring the U.S. Navy to abandon the islands of Vieques and Culebra. She remained a target of the various local and federal counterintelligence agencies in Puerto Rico until the day she died at age seventy-four.

Coming of Age in Lares

Carmín Pérez was born on September 14, 1929, in "La America," in barrio Buenos Aires, Lares, Puerto Rico. She lived up to her teen years in the municipality of Lares, where her father Juan Eduviges Pérez owned a farm, but earned a living as a merchant, while her mother María González stayed home to care for the children. She recalled her childhood as one "full of adventures: climbing trees, throwing stones, and getting into mischief with other kids."[1]

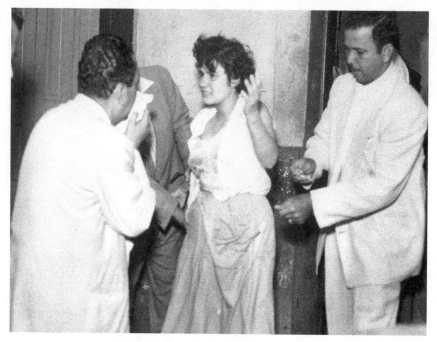

Carmen Maria (Carmin) Pérez being handcuffed in San Juan. March 6, 1954.

She attended elementary and middle schools in the rural outskirts of Lares but graduated from the high school in town. She recalled that as a teen she already had an interest in politics, and every September 23rd she and a group of friends would pressure the school to "shut down" and let the students go to the town's plaza to celebrate "El Grito de Lares" (Puerto Rico's cry of independence, 1868). She said that her love of homeland was born during that time.[2]

Sometime in 1949 (after she finished high school), she and her mother moved to Old San Juan to live with Carmín's brother. Her father did not come along, for reasons she did not care to disclose. She was "happy to discover that her new home, on Sol Street, was only a short distance from the Nationalist headquarters" (also called the Nationalist Club), the place where Pedro Albizu Campos settled with his family shortly after he returned home from prison in December 1947.

Joining the Nationalist Party

Pérez joined the Nationalist Party unofficially in 1949, shortly after she arrived in San Juan with her mother. She explained: "One day, I went for a walk along Sol Street with my mother and saw the flag and the Nationalist Club, so the next day I went there, knocked on the door and walked in. In other words, I entered the [the Nationalist Party] through the front door," she said with a grin. Yet in one of his testimonies after he was arrested in 1954, Gonzalo Lebrón told prosecutors in San Juan that on September 23, 1949 "Carmen María Pérez asked to join the Lares Nationalist chapter, which I was assigned to reorganize by Don Pedro Albizu Campos." He added that he and another member of the Party had "vouched for her, and that very day she was inducted into the Nationalist Party just hours before the leadership of the Lares Junta was appointed."[3]

For her part, Pérez explained that the day she walked into Albizu's home she was "supposed to be going to school" [she was then enrolled in Colegio Ramírez, a secretarial school], but felt she could learn more by visiting Albizu instead. She recounted that she had met Albizu Campos in Lares a few months earlier (September 1948) when he went there to speak in honor of the men who led the uprising of 1868. She recalled that she and a girlfriend had approached him as he was leaving the Catholic Church, and "he was very kind and kissed us on the cheek, saying he was very happy to meet us."[4]

She reminded him of that meeting when she walked up to his place and he assured her "that he remembered the incident." He made her feel welcome, she said, so she continued to visit him regularly, "at first, after school let out and then instead of going to school." Eventually, he grew used to her presence, she said, and put her to work: clipping newspaper articles, filing and posting his mail. It was probably because of this work that the island's Internal Security (I.S.) agents later described her as Albizu's personal secretary. She never saw herself as such, she said, she "merely helped him with chores which needed to be done."[5]

She remained at Albizu Campos' side from 1949 onward because she considered him "a great leader, totally committed to the struggle of Puerto Rico's independence." She admired him, she said, because of "his qualities as a man, who endured with valor untold challenges: from economic deprivation (after his lawyer's license was revoked in 1936) to the 'tortures' he suffered in prison and later in his own home. He survived economically, she added, thanks to the generosity of friends and comrades who brought him "small sums of money to cover the Nationalist Club's rent and pay for his family's basic necessities."[6]

She dismissed the importance of her own role in securing some of these funds. According to local I.S. agents, Carmín Pérez, Isabel Rosado, and Doris Torresola, among others, were often "seen at Nationalist Party events, collecting members' dues or soliciting funds from the audience," which they then delivered to the Albizu family for its economic survival. She said Albizu himself "lived with very little," and at one point Isabel Rosado had bought him a pair of shoes because his feet were so swollen he could not fit into the only pair he owned. She lamented how much he had suffered as a result of the "radiation experiments" he suffered in prison. She wished she and others had done more "to ease the pain and swelling of his legs and stomach he endured as a result of the radiation experiments." She marveled at how he "never asked for anything for himself" and how he appreciated every little kindness he received. "He was a person who lived with great dignity," she added. (Others would say the same about her many years later.)[7]

She described Albizu also as an intelligent, religious man, who survived his long imprisonments thanks to his "curiosity, faith in God, and sense of humor." She recalled that during the time he was jailed in La Princesa, "he would sing and whistle during the one hour of recreation he was allowed." And since he was not permitted to keep a watch, he had come up with a system of tracking the movement of the sun (with two pieces of cardboard) so he could tell the time of day. Engaging in these activities, he had told her and Doris Torresola after he was released from prison in 1953, had helped him to take his mind off his troubles during that incarceration.[8]

She admired him also: "Because he gave women the opportunity to lead, and treated them as equal partners in the struggle." Not all the men in the Party were like him, she conceded, "but they always respected us because of Don Pedro." Though males predominated in the Party's leadership," she noted, "there were women, such as Blanca Canales, Doris Torresola, and Lolita Lebrón, who also occupied important roles." The post of treasurer, she added, was often held by a woman, and women were also invited to sit with Albizu at the presidential table during annual Party meetings. Others, namely Isabel Freyre, Carmen Rosa Vidal, and Olga Isabel Viscal were known to speak in public, she said. "Not me," she explained, shaking her head, "because I never wanted to be out in front. Besides, speaking in public is for those who have something to say, which I did not." In retrospect, she agreed that, "not enough women were appointed or elected to leadership positions in the Party, though they were the ones who kept it going while the male leaders were in prison."[9]

First Arrest and Imprisonment

Her devotion to Albizu and the cause he espoused resulted in several arrests for Carmín Pérez, the first of which occurred on October 30, 1950 when she was just twenty-one years old. She was in the Nationalist Club on the afternoon of October 30, 1950 when a group of forty police officers and detectives arrived at the corner of Sol and Cruz Streets (Old San Juan) with orders to arrest Albizu Campos, who was suspected of having ordered the attacks against the Governor's residence, La Fortaleza, and various police stations throughout the island. She was arrested, she said:

> Because by then the revolution had started and the Republic [of Puerto Rico] had been proclaimed in Jayuya. The police surrounded Albizu's place, and I was there with Doris Torresola and a man called José (from Utuado), who did the cleaning. He was on the stairwell when the police began shooting at us from the street below, and pushing the people on the street against the walls and threatening them with their guns. They wanted to kill Albizu, but Doris got in front of him and she was shot in the throat.[10]

When asked, "Were you shooting?" She replied, "We were all shooting and that's when [Police Lieutenant] Astol Calero tried to kill Albizu and Doris got in front of him and was shot instead. She saved Albizu's life," she added.[11]

"Where was Doris standing when she was shot?" I persisted. "By the window facing Cruz Street, where the flag was flown; that's where Astol Calero was shooting at," she replied though she was not sure if she observed this or heard it later when Lieutenant Calero testified at her trial, in which he said, "his plan was to kill Albizu, and he had aimed at his heart." She said, "Had it not been for Doris stepping in front of Albizu he would have been killed because he did not protect himself."[12]

"So Albizu was also shooting," I observed. "We were all shooting," she confirmed. "Is it true that Albizu had an arsenal in the apartment?" "Nah," she replied, "If we had had the arsenal the police claimed, the story would have been different. We had only a few pistols and small revolvers, defense weapons mostly, because the bombs we had didn't work." She wouldn't divulge how they got their firearms but conceded that they had been hard to obtain. Asked, "Where did you learn how to shoot?" She replied, "My father had all sorts of firearms and I learned to shoot by watching him and my brother hunt pigeons." (It should be noted that "pigeon hunting" was a fairly standard reply the Nationalists gave when the authorities questioned them.) "Weren't you trained to shoot by the Nationalist Cadets?" I persisted. "No" was her only reply.[13]

She said that sometime in the afternoon of October 30, "during a pause in the shooting," Albizu had asked her and Juan José Muñoz Matos (a Cadet of the Santurce Junta, who snuck into the apartment, despite the police siege) to take Doris to the hospital. Before that, she recalled, they had been "pressing cotton balls into the wound to stop the bleeding." After Albizu gave the order, she and Muñoz Matos "half-carried" Doris down the stairs and once outside, they (the two women) boarded a 'public service car, which took them to the hospital. "A policeman accompanied us to the hospital, she recalled, but Muñoz Matos was arrested immediately."[14]

When they reached the municipal hospital on De Diego Avenue, "Doris was placed under police custody and I was arrested, and taken to Police Headquarters at stop 4" [Puerta de Tierra]. There a policeman threatened to hit her, she said, and she became so incensed that she dared him: "Well you better get started because if you hit me you'll have to kill me." She had to act tough, she explained, because she was not about to let anyone intimidate her. "After that," she said with a satisfied grin, "they calmed down and took me inside."[15]

She was detained at the Puerta de Tierra station for a few days before she was interrogated and then sent to La Princesa (San Juan's District Jail). At the station, she recalled seeing other detainees, among them several women she had never met. A few of them were questioned and then released, she explained, "because they hadn't done anything the authorities could charge them with." Among those detained and released without being charged, she said, were: Nieves Padilla, a member of the Independence Party and the Nationalists: Juanita González Bouillerce and Carmen Rosa Vidal. Another woman she saw there was Julia de Burgos' sister, "who was brought in with her two kids; the mother carrying the baby and the older child carrying the diaper bag and a bottle." (She would not give the woman's name or any other details about her until I turned off the tape recorder, a request she made several times during our interview.) "The police station was crowded, and there was no place to sit so, after a while we had to lean against the wall or sit on the floor if we got tired of standing," she added. "The men in the group were stripped of their wallets and belts and kept in check at bayonet point by several police officers."[16]

When asked, "Is it true that you slapped the warden of La Princesa?" She replied "Yes, because he came up to our cell with several guards in tow to shut down the only window in the place, and when we objected he threatened to send us to the calabozo (confinement cell)." The reason the warden of La Princesa ordered the window shut, explained Ruth Reynolds in another interview, was "Because Olga Viscal and Carmín Pérez yelled down from the window to Doris Torresola's mother that we were all fine." Pérez explained that she and Olga Viscal had in fact called out to Doris' mother when they saw her pacing along Paseo La Princesa, "because the poor woman was hoping to catch a glimpse of her daughter since visits to the prison were prohibited." Imagine how she felt, she added, "she had lost her son Griselio [in the attack of Blair House, November 1, 1950], had her other son [Elio] in jail [because he led the rebel troops in the attack against Jayuya] and a wounded daughter in La Princesa! So we decided to yell to her that we were all fine."[17]

Since that window was "the only source of light and ventilation," Pérez said, she and Doris "were so upset that we reached across the room and slapped Bravo and one or two of his guards." Not ready to have his authority challenged the warden [ex-Nationalist Juan S Bravo] made good on his promise the next day and had them [Pérez and Viscal] transferred to the Women's Wing of the Arecibo prison, where they were in fact confined to two tiny calabozos. (Doris Torresola remained in La Princesa because she was due at her first trial, along with Pedro Albizu Campos, she added. Ruth Reynolds and Isabel Rosado were sent later to the Arecibo jail.) "They took us out of La Princesa," Pérez continued, "through the back door of the jail, and put us in three armored cars, with three cars in front and three following behind, plus a helicopter flying overhead. All of that fuss because they feared that we might be planning to escape and that was the reason we had yelled down to Doris's mother."[18]

Life in Arecibo's Jail

Life in Arecibo's District jail had its challenges as well. According to what Warden J. González Lebrón explained to the Department of Justice, the institution was overcrowded so he had been forced to house the Nationalist women together in two makeshift cells on the top floor of the Women's Wing. It was the best he could do, he explained, given the orders he had received "to keep the Nationalist women isolated from the rest of the imprisoned population." For Pérez and her comrades "living together in the makeshift cells worked out relatively well," she said, "because we had each other." Their main complaint, she recalled, was being confined to those rooms twenty-three hours a day, without visits from their relatives, or contact with the outside world, except for the occasional visit from their lawyers.[19]

The makeshift cells where they slept became extremely crowded after the warden sent in two bunk-bed sets and a cot, Pérez recalled. As the youngest, she said, she offered to take the cot, "which was placed next to the toilet." At least "we had beds, and the cells had toilets," she said with a shrug, "because in Vega Alta (the next women's prison where they were sent years later) inmates in solitary confinement had to sleep on the floor because no bed was provided, and had to use a hole in the ground because there was no toilet." Until Doris joined them at the Arecibo jail, Pérez said, she had roomed only with Ruth Reynolds while Olga Viscal and Isabel Rosado occupied the other tiny cell.[20]

The other Nationalists there (Monserrate "Monse" Valle, Juanita Ojeda, and Leonides Díaz), she said, "Were housed in another small room on the second floor of the Women's Wing, probably because they were brought to that prison earlier." She hadn't known any of the three women prior to their incarceration. She wasn't sure why Valle had been arrested, but suspected (as did Isabel Rosado) that Valle had been "detained because of her husband Tomás López de Victoria" (the Nationalist accused of leading the attack against Arecibo's police station). "Was that the only reason why she was incarcerated?" I asked. "Oh no, she was also a Nationalist, but I don't think she was involved in the uprising."[21]

In Arecibo, she said, she came to know and admire Leonides Díaz "for her revolutionary history." She recounted a story (as did Isabel Rosado) that Doña María Díaz (Leonides's mother) had sharpened a machete and given it to her thirteen year old son with instructions "go and defend the homeland." She recounted also that Leonides Díaz "had stood up to the arresting officers," when they came asking for her husband and sons, saying: "They are out defending the homeland because independence will not come on a silver platter." (It should be noted that there are several versions of this story attributed to Leonides Díaz or to her mother.) "Was that the only reason why Leonides Díaz was put in jail?" I asked. "No," she replied. "She was a Nationalist, a woman of great character. Her whole family was in the revolution: her brother, her nephew, her husband and her three sons. They were all arrested and sent to prison along with her, and she was later convicted and sentenced to life in prison."[22]

"Why do you think the revolution didn't succeed?" I asked several hours later. "Because it was aborted because it began ahead of schedule. And because we didn't have enough weapons to fight against the powerful enemy." They had gone ahead, she added, "Because we had to resist and show the world that we did not want to be slaves." Not to act would have meant "that we accepted the ELA (Commonwealth) government, which was nothing more than another form of colonialism." They had to resist, she said, "Because Albizu's life had been threatened by the United States' Secretary of Defense who had ordered he'd be taken dead or alive." And those orders, they had been told "were going to be implemented on October 26 [1950] where the police would try to kill him at the activity in Fajardo. The plan hadn't succeeded "because Albizu was alerted and he took steps to avoid his capture. But after some of his escorts were arrested that evening, we feared that Albizu would be next."[23]

"So, in some ways it was like what happened in Lares in 1868?" I interjected. She nodded.

"Was Albizu planning to lead any of the revolutionary fronts?" I asked. "Well, he didn't want to leave San Juan because he was always being followed (by the I.S. agents) and he didn't want to expose the others. It was not that he didn't want to fight [as it was later claimed by the Governor]; he was waiting for the revolution to start so he could join. But there was no time! It was not that he did not want to fight! He fought, there on Sol Street, and later in 1954, but that is another story."[24]

Apparently unhappy with my line of questioning, she steered the conversation back to the women who were held in Arecibo and said that the elderly poet Trina Rodríguez de Sanz, (la Hija del Caribe) had spent at least one night in that jail. "It seems," she explained, "that her son had connections at the top and had her released the following day." There were many others "from Cabo Rojo, San Germán, Ponce, and Vieques (whose names she couldn't recall), she said, but "there were many women in the movement who were never caught." (She provided some of their names later.)[25]

Absolved by a Jury, 1952

Shortly after her own detention, Carmín Pérez was arraigned on two felony counts: attempted murder; and one violation of Law #53 (conspiring with others to depose the island's government by force and violence). Though the colonial law guaranteed the accused the right to a "speedy trial" (within six months from the time of the arrest), the proceedings in Pérez' case (for the charge of attempted murder) did not take place until fifteen months after her arrest. Yet having her case go to trial so many months later proved helpful because by then Albizu Campos and Doris Torresola had been tried and absolved of a similar charge. Her defense used that precedent to get her absolved also.[26]

The second trial (for the alleged violation of Law #53), took place in July 1952, in San Juan's District Court, with Judge Julio Suárez Correa presiding. The defendants in this case, in addition to Carmen María Pérez were: Doris Torresola, Alvaro Rivera Walker, and Juan José Muñoz Matos. The defense was conducted by A. Reyes Delgado and Julio Burgos Mundo. The prosecution, as in previous similar cases, was headed by Special Prosecutor José C. Aponte with the support of several others, in this case Baldomero Freyre. The prosecution followed a pattern established earlier: calling an excessive number of policemen and undercover agents to the stand to testify, identify photographs or verify surveillance reports about the actions for which the defendants stood accused. Much of the information revolved around their presence at Nationalist Party events and meetings, in violation of the Gag Rule (Law #53), enacted in

1948. Even attending masses for the fallen and visits to their tombs were considered violations of the 1948 statute.[27]

Though the defense repeatedly objected and called on the prosecution to stick to the facts of the case, the jury tendered a guilty verdict for three of the four defendants. To everyone's surprise, Pérez was absolved, despite the fact that she had been accused of the same charges as the others. She was free to go, Judge Suárez said, but her three comrades were to return to jail, to await sentencing. Stunned by the outcome, Pérez asked the judge to send her back to jail with her comrades. He consented to let her spend that night in jail, but said she would be released the following day. Thus, on July 19, 1952, Carmín Pérez walked out of La Princesa a free woman. (Some later speculated that she had been absolved because her father was "a big supporter" of the Muñoz government and had exerted pressure to have her released because of her young age.) The fact remains that by the time Pérez was released in July 1952, she had served nearly twenty months in prison before she was brought to trial.[28]

Asked about the conditions in prison, she exclaimed, "they were terrible everywhere." Adding "while I was in the Arecibo jail my mother died and no one told me about it for many weeks so I could not attend her burial. There was no chance to say good bye." Still stung by the experience, she asked to no one in particular: "Why couldn't they allow me to say goodbye to my mother?" In Arecibo, she explained, "we were locked-up twenty-three hours a day and deprived of contact with the outside world for many months, while in La Princesa we were deprived of air and light, after the warden had the only window in the cell shut." There they were also "subjected to electric shocks and noise vibrations," which robbed them of sleep and rest, she explained.[29]

"What was the food in the prison like?" I asked. "Simply awful," she replied. "In the mornings we were given coffee with milk, or sometimes black, and a piece of bread, or porridge, when it was available." The noon meal consisted of rice and beans, which sometimes were cooked with pig's feet. "The problem with the pigs' feet was that they generally had worms." The food was awful beyond words, she repeated. "What about fruits and salads?" I persisted. "Hardly ever," she replied.[30]

Did you or the others become ill as a result of the poor diet?" I inquired. "I never did, thank goodness, but Doris and Olga got sick. Doris especially needed better food because she had asthma." Then, when they got to know Doña Leonides, she would often bring the left over soup from the one "she made for the inmates on special diets."[31]

"Was sexual harassment ever a problem in any of the jails?" I continued. "No, goodness no, that never happened to us" (again motioning that I should turn off the tape recorder). And then explained "the Nationalist women were never bothered in that manner," but there were cases "of inmates, the ones who worked on the prison grounds, who were taken out at night by some male guards and brought back in the next morning." But the Nationalist inmates, she reiterated, "were always respected by the guards and seen as 'protectors' by the other inmates." They would complain to them, she said, "and we would go to their defense." Isabel Rosado, especially, had always defended the "common prisoners," she added, and for that she was named "the inmates counsel" by the guards and some administrators.[32]

Second Arrest and Imprisonment

After her release from prison in July 1952, Carmín Pérez lived only a short time as free woman before she was arrested again on March 6, 1954. During the short reprieve she continued to do political work, and after Albizu Campos was released (September 1953), she said, that she Doris Torresola and José Rivera Sotomayor took turns taking care of him "because he was already very sick due to the tortures he had suffered in jail." He was so ill, she added, "that [Governor] Muñoz Marín decided to pardon him, for fear that he might die in jail and become a martyr to his followers."[33]

Once out of prison, she was kept under strict surveillance by local undercover agents (I.S.) and a host of informants paid for by the FBI office in San Juan. Thus, shortly before Albizu returned home, an informant reported to the FBI office in San Juan that, "Carmín Pérez was trying to purchase a gun for herself," while I.S. agents reported to the Chief of Police (Salvador T. Roig) and he, in turn, alerted the Governor, that Carmen María Pérez, Doris Torresola, and others "were plotting a prison break-in to liberate Albizu Campos and other incarcerated leaders." Once Albizu was released from prison, those rumors were put to rest, only to give birth to others, which claimed that Carmen María Pérez and Doris Torresola, among others, "were aiding Albizu Campos in his plans to unleash a second revolt."[34]

The fact that she lived in Albizu's home and "regularly attended Nationalist Party activities" were cited by the undercover agents as evidence that she was still "a very dangerous subject." They wrote that while Albizu was incarcerated, she had returned to the Nationalist Club and "apparently lived there because she had the keys to the place." And that she had often been seen waiting outside the prison gate, with packages for Albizu, which she sent to him with those allowed to visit because she was not allowed in the prison. They reported that "the packages generally contained food, items of clothing and toiletries" [not provided by the prison]. But that after Albizu returned home, she had devoted most of the time "to caring for him." According to one informant, who frequently visited the Nationalist Club, Pérez and Torresola "laid awake all night, checking up on Albizu, to make sure he was still alive." Other times they had been observed "crying because they thought their leader was dying." Pérez confirmed that observation, saying "after Albizu became gravely ill we didn't let him sleep more than twenty minutes for fear that he wouldn't wake up."[35]

After Lolita Lebrón and three male companions attacked the United States Congress on March 1, 1954, the I.S. agents in San Juan reported that Pérez, Torresola, and Albizu had been "conspiring with the attackers." No evidence was ever found to link either of the two women to the plot, and Pérez dismissed the claim, saying that she "knew nothing about those plans." But since she lived in Albizu's home and was there the morning of March 6, 1954 "armed and ready to defend her leader," she was arrested by the police officers who were given orders "to arrest Albizu and his companions." Albizu was to be returned to jail for having "violated the terms of the pardon granted by the Governor," and the others for alleged violations of the newly amended Law #53. (Details of the amended statute are included in the section devoted to Isabel Rosado in this book.)[36]

The orders for all the arrests, according to FBI Special Agent in Charge (SAC) in San Juan, Richard Godfrey, were signed by several San Juan district court judges the evening of March 5, 1954, at the conclusion of a meeting which took place in the Governor's office, and which he also attended earlier that afternoon. He explained to his superior in Washington, Assistant FBI Director Belmont that he had been summoned to the Governor's mansion, and when he arrived at 4:00 p.m., he found the Governor, Luis Muñoz Marín chatting with the Secretary of State,

Roberto Sánchez Vilella, Secretary of Justice, José Trias Monge, and the Chief of Police, Salvador T. Roig. One of the topics the Governor had introduced during his presence, he said, "was the impending arrest of Albizu Campos and 25 to 30 others based on a list the Government had compiled of the most dangerous Nationalists on the island." (The actual number of suspects arrested over the next two days was thirty-eight, a few of whom were members of the Communist Party.)[37]

The Governor had then explained that "the arrests would be carried out in as simultaneous a manner as possible, beginning at 6:00 a.m. the following morning, March 6 [1954]." He had also explained that, the "warrants were being drawn, charging violations of Law #53, as amended," [which Godfrey described "as almost an exact copy of the Federal Smith Act"]. Governor Muñoz had also said that "prosecutions would proceed on the theory ... supplied to him by the Secretary of Justice of Puerto Rico that in view of the circumstances and the violence which had ensued on Monday afternoon last, in Washington, membership and active participation in the program of the NPPR [Nationalist Party of Puerto Rico] was sufficient to sustain prosecution under the interpretation of the Commonwealth statute."[38]

The wider interpretation of the amended local statute would have sufficed to arrest all of Albizu's companions. But based on her own admission, Pérez and the others in the Nationalist Club had "fought back when the police began shooting." Their goal, she said, "was to protect Albizu, who was sick in bed, from flying bullets." For that reason she and the others "had moved Albizu from his bed and laid him on the floor." Asked: "Was Albizu also shooting?" She hesitated, and then replied: "He got out of bed and joined the fight." (It should be noted that Isabel Rosado said during our interview that "Albizu Campos was too ill to fight and couldn't do anything.") "He wanted to fight," Pérez declared, "and he got out of bed and began shooting." According to the official reports and the news articles by reporters on the scene, Albizu's companions kept the police at bay for several hours, "shooting sporadically," according to Pérez, because they "needed to conserve bullets."[39]

In his report to the Governor, March 11, 1954, Police Chief Salvador T. Roig, indicated that Albizu and his companions had "refused to surrender" and that had required "the arresting officers to shoot several tear gas bombs into the apartment ... to coax them out, and thus avoid the errors that were made in 1950." (On that occasion the capture of Albizu and his companion, Alvaro Rivera Walker, took four days.)[40]

Pérez recalled that when she and Rivera Sotomayor noticed that "Don Pedro, Isabel, and Doris had fainted from the gases," they went outside to alert the journalists that their comrades were still alive. "Why was that necessary?" I asked. "In case the police broke into the apartment and killed them," she replied. Yet in the unedited testimony of Rivera Sotomayor, published by *Claridad* in 2003, he claimed that Carmín went out that morning (March 6) to buy ointments to reduce the pain in Albizu's legs. According to a journalist on the scene, Rivera Sotomayor was "seized" the minute he came out, "pushed into ... an alleyway and beaten to a pulp by some of the arresting officers." (The snapshots accompanying the article showed Rivera Sotomayor's bloody face and clothing.)[41]

Pérez said she was "grabbed" and had her "blouse ripped by one of the officers. He ripped my blouse," she explained, and left my chest exposed, except for my brassiere." The act made her "so angry" that, she "slapped one of the officers" who was trying to handcuff her. "I needed my hands free, she explained, "so that I could cover my chest." He, meanwhile, began to "yell obscenities," while he handcuffed her, she added. Asked by the defense about the blouse-ripping incident (during one of the proceedings a few months later) Captain Benigno Soto [head of I.S. Division and the person in charge of the detectives on the scene] replied that he was "unaware" the accused had her blouse ripped. But he did recall that "she had to be restrained because she was prone to slapping people."[42]

Reporting on the arrest of March 6, 1954, Chief Roig stuck to the version of the charges reported to him by Police Lieutenant Astol Calero, namely that the arresting officers had "found sixteen bullets in Pérez's pockets, five in one and eleven in another." Based on that account, the prosecution would later claim that "Pérez had been in possession of a .38 caliber pistol the morning of March 6, 1954." Two months later (April 1954), the prosecutor established that she had never been authorized to "own a firearm," a fact he used to add the charge of violation of the island's Arms Statute to the earlier charge of attempted murder.[43]

The morning of her arrest, Pérez said, she was taken directly to the Arecibo jail, "still with her brassiere exposed." There a male guard had made fun of her and she "was so ashamed and furious," that she "slapped him as soon as the handcuffs came off." Shocked by her action, "he threw a pair of handcuffs at my face and tried to strangle me," she said. But then another guard, who knew her from her last incarceration, "intervened and forced him to release his grip and let me go," she added. She couldn't remember if she had been punished that time. "Whatever happened," she said with a shrug, "I would not have cared because I had already exacted my revenge for what he had done." She was then twenty-five years old.[44]

About the morning of March 6, she recalled, that after she and Rivera Sotomayor left Albizu's apartment, "a group of policemen and detectives rushed upstairs to his place, and finding the door locked, smashed it with an axe." The man wielding the axe, she said, was Dudley Osborne, a Captain in the island's National Guard, who should not have been part of a police mission, according to her defense attorneys. She remembered hearing that "Osborne hated Albizu so much that he wanted him dead" and that's why he was carrying a rifle with a fixed bayonet when he went up the stairs to Albizu's place. "He intended to kill Albizu but [Police Lieutenant] Astol Calero (the person in charge of the police officers) stopped him," she said. In his report to the Governor, Chief Roig said that: "Osborne was taken along on the arresting mission because he had "repeatedly volunteered," and because the officers "thought they might have a need for a brawny fellow."[45]

When Captain Benigno Soto was asked by the defense to explain the reason for Osborne's presence in the arresting mission, he said, he had "no idea." But when the same question was posed to one of his junior officers, he said that Captain Soto was "the one who authorized Osborne to be there." Probably in anticipation that Osborne's presence would become a thorny issue, Chief Roig tried to justify his actions by telling the Governor that, "he was quite useful" because he not only "wielded the axe that smashed the door leading to the Nationalist Club but carried Albizu out of the apartment on his shoulders."[46]

Arraignment, Trials and Incarceration

At the end of April 1954 Carmín Pérez and her three companions were arraigned on three criminal counts: attempted murder, illegal possession of a firearm, and one violation of the amended Law #53. According to various documents, the bails set against her amounted to $35,000. But as it often happened in these cases, the sums of her various bonds were appealed and reduced to $14,000. This time three individuals came forth to post the required bonds and she was released temporarily, in September (1954), until her cases came to trial.[47]

She couldn't recall what she did during the three months she was out on bail, but the Internal Security (I.S.) agents on her trail reported that as soon as she was out of jail she began to raise funds to pay the rent for the Nationalist Club. She had also returned to "leave packages, and occasionally a money order, for Albizu Campos at whichever jail he was in." According to the same agents, "the most likely person to deliver the packages to Albizu in jail was "his 'half-sister' Ana María Campos, who came from Ponce to see him [because] his wife and children lived in Mexico since 1948" [they later moved to Havana, Cuba].[48]

The first trial for Pérez and fourteen others similarly accused of violations of Law #53 took place in Arecibo's District (then called Superior) Court, between December 1954 and February 1955. The fact that the fifteen accused were tried outside San Juan, where the alleged crimes had presumably been committed, has never been adequately explained. The apparent judicial aberration has led to a few interesting speculations. One of them claims that the Governor "pressured the Department of Justice to relegate the case to the backwater Court of Arecibo in order to reduce its publicity." Another holds that the Department of Justice "assigned the case to Judge Rafael Padró Parés, a man known for his antipathy toward the Nationalists and other dissenters, expecting he would probably punish those convicted to the maximum penalty allowed by law." Without evidence to support either of these speculations, I chose to read the accounts reported by the press.[49]

According to reports published in *El Imparcial*, Judge Padró followed the same pattern he had employed in the 1950 cases: allowing ample latitude to the prosecution while restraining the defense. He permitted the prosecution to call an excessive number of government witnesses, most of them detectives and policemen, and let them introduce information the defense called irrelevant to the case at hand. The journalists covering the trial reported that, while the focus of the investigation should have been limited to the defendants' actions between December 20, 1950 (when Law #53 was amended) and March 6, 1954, the day of their arrest, the Judge had accepted as evidence details dating back to December 1947, when the Gag Rule hadn't yet been enacted much less amended.

Such evidence, they explained, was accepted, over repeated objections from the defense.[50]

Despite the attorneys' dogged defense, petitions for a new trial, rebukes of the Court for its partiality, and final appeals for clemency, fourteen of the fifteen defendants were convicted as charged by the jury, which took less than three hours to deliberate the case. The speedy results, wrote one journalist, surprised even the Judge and provoked all sorts of jokes right there in the Court. Nonetheless, the Judge accepted their verdict and limited his remarks to setting the date, May 31, 1955, as the day for sentencing.[51]

Among the fourteen convicted in Arecibo in February 1955 were six women: Carmen María Pérez González, Doris Torresola Roura, her sister Angelina Torresola de Platet, Isabel Rosado Morales, Juana Mills Rosa, and Juanita Ojeda Maldonado. It should be noted that neither Leonides Díaz nor Olga Isabel Viscal had been arrested in 1954 because they were still serving the sentences handed down to them in connection with the uprising of 1950. In fact, during September 1954, when Pérez and her codefendants were out on bail awaiting trial, Viscal and Díaz were transferred (from the Arecibo prison) to the newly built penal facility, the Escuela Industrial Para Mujeres, in Vega Alta, Puerto Rico. Similarly, Ruth Mary Reynolds, one of Pérez' cellmates in San Juan and Arecibo between 1950 and 1952, also escaped arrest in 1954, possibly because she had moved back to New York City shortly after she was released on bail while her case was appealed. (Details of Reynolds' case are discussed in a section devoted to her in this book.)[52]

Before sentencing in Arecibo was rendered, Pérez and three of her comrades were again brought to trial, this time in San Juan's Superior Court, for the counts of attempted murder and illegal possession of a firearm. In the meantime, her defense attorneys continued to file a variety of motions. One of them requested a new trial, on grounds that she had been "wrongfully convicted" at the Arecibo Court. Another requested that she (and several others) be released on bail until a new trial was held. A third petitioned the court to ask the stenographer to provide, free of charge, all transcriptions of the proceedings. The motions were all denied and Pérez and four of her female comrades were sentenced by Judge Padró Parés to prison terms of seven to ten years. The four sentenced in this fashion were: Doris Torresola, Juana Mills Rosa, Juanita Ojeda Maldonado, and Isabel Rosado Morales. Of the six women convicted in Arecibo, only Angelina Torresola de Platet received a relatively shorter prison sentence of three to seven years. It is not clear why Mills and Maldonado, who had not been at the Nationalist Club or engaged the police in the shoot-out the morning of March 6, 1954, should have been sentenced the same as those who had. They were not guiltier than Angelina Torresola de Platet who was also at home but received the shortest sentence of the female group.[53]

Convicted also in San Juan on the counts of attempted murder and illegal possession of a firearm, Pérez was again sentenced to prison. On June 18, 1955 she received sentences of six months for the one violation of the island's Arms Statute and one to two years for the crime of attempted murder. Since the latter sentences were to be served concurrently with the seven-to-ten year sentence handed down by Judge Padró Parés, she could be expected to be imprisoned a minimum of eight and half years to a maximum of twelve and half years.[54]

Once sentenced, Pérez was sent to the Escuela Industrial Para Mujeres in Vega Alta, Puerto Rico, where she soon joined her old comrades Leonides Díaz and Olga Viscal, before the two were released from prison. She later shared a cell with Blanca Canales, when she was sent to Vega Alta prison in 1956 after serving a term in Alderson, West Virginia. According to the Escuela's records, "the Nationalist inmates" were housed in "Maximum Security," an area generally reserved for mentally ill prisoners. (Details of that prison's conditions are discussed in another section of this book.) One anecdote worth mentioning, according to Carmín Pérez, was that "one time 'las locas' (the insane) went on a rampage and set fire to the cellblock, but made sure to skip our rooms," she said, still amused. "They would not harm us," she added, "because we protected them when they got in trouble with the administration."[55]

Apparently, Pérez adjusted to the new environment by keeping busy. According to several guards' reports, she alternated her job assignments between teaching literacy classes, working in the library several afternoons a week and helping Leonides Díaz in the kitchen. During the time she remained in that prison her family tended to visit regularly. Her father Juan E. Pérez and his new wife, Ramona Rodríguez visited about once a month and always brought her fruits and vegetables from their farm in Lares. Her brother, Jorge Luis Pérez and his wife Gladys Machicote, who lived in Isla Verde (a sector of San Juan) visited more often, sometimes two or three times a month. They also came bearing foods not easily available in prison, such as eggs, canned milk, plus fruits and vegetables, which she later shared with her cellmates.[56]

But despite her best efforts to stay away from the guards, she was reported to the administration twice. On January14, 1957, she and Blanca Canales were reported by Sra. Salazar for disobeying her orders. According to the guard's own report, she woke up Pérez and Canales at 6:00 a.m. on January 1 and had them clean up their rooms. Since there was still time before breakfast was served, she "gave them soap powder from the pantry and asked them go clean the Youth Area. They reacted in a disrespectful manner, saying they were being treated like pigs." Pérez had said "not to ask her to do anything more and appeared to be in a foul mood through lunchtime." The report was sent to the Assistant Director, Crucita Arzuaga, who would determine whether the offense merited being referred to the Disciplinary Board, headed by her superior, Lydia Peña de Planas. But on January 16 (1957), Arzuaga went to Pérez and Canales' cell, "to hear their version of the story." Apparently, what they said was sufficiently convincing because Arzuaga dropped the matter "after reviewing the prison's rules and regulations and admonishing the two women about the sort of behavior the institution required." In a confidential report she sent to her superior, she indicated that the incident could have been avoided had Guard Salazar been "more tactful in the manner she presented the request." In her view there was "no need to take the matter any further."[57]

Pérez was again reported on August 18, 1959. On that occasion a male guard named Juan Otero claimed that he had asked Carmín Pérez whether she had permission to be out in the field picking "acerolas" (a type of tart cherry grown in Puerto Rico) and she had "replied in an insolent manner that she was not about to let herself starve in this place." And then goaded him, saying: "go ahead and report me because I no longer give a damn!" He said he "called her to attention because this was not the first time I have seen her out in the fields, picking acerolas, without authorization." He had tried, he said, "to tell her that not even the inmates assigned to work the prison grounds were authorized to pick the acerolas." But since she had "continued with her insolence" he reported his complaint to Sra. Rosa. This time the case was handled directly by Lydia Peña de Planas the following day. She summoned Carmín Pérez to her office to tell her version of what had transpired. Apparently, she made a good case because the matter was dropped "after a review with the inmate about the rules and regulations of the institution and the proper way to behave when a guard called her to attention." But after this incident, the Director said, "I instructed the farmhand to pick the acerolas and bring them to the kitchen so they can be shared by everyone."[58]

Life as a Free Woman, 1965–2003

Carmín Pérez remained in the Vega Alta prison until November 15, 1965, when she was eventually released thanks in part to a habeas corpus filed by Isabel Rosado. (Details of the events that led to their release are explained in the section devoted to Rosado in this book). At the time of Pérez' release, she had served nearly eleven years of the twelve and half year combined sentences she received in 1955 for three convictions. By then the law for which she (and others) had been convicted had been abolished for more than eight years. The obvious question that arises is: Why wasn't she released from prison a lot sooner, if her longest sentence was due to a law which had been abolished? The official records do not provide an answer.[59]

By the time Pérez left prison, Albizu Campos had died (April 1965), and the place she called home before her 1954 arrest had disappeared. Her closest comrades: Doris Torresola and Isabel Rosado once released had gone their separate ways. Torresola was temporarily interned in a Psychiatric Hospital and then went to live under her sister's care in Hato Rey. Rosado returned home to Ceiba and continued her political work from there. They would see each other from time to time at Nationalist and other groups' activities, but with Don Pedro gone and others dead or still in prison, the movement was no longer as strong as it once had been.[60]

Radicalized by her prison experience, Pérez soon began to collaborate with other activist groups and joined in their demonstrations. She became especially devoted to the groups calling for the release of all Puerto Rican political prisoners still held in local and United States prisons. She also joined (along with Isabel Rosado and Lolita Lebrón) a pacifist group that was pressuring the United States Navy to leave the islands of Culebra and Vieques. She supported the struggle of the landless who were being evicted from subsistence plots they had seized in Humacao, Puerto Rico. Along the way she also joined the Socialist League, a new pro-independence group founded by Juan Antonio Corretjer, a former associate of Albizu Campos. The group's open admiration of Fidel Castro and Socialist Cuba made her a perennial target of the counterintelligence programs, extended to Puerto Rico. As federal funding for such programs increased, the Puerto Rican Police Department became better financed and was able to revamp its undercover units and send some of its top men to be trained in counterintelligence operations in the United States and Panama. The added resources in turn enabled the much-improved secret police to keep Pérez and all other dissidents under strict surveillance.[61]

Despite the daily harassment and threats to her life, Pérez said, she survived economically, thanks to friends and admirers who employed her, or helped her to find work. According to an article published at the time of her death, she had worked the last five years of her life at the Puerto Rican Bar Association (Colegio de Abogados de Puerto Rico), located in Miramar, a sector of San Juan.[62]

What is not clear is: Why was she, of the surviving Nationalist women, the least honored during her lifetime? Some have suggested that she was "too modest" to accept any invitation that sought to sing her praises and that she avoided public appearances." Others said that she was "too devoted to the cause of independence to be concerned with fanfare." Both could be true, for she seemed to be a shy woman. Yet there is a record that in 1997 she accepted an invitation, held in barrio Mariana, Humaco (Puerto Rico) in which she was one of "three heroines" being honored. The other two were Lolita Lebrón and Isabel Rosado. The organizer of the activity, Attorney Alejandro Torres, spoke eloquently about the "three heroines" in attendance, but failed to call any of them to the podium, or gave them a chance to speak. It appears from the article (he later sent to Claridad) that everyone, including the "heroines" were satisfied to have him speak for them.[63]

Pérez died six years after that event, on April 4, 2003, at the age of seventy-four. The cause of death was attributed to long-standing complications of a diabetic condition, according to the daily El Nuevo Día. News of her death led friends and admirers to register their thoughts through various means. The photographer Alina Luciano, for example, wrote a touching account about a day she had spent following "a reluctant Carmín through much of Old San Juan" hoping she would agree to be photographed. When she finally "consented," Luciano said, she could not "get her to pose or smile." And in the end, the snapshot she had selected from the stack she presented was one in which she "looked very serious," Luciano said. In an unedited testimony, sent to *Claridad* by Carmín's old comrade-in arms José Rivera Sotomayor, he described her "as totally devoted to Albizu Campos and to the cause of independence." He wrote that on March 6, 1954, she left the Nationalist Club in order "to get the ointments needed to ease the burning pain in Albizu's legs." He said that, "Carmín lived with very little, just as Albizu Campos did, and like him, gave the little she had to anyone who needed it."[64]

At the Colegio de Abogados, where a viewing of the deceased was held on the morning of Saturday, April 5, 2003, the Bar's ex-president, Eduardo Villanueva described her as "an example for generations to come." He also spoke of her humility and kindness towards others. Another who described her virtues was Carlos Gallisá, a well-known member of the Movimiento Pro-Independencia (MPI). In closing, he told the audience, "one day when the people of Puerto Rico are able to write their own 'unadulterated history,' they will recognize [Carmín Pérez] as one of the heroines who gave her life for the homeland."[65]

The Cuban Communist Party also sent a message of condolence to her friends and relatives. Filiberto Ojeda, commander of Los Macheteros, sent a touching message, which promised that Carmín "will never be forgotten." *Claridad's* publisher, Alida Millán Ferrer, confessed later that all throughout the ceremony at the Bar's Association, she kept thinking: "if Puerto Rico were independent, Carmín would be buried as a commandant, with all the honors due a revolutionary." Reporter Cándida Cotto, who followed the funeral procession from San Juan to the Lares plaza ("Plaza de la Revolución"), said that "hundreds of persons came to Lares to pay their respects" to Carmín. In the crowd, she saw Rubén Berríos Martínez, president of the PIP (Partido Independentista Puertorriqueño), Juan Mari Bras, founder of the MPI (Movimiento Pro-Independencia), and the town's mayor Luis A. Oliver, a PDP (Popular Democratic Party) member. Neither of the three spoke, she said, since that honor was given to her mentor and idol Lolita Lebrón. Lolita, she wrote, took the opportunity to remind the youth to carry on Carmín's revolutionary struggle and not to rest until independence was achieved.[66]

Energized by Lebrón's patriotic words, twelve-year-old Gustavo Sánchez recited a poem ("Mi Capitán") by Carmín's friend and comrade, Juan Antonio Corretjer. Then everyone followed the funeral procession to the municipal cemetery, singing Carmín's favorite patriotic songs while the musicians honored her request by playing the Hymn of Lares and the national anthem, La Borinqueña. Amid music and songs, Cotto said, "the heroine was finally laid to rest next to her late mother" [Doña María González]. The moment had finally come for Carmín to be near the mother she lost fifty-three years earlier.[67]

4. Ruth Mary Reynolds (1916–1989)

Preface

Ruth Mary Reynolds, a native of Terraville, Lawrence County, South Dakota, was born on February 29, 1916. Her father worked as a manager at the Home State Mining Company, a cyanide plant in the region. Her mother stayed at home to care for the family, though she had been a schoolteacher before she married.[1] In 1877, the maternal family migrated to Terraville from Kentucky, though like most settlers in the town they traced their ancestry back to Europe. The land where the town was founded, her father said, had belonged to the Sioux Indians until 1876.

Ruth commented that her childhood had been a happy one. She grew up roaming the Black Hills near Terraville, enjoying Sunday and holiday picnics her mother organized for the family. She recalled gathering beautiful flowers in the summer and skiing during the winter. She attended the Methodist Church, one of the three religious institutions in town. Though the family had limited resources, she said, her mother insisted that the children get a good education.

Ruth Reynolds in San Juan's District Court shortly after her arrest. November, 1950.

And when Ruth graduated from high school she was sent to Dakota Wesleyan University (1933-37), a Methodist-owned school from which she graduated with a B.A. degree in English, in hopes of becoming a high school teacher.[2]

A bright, competitive student, she was elected to the Student Council to represent the "Women's Self-Government Association." That position, she said years later, would help her understand the Commonwealth Government of Puerto Rico, for it offered little power with which to make any significant changes. The environment at the university, she said, was "much too restrictive since Methodists tend to say no to any form of independent expression." With her in the lead, however, the women extracted a few concessions, but only after a brief confrontation with the administration. That minor triumph, she said, came at a price for her because the Elder she had challenged made sure she didn't get a teaching position anywhere near her home after she graduated.[3]

Following a frustrating search that lasted the entire summer, she said, she took the only job available to her (1937-38), teaching at the Rosebud Indian Reservation, far away from home. But while that job was far from what she "had envisioned," she said, "It was the job I needed, for it allowed me to witness first-hand the many injustices our government committed against some of its people." The following school year (1938-39) she found a new job on a ranching community, closer to home. The school in that area, she said, was built on land white settlers leased from the Indians because they had none of their own. That experience, she explained, also taught her about the "privations poor whites experienced in the Dakotas." Without a job prospect for the following year, she opted to borrow money and go to Northwestern University, in Evanston, Illinois, to pursue a graduate degree. In Evanston, she was introduced to Pacifism and to volunteer work in an urban (mostly African American) area.[4]

Moving to New York: Meeting Pedro Albizu Campos

Armed with a master's degree in English literature, an awakened social conscience, and some experience in volunteer work, she arrived in Manhattan the summer of 1941, to take part in a training course on Pacifism being offered at the Harlem Ashram. At the time she was in search of "something meaningful to do," because by then she had become "frustrated with the inaction of my church." The Harlem Ashram, she explained, was founded the previous year (1940) by Ralph Templin and Jay Holmes Smith, two Pacifists who had been evicted from India by the British government for their devotion to Mahatma Gandhi's pacifist philosophy of non-cooperation.[5]

At the Ashram, she found a community of like-minded souls who spent the greater part of their days doing "amateur social work" in East Harlem, and the rest of the time organizing protests in demand of social change. In their company she was able to hone her organizing skills and to attend demonstrations in demand of social justice. At the Ashram she also met several Puerto Ricans, including a Baptist minister named Hipólito Cotto Reyes, who challenged her and her peers to examine their narrow political views. He applauded them, she said, for "our support of India's struggle for independence from Great Britain, but challenged us to examine the situation of Puerto Rico, a Caribbean island held in bondage by the United States."[6]

She confessed that until they met Reverend Cotto Reyes they "knew nothing about Puerto Rico or its situation" and what he told them "hit us between the eyes because we didn't have the slightest knowledge about what our government was doing in Puerto Rico." We knew only about a couple of war resistors [Cesar Torres and Julio Pinto Gandía] who were in prison because they would not register for the U.S. military draft. Though Reverend Cotto Reyes was not a Nationalist, he was fond of Pedro Albizu Campos, whom he and his brother (also a pastor of another Manhattan church) visited at Columbus Hospital. After their initial encounter, she said, the Reverend went to the Ashram a few times "to enlighten" them about U.S. Puerto Rican relations.[7]

His visits gradually led the group to reconsider what to do about Puerto Rico. On the one hand, they "as Pacifists, opposed all imperialism, especially that of our own government," but on the other were also "disconcerted by the fact that Puerto Rican Nationalists believed that "there were times when violence should be answered with violence." In the end, her peers agreed that "there was no logic in taking a position of liberty for other peoples half way around the world, without taking a position of liberty for those our own government is oppressing." They resolved that "Puerto Rico must be free and that we had to incorporate that [struggle] into our program in some way or other."[8]

"Then, during the summer of 1943," Reynolds said, "one of our boys, Al Winslow, who had been imprisoned in Petersburg, Virginia for refusing to register for the draft, was released, and he returned to the Ashram. A few days later he asked us if he could bring a fellow inmate to dinner." The man in question turned out to be Julio Pinto Gandía, "a Puerto Rican Nationalist who was Albizu Campos' right hand, and who at one point had presided over the Nationalist Party of Puerto Rico" after the Ponce Massacre. "He was a very good man and the first Nationalist I ever knew," Reynolds said. Pinto Gandía continued to educate them further about Puerto Rico and to encourage them to go meet Albizu Campos. "It was then that the group decided that Jay [Holmes Smith] should be the one to visit Albizu Campos, in order to explore further the question of Puerto Rico's independence." He returned to the Ashram "totally entranced by Albizu's character, intellect and personality," Reynolds recalled. Yet she postponed visiting Albizu for a few months, "in part because (she) was busy assisting the director of the Ashram, and partly because (she) felt that Smith's presence was sufficient representation from the group." In February 1944, she "yielded to Pinto Gandía's pressure and went to meet Don Pedro," who by then had been at Columbus Hospital a few months.[9]

Like Jay [Holmes Smith], she returned "enchanted with Albizu's personality, goodness, intelligence and his absolute dedication to the independence of Puerto Rico." They became friends, she explained, and "stayed in contact almost daily" while she worked through a few issues. Though she believed Puerto Rico had the right to be independent, she wasn't sure how it would "survive economically, if it was so dependent on the United States." She had witnessed the poverty of the Indians on the Rosebud Reservation and the privations experienced by the poor whites in the ranching community in South Dakota. She had seen also "the ill effects produced by poverty and racial discrimination in the African-American community of Evanston, Illinois. If she were to take a stand on the issue of Puerto Rico's independence, she would need to know more. To that end, she went to the New York Public Library and spent a few months reading all she could find about Puerto Rico.[10]

Meanwhile, by July 1943, Jay [Holmes Smith] and other Ashram members had decided that: "having the United States hold Puerto Rico was an outrage" and that it was time for them to found a support organization, later known as the American League for Puerto Rico's Independence. Smith was elected president of it, "Because he had worked in India and was also at an age people would listen to [him]," she explained. She was elected Executive Secretary, in part "because she was still too young (she was then twenty-seven years old) and did not have the stature needed to be followed." The decision to elect her secretary, she said, was in part "because at the time people did not think women could be major political players. One could be the secretary and type letters," she added, "but not be the leader." But Don Pedro was different; "he always kept pushing me because he saw that I had some intelligence and determination." She reiterated that regarding the American League for Puerto Rico's Independence Jay Holmes Smith was "a pivotal figure." What neither of the two budding leaders could predict then was that Reynolds would in time eclipse Smith because once she made the decision to support Puerto Rico's independence, she never wavered.[11]

Travels to Puerto Rico

In 1945, while Albizu Campos was still in New York City, Ruth Reynolds went to Puerto Rico, and during that trip interviewed the top political leaders, including Senate President, and soon-to-be Puerto Rico's first elected governor, Luis Muñoz Marín. She interviewed also several top administrators, including the Secretary of Justice, and the Chancellor of the University of Puerto Rico. She spoke with a few persons who claimed to have direct knowledge of the Ponce Massacre, including Ponce's past district attorney, Rafael Pérez Marchand, and his sister Dr. Laura Pérez Marchand. The former, she said, had chosen to resign his post in 1937 rather than "be complicit in the travesty of justice that followed the massacre." The latter had helped the wounded brought to the Pila Clinic where she worked as a physician. In 1946, with Reynolds' help the League presented a brief to the United Nations, charging that the United States treatment of Puerto Rico was in violation of the "Declaration Regarding Non-Self-Governing Territories," set forth in Chapter 11, Article 73 of the United Nations Charter.[12]

By the mid-1940s, she had become a target of New York's Secret Service and the City's FBI office. According to several of their reports, Reynolds was actively involved promoting the agenda of the American League for Puerto Rico's Independence. They asserted that she also translated into English many of the position papers Pinto Gandía presented to members of the United Nations interested in the case of Puerto Rico. They wrote that she met regularly with Albizu Campos and other Nationalists. In October 1948, she returned to Puerto Rico, where she became a target of Puerto Rico's Internal Security (I.S.) division, which reported her arrival, though not the reason for her visit. The purpose of that trip, Reynolds explained years later to interviewer (Blanca Vázquez at the Center for Puerto Rican Studies at Hunter College) "Was to gather information for a book I wished to write about the 1948 student strike at the University of Puerto Rico." She was particularly interested, she said, in establishing the reasons why the student leaders had been expelled and the University had shut down during the last month of the spring semester.[13]

By 1948, Albizu Campos had returned to Puerto Rico (December 1947) and she seemed eager to work with him. The one thing she did not do, she said, was to join his political party, or any other, "because as a North American I thought my role was to support those working for Puerto Rico's independence, but not to tell any of them how to do it." For that reason, she also never joined the Partido Independentista Puertorriqueño (PIP), founded by Gilberto Concepción de Gracia, in 1946, which promised to bring independence to the island via the ballot. She reiterated the point that she disagreed with the Nationalist position, which held that "there were times violence should be answered with violence."[14]

Reynolds' association with Albizu Campos and other key Nationalists on the island also made her "persona non-grata" in local government circles, as well as a target of the FBI, one of the five surveillance groups operating in Puerto Rico by the 1940s. By the fall of 1949, she had a growing police file or carpeta (#1340) and several undercover agents trailing after her. On October 3, 1949, for example, Internal Security Commander Jorge Camacho Torres reported to the Chief of Police, and he in turn informed the FBI office in San Juan, that Ruth Reynolds was "now living in Bayamón, in Juan Alamo Díaz's home." (Alamo Díaz and his wife Germana Bilbao had lived temporarily in the Bronx, New York during the 1940s and had taken Albizu to live with them when he was Columbus Hospital.) Camacho Torres instructed agent Vicente Cáceres to follow Reynolds during the time (one month) she stayed in Bayamón and report to him. Cáceres wrote the same day that Reynolds arrived in

Bayamón that morning (October 3). He said he had "seen her when she got off the bus in front of the Cafetería Bilbao, where she was met by Juan Alamo Díaz. There, "the two had spoken for a few minutes, before she continued on her way to Alamo's home, located at Calle Tió # 4, where she arrived around 10:00 in the morning."[15]

Generally, I.S. agents on a suspect's trail were assisted by a host of informants, some of whom were close relatives of the persons being trailed. In this case the informant turned out to be Juan Alamo Díaz' brother, Pedro [Alamo Díaz], who reported to agent Cáceres "that on September 23 (1949) Ruth Reynolds had gone with his brother (Juan) to the celebration of El Grito de Lares. He claimed he saw them drive off in Juan's car earlier that morning. On his own, Cáceres discovered that, "Ruth Reynolds had left Alamo Díaz's home on October 4th, "presumably," to visit the Nationalist Club in San Juan." He added that he was still following a lead "to see if the subject (Reynolds) was the same person who had been observed photographing the events in Lares."[16]

On October 29, Cáceres was again instructed by Commander Camacho Torres to report on the whereabouts of Ruth Reynolds. He specifically wanted to know whether "Miss Reynolds has left Bayamón" because he had received information "that she boarded 'a public service car' around 11:40 that morning, carrying two suitcases." He sent similar instructions to his men at the airport, asking them "to investigate whether Miss Reynolds has left the island." After several more orders from Commander Camacho Torres, detective Angel Rodríguez and agent Cáceres reported that Reynolds was still on the island, but had "gone to Ciales, and was staying at the home of the well-known Nationalist, Carlos Vélez Rieckehoff." (Vélez Rieckehoff had also lived in Manhattan during the 1930s and 40s. He was in fact the New York Junta leader who inducted Rosa Collazo into the Nationalist Party in 1935.) The two agents reported to Camacho Torres that Reynolds was still in Vélez Rieckehoff's home on November 7 (1949) and that she had brought along a typewriter in addition to two suitcases. The surveillance reports go on and on about the activities Reynolds attended, the persons she visited, or talked to during the two years she lived in Puerto Rico prior to her arrest. The data gathered through this process proved useful to the island's Department of Justice when it chose to build a case against her in connection to the Nationalist revolt of October (1950).[17]

Arrest and Incarceration

On November 2, 1950, Ruth Reynolds was arrested at 2:00 in the morning. According to a letter she sent to her sister Helen, she "was asleep in Cataño" (a municipality across the Bay of San Juan) when the arresting officers came, pounding on her door. She was then a guest of the well-known Nationalist Paulino Castro Abolafia, and was staying at a small apartment the family owned in the back patio of their residence. She said she awoke when "a group of about forty policemen and National Guards called her name, saying they had orders to arrest her and search the place. She asked to see their search warrant, which they promised to show her later, but instead proceeded to arrest her and impound her property, including her finished manuscript on the strike at the university. That same night, she added, the officers also arrested Paulino Castro and his son and then took all three of them to police headquarters in Puerta de Tierra (San Juan).[18]

According to the judicial records, two events had led to her arrest. The first, they claimed, was due to the fact that she taken a ride, on October 26 (1950), with three Nationalists: Rafael A. Burgos Fuentes, José Mejías Flores, and Eduardo López Vázquez, who were carrying arms intended to help the revolt which occurred four days later. The second they attributed to the reports of three I.S. agents, who claimed that they had "seen her take the Nationalist oath (to give life and fortune in defense of Puerto Rico's independence) at the Party's annual assembly, on December 18, 1949, in Arecibo (Puerto Rico). Regarding the first event, the arresting officers explained that they had stopped the car in question "because the driver had run a red light." They had then "asked the driver and three passengers to step out of the car while they searched it, and when firearms were found, they had taken all four to police headquarters (in Puerta de Tierra) for questioning." Reynolds replied to the first accusation, saying that she "had accepted the ride because by the time the Fajardo activity ended that evening the buses had stopped running and (she) needed to get back to San Juan." She added that, she didn't know there were arms in the car because she "was not in the habit of inspecting the trunk of a car before I accept a ride." (The comment didn't exactly endear her with the interrogators.)[19]

The trip back from Fajardo, she told a few friends in the United States, had been uneventful until the police intercepted the car around 1:00 in the morning, as they were approaching San Juan. The police had searched the car and taken them to headquarters, where they had been kept until 4:00 in the morning, before they were released with instructions to return at 2:00 that afternoon for further questioning. During the afternoon session, she again admitted she had taken a ride with the three Nationalists, but repeated that she "had no idea" they had arms in the trunk of the car. She said again that she had never been a member of the Nationalist Party. She tried to persuade her interrogators that she was a Pacifist and would never condone any act of violence. Regarding the second accusation, she admitted attending the Nationalist Party assembly in Arecibo (December 18, 1949), but emphatically denied "taking the Nationalist oath, the agents claimed."[20]

But nothing Reynolds said in her own defense made any difference to the interrogators, who as members of the first newly elected Puerto Rican government, were exercising newly acquired powers, powers which were now being threatened by a group of "subversives" she was known to support. They intended to send her to prison, for even "if she wasn't directly involved in the revolt," she had until a few days earlier collaborated with the group "whose expressed intent was to overthrow the island's government by force and violence." Such collaboration, they explained, was not only "a disregard for the well-being of the peaceful Puerto Rican society, but a violation of the laws of the land (especially Law #53). Thus, on November 12, 1950, after ten days of detention in Puerta de Tierra and numerous interrogations by district attorneys and FBI men, Reynolds was taken to San Juan's District jail, La Princesa. According to a letter her Defense Committee circulated in the United States in 1951, she had been detained in November 1950, but not indicted until the following February. This, Reynolds had said, was an open violation of a local statute, which stipulated that a suspect had to be charged, or released within forty-eight hours of his or her arrest. But, according to a May 12, 1951 "Memorandum" sent by Special District Attorney José C. Aponte to the island's Secretary of Justice, Reynolds was charged on November 12, 1950 and assigned bail in the sum of $25,000. She was unable to post bail and was sent to San Juan's District jail to await review of her case. He added that she had been indicted on January 3, 1951." (Either way, Reynolds' claim points to a common practice in which the Puerto Rican judicial system suspended or outright violated the basic guarantees of its political prisoners during the 1950s.)[21]

Once at La Princesa, Reynolds said, she was taken to a cell already occupied by three comrades (Carmen María Pérez, Olga Isabel Viscal, and Doris Torresola). The latter she explained, arrived a day or so later, and Blanca Canales several days after that. Isabel Rosado, the sixth Nationalist to join them in that cell, did not arrive until the following January (1951). That cell, (as Carmen María Pérez already explained) had its only window sealed because she and Olga Viscal "had greeted Doris Torresola's mother" when they saw her on the street below, hoping to catch a glimpse of her daughter. (For details, see the section devoted to Pérez in this book.) The lack of ventilation in the cell, Reynolds said, made life intolerable for her and two others "with medical conditions." Doris Torresola, she said, "was the most affected by the lack of ventilation because she had asthma and was recovering from a gunshot wound." Olga Viscal "was affected also because she suffered from epilepsy." While she, (Reynolds) had "a chronic sinus condition." Only Carmín [Pérez], in her view, "seemed fine, perhaps because she was very young and in good health." The window incident, Reynolds added, caused Pérez and Torresola "to slap the warden," and that in turn provoked him to ship the two to the Women's Wing of Arecibo's District jail the following day. She stayed behind one more day and then joined them in Arecibo, while Doris Torresola was kept in San Juan because she was scheduled to go to trial within a few days.[22]

Life in Arecibo's District Jail

In the Arecibo jail (as Pérez and Rosado have already explained), they were confined to two tiny rooms, which had previously served as isolation cells. Reynolds does not dispute her comrades' comments about the overcrowding, twenty-three-hour a day lock-up, or the poor diet in that prison, but chose instead to provide an assessment of the prison staff. In her view, the men and women who worked in the Arecibo jail were "more humane" than their counterparts in La Princesa. (It should be noted that after her comrades were sent to the women's prison in Vega Alta, they revised some of their views regarding the Arecibo staff.) In Arecibo, Reynolds noted, the warden J. González Lebrón and his wife Doña Segunda (who worked there as a guard) "did their best to honor our requests within the constraints of prison regulations." She recalled that whenever the Nationalist women "had to see the prison doctor, the warden had his wife accompany them, to ensure that they we were not subjected to any physical examination they didn't want." As a result, Reynolds said, none of them had "been subjected to the routine pelvic examination" other inmates had to go through. "The prison staff," she concluded, "always treated us with respect and consideration." Reports from the prison physician, Dr. Arturo Cadilla, concur with one of Reynolds' assertions. He wrote to the Superintendent of Prisons that none of the Nationalist women he treated "has ever consented to undergo the pelvic exam or even undress, or have her chest examined. They did, however, consent to have chest x-rays and blood work done, when necessary. Reynolds added that her cellmates were "so private that they wouldn't undress in front of anyone, or shower with the other inmates." To accommodate their wishes, she said, "the warden had set aside a special hour for them to shower, separately, after the other inmates had finished." (Isabel Rosado recounted in another interview, that she and her comrades generally showered between three and four in the afternoon.)[23]

Reynolds' main complaint about the Arecibo prison was the diet, which basically consisted of rice and beans for lunch and dinner and black coffee and bread for breakfast. Occasionally codfish was served, or pig's feet or corned beef were added as a flavoring to the rice or beans, Reynolds said. Accustomed to a diet high in animal protein, plus fruits and vegetables, she said, she began to lose weight and feel unwell within the first two months she was in prison. She brought up the case of her weight loss to the warden of Arecibo, but before he could send her for the required medical evaluation in such cases, she and her comrades were called back to the San Juan prison, presumably to serve as witnesses in the upcoming trial of Doris Torresola and Albizu Campos. She would discover later that Albizu had requested their presence at his trial, in hopes of giving them a break from their isolated existence in the Arecibo jail. He thought he was doing them a favor. Reynolds recalled that on February 7, 1951, at lunchtime she, Pérez, and Viscal had been told by a guard they should get ready to go to La Princesa that afternoon. They weren't told the reason for the trip.[24]

Ordeals in San Juan's District Jail: La Princesa

According to a testimony Reynolds wrote in the fall of 1951, and revised in June 1952, they arrived at La Princesa, around three in the afternoon (February 7, 1951) to the surprise of the warden who hadn't been told to expect them. A few phone calls later, he learned they were there to stay for the duration of the trial, so he ordered three additional Army cots for the new occupants of the cell. When the cots arrived, Reynolds said, he took them "to the upper floor of the prison, through a room known as 'la escuelita' to an inner room beyond." There, they found Blanca Canales in a "pantry-size alcove" they called 'la alacena.' They hadn't yet settled in, Reynolds wrote, when the warden "came up again, this time accompanied by a woman he introduced as Evelyn Emry. When asked, "Why was this woman to be left with them?" he had replied that Emry had been arrested "for abuse of confidence; she had failed to pay a bill of nearly two hundred dollars at the Pan American Guest House." He claimed also that he had "no other place to put her." Her comrades became suspicious and asked each other: why would a woman charged with such a minor offense have to be left in a cell with political prisoners? Was she there to spy on them, even though she insisted she "did not know Spanish?" Canales sent a note cautioning them to be mindful of what they said in Emry's presence. At first, Reynolds said, Emry was reluctant to stay in the cell, "but once she saw that I, too, was American, she relented, and in time told me the story of her life."[25]

In essence, Emry told Reynolds that she had been adopted at birth by a couple in Kansas and still had her adoptive mother living there. Her mother wanted her to live with her, but she wouldn't hear of it because they didn't get along. She said she had graduated from the University of Kansas, and after a while had started working for the United States government in Prague, Czechoslovakia and then at the U.S. Consulate at Frankfort-am-Main, Germany. She claimed she had been fired from the last job because the American Ambassador did not like her and had accused her of sympathizing with the Communists, after she began dating his son. From Germany she had gone to Paris, where U.S. officials had tried to poison her and then had accused her of being mentally ill and sent her to a mental hospital in New York. After she was released from that hospital she had returned to Kansas, where she had convinced her adoptive mother to send her to Latin America to recuperate. And after a trip through the West Indies she had come to Puerto Rico, where she hoped to stay and learn Spanish. But those plans had now been aborted by her arrest, which she claimed not to understand since she had left her luggage, which was worth more than what she owed the Pan American Guest House. Reynolds recalled that after hearing Emry's life story, she wasn't sure what to believe.[26]

So ten days later, when Emry was called down to the warden's office, Reynolds said, she looked through her belongings, and found two U.S. Passports in Emry's name: "one authorizing her to travel through non-Communist Europe, in 1945," and the other which "identified her as an employee of the United States Consulate at Frankfort-am-Main, Germany." So far, Reynolds declared, "The passports confirmed, the part of the story that she had worked for the U.S. government, "a discovery that only increased our suspicion that Emry's purpose in our cell was to spy on us." They decided to watch her closely.[27]

After a few days, they noticed that Emry's behavior grew increasingly more "bizarre" the longer she stayed in the cell (about three weeks). For example, she spent most of the time "lying in bed, moving her lips, as if she were talking to herself. Many times she would laugh out loud and then cover her mouth with the sheet to stifle her laughter. Every few days, she would be called downstairs, but she always seemed to know ahead of time, even though no one had come to warn her." On those occasions, Reynolds wrote, "she would get up, shower, dress and get ready before the guard came for her." After a while, she said, her cellmates had begun to joke "that perhaps Emry had a listening device in her vagina." Then on February 26 or 27 (1951), they noticed that Emry's luggage (which she had ostensibly left behind in payment for the bill she owed at the guest house) was brought to her as she was getting ready. Reynolds then asked the guard where they were taking her, and he had said: "she is being taken to the airport." After Emry left the cell, Reynolds found "a torn post card on her bed, addressed to a Mrs. Young in Kansas," in which she had written that she was "in La Princesa, being tortured by electricity and de-sexed by radio."[28]

A few days after Emry was taken from their cell, Reynolds began hearing voices, always late at night, which appeared to be coming from the warden's office, the room directly below their cell. They were distinctly "the voices of American men," she said. She heard them every night, for about a week, as they discussed various topics, including the case of a person they had been following and who was proving elusive. She re-named one of the voices "Loudmouth" because of the loud tone in which he complained about everything in Puerto Rico. One night he was telling another (a quieter sort) that "the Puerto Rican government had locked up people without having good cases against them." Then after a week of the late night chatter, the voices were gone and the place grew quiet. Shortly thereafter they were sent back to the Arecibo jail and she forgot the incident until she was brought back to that same cell at the end of July 1951since her trial was scheduled to begin in early August.[29]

She described the period (July 30 to mid-September 1951) she spent at La Princesa as a "horror." Recalling the lack of ventilation in the cell she had occupied four months earlier, she asked the assistant warden who greeted her whether she could stay in the open gallery until another room could be found. He agreed, and she then "spent two days and nights in the company of hundreds, perhaps thousands of bed bugs, on the filthiest army cot I had ever seen," she said. And then on August 1st she was transferred to the alcove where her torments began.[30]

At first, she noticed "nothing strange about the alcove," but within hours, she said, she began to hear "noisy vibrations, like those produced by the motor of an old refrigerator," which seemed to be coming from the floor below. The following day she heard the noisy vibrations again and then began experiencing "mild electric shocks at the base of my head." That weekend, she again heard the distinct voice of "Loud-mouth," who this time was ranting about the Pacifists, calling them "agents of Albizu Campos." He appeared to be instructing someone "not to allow them to land in San Juan" and describing Conrad Lynn (her de-fense lawyer) in objectionable racial terms. He continued ranting all day, Reynolds said, making it hard for her to concentrate on preparing her defense. Yet she was surprised that she managed to sleep "despite the mild electric shocks" to her head.[31]

She remained alone in the cell until August 13 (1951) when Pérez, Torresola and Viscal were brought back from Arecibo and housed in the larger cell adjacent to the alcove. Since the door of that cell was now closed, the alcove was left without ventilation, she said. But, she didn't complain because she was glad to have comrades nearby again. Within a day after their arrival, "they, too, began to complain about odd sensa-tions and noises" they hadn't experienced the last time they were there. They compared notes, and she told them that she had also been experiencing them, and that more recently she had been hearing conversations, which seemed to be coming from the floor below. The others said they hadn't heard any voices, so she decided to keep those details to herself, for fear they might think she was losing her mind. Then on August 15, she said, there was a "hurricane scare," and during a trip to the bathroom she overheard a guard asking another how they were supposed to "protect the x-ray machine from the winds." The comment struck her as odd because she hadn't known the prison owned such a machine. A little later she heard men on the floor above, nailing boards across the windows (a common precaution the islanders take in times of hurricanes). Paint and dirt, she said, dirtied her bed and the floor, and that led her to wonder whether "the x-ray machine was kept above the alcove."[32]

The next day (August 16) her three comrades were sent back to the Arecibo jail and she was again left alone. That Thursday the San Juan District Court adjourned for the weekend, she recalled, so her trial was again postponed. She decided "to use the time to prepare for the trial, now rescheduled to begin on Monday morning." But by early Saturday morning "Loudmouth" was ranting about Albizu and the two Pacifists (Ralph Templin and Ernest Bromley), who had flown to Puerto Rico to attend her trial. At one point Loudmouth had pretended that her friends and Conrad Lynn were downstairs, asking to visit her, but that he had given orders to send them away because "visits weren't allowed on Saturday." (She later discovered that this had never happened because the three men had left San Juan for the weekend.) After listening to his rants for a few hours, she decided to send Conrad Lynn a telegram, only to hear the contents of it read back to her by Loudmouth. (The telegram was never sent, she said, even though she had paid for its delivery.)[33]

She continued listening to Loudmouth everyday that weekend, though at times other "voices" appeared. These told her they were there to counsel her "to desist from your mistaken ways." They said they were there for her benefit because they knew her "potential and wished (she) would use it to help the United States." At times they suggested ways in which she could be useful to the U.S. government in Puerto Rico and in Latin America. But that collaboration, they reminded her, could only take place if she agreed "to abandon Albizu Campos and his group." The most disturbing of the new voices, she wrote, was one pretending to be a psychiatrist who wanted her to know how much her family worried about her. He gave such precise details about the various members of her family, she wrote, that she "almost believed him." The other voice that unnerved her was one who pretended to be the pastor of the church she attended in Manhattan. That voice, she said, questioned her devotion to her faith and urged her "to repent, repent … repent" and return to the Christian fold. The worst part about the voices, she said, was the way they would trail off, while repeating a particular phrase. That mental exercise, she noted, left her "half-dazed" and caused her to fall into "a restless, hypnotic sleep." The voices, the noise, and the electric shocks continued until the trial ended. Thankfully, she said, the "diabolical experiments" were interspersed with brief periods of rest. By the time she appeared in Court each morning, she was "exhausted, yet relieved to be away from the cell."[34]

Towards the end of August, she said, she was experiencing kidney problems, but was too frightened to take the medication Dr. Hazim, the prison physician at La Princesa, had prescribed. She feared that it might cause her to hallucinate during the trial, but took the script, in case she was able to fill it once the trial ended. But the trial was again delayed, as the Court adjourned the last Thursday of August, in observation of the upcoming Labor Day weekend. For her, that weekend was pure "torture" because she had to contend with "the voices from the moment (she) returned to the cell." This time the men at the other end began to make their suggestions through repeated chants. One of the voices suggested that she could escape her "impending fate of being confined in a Puerto Rican jail, eating those damned rice and beans, those damned rice and beans … rice and beans, for years on end, for years on end." They chanted also that "Conrad Lynn wouldn't be able to save her … couldn't save her … because he knew nothing about the law, knew nothing about the law." They chanted also that the best thing for her to do was to "come to your senses … come to your senses … come to your senses" and "come to work for the U.S. government, the U.S. government and save yourself … save yourself." Then a harsher voice appeared, and while speaking normally, began to question her "virginal claims" and to accuse her of having had love affairs with both Albizu Campos and Conrad Lynn. She said that voice went on to describe the "private parts" of her body in the "most objectionable language." She was so distraught by that voice, she wrote, that she attempted to pray, only to hear "the voice" mock her effort. She then tried to translate a passage from the Bible into Spanish and again heard the voice laughing while correcting her. It was at that point, she said, that she "realized that someone evil must be watching me and see every move I make." Overwhelmed by "the monstrosity" of what was being done to her, she mouthed the words "Peeping Toms," and that caused the voices "to explode in riotous laughter." It took a great deal of struggle, she said, not to succumb to the fear and helplessness she felt. She prayed and hoped the trial ended soon.[35]

Conviction and Incarceration

According to the reports filed by Police Lieutenants Carlos Guadalupe and Juan Rodríguez Pérez, the trial of Ruth Reynolds (and the three Nationalist men who had traveled with her from Fajardo to San Juan on October 26, 1950) ended at 9:45 in the evening on September 5, 1951. Reynolds' trial, according to other official records, differed only in that the proceedings were conducted in two languages: English and Spanish. Otherwise, the San Juan District Court followed the same practice followed in other Nationalist proceedings: allowing the prosecution to call numerous witnesses in hopes of convincing the jury that Reynolds and her codefendants "had conspired with individuals, whose known intent was to overthrow the island's government." Representing the interests of the People at the trial were five Special District Attorneys (José C. Aponte, Guillermo Gil Rivera, Baldomero Freyre, Angel Viera Martínez, José Dávila Ortiz), and twenty-one witnesses, nineteen of whom were detectives and policemen. One was a former Nationalist (Guillermo Hernández Vega, who had already testified against Pedro Albizu Campos, Leonides Díaz, and others) and the other was Francisco Viscal, the disgruntled father of the well-known Nationalist, Olga Isabel Viscal. According to his testimony, Reynolds had been "a bad influence on (his) two girls." He recounted in Court what he had already told one of the district attorneys months earlier. He said that Reynolds had come to his house (in Puerto Nuevo, Hato Rey) one evening in 1948 and taken away his underage daughter Irma (Viscal) to Albizu Campos' home. He was not sure whether the man who drove Reynolds to his residence was armed or not. He added that Reynolds had also influenced his daughter Olga to become involved with the Nationalists and that was the reason why she was now in jail. Fortunately, he said, he had rescued Irma in time, and she was now a married woman.[36]

During cross-examination, two of Reynolds' attorneys (Juan Hernández Vallé and Francisco Hernández Vargas who assisted Conrad Lynn) challenged Viscal's testimony. They told the Court that Irma Viscal had been the one who asked Miss Reynolds to take her away from her home because her father was in the habit of beating her. They added that, after Miss Reynolds "rescued her, she took her to the Albizu family for her own safety." Olga had come on her own to Albizu's home, looking for a place to stay. And at that point, Albizu had asked his trusted friend Raimundo Díaz Pacheco "to take both girls to his family home," where they could be supervised by his wife. They had stayed with the Díaz Pacheco family for a few weeks, the lawyers stated. Then Irma had found a job and rented an apartment in Río Piedras and taken Olga to live with her. Given the events just described, could Mr. Viscal explain: Why had his girls chosen to go and live on their own rather than return to the family home? Wouldn't their actions suggest that they had left of their own accord and not because of Miss Reynolds' influence? Miss Reynolds, they argued, was not responsible for anything his girls had done. In the end, Viscal's testimony produced a mixed reaction in the jury: it called into question Ruth Reynolds' morals for having helped Irma Viscal escape the family home but presented the Viscal sisters in a negative light, an outcome their father had not intended.[37]

Eager to have Reynolds convicted of "helping the Nationalist lunatics" the prosecution laid aside Viscal's testimony and concentrated on the I.S. agents' claims: that she had pledged her life and fortune in support of Puerto Rico's independence, which represented a violation of Law #53. Because of their elaborate arguments regarding that accusation, the jury absolved Reynolds and one of her codefendants (Mejías Flores) of the first count (transporting weapons to aid the revolt of October 30) but convicted the other two travelers: Rafael Burgos Fuentes (the driver of the car) and Eduardo López Vázquez (the other passenger). The two convicted were later sentenced to prison terms, ranging from one month to five years and one day to two and half years, respectively. Reynolds, on the other hand, was convicted of the second count (pledging life and fortune in support of Puerto Rico's independence at the Nationalist assembly of 1949) and was sentenced on September 7, 1951 to a prison term of two to six years. Since Puerto Rico did not yet have a separate prison for women, she was sent back to the Women's Wing of the Arecibo district jail to serve her term.[38]

Displeased with the outcome of the trial, her defense team filed a motion, challenging her "wrongful conviction." But as the judicial system seemed in no hurry to revisit her case, her attorneys then filed another motion, requesting that she be released on bail until the case came up for review. The District Court complied with the second request, and in February 1952 summoned Reynolds to San Juan for a hearing regarding bail. The sum, which was initially set at $25,000 was slightly reduced to $20,000, provided that half of it was paid in cash. Because of the exorbitant sum, it would take nearly three months to find three individuals who could post the bonds required. In the meantime, Reynolds had to make the best of her life in the Arecibo prison.[39]

A New Chapter in Arecibo's Prison

According to Reynolds' account, she and seven other Nationalist women, also confined to that jail, were no longer able to return to the isolation cells they had occupied months earlier. They were instead sent to the open gallery to share their lives with more than one hundred "common prisoners." The gallery space the female inmates shared, explained the Interim Superintendent of Prisons when he visited two months later, had been designed to hold eighty inmates at most and now held one hundred and nineteen. The gallery was so crowded, Reynolds recalled, that some inmates had to sleep on the floor because there wasn't enough floor space to accommodate the Army cots needed. At night, when everyone had laid down, she added, there was hardly any place to move around if one needed to use the toilet. The place was also "so noisy" that after a few days there she and her comrades had begun to "feel nostalgic" for the old isolation cells (calabozos). But those rooms, they had been told, had reverted to their old usage: (to punish inmates who had broken prison rules). Fortunately, Reynolds recalled, she and her comrades hadn't stayed in the gallery very long because two months after she arrived the warden had assigned them a large room of their own. The reason for the change of quarters, Reynolds explained, was that she and Monserrate Valle had been placed on the prison's "special diet" (the one generally reserved for inmates who were ill). He had told them that it might be best if all of them lived together in one place where they could prepare their foods without eliciting envy from the others.[40]

In reality, the case of Reynolds' "special diet" had taken a circuitous route. From the start, she had been complaining to her friends in the United States about the awful prison fare she was served, and they in turn had written to several congressmen, the Secretary of the Central Committee for Conscientious Objectors, Lyle Tatum, and a lawyer in Philadelphia, named Walter C. Longstreth. In December 1950, one of the congressmen, House Representative John S. Wood, had written to Governor Luis Muñoz Marín, inquiring about Ruth Reynolds' incarceration. The Governor then rerouted the letter to the Puerto Rican Department of Justice, which in essence limited its reply to describing the charges that had led to Reynolds' incarceration. The reply also took care to quote the portions of Law #53 she had allegedly violated. Then in October 1951, a month after Reynolds was convicted, Lyle Tatum also wrote to the Governor, asking about the diet and conditions of the island's prisons. Yet the most interesting letter on Reynolds' behalf was sent in late October (1951) by Attorney Longstreth to the Secretary of the Interior, Oscar L. Chapman.[41]

In that letter, he addressed several of Reynolds complaints and suggested that Secretary Chapman order an investigation into the conditions of Puerto Rico's prisons. He reminded Chapman that "Reynolds is a citizen of the USA and should not be treated as she has been, regardless of her crime." He added that, "prior to her conviction she was confined in a filthy room without light and now she and seven other political prisoners are confined in a large room with 119 prisoners." He explained that "Reynolds had weighed 154 pounds at the time of her arrest and was now (October 24, 1951) weighing only 115 pounds because she was fed only beans and rice." He contended that "the treatment of prisoners in Puerto Rico is inhuman and should be changed forthwith." Thus, he was recommending that Chapman "send one of your trusted observers to Puerto Rico to carry out the investigation and not to rely on anyone connected with the prison system on the island." He concluded that, "Puerto Rico is a territory of the United States and our government is responsible for conditions there ... and should cease to rule it if we cannot maintain decent conditions."[42]

Whether Longstreth's letter or any other (all of which were rerouted to the Secretary of Justice and from there to the Department of Prisons) led to her new diet and improved living conditions is a matter of conjecture. Yet the fact remains that shortly after Reynolds returned to the

Arecibo prison after her conviction, the newly appointed Secretary of Justice (Víctor Gutiérrez Franqui) opted to investigate her claims. First, he sent orders to the Arecibo warden (González Lebrón) to have Reynolds medically evaluated, "to determine whether she qualifies for the special diet assigned to inmates who are in ill health." Next, he sent the Interim Superintendent of Prisons, Rafael N. Rodríguez to Arecibo to meet with the warden, the prison physician (Arturo Cadilla), and Reynolds herself, and take steps to correct the situation, as well as report his findings. On November 5, 1951, Rodríguez reported to Interim Attorney General, Federico Tilén that he had met with the parties concerned, and according to the medical results, Reynolds was "basically in good health." And though she had "lost some weight," the physician stated, "it was not as much as she claimed." Nonetheless, they had agreed that "since Reynolds is not Puerto Rican and thus not used to the basic fare of rice, beans and codfish, she could benefit from a change in diet." The doctor had also suggested that "she should also take a few vitamins" in addition to the new supplements of eggs, milk, fruits and canned meats and vegetables.[43]

The warden, Rodríguez wrote, had been amenable to the changes recommended, provided Reynolds (like all others inmates on the special diet) agreed to pay for the additional items because he simply did not have funds in his daily meal allowance (35 cents a day per inmate) to cover the extra cost for everyone on the special list. Reynolds (and later Monserrate Valle) had agreed to pay for the extra foods, and the warden promised to have the additional groceries delivered to their cell once a week. Rodríguez added that since he also found "the gallery was much too overcrowded," he had suggested and the warden had concurred, "to vacate the sewing room (a space of approximately 20 feet by 20 feet, conveniently located next to the kitchen) and use it to house the eight Nationalists, so that Reynolds and any other (Monserrate Valle) could prepare their supplementary meals away from the prying eyes of the other inmates." (It is likely it was in that new space where Leonides Díaz prepared the nightly soups, which were described by Carmen María Pérez and Isabel Rosado in their interviews.)[44]

Her comrades, Reynolds declared, were delighted with the new housing quarters because they now had "access to clean sheets and beds." They were also glad to be "farther away from the noise of the open gallery." The peace and quiet the room offered, Reynolds continued, had been a welcome relief for Leonides Díaz, Monserrate Valle, and Juanita Ojeda in particular because they had spent the longest time in the open gallery. For Leonides Díaz, it had the added advantage that she could practice her Spiritualism undisturbed and hold an occasional séance in which she appealed to the spirits of dead Nationalists to guide her." Reynolds said she attended one of the séances but was not convinced in part because she could not understand how one could be a Christian and a Spiritualist at the same time. Yet she did not criticize Leonides, whose politics she greatly admired. She noted also that just as they were getting used to their new quarters, the warden of Arecibo (J. González Lebrón) died of a heart attack and they had been left to wonder what would happen when a new warden came on board. They went to the wake to pay their respects, she said, and were surprised "to see inmates openly crying as they filed past the coffin." Shortly after the funeral, they were relieved to discover that the new warden was Don Balbino González, a person they had known briefly when they were first sent to La Princesa. "He was a decent man, a straight-talking man who never promised what he couldn't deliver," Reynolds said. "We grew to like him," she added, "because he did not interfere with our living arrangement or special diets."[45]

Free on Bail: Awaiting Resolution of her Appeal

In June 1952, Reynolds was released on bail, pending resolution of her appeal. She stayed in Puerto Rico a few days, long enough to arrange her return trip to New York City. She had no money, so she went to see Carlos Vélez Rieckehoff, in Ciales, and he in turn took her to a local businessman (one of the three who had posted her bail) to secure the funds for her plane fare. By the third week of June she had left the island undetected to the dismay of the Puerto Rican authorities. Back in Manhattan she found that her friends had sublet her apartment while she was in prison, so she took a room in the old building where the Harlem Ashram had been. Conrad Lynn offered her part-time work at his legal firm at West 125th Street until she found a better position. Working for Lynn, she said, had the advantage that she could keep track of her appeal as it wound its way through the legal channels of Puerto Rico.[46]

After nineteen months in prison and a few more in a boarding house, she was eager to have a place all her own, and gladly moved to her apartment when it was finally vacated. Yet having to pay the rent on her own, in addition to other bills meant she also had to find full-time employment. She found a job she liked, doing secretarial work, only to lose it a few weeks later when the FBI paid a visit to her employer. The pattern was repeated so often that she decided it would be best to take two part-time jobs instead. That way, she reasoned, if she lost one job, she could still have some income coming in while she looked for another. The agents who had her fired, she said, generally waited for her out on the sidewalk, to ask her the same old questions, and suggest ways how she could change her situation. All she had to do, they said, was to agree to collaborate with them and come to work for the United States government. They trailed her so often, she said, that they knew where she lived, where she went, and who she saw. Yet she never wavered in her support of Puerto Rico's struggle for independence, according to her friend and colleague, Jean Zwickel. In fact, among the first things she did when she returned to Manhattan in 1952, Zwickel said, was to revive (and rename) the American League for Puerto Rico's Independence, created nine years earlier under the leadership of Jay Holmes Smith but which had been disbanded after Reynolds was imprisoned.[47]

As the spokesperson for the new organization, she called "Americans for Puerto Rico's Independence," she attended numerous meetings and in 1953 went before the United Nations' General Assembly to challenge the United States claims that Puerto Rico was a self-governing territory. She also petitioned the United Nations to establish a permanent commission to investigate the case of Puerto Rico and study the treatment the advocates of independence were accorded in Puerto Rico's prisons. She also focused on trying to get Albizu Campos released from prison. To that end, she wrote to old friends in Pacifist circles and got them to publish her articles and opinion pieces about Puerto Rico, its colonial dilemma, and Albizu's deteriorating health due to the ill treatment he received in prison.[48]

Then on March 1, 1954 Dolores (Lolita) Lebrón and three male companions attacked the United States Congress and Reynolds felt that all her efforts to help Albizu and Puerto Rico's independence had come to a dead-end because earlier supporters were now afraid of being linked to the Nationalists. The Cold War, the McCarthy hearings, and the general fear that characterized the period, she said, caused many of her friends "to run for cover" after the attack on Congress. In reality, they had reason to worry because within days after the attack, ninety-one Nationalists were called in for questioning by three grand juries established in New York City. Of those, thirteen were later indicted on suspicion of "conspiring" with the attackers. Similarly, in Puerto Rico more than three dozen were arrested on the pretext that they had had probably known about the impending attack and thus violated Law #53, (known in the United States as "the little Smith Act"). The day after the attack on Congress, several FBI agents visited Reynolds' employers in order to have her fired. One employer did as he was told and fired that very day, but the other, a Jewish man who had escaped the horrors of Hitler's Germany, refused to be intimidated. According to what Reynolds was told later, he had asked her supervisor whether Reynolds had been discussing politics at the office. When he was told that she hadn't, he had said, "in that case let her work because what she does after she leaves here is her business."[49]

The FBI men were waiting when she finished work that day, she said. They wanted to know how well she knew Lolita Lebrón and her three companions because they had information that she had visited Lebrón's home sometime in February. She admitted that she had gone to dinner at Lolita's place with her friend Pinto Gandía but insisted that she hardly knew her because Lolita apparently had joined the Nationalist Junta of New York while she (Reynolds) was living in Puerto Rico. That day was a very cold day in New York, Reynolds explained, and she was in no mood to stand on the sidewalk to answer the FBI's questions. So she tried to get out it, saying that she had to get to the Fulton Market to buy food for her cats before it closed. They offered to drive her there, which she accepted, and when they arrived one of the agents went to buy the cat food, while the other continued to interrogate her. In general, he just repeated a variation of the same questions, but then asked whether she might be persuaded to testify against Lolita or any of the others. She told him "what they already knew" that she had known Rafael Cancel Miranda since he was a teen, and that he had been sent to prison for failing to register for the military draft. With the others, she said, she only had "a nodding acquaintance." No, she had not heard about any plan to attack the Congress. Besides, that would not be an action she would have condoned because she was a Pacifist. Apparently they were convinced because instead of arresting her, they drove her home.[50]

In retrospect, she thought the reason she was not arrested that day was because the FBI already knew from Gonzalo Lebrón (the Nationalist turned collaborator) that she was opposed to what the Nationalists had done "since he was probably wearing a wire" when he spoke to her. She said she told him she was angry for what the attackers had done because with that action they had destroyed years of diplomatic efforts to help Puerto Rico become independent and Albizu Campos released from prison. She had made it clear that she did not condone violence, regardless of its origin and would never forgive the attackers for what they had done. At the time, she said, she had no reason to suspect Gonzalo because it was not yet known that he had betrayed everyone. She had been worried that she might be arrested at any moment, as Rosa Collazo and others had been. She wondered also whether the Puerto Rican authorities could re-arrest her given that her appeal was still pending resolution at the Puerto Rican Supreme Court. They had rearrested five of her former cellmates, she reasoned, even after they completed their sentences. Albizu Campos, too, had been sent to prison when the Governor revoked his pardon.[51]

Yet despite her fears, she agreed to testify for the defense during the attackers' trial in the Southern District Court of New York in October 1954. She said in Court what she had told the FBI, and what the authorities already knew, that she was not a Nationalist, though a few of them were her close friends. She divulged nothing, she said, that could incriminate the attackers, "for they had done that on their own." She was not like Lolita's brother, she said, "the louse who had betrayed his own sister and his friends." She was sad for her dear friend Pinto Gandía who was convicted on charges of conspiracy, even though he had "opposed the attackers' plan" from the start. Gonzalo knew this and said as much in Court, but the prosecution had already made its deal: only Gonzalo and two of his men would get suspended sentences and in exchange they would divulge the Nationalist plans. In the end, Gonzalo and two of his men received six-year suspended sentences.[52]

Conviction Revoked in Puerto Rico: Reynolds Freed

In November 1954, approximately a month after she testified in New York at Lolita Lebrón's trial, the justices of the Puerto Rican Supreme

Court revoked Ruth Reynolds' conviction. The justices said they had reached their decision on the basis that "it would not have been a criminal act for Miss Reynolds to take the [Nationalist] oath (if she had) on December 19, 1949." That decision, Reynolds declared, had taken more than a year and represented a great deal effort on the part of her attorneys, Conrad Lynn and his associate in Puerto Rico, the distinguished constitutionalist, Santos P. Amadeo. The justices, she explained, were probably reacting to the news that her attorneys would pursue her case all the way to United States Supreme Court, if necessary. Lastly, they could have also been influenced by the opinion published by the American Civil Liberties Union (ACLU) in its July 1953 bulletin. According to her recollections, the ACLU had been reluctant to become involved in her case until recently, claiming that it couldn't "meddle in Puerto Rico's internal affairs." Yet she added tartly, the ACLU director, Roger Baldwin, hadn't considered it a problem to visit Puerto Rico's Governor and advise him on how to reduce the negative image his administration had created before the United Nations and the world. But now thanks to Conrad Lynn's relentless pressure, and Santos Amadeo's announcement earlier that year that he and a few colleagues were planning to start a civil rights organization in Puerto Rico (to investigate the civil rights violations committed by the government), the ACLU had finally agreed to participate in her case as "amicus curiae." A year earlier, she continued, the Muñoz administration had secured approval from the United Nations for the island's new political formula, the "so-called self-governing status, known as the Commonwealth of Puerto Rico."[53]

The opinion published by the ACLU in July 1953, reported the local daily, El Imparcial, had enabled Reynolds' attorneys to file a motion with the island's Supreme Court, "requesting that it overturn Reynolds' conviction." They argued, as the ACLU had done, that "taking an oral oath" at a public event did not constitute legal grounds to condemn her. They explained that Reynolds had been "convicted on the basis of 'one line' of a long oral speech," pronounced by Pedro Albizu Campos in Arecibo (December 1949) in his effort to raise funds for his Party. They explained, as the ACLU had done, that "if such a conviction were upheld, no citizen would ever be safe to approve an oral resolution without first having to analyze every sentence of the text proclaimed." In the end, the ACLU made clear that its interest in Reynolds' case "was not based on any political view, but in the defense of her constitutional rights." Whatever the justices' motives, they ruled in Reynolds favor and revoked the lower court's conviction. They set her and two others (Burgos Fuentes and López Vázquez) free but said their decision did not extend to others also convicted of violations to Law #53. These would have to appeal their case, one by one, as Reynolds had done. As a result, the next person to have her case overturned, after a lengthy legal process (this time spearheaded by Santos P. Amadeo) was Leonides Díaz, the Arecibo matron also wrongfully convicted and sentenced to more than 490 years. The others convicted of violations of Law #53 remained in jail until the statute was abolished by the Puerto Rican legislature in August 1957. Some have credited the abolition of Law #53 to Governor Luis Muñoz Marín, who in February 1956 established a Civil Rights Committee (to investigate the civil and human rights abuses of his own government) and upon receiving its report persuaded the legislature to abolish the troublesome statute. Others have claimed that after the United States Supreme Court abolished the Smith Act, Puerto Rico had little choice but to abolish its own "little Smith Act."[54]

Last Decades of Reynolds' Life

Shortly after her case was resolved, Reynolds flew back to Puerto Rico, in order to attend the trial of fourteen comrades (six of them former cellmates) who had been rearrested in March 1954 for alleged violations of Law #53. Since she had been in Puerto Rico the month before and was short of funds, she accepted a $100 money order sent to her by Doris Torresola, according to an I.S. report. This time, she stayed in Juanita Ojeda's home in Río Piedras because she lacked funds to rent a hotel room, reported the same agents. Ojeda, too, had been rearrested in March 1954, but was then out on bail awaiting a review of her case. The proceedings for all of the accused were slated to begin in December at the District Court of Arecibo, and Doris Torresola had expressed a desire to see Ruth one more time before she "was put away for many years." Reynolds stayed only for part of the proceedings, which lasted from mid-December 1954 through February 7, 1955 because she was due at work. Her comrades said they were grateful for the visit. As expected, they were all convicted and sentenced to long prison terms and would not see Reynolds again for many years.[55]

I found no evidence to indicate that Reynolds ever visited her women friends at the Vega Alta prison even though she visited Puerto Rico several times while they were incarcerated. She did, however, support the various groups that were calling for the release of the Nationalist prisoners. There are photographs of her picketing in front of the Vega Alta prison in August 1963. Five years earlier (December 27-31, 1958), she led a march from the southern port of Guánica to the northeastern city of San Juan. The purpose of that march, she told the press, was to protest the ongoing occupation of Puerto Rico by the United States.[56]

From her return to New York until her retirement, she worked as assistant librarian and archivist at the New York Psychoanalytic Institute, the same employer who had refused to fire her when the FBI demanded it in March 1954. Until the mid-1960s, she flew often to Puerto Rico in hopes of getting Albizu Campos released from prison. She visited him once in 1963 at the Presbyterian Hospital, where he was kept under tight surveillance after he suffered a major stroke in prison. It is not clear whether she saw him after he was pardoned by the Governor, shortly before he died (April 21, 1965). She flew back to San Juan to attend his funeral and join his wife and daughters in the seventy-two hour vigil that followed Albizu's passing. She said she was amazed and gratified to see the enormous crowds that came to the various places where Albizu's body laid in state. She mourned and prayed with the thousands who attended the two masses that were said for his soul. Then, after she returned to New York and had had time to reflect on her loss and the meaning of Albizu's life, she wrote a beautiful eulogy in his honor. It reads in part:

The body lay in state, and the people came. They came in white linen suits—the dress of 'gentlemen' in the tropics— and they came barefoot and with holes in their shirts. Small shoeshine boys left their trade to come, and old people tottered in on canes. The crippled came in wheelchairs, children in their school uniforms. Ex-governmental officials came and ex-political prisoners. Persons who staunchly shared with Don Pedro forty years of persecution were there; hundreds who had deserted him in hours of peril were also there, demonstrating publicly at last the true affection of their hearts. All Puerto Rico was represented. During seventy-two hours, sixty-five thousand memorial ribbons were distributed, and thousands of mourners left without them because they could not be prepared fast enough to keep up with the demand.[57]

After the long vigil, starting the procession became a complicated affair because the multitude was so large that it had to backtrack about a mile in the opposite direction in order to allow the mourners to follow the bier. She explains:

> First in line was a sixty-piece band, playing alternately Bach's Passion Chorale and Puerto Rico's National Anthem, La Borinqueña. Then followed a long line of women and girls bearing the floral arrangements.... Then came the close relatives and intimate friends, among whom I was privileged to be included. Then came the coffin, carried on the shoulders of

†

PEDRO ALBIZU CAMPOS

HA FALLECIDO

A las 9:30 P.M. del 21 de abril de 1965

Su viuda Laura Meneses de Albizu Campos; sus hijos Pedro Albizu Campos Meneses (Ausente) Rosa Albizu Campos de O'neill (ausente) y Laura Albizu Campos de Meneses, sus hijos políticos Mercedes Espiñeira de Albizu Campos (ausente) Luis O'neill Rosario (ausente) y Carlos G. Meneses (ausente); sus sobrinos, nietos y demás familiares su fiel y consecuente amiga Juanita Ojeda; Los Doctores Ricardo Cordero, Cuello y Rodríguez, suplican una Oración al Todopoderoso y asistir al Acto del Sepelio que tendrá lugar el domingo 25 de abril a las 2:00 PM; partiendo la comitiva fúnebre desde el Ateneo Puertorriqueño hasta el Cementerio de San Juan acto por el cual quedarán agradecidos. Los restos mortales permanecerán en Capilla ardiente en la Funeraria Jensen Pda. 26, Santurce, hasta el sábado 24 de abril a las 2:00 PM, hora en que será trasladado al Ateneo Puertorriqueño, donde recibirá Honras Fúnebres hasta el domingo 25 de abril a las 2:00 P.M. que se procederá al Sepelio.

JENSEN

Death notice of Pedro Albizu Campos, April 21, 1965. Among the persons listed is Juanita Ojeda (who is described as his loyal friend).

strong men, eager to perform this last small service. Then
came the people, thousands upon thousands, so that at the
highest point of the journey ... we could hardly see the beginning of the procession entering Old San Juan, and the end of
it was not visible at all.

All along the route, the crowd paid tribute. At the Cathedral, the Arch-
bishop Luis Aponte had personally offered to officiate a Mass of Response
for Don Pedro, but he had to leave after having waited two hours for the
procession and the mass was held without him. And when the procession
finally climbed the hill to the top of San Justo Street, the priests at the
old San José Church, on the plaza by the same name, asked to be allowed
to hold another Mass of Response for Don Pedro. The widow agreed.
Then the procession walked downhill to the Old Cemetery by the sea
wall bordering El Morro and Albizu's body was finally laid to rest next to
the tomb of José de Diego, "the first of that century's independence leaders he had come to admire."[58]

Over the next twenty years she attended numerous activities in support of, and sponsored by Nationalists and other independence advocates
who strove to keep the struggle alive in New York City and Chicago. In
1977, she made a presentation before the United Nations' Decolonization
Committee in support of Puerto Rico's independence. Among her writings one finds copies of the speeches she gave at many Nationalist activities in her uniquely accented Spanish. In some of these she discussed
various aspects of Puerto Rico's history and in others the importance of
El Grito de Lares, or its counterpart, the Nationalist Revolution of 1950.
Oftentimes she was invited to speak about Don Pedro or other Nationalist
leaders, but occasionally, she was there as one of the leaders honored.[59]

Between 1985 and 1986, she sat for 112 hours with Blanca Vázquez
of El Centro de Estudios Puertorriqueños, at Hunter College of CUNY
for taped-recorded interviews. The transcripts of those interviews provide
rich information about the forces that informed her life: from her family
to her Christian Faith, to her discovery of Gandhi's Pacifism, to her actions for social justice. They help us to understand the motives that led
to her involvement in Puerto Rico's struggle for independence. They
speak also to her loyalty to Don Pedro and other independence advocates
who befriended her along the way. And they also make evident her unwavering love for the United States. The conversations illuminate the

point that everything she did was motivated by the principles of democracy and fairness she believed had shaped her nation. Given her deeply held beliefs, she said, she could not condone her government's colonization of Puerto Rico, one against which she would struggle until her dying day. And now as death loomed near, she wanted to leave a record of that struggle so that future generations would not forget. For that reason, she also participated in oral history projects at Columbia University and the Schomburg Center for Research in Black Culture at the New York Public Library. And shortly before she moved back to South Dakota, she donated her entire collection (of books, manuscripts, letters, newspaper clippings, police files, and photographs, among other items related to Puerto Rico's history and the Nationalists) to the Centro de Estudios Puertorriqueños at Hunter College. The Centro subsequently published her manuscript on the strike at the University of Puerto under the heading, *Campus in Bondage: A 1948 Microcosm of Puerto Rico in Bondage.* Since then the Centro staff has honored her memory by processing the collection she gave them (The Ruth Reynolds Papers) and making it available for our benefit.

In 1987, already ill with cancer, she returned home to the Black Hills of South Dakota, to be closer to her family and the place that had shaped her life. She died there two years later, on December 2, 1989. According to the heartfelt articles published by the newsweekly *Claridad* weeks later, she was loved by many in Puerto Rico. Though most of the tributes sent in by her admirers focused on recounting the highlights of her life's history, some also recounted touching anecdotes about the moments they had shared with her in or out of prison. Most recalled her courage, her loyalty, and the work she had done in support of Puerto Rico's independence. Albizu Campos' granddaughter Rosa Meneses Albizu recalled that one of Reynolds' distinguishing traits was her loyalty to her friends. She remembered her at her grandfather's funeral and was grateful she was there accompanying her grandmother through the difficult ordeal. "Ruth," she said, "loved Puerto Rico deeply and understood the justice of its struggle."[60]

Another who remembered her with great affection was Jacinto García Pérez, then president of the Nationalist Party. He recounted an anecdote Reynolds had told him about her time in prison. She said that one day the warden of the Arecibo prison had called her "mija" (mi hija, my child) in his attempt to get her to eat the rice and beans she disliked.

Not yet familiar with the Puerto Rican custom, she took it literally, she said, and shouted back: "I am not your daughter, and your are not my father because if you were, you would bring me a steak with lots of french fries."[61]

Isabel Rosado, who had spent more than a year in prison with her, said that Reynolds' humor had helped them to overcome difficult moments in prison. In a tribute she wrote, she added, that Reynolds had often said: "The greatest honor of my life is to be in prison with you who are defending your homeland." Rosado described Reynolds as "a woman who believed deeply in the justice of Puerto Rico's struggle for independence."[62]

Oscar Collazo, the Nationalist who survived the 1950 attack of Blair House, wrote that Reynolds had worked hard to get the United Nations to understand Puerto Rico's colonial plight. He recalled that she had translated into English many of the position papers Pinto Gandía presented at the United Nations on behalf of Puerto Rico [after the Nationalist Party lost its Observer Post in that institution in 1950].[63]

Lolita Lebrón, as the poet she was, said it best when she described "the great sadness Reynolds' death has left in our hearts." She called her a "noble North American woman who is as much a Puerto Rican heroine as all the other national heroines." Adding, "Though Reynolds has died, her spiritual presence has not vanished; she lives on in the great works she performed on behalf of Puerto Rico's independence."[64]

5. Isabel Rosado Morales (1907–2015)

Preface

Isabel Rosado Morales, better known as Isabelita Rosado, spent nearly thirteen years in three Puerto Rican prisons for her political beliefs and actions. A native of Ceiba, Puerto Rico, she was born into a loving family in the rural barrio of Chupacallos on November 5, 1907. She was the fourth daughter among seven siblings, which included three younger brothers. Her father Simón Rosado owned a small plot of land, where he grew vegetables and other edibles with which he supplemented the income he earned working in the sugar fields. Her mother Petra Morales stayed home to care for the growing family. In addition to her household chores, she helped her husband plant the vegetable garden and care for the animals the couple raised to supplement their family's diet. Neither parent had gone to school, but made sure their children did, and even provided room and board to one of their teachers. During her childhood, Rosado said, she often saw the teacher repay her parents' kindness by reading to her mother in the afternoons or to the family during the evenings.[1]

School and Work in Eastern Puerto Rico

Isabelita Rosado completed elementary and middle school in the rural barrios of Ceiba and Naguabo, but in order to attend high school she had to travel to the neighboring town of Fajardo. At eighteen, she had earned a high school diploma and was "selected to attend a one year teacher-training course offered at the University of Puerto Rico." The university, she explained, had been looking for students with at least a 10th grade education, to train and send to staff the rural schools of Puerto Rico. She completed the training course by the summer of 1926, but was not hired that year, "Because my father did not belong to the right polit-

Isabel Rosado being dragged out, unconscious, from the the Nationalist Club in San Juan, due to the gases thrown by the police. March 6, 1954.

ical party," she said. She continued studying on weekends towards a bachelor's degree and was hired the following year (1926-27) by a rural school in Naguabo, thanks to the help of the region's school superintendent, Francisco Colón Gordiany.[2]

She remained in the teaching field for the next fourteen years while she completed a B.A. and various courses in the field of social work. In 1940 she left teaching and became a visiting social worker in the eastern towns of Ceiba, Fajardo and Naguabo, even though she still lacked certification in the field. In fact, she did not receive her Social Work license until April 12, 1950, according to a document that was submitted to the judicial authorities by the Examining and Registry Board of Social Workers in Santurce, Puerto Rico. The document had apparently been requested by one of the prosecutors shortly after she was arrested in January 1951. According to Rosado's testimony, both of her working licenses (teaching and social work) were revoked soon after she was convicted in April 1952, which meant she could never again teach in Puerto

Rico's public schools or work in any government social service agency.[3]

Working among the poor in eastern Puerto Rico all those years, Rosado said, helped her to understand the island's problems and clarify her political views. Thus, by the time she joined the Nationalist Party in 1937, she did so with the full understanding that the Party's goals coincided very closely with her own. Already deeply committed to helping the poor she served, she felt that the only way to create an equitable society in Puerto Rico was to set the island free from its colonial rulers. From 1937 till the day she died in 2015 she remained a steadfast supporter of the Nationalist Party ideals and its quest for Puerto Rico's freedom. Her devotion to the Party, its principles, and its leaders would eventually result in several arrests and imprisonments for her, the first of which occurred in 1951, when she was forty-four years old, and the last in the year 2000 when she was ninety-three.[4]

Joining the Nationalist Party: Meeting Albizu Campos

According to a self-published testimony and various interviews Rosado granted over the years, she became motivated to join the Nationalist Party after she heard the news that nineteen unarmed Nationalists (most of them women and children) had been assassinated and more than one hundred injured in the southern city of Ponce by the colonial police. The event, which later became known as the "Ponce Massacre" took place on March 21, 1937 (Palm Sunday) when a group of Nationalists congregated on the Ponce plaza in order to protest the arbitrary conviction and ten-year prison sentence levied against their leader, Pedro Albizu Campos by the U.S. Federal Court in San Juan. (For details about the Ponce Massacre, see the section devoted to Dominga de la Cruz in this book.)[5]

The "injustice committed against the Nationalists in Ponce," Rosado said, "was what motivated me to join the Nationalist Party in 1937, and other injustices and the abuse of power by those in government reaffirmed my life-long commitment to the cause of independence." She said she originally joined a chapter of the Party in barrio Daguao (a rural area between Ceiba and Naguabo in eastern Puerto Rico) and had been sworn in by its president Ignacio Rodríguez. "Rodríguez," she said, "taught me that only an independent Puerto Rico would allow its leaders to create a more equitable society." He taught her also about the importance of General Antonio Valero Bernabe, a Fajardo native who had fought alongside Simón Bolívar in South America's wars of independence. "And Rodríguez' wife," she recalled with a smile, "reminded us that no country had ever won independence without armed struggle."[6]

She had been a member of the Nationalist Party for about nine years when she was first introduced to Pedro Albizu Campos. "That momentous event," she said smiling, "occurred in the summer of 1946 when I went to visit a friend of mine who lived in the Bronx." That friend later took her to "a place in El Barrio (East Harlem) where Don Pedro used to meet his followers after he was released from Columbus Hospital." During that trip, she also met several other important figures, including Ruth Reynolds, a personal friend and advocate of Albizu Campos in the United States, Thelma Mielke, who later became the Nationalist Party Observer at the United Nations, and Juana Mills, a devoted follower of Albizu, who took great pride in preparing his meals because he had suffered a heart attack in Atlanta, Georgia's federal prison.[7]

According to Puerto Rico's I.S. agents, Rosado was "a known presence" at Nationalist Party activities and meetings by the 1940s, but her participation in Party events increased significantly after Albizu Campos returned home in December 1947. They reported that between 1948 and 1950, they often saw her "distributing Party literature, selling pamphlets or books that extolled the virtues of independence, or collecting members' dues or donations from those in the audience." The funds she and others collected at these events, they claimed, were then delivered to the Nationalist Party headquarters, where they were employed to pay the rent for the Nationalist Club, located at the corner of Sol and Cruz Streets, and to support Albizu Campos and his family. In one of the photographs the police took of Isabel Rosado in 1948, she appears sitting to the right of Albizu Campos at the presidential table during the Party's Annual Assembly held in San Juan that year.[8]

The photographs and reports filed by the I.S. agents would later be used by the prosecutors to try to convince the jury that she had been a sworn enemy of the Puerto Rican government for many years. They tried to link her to the six to eight activities the Nationalists held throughout the year in order to honor their heroes or mourn their dead. (Generally, these took place on February 23, in Utuado, March 21 in Ponce, April 16 in Santurce, September 23 in Lares, October 12 in Cabo Rojo and October 26 in Fajardo.) They also gathered in the southern port of Guánica every July 25 to protest the occupation of Puerto Rico by United States since 1898. Every December they held their annual assembly in which the membership elected (or re-elected) Party leaders. The I.S. agents attended all those activities and kept lists of the attendees. After the uprising of 1950, the authorities placed much emphasis on two Nationalist events Rosado had attended: the Annual Party Assembly, held in Arecibo, December 18, 1949 and the commemoration of late General Valero de Bernabe's birth, held in Fajardo on October 26, 1950. These two events, the authorities argued, linked her to the planners of the uprising. Asked whether the agents' claims were accurate, she replied, "No, they always exaggerated. I attended a lot fewer events than they claimed, not because I didn't want to, but because I worked during the week. I also didn't have a car."[9]

Asked if she knew Blanca Canales then, she replied, "We had a nodding acquaintance because we both worked for the same employer (the Puerto Rican Department of Social Services), but we didn't know anything about each other's politics. That happened later, after I met Albizu Campos in New York City [1946], and he asked me to convey his greetings to Blanca." Did she know Carmen María Pérez and Doris Torresola? She wasn't sure when she met them, but guessed that was "probably after Albizu Campos returned to Puerto Rico." She would see them at the Nationalist Club whenever she visited Albizu. According to the I.S. agents, she visited Albizu less frequently before her arrest.[10]

Rosado's First Arrest: January 1951

The day the Nationalists revolted in San Juan and other cities and towns throughout southern and western Puerto Rico, Isabel Rosado was at work in eastern Puerto Rico. But though she was nowhere near any of the scenes of violence, she was arrested in January 1951, on grounds that she was a member of the Nationalist Party, whose leaders proposed to make Puerto Rico independent, "by force and violence, if necessary." According to one informant, Rosado had said: "No country has ever won its independence without a struggle and bloodshed." She claimed not to remember having made the statement. But regardless of the informant's claim, the police were authorized to detain her "on suspicion that she had violated the newly amended Law #53" by the mere act of belonging to the Nationalist Party, which had been declared a "subversive" group by the authorities. In the law's previous incarnation, it made it a crime "to advocate, preach, write, or conspire with others to overthrow the island's government or harm any of its dependencies." The amended version of that law (December 20, 1950) made it a crime "to belong" to any subversive group.[11]

The fact that Isabel Rosado "belonged" to the Nationalist Party meant that she could be detained and interrogated on the theory that she supported the Party ideals and (probably) the uprising. By the time she was arrested, the authorities had already detained more than a thousand others believed to have supported the Nationalists at some point. Though more than eight hundred of those detained had to be released for lack of evidence on which to charge them, they were photographed and fingerprinted, as if they had committed criminal acts. According to an investigation conducted by a Civil Rights Committee established by Governor Luis Muñoz Marín in February 1956, his government had indeed violated the civil and human rights of hundreds of Puerto Rican citizens following the Nationalist uprising. Nevertheless, many of those released were kept under police surveillance for many years, in open violation of their rights to privacy. Some of them lost their jobs or businesses due to the constant harassment by the undercover agents.[12]

In Rosado's case, it took the authorities nearly two months to build a case against her before she was arrested on January 3, 1951. Rosado recalled those days, "On October 30, 1950, I was visiting a school in the outskirts of Fajardo and did not know 'the revolution' had started until I came back to the principal's office that afternoon." Upon hearing the news, she said, "I tried to get to San Juan to see what I could do, but the roads were blocked so I went to visit some friends instead. Then several days later two secret agents (she believed were FBI men) visited the school where I worked in Fajardo and questioned me in the principal's office." She described the agents' questions as a fishing expedition. "They had no case," she said, "so they let me go." She went back to work, but in the afternoons and weekends she would visit the families of comrades who were imprisoned and sometimes would organize fundraisers to help pay for their legal fees. Other times she would give the funds to their families so they could buy food. During that time, she remembered being followed everywhere she went by I.S. agents, though she never allowed their presence to intimidate her, she said. In fact, she continued to carry a Puerto Rican flag in her purse, even though she knew that carrying the flag constituted a crime under Law #53. "Perhaps it was my defiant attitude," she said, "that gave them the excuse to have me arrested."[13]

On January 2, 1951, the day before her arrest, she said, a policeman she knew in Fajardo came to the school (Antonio Valero) where she was handing out toys, and told her that she had "to report to the police station." Suspecting she would be arrested, she told him, "I will go there as soon as I finish what I am doing and have had time to eat lunch." He did not insist and just sat and waited for her. Once she finished her task, she said, she went out and "made sure to eat a good lunch, in case I was arrested and that was my last meal for the day." She also borrowed ten dollars from a colleague, she added, "just to have some cash on me if I was arrested." She then followed the policeman to the station. To her surprise, she said, she was released after she was questioned. "But that reprieve," she said smiling, "was short-lived because I was arrested the following day after school let out." She explains:

> I was waiting for the bus with a few other women teachers when an unmarked black car, one of those used by the secret police, approached and asked me to get in. I refused and instead boarded the bus that had just arrived. The driver of the black car then drove alongside the bus and asked the bus driver to follow him to the Fajardo police station. The women on the bus became frightened and asked me to explain why we were being followed and I said, 'Because I am a Nationalist.' They then asked me to get rid of any evidence that might incriminate me, but I told them that I couldn't, "Because all I have on me is a Puerto Rican flag which I will never give up.[14]

The bus driver dropped her off at the police station, where she was arrested on two violation counts of Law #53. Later that evening she was taken to San Juan's district jail, La Princesa. She remained in that jail for a few weeks until she was transferred, along with cellmates Olga Isabel Viscal and Carmen María Pérez, to the Women's Wing of Arecibo's district jail. She explained that Blanca Canales and Doris Torresola had stayed at La Princesa because their trials had begun, and that Ruth Reynolds was sent to Arecibo's jail a day later because she had been expecting a visitor.[15]

Life in Prison, January 1951–April 1952

According to Rosado's self-published testimony and several interviews she granted over the years, the most memorable event she witnessed in La Princesa in February 1951 was the arrival of Evelyn Emry. Emry later told Ruth Reynolds that she had worked for the American government in Europe during the 1940s but had fallen out of favor and had her life threatened. According to the warden of La Princesa, who brought her to the overcrowded cell the Nationalist women shared, Emry had just been arrested in San Juan for failing to pay her bill to the Pan American Guest House. He failed to explain why he was placing her in their cell for what seemed to be a petty crime, Rosado said. "Her presence among us made us suspect that she might be there to spy on us." In time, however, she came to believe that Emry was probably there to be used as "a guinea pig in the radiation experiments that were later used on Albizu Campos, Doris Torresola, and Ruth Reynolds." Asked whether she had been exposed to the radiation experiments reportedly conducted at La Princesa, she replied, "No, I never was subjected to those diabolical experiments." But added that she had "experienced a 'radiation wave,' aimed at Albizu, one afternoon when I was at his home, writing a letter for him." She explained, "I saw a blue ray of light shoot through one of the windows and then felt an electric shock, which made me feel as if my feet had been nailed to the floor." The sensation of that shock continued, she said, even after she went out of the apartment to post the letter.[16]

The admission process at the Arecibo jail, Rosado said, "involved the typical dehumanizing and humiliating body search, commonly practiced by the island's prisons." After the registration process was completed, she added, "We were placed in solitary confinement, ostensibly to help us adjust to prison life." In her view, "this was simply another controlling practice widely employed by the prison staff to subdue newly arrived inmates or to punish those who violated institutional rules." (For other details about the Nationalists' experiences in the Arecibo jail, see the sections on Ruth M. Reynolds and Olga Viscal included in this book). She explained, "We were housed together in two tiny rooms, on the top floor of the jail and kept there for many months, without contact with our relatives or the outside world, except for the occasional visit from our lawyers." The warden in charge, J. González Lebrón, wrote to his superiors that he had been forced to place the newly arrived Nationalist women in two makeshift cells because the prison was overcrowded and he lacked space in which to house them, according to the court's recommendation. He was aware, he said, that the Nationalists were supposed to be separated not only from the "common criminals," but from each other until their cases came up for review, but there was nothing else he could do.[17]

From Rosado's perspective the worst problem she experienced in the Arecibo jail was being locked up twenty-three hours a day. She recalled that she and her comrades were let out one hour every afternoon, which they used to walk, take the sun, and shower. "Without each other's company," she said, "we would have died of boredom in that jail because we had absolutely nothing to do," except talk to each other or read letters sent by relatives. After Doris Torresola joined them, Rosado said, she would entertain them with her stories or funny letters she received from her brother-in-law Alfredo Platet. Rosado said that they were grateful for the care packages they received from their relatives, which helped to supplement the prison's dreadful diet. She recalled that they looked forward to the fresh fruits and vegetables Carmín Pérez's father sent from his farm in Lares since these were foods that were never served by the prison's kitchen. From time to time, she said, she also received fruits in syrup or coconut candy that her sister Aleja made for them. Olga's and Doris' relatives would often send them canned milk and other canned foods which they always shared with the others. In general, Rosado had fewer complaints about the Arecibo prison than she later had about the one in Vega Alta. She described the Arecibo guards' treatment of the inmates as generally "courteous and humane," in comparison to the ones at the "so-called Escuela Industrial Para Mujeres" in Vega Alta. It should be noted that Carmen María Pérez and Olga Isabel Viscal who roomed with Rosado in Arecibo had much harsher things to say about the place.[18]

The best thing that happened to her in the Arecibo jail, Rosado said, was "meeting Leonides Díaz" (Doña Leo, as she affectionately called her). She said she admired Doña Leo because she was "an excellent wife and mother who spent many hours knitting in order to generate funds that she would then give to her sons and husband, also imprisoned in the same jail, so they could buy toiletries and other items the prison didn't provide. For her part, she said she was "grateful to Doña Leo for the many times she mitigated our hunger with the soups she made" with leftovers she gathered in the kitchen. "Dinner in prison," she said, "was

served at 4:30 in afternoon, so by eight o'clock we were always hungry."
At the Arecibo prison, she recalled also meeting Monserrate Valle and
Juanita Ojeda. "Valle," she said, "was married to Tomás López de Victoria, the person who led the Nationalist attack on Arecibo." She explained,
"Although Monserrate was also a Nationalist, I think she was arrested
because of what her husband did, and that was probably the reason she
didn't go to trial, but I am not sure." The one thing she remembered
about Valle was that "she laughed a lot at our stories." She had no stories
to tell about Juanita Ojeda, except that she was from Utuado.[19]

Though legally Rosado was entitled to be released, if bail was posted,
that did not happen and she remained behind bars until her case came
up to trial in April 1952. Originally her bail was set at $25,000, but the
sum was reduced to $10,000 upon appeal. A few days before her trial
began she was sent from Arecibo's jail to La Princesa in San Juan, possibly
to shorten the daily commute that would have been required to reach
the District Court of Humacao, in eastern Puerto Rico. I found few details of Rosado's trial, perhaps because by then the novelty of court proceedings involving Nationalists had worn off. Yet according to Rosado's
recollections, the Humacao District Court was "jam-packed" with relatives, neighbors and well-wishers who had known her as a teacher or as
a social worker over the past twenty-four years. The prosecutors, she
said, followed the well-established pattern of other trials and called in
more than twenty policemen and undercover agents to testify against
her. Some of those witnesses, she said, "lied outright about things I had
supposedly done and places I had been." They said, and she concurred,
that she had attended several religious services in San Juan and Río
Piedras' churches in memory of comrades who fell during the attack on
the Governor's palace, La Fortaleza. She also agreed that she had often
deposited flowers on the tombs of fallen comrades, but failed to see how
attending mass or visiting the tombs of patriots could be considered a
crime. A few of the people's witnesses also claimed that she had supported the attackers who sought to overthrow the island's government
by force and violence the previous October. In the end, she was convicted
of one count and exonerated of the other. Conviction of any violation of
Law #53 carried a potential prison sentence of one to ten years, the
length of it to be determined by the presiding judge. In this case, Rosado
said, she had been lucky to have been tried in a town where people knew
her to be innocent of the exaggerated charges levied against her. She felt

that perhaps the presence of so many well-wishers in court might explain why the judge had sentenced her only to the time served, one year and three months. "So, it happened that I was released the same day that I was sentenced," she said.[20]

Life as a Free Woman, 1952–1954

Finding work with a prison record was an ordeal, she said, especially after she discovered that her teaching and social work licenses had been revoked by the state shortly after she was arrested. Unable to work in either of her two professions, she took a proofreading job at the daily newspaper *El Imparcial*, only to have that job disappear a month later when she attended a Nationalist demonstration in Guánica (July 25, 1952) to protest the island's occupation by United States since 1898. Unemployed once again, she went back "to knitting baby clothes and booties in order to generate some income." A few months later (she is not sure of the exact date) she found a job, teaching at a Catholic school in Cataño (the municipality just across the Bay of San Juan) thanks to the help of friend and comrade Paulino Castro.[21]

It was during this time, that she became "a nomad," she said, because "after so many months in prison I had an urge to keep moving." She would wander off to Arecibo and other far-flung places to visit the families of those still incarcerated. She especially loved visiting Leonides Díaz's mother, Doña María Díaz, who delighted her with stories of earlier times. She once told her that she had "ordered her (thirteen-year-old) son to grab a machete and go and defend the homeland's honor." Doña María also told her about the "many abuses" that had been committed by the invading American troops in 1898. (I recounted that story in the section devoted to Leonides Díaz.) In addition to those visits, she attended various island-wide Nationalist activities, "because all that prison accomplished was to reinforce my Nationalist ideals," she declared. After Albizu was released from prison in September 1953, she would also visit him at his home. In fact, the day before her second arrest (March 5, 1954), she spent the night at Albizu's place at the corner of Sol and Cruz Streets. Fearing that Albizu might be arrested at any moment due to the Nationalist attack on the United States Congress five days earlier, she said she went to his home "to provide support." Though poorly armed, she said, she was on hand when the police arrived at 6:00 a.m. on March 6, with orders to arrest him and his companions.[22]

Rosado's Second Arrest and Imprisonment

On March 1, 1954 a group of Nationalists led by Lolita Lebrón opened fire on the floor of the House of Representatives of the United States Congress, wounding five congressmen. An alert journalist in Puerto Rico obtained an exclusive interview with Nationalist leader Pedro Albizu Campos, in which he stated, among other things, that the attack had been "an act of sublime heroism." Though he placed his remarks in a broad historical context, the only message that was highlighted by the government was that he had praised the attackers. Claiming that he had probably planned and ordered the attack on Congress, Governor Muñoz Marín used the occasion to revoke the pardon he had granted Albizu Campos six months earlier. The same claims also became the basis for the Justice Department's orders to have nearly three dozen people arrested, including nine members of the Communist Party (seven men and two women). The Nationalists were detained on suspicion that they had violated the amended version of Law #53 and the Communists on suspicion that they supported the Nationalists.[23]

The fact that none of the accused, except possibly Albizu Campos, had previous knowledge of the attackers' plans was immaterial to the judges who signed the orders of arrest the previous day (March 5, 1954), according to an FBI report submitted later that afternoon by the SAC in San Juan. He told his immediate superior, first by telephone, and then in writing, that at 4:00 in the afternoon (March 5), he had been summoned to the Governor's office. With the Governor he found various members of the Cabinet who proceeded to discuss the impending arrest of Albizu Campos and others when he arrived. The rationale for their arrests, he learned, was provided by the Department of Justice, which claimed they could be arrested for violations of the newly amended Law #53. The amended law, as indicated earlier, made it possible to arrest any suspect known to "belong" to any subversive organization. He reported also that he had been asked to share any information he might have on the suspects, but that he declined after he explained that his office "could not intervene in the internal affairs of island's government."[24]

Since Isabel Rosado had never stopped "belonging" to the Nationalist Party (a subversive group), she was one of those targeted for arrest that afternoon. According to a SAC San Juan Quarterly Report (August 1-October 31, 1953) shared with the FBI offices in New York City and Chicago, Rosado was suspected of being the messenger who delivered Albizu's order (for the attack on Congress) to the Nationalist leaders in New York Junta in October (1953). Reportedly, once in Manhattan, she met with Julio Pinto Gandía, Lolita Lebrón, and her brother Gonzalo Lebrón, who was summoned from Chicago"[25]

A bulletin the Puerto Rican police shared with the FBI, in September 1953, reported that Rosado had often collaborated with Albizu Campos. It gave as example the fact that she had gone "to La Princesa with Antonio Moya Vélez to pick up a small refrigerator and fan he had left behind when he was released from prison."[26] Another I.S. bulletin the Puerto Rican police shared with the FBI offered a description of Isabel Rosado "as a native of Ceiba, white, 5 feet 6 inches tall, weighs 140 pounds."[27]

The fact that Rosado was found in Albizu's apartment the morning of March 6, 1954, following an armed confrontation with the police, helped to seal her fate. Also arrested at Albizu's place that morning were: Doris Torresola, Carmen María Pérez, and José (Pepe) Rivera Sotomayor, according to a March 11, 1954 report sent to Governor Luis Muñoz Marín by Chief of Police, Salvador T. Roig. He told the Governor that the arrest of Albizu Campos and his companions had been "executed, as planned, at 6:00 in the morning on March 6." The arresting officers, he wrote, had surrounded the apartment at the corner of Cruz and Sol Streets in Old San Juan, and then used a bullhorn to notify Albizu Campos and his companions that they were under arrest and had to surrender. But the response from the apartment had been "a barrage of bullets," which had "forced the officers to fire back in self-defense." Since the Nationalists had failed to surrender two hours later, Roig said, the officers threw a few tear gas bombs into the apartment "to coax them out" and thus avoid the mistakes made four years earlier.[28]

According to Rosado's recollections, she and the others in Albizu's place had been "expecting a police raid and had moved the refrigerator to block the front door" shortly before they got the order to surrender. And since Albizu was quite ill, they had "taken him from his bed and laid him on the floor, to keep him safe from the flying bullets." Then she, Carmín [Pérez], Pepe [José Rivera Sotomayor], and Doris [Torresola] had "exchanged" gunfire with the police. Asked: "Wasn't Albizu also shooting?" She replied, "No, no, he couldn't. He was too sick and he was lying on the floor." (I should note that in another interview Carmen María Pérez said that Albizu had "gotten out of bed and was also shooting.")[29]

Carmín Pérez recalled that as the tear gas began to fill the apartment, she and Rivera Sotomayor, fearing for their comrades' lives, had walked out to the street "to let the press know that Albizu, Rosado, and Torresola were unconscious but still alive." A journalist on the scene wrote that the minute the two walked out, "Sotomayor was pushed into a nearby alley and beaten to a pulp by the police before he was handcuffed and loaded into the police wagon" while Pérez was handcuffed as soon as she walked out of the building. Based on Chief Roig's report, once Pérez and Sotomayor walked out of Albizu Campos' apartment the officers rushed up the stairs and "National Guardsman Dudley Osborne broke down the door with an axe." Osborne, he said, had repeatedly volunteered for the mission and was taken along "in case a brawny fellow was needed." Osborne was useful because he also carried Albizu on his shoulders out of the building, according to Chief Roig.[30]

All Rosado remembered of that day was waking up in the municipal (Santurce) hospital and being told she was under arrest, before she was driven to the Arecibo jail. In that instance, she was charged with attempt to commit murder; one violation of Law #53; and one violation of Article 6 of the island's Arms Statue. Bail was set at $35,000 but later reduced, upon appeal, to $14,000. This time, she spent six months in jail before she was released on bail (September 1954) until her case came to trial in December 1954 (though she often said the trial had started in November). No longer able to find work due to her latest arrest, she said, she returned to knitting baby clothes and booties.[31]

For reasons that are not altogether clear, the proceedings against her and fourteen others, including another five women, were held in the District Court of Arecibo, instead of San Juan, where their alleged crimes had been committed. The presiding judge in this case was Rafael Padró Parés, a man known for his severity and his dislike of the Nationalists. The lawyer leading Rosado's defense was Francisco Colón Gordiany, the old school superintendent who two decades earlier had helped her find a teaching job. But despite his dogged defense, which led to more than one run-in with the judge, she was convicted on all three counts, on February 8, 1955, and sentenced the following April by Judge Padró Parés to seventeen years in prison.[32]

She was later transferred to the newly built women's prison, the Escuela Industrial Para Mujeres in Vega Alta, Puerto Rico. That prison, according to Rosado was "a horror" despite its "grandiose name Escuela Industrial," she said angrily. "That was no school because no school would ever tolerate the type of cruelties I witnessed in that place." She recalled that on many occasions she had risked her own safety, in order to protect the women "who were sent to the 'calabozos' (also known as confinement cells) and abandoned there for days on end, despite regulations to the contrary." Those "dark holes," she declared, "were so narrow that no bed, not even a cot, would fit, and the inmate sent there was forced to sleep on the dirt floor. The place had no showers or running water, so the guards would hose down the inmate, sometimes still wearing her clothes, whenever they felt she needed to bathe. No towel was given to dry her body or rags with which to dry the floor." The resulting humidity from the heat and water hosed in, she said, attracted swarms of mosquitoes, adding to the misery of the place. The 'calabozo' also lacked toilet facilities, she added, "and if the guard on duty did not respond when called, the inmate confined there had to use a hole in the ground when the need arose." And though meals were delivered to "those dark holes," she explained, "drinking water was not always provided, and the inmate was forced to beg for it" from the next guard on duty. That was the case of Genoveva Flores, a mentally ill inmate who after spending several days in one of those 'holes' spent hours one evening trying to get the guard on duty to bring her water. Since Rosado couldn't sleep "because of Genoveva's cries," she interceded by offering the guard a paper cup in which to give Genoveva the water. The reason the guard was reluctant, Rosado explained, was because often times inmates used the empty cups to bang on the metal rails. When the guard finally acquiesced, Rosado said, "She found Genoveva in the midst of giving birth, with the child's head already showing between her legs and at that hour she had to rush her to the hospital."[33]

For her advocacy, Rosado said, she had earned the scornful title of "la abogada de las presas" (the inmates' counsel) among the guards and received a warning from the prison's director, who told her she shouldn't bother because the "inmates do not appreciate it." She also told her that "some inmates have to be sent to the calabozo until they adjust to prison life." To which Rosado reportedly replied, "How can they adjust when they are kept in such onerous conditions?" Apparently the director was referring to Genoveva, who days earlier had flooded the entire cellblock in Maximum Security (where the Nationalists and the mentally ill inmates were housed) by stuffing the toilet with paper. When asked by Guard Soto who discovered the problem, why she had done it, she reportedly said "because I was angry because I couldn't sleep." It turned out that her cellmate, Conrada Osuna, another mentally ill inmate, had spent the entire night singing and didn't let her or Gladys Quiñones sleep. Apparently Genoveva was sent to the calabozo following the reports of guards Soto and Ithier. What is evident from Rosado's and the guard's reports is that Genoveva, in addition to being mentally ill and near giving birth, was also sleep deprived when she was sent to the calabozo. What no one explained was how long Genoveva had been in prison when she became pregnant.[34]

Though Rosado and her comrades were housed in Maximum Security, a section of the Psychiatric Building reserved for the mentally unstable, they were never sent to the dreaded confinement cells. In her case, Rosado suspected, that was probably because she had warned the administration that she "would resist" if anyone attempted to send her to any of those "horrific places." She said she disliked the Vega Alta prison so much that she had requested to be sent back to the Arecibo jail, where "conditions were more humane." Her request was ignored and she remained in the Vega Alta prison for eleven more years. Over time she apparently adjusted to her new surroundings because according to several guards' reports, she often volunteered to work in the library or to teach the literacy classes. According to the same sources, neither Isabel nor any of her comrades was ever assigned hard labor, such as weeding the gardens or cleaning the prison floors. Occasionally, Leonides Díaz and Carmen María Pérez were said to have volunteered to work various shifts in the kitchen. Rosado said she never liked the kitchen because "I didn't know how to cook."[35]

In 1965, the Puerto Rican legislature appointed a Commission, headed by the Secretary of Justice, Rafael Hernández Colón, in order to investigate ongoing complaints from various prisons. Rosado said she took advantage of the Commission's visit in September 1965 to personally hand the Secretary of Justice a Habeas Corpus she had drafted on her own behalf. The Secretary, she explained, followed up on her request and she was freed on December 9 that same year. Possibly since she had already served the majority of her sentence, and Law #53 had been revoked eight years earlier (August 1957), the newly elected administration of Roberto Sánchez Vilella saw no purpose in keeping her in jail any longer. It should be noted also that Governor Sánchez Vilella made it a point to release not only Isabel Rosado but other Nationalists who were still incarcerated for crimes related to the revoked statute and/or to the uprising of 1950. One of those he also released at the end of August 1967 was Blanca Canales, one of the Jayuyans convicted (erroneously in her case) and sentenced to life in prison for the death of police officer Virgilio Camacho.[36]

Life as a Free Woman, 1965 to 2015

Already fifty-eight years old and suffering from diabetes and other ailments, Rosado found it much harder to find employment upon her second release from prison. She returned to knitting children's clothes and booties until she was "old enough to collect social security," to which she had contributed for more than twenty-four years. She was denied the benefits the first time she applied at the district office in Fajardo. She appealed her case in San Juan and was subsequently paid retroactively the sum of $1,000. She said she used these funds to attend a conference in Cuba (1974). Though she did not meet Fidel Castro or any of the major Cuban figures, she said, she enjoyed the trip immensely because she was able to "see for myself the many achievements of the revolution." Because of her experiences at the Vega Alta prison, she said, she was most impressed by the "humane care and advanced treatment offered to the mentally ill at Havana's Psychiatric Hospital."[37]

During the next two decades Rosado also traveled to the United States, generally to visit political prisoners, among them Lolita Lebrón, Oscar Collazo, Alicia Rodríguez, and others. On one occasion she traveled to the Dominican Republic, though she did not disclose the purpose of that visit. Asked by journalist Miñi Seijo how was she able to afford these trips, she replied rather obliquely: "the funds always appeared." Perhaps, as was the case of Rosa Collazo, her trips were financed by comrades' donations.[38]

In addition to her travels, Rosado attended various meetings and demonstrations, organized by the Nationalists and other groups that were demanding the release of the Puerto Rican political prisoners still incarcerated in the United States. For years she also conducted her own campaign in favor of prison reforms in Puerto Rico. She was jubilant when in September 1979 President Carter pardoned Oscar Collazo, Lolita Lebrón, and her three companions, all of whom returned to Puerto Rico two days later. She would later work with them for many years on the cause of Puerto Rico's liberation. Though she never fully abandoned the struggle for prison reform, she also devoted a great deal of time to other causes. In the 1970s, for instance, she joined PIP President Rubén Berríos and others in their struggle to aid the residents of Culebra to oust the U.S. Navy from the island. And though the movement's participants employed the pacifist tactics of civil disobedience, they were arrested every time they "trespassed" on naval grounds. The fact that the U.S. Navy left Culebra in 1975 made her feel "enormously satisfied" to have been part of that struggle.[39]

She later joined the pacifists in their struggle to push the U.S. Navy out of Vieques and was arrested twice "for trespassing on U.S. military property." In 1979, according to Miñi Seijo, Rosado was dragged from Cabo Manuel (Vieques) by three military men and one woman and handed over to the municipal police on the pretext that she "looked drunk." (Isabel was a diabetic and was experiencing low blood sugar, which gives the appearance of drunkenness to those unfamiliar with the disease.) Like the others also arrested, she was fined and released with a warning to stay out of U.S. military grounds. Though the Vieques struggle took longer to succeed than the Culebra struggle, Rosado never relented and was arrested again 2000. A photograph of that arrest shows her face down on the ground, with a hefty policewoman's knee pressed on her back, while she was being handcuffed. Rosado was ninety-three years old at the time.[40]

At the time of the 2000 arrest, she had spent more than six decades of her life struggling on behalf of Puerto Rico's independence, demanding justice for the poor, calling for the release of Puerto Rican political prisoners, and advocating for prison reforms. She had marched with the landless when they were threatened with eviction from the plots they occupied in Río Grande, and with university students when they protested tuition increases or demanded educational reforms. She had also worked with religious and civic groups calling for world peace and

the end to nuclear proliferation. She was held in
great esteem by the many
who occasionally honored
her and declared her "an
icon of the liberation
struggle" they hoped to
emulate. All who knew
her said they admired her
for kindness, sense of fairness, and her political
ideals.[41]

When she could no
longer travel or attend
their demonstrations, they
went to see her at the residence for the aged, in
Ceiba, where she lived the
last years of her life. In
that home, she was lov-
ingly cared for not only by

Isabel Rosado being arrested in Vieques.
(Souce: Vieques, Fotomemorias de una lucha)

the staff, but by her devoted nephew, Radamés Rosado, the young man
she raised as the son she never had. Her visitors later reported that he
not only came to see her, but that he arranged her schedule so that others
could visit her while he also ensured that she had time to rest. A few visitors often found Isabel "beautifully dressed, with a flower in her hair."
They commented on Isabel's "unwavering commitment to the cause of
independence," and the fact that she "had not become bitter or cynical
after spending so many years in prison."[42]

Isabel Rosado died peacefully among friends, on January 13, 2015, at
age 107. The news of her passing spread rapidly over social media, and
by the next day hundreds had congregated at Club Cívico La Seyba in
Ceiba, Puerto Rico. They went to pay their respects to the woman they
had followed, loved, and admired for many years. The viewing of their
beloved leader was organized by the Comité Isabel Rosado (a group authorized by her to continue her social and political work in her hometown). Those too far away to attend the funeral services tweeted on social
media or expressed their condolences via the press. Politicians and civil

servants, in particular, were eager to recognize the importance of the leader she had been. In San Juan, PIP Senator María de Lourdes Santiago said: "For us, the independentistas, Doña Isabel represents an ongoing faith which has never been broken, a faith that represents the best Albizuista tradition." The electoral commissioner Juan Dalmau stated: "Doña Isabelita was a great patriot ... who struggled for the liberation of our homeland and suffered for that ideal. She was also a humble devout Christian." While in New York, City Council Speaker, Melissa Mark-Viverito, according to the *Daily News*, tweeted, "Isabel Rosado is an icon and a patriot ... who supported the Vieques struggle and groups calling for the release of Oscar López Rivera [the longest held Puerto Rican prisoner in the United States]." Both are causes she said she also supported.[43]

On January 15, two days after Rosado's death, a Mass of Response was held for her at the Parroquia San Antonio de Padua in Ceiba, where Bishop Eusebio Morales said: "We wish to remember Isabelita whose mission was to serve others. She was a woman who loved this country and knew how to live with passion and joy within the Christian faith." After the Mass ended, a group of women accompanied by hundreds of mourners, carried Isabel's coffin through the streets of Ceiba "singing patriotic songs." Along the way the crowd stopped at the modest wooden house where she had lived for decades on Escolástico López Street. "They placed the coffin in the tiny living room," a journalist wrote, "while outside the 'pleneros' improvised songs about the transcendental figure the teacher and social worker had been." Then the mourners resumed their march to Ceiba's municipal cemetery, where she would finally be laid to rest. "There were no flowers," observed the journalist, "for that was what she had requested." Instead she had suggested that those who wished to remember her would do better to send a donation to the Comité Isabel Rosado.[44]

Though several persons were eager to eulogize her at the cemetery, only two ex-political prisoners, Rafael Cancel Miranda and Alicia Rodríguez were granted the privilege. Cancel Miranda summarized his views by describing Isabel as a triumphant woman. "She triumphed," he said, "because she was never broken. They [referring to her jailers] were never able to bring her to her knees ... she left us the flower of justice in our hearts." Alicia Rodríguez, who had received a visit from her in 1984 during her time in prison, said: "Isabel is a transcendental figure who is loved and admired by many." She said what many in the crowd were feeling: "I have come not to say goodbye, but to feel your presence … as I did when you visited me. That was an experience filled with love and tenderness."[45]

6. Doris Torresola Roura (1922-1972)

Preface

Doris Torresola Roura was arrested twice for her participation in the Nationalist events of the 1950s. She was the only woman in her group who was shot during the insurrection of October 30, 1950. She nearly died, in part because the arresting authorities did not authorize surgery for a few days, and then did not permit the hospital to administer the antibiotics she needed. She finally received those at San Juan's District Jail, La Princesa eleven days after she was shot. She was convicted of having violated Puerto Rico's Gag Rule, Law #53 and spent three years in Arecibo's district jail. She was arrested again five months later, March 6, 1954, for her participation in a shootout with San Juan's Police when they arrived at the corner of Sol and Cruz Streets, with orders to arrest Albizu Campos for his alleged role in the attack on the U.S. Congress five days earlier. This time Doris was convicted on several felony counts and sentenced to serve seventeen years in jail. She went mad in prison (ostensibly due to a drug administered to her in the women's prison in Vega Alta) and had to be released to a psychiatric hospital before her term expired. Since her tragic death in February 1972, she has been considered a heroine of Puerto Rico's struggle for independence.

Childhood in Jayuya

Doris Torresola Roura was born either January 28 or March 1, 1922, according to Janet Martínez, who noticed a discrepancy in the recorded date of her birth. She was born in barrio Collores of present-day Jayuya, where her parents, Clodomiro Torresola Vargas and Rosalina Roura Rivera, owned a small family farm until 1927. That year, stated Stephen Hunter and John Bainbridge, the family fell on hard times and Don Clodomiro moved his wife and four children to barrio Coabey, where

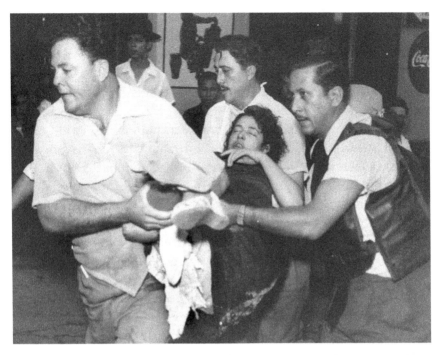

Doris Torresola being dragged out, unconscious, from the Nationalist Club in San Juan, due to the gases thrown by the police. March 6, 1954

he, and later his sons, would work for their keep on a farm owned by his sister, Consuelo Torresola, and her husband Rosario Canales. Don Rosario and his wife Doña Consuelo were the parents of Blanca Canales, the revolutionary leader who declared Puerto Rico a republic in October 1950. Coabey, where Doris and her siblings were raised, is about four kilometers (2.5 miles) distant from the town's center.[1]

Doris's mother, Doña Rosalina Roura, "was a short, thin woman, but one with great fortitude and strong character," according to her oldest daughter Angelina Torresola. These traits would serve her well years later, when one of her four adult children was killed and the other three were sent to prison for their deeds in the Nationalist revolutionary struggle which sought to liberate Puerto Rico from the United States. The daughter explains: "There came a time when my mother had none of her children because even I was sent to prison for six months. But, she never complained because in her mind her children had done what they had to." Sigfredo Rodríguez Orama, a family friend and neighbor, concurred with Angelina's view. "Doña Rosalina," he said, "didn't complain because she was convinced that her children had performed their duty."[2]

While her children were still young Doña Rosalina enjoyed a relatively peaceful life, as did many rural women of her time. She spent most days caring for her home and family and helping her husband Clodomiro tend to their small farm. Angelina recalls that her family planted a variety of food crops, especially tomatoes, a favorite plant of Jayuya farmers.[3]

The barrio children, especially the Torresola boys, enjoyed roaming the lush, green valley of Coabey, a region shaded from the hot tropical sun by the imposing mountain peaks Tres Picachos. They especially enjoyed swimming in the placid waters of the nearby Río Grande of Jayuya, according to Heriberto Marín who often joined them in these outings. The municipality of Jayuya, however, did not exist as a separate entity until 1911, when a few leading families wrested the region from neighboring Utuado and incorporated a new town. Soon thereafter, the town's founders organized a city council and selected Don Rosario Canales (Blanca Canales' father) as its first mayor.[4]

The Torresola children resumed their studies in Coabey's schools. The oldest (Angelina) enrolled in the seventh grade, but did not go beyond middle school, in part because she married and left home at sixteen, and partly because the town did not yet have its own high school. The first high school in Jayuya was established between 1936-1937 when a few leading families in town pressured the Board of Education to approve the Jayuya Extension High, which began by offering classes in a rented space above a store in the center of town. Until then only those students who could afford it went to Utuado High, according to Angelina. Friend and neighbor Sigfredo Rodríguez Orama recalled that Doris and her cousin Gladys Torresola were among the first in the barrio to attend the newly established high school. Vionette Negretti reported that Doris probably graduated from Jayuya's Extension High School in 1940.[5]

"Doris not only attended high school but was an excellent student," noted Rodríguez Orama. "She was so smart and so proficient in English that the teacher, Mr. Colón, often called her to the front of the class to explain the day's lesson to the other students."[6]

In addition to her school performance, Doris also stood out, "as the only black-haired member of an otherwise light-skin, blond-hair family," said Heriberto Marín. She grew up to be "a woman of great beauty many of us would have been pleased to date," added Rodríguez Orama. But while she lived in Coabey, she only dated Arcelio Torres. But that relationship did not last long, the neighbors said, because Torres returned home "mentally ill" from World War II. Neighbors and relatives also told Negretti that during her youth, Doris had been "the life of the party," because in addition to being "a great dancer, she had a great sense of humor and could make everybody laugh."[7]

Angelina, in whose home Doris lived many years of her adult life, recalled that Doris had also suffered a great deal during her life because of an asthmatic condition she contracted during childhood. That condition, stated Janet Martínez, would not only haunt Doris the rest of her life, "but later became a convenient tool of torture at the hands of her jailers."[8]

Joining the Nationalist Party

According to an official document found at Puerto Rico's General Archives (AGPR), Doris Torresola became a card-carrying member of the island's Nationalist Party on November 26, 1947, when she was twenty-five years old.[9]

Yet her friend Heriberto Marín stated that Doris' interest in the Nationalist Party probably dated back to the early 1930s when she and her family first met Pedro Albizu Campos. Marín told Hunter and Bainbridge during an interview that Don Pedro had first visited the Canales-Torresola clan in 1932, when he was preparing to participate in that year's general elections. Angelina Torresola and her cousin Blanca Canales tend to agree with Marín's recollection of Albizu's visit and impact on the family. In one of her many interviews, Angelina said that Albizu first visited her parent's home in 1932 at the invitation of Blanca Canales. For her part, Canales explained that she had initially met Albizu while she was a student at the University of Puerto Rico and had been so impressed with his views of Puerto Rico's colonial problems that she invited him to visit her family.[10]

"Albizu's visit," Angelina explained, "changed the family's world view. Before Blanca began to interest us, I don't remember politics being spoken about a great deal in my home." But "after Don Pedro came ... well ... that's when an impression was made on all of us. The family became fond of Don Pedro and he became fond of us; he treated us, the Torresola family, like his own family." As the affection between the parties grew, the Canales-Torresola clan began to welcome Albizu Campos and his family into their homes for extended periods. In 1948, for example, shortly after he returned to Puerto Rico from a ten-year absence (1937-1947), six of them spent in federal prison, he spent nearly three months in Blanca Canales' home. It was there, according to Canales, where he first disclosed to her his plans for the "revolution" he envisioned.[11]

During his extended visits to her home, Albizu was free to meet with other Party leaders to plan and accept their financial contributions, out of earshot of the secret agents who followed him everywhere. At Canales' house, he was protected by a select guard, headed by twenty-eight year old Elio Torresola and his twenty-three year old brother Griselio. The guard, which operated out of the Canales' basement, included many of Griselio and Elio's friends. The best known among them were World War II veteran and university student Carlos Irizarry, his cousins Fidel and Mario Irizarry, and the Morales brothers, nicknamed "Los Mencha." Heriberto Marín, then eighteen years old, was also a member of the select guard, according to his own account. Carlos Irizarry and Elio Torresola, Blanca Canales reported in a testimony she wrote in 1967, were "the braves who led the revolutionary troops against Jayuya on October 30 (1950)."[12]

Move to San Juan: Caring for Albizu Campos

During the summer of 1948 the Canales-Torresola families became to-tally devoted to Albizu's liberation project. Within that group, noted Heriberto Marín, "the most devoted was the beautiful, twenty-six year old Doris Torresola."[13]

Doris' devotion to Albizu Campos was so great that in May of 1950 she made an unusual decision, for a single woman of her day, to leave her home in Coabey and move into his home, which also served as the Nationalist Party headquarters. Her arrival at Sol and Cruz Streets, re-ported the FBI office in San Juan, coincided with the departure of Albizu's wife, Peruvian-born Laura Meneses, and their three children for Havana, Cuba. An informant close to the Albizu household "advised" the local Division of Internal Security that soon after Doris arrived at his home Albizu appointed her housekeeper and secretary. When asked by Janet

Martínez, "How did your mother react to Doris' decision to move in with Albizu Campos?" Angelina replied, "Mother agreed with her decision because she was worried about Don Pedro's health. She felt that since his family had left he would need someone to look after him."[14] One wonders how comfortable Doña Rosalina felt, given that she also sent along Doris' unmarried uncle (Raúl Torresola) on the veiled excuse that he might be of help to Don Pedro (Albizu Campos).

Regardless of the motivations that led Doris to move to Albizu's home, she found upon her arrival that he was far from alone. There were always people around him eager to fetch his mail or run his errands. Among those who visited his home daily was eighteen-year-old Carmen María (Carmín) Pérez González. She said during an interview that she began visiting Albizu in 1948, when her mother moved to Old San Juan. She explained that she would happily skip school in order to spend the day in Albizu's company because she could learn more from him in one hour than she could during a whole day in school.[15]

Carmín Pérez, like many of Albizu's followers, confessed that she was originally attracted to the Nationalist Party by one of his "mesmerizing speeches." She recounted with great fondness the impression Albizu had made on her the first time she heard him speak in the Lares plaza. "It was September 1948," she said, "and he was there giving a speech in honor of the town's rebels who had proclaimed the first Puerto Rican republic in 1868." Determined to talk to him she "armed (herself) with valor" and followed him, as he left the stage. She caught up with him as he was about to cross the plaza, and to her surprise, he not only stopped to talk to her, but "was very friendly and even kissed me on the cheek, she said." Half a century later she was still savoring the moment.[16]

The arrival of Doris and her uncle at the Nationalist Headquarters did not in any way displace Carmín from Albizu's life. On the contrary, she explained, "after Doris and Raúl came, Don Pedro was better served because the three of us would divide the tasks of caring for him and his home." The two women, she recalled, took charge of the cooking, cleaning, washing and caring for Albizu's health, while Raúl was left to run errands. When Doris assumed the role of housekeeper, she took on the responsibility of the home's finances, while in her role of secretary she scheduled Albizu's appointments and screened his visitors. But when his health began to falter, she and Carmín divided the tasks of caring for him around the clock, when necessary. According to Isabel Rosado, another frequent visitor to Albizu's home, Doris and Carmín "were totally devoted to Don Pedro."[17]

Her Political Star Rises

By the fall of 1950, the FBI SAC (Special Agent in Charge) San Juan reported that "Doris has become a member of Albizu Campos' inner circle" and as such, she has "trained in the use of firearms" and has also vowed to "lay down her life to save his, if the need arises." A few months earlier, local undercover agents notified their superiors that Doris was often observed at Nationalist Party functions, collecting fees and soliciting donations from members and affiliates. Those funds, they learned through their informants, were donated to the Albizu household to cover monthly expenses and pay the rent for the Nationalist Club (the place where Albizu and his companions also lived). The informants had also said that Doris probably belonged to the Nurses Corps (the auxiliary female wing of the Cadets of the Republic), whose expressed function was to stand ready to help their comrades in times of peril.[18]

Prior to Doris's arrival, the housekeeping post at Albizu's home had been occupied by his wife, Doña Laura Meneses, according to Irma Viscal. In a signed deposition Viscal gave at the San Juan District Court, on November 9, 1950, she disclosed that she had temporarily lived in Albizu's home in 1948 when she first joined the Nationalist Party at age seventeen. She claimed that she later left Don Pedro's house and the Nationalist Party because she had become "disillusioned" with the heavy-handed manner in which Albizu's wife spent the funds that she (Viscal) and others collected at Party events. She accused Doña Laura specifically "of using Party funds to purchase expensive items for the household, special foods for her family, and even haircuts and beauty treatments for herself." This disregard for their fundraising efforts, she claimed, was partly the reason why she abandoned the Party and returned home when her father (Francisco Viscal Bravo) came looking for her. It should be noted, however, that by the time Irma Viscal was brought in for questioning, her sister Olga Isabel Viscal had been apprehended and sent to San Juan's District Jail, La Princesa. Most likely she would have run the same fate had she not chosen to collaborate with the authorities.[19]

Doris' Role in the Uprising

On the morning of October 30, 1950, small groups of Nationalists took up arms against the colonial government in half a dozen municipalities throughout Puerto Rico. At noon that day a handful of them stormed the Governor's mansion, La Fortaleza. Their attack was effectively repelled and all but one of the attackers were killed on the spot. Later that afternoon Doris Torresola was shot while she stood on the balcony of Albizu's home. Who shot Doris and why? According to Carmín Pérez, a witness and participant in that day's events, "a few minutes after midday on October 30 a group of heavily armed policemen arrived at the corner of Cruz and Sol Streets, calling on Albizu Campos to surrender. They said they had orders to take him to Police Headquarters, to answer questions about the violent acts perpetrated by his followers earlier that day." They believed that Albizu was the mastermind behind the upheaval, according to Carmín Pérez. "But why did they shoot Doris?" I asked. "Because," Pérez explained, "she was in Albizu's apartment that day and went out on the balcony to see who was yelling his name. And when she did that, one of the policemen took aim and shot her through the throat." For its part the Police Department reported a few days later that the officers at Sol and Cruz "had fired in self-defense after Doris and Albizu had thrown fire bombs at their car in an attempt to assassinate them."[20]

"After Doris was shot," Carmín continued, "she fell on the balcony floor bleeding profusely [and] … we (referring to herself and Juan José Muñoz Matos, a university student who had snuck into Albizu's apartment around 1:00 p.m.) pulled her back into the apartment and closed the door." There they kept trying to contain the bleeding by pressing swabs of cotton against the wound "until there was a lull in the shooting and Albizu asked us to take Doris to the hospital." But since there wasn't "anything in which we could transport her, we placed ourselves on either side of Doris and half-carried her down the stairwell," she added. The moment they reached the street they were promptly arrested, though to her surprise, the officers did not stop them from taking Doris to the municipal hospital (then located on Avenida De Diego in Santurce). After they left Doris at the hospital, she said, she and Muñoz Matos were taken to Police Headquarters in Puerta de Tierra and left there many days before they were interrogated.[21]

Until Albizu surrendered, on November 2, 1950, Doris remained the primary target of the judicial investigation that followed the uprising. According to her own account, she was repeatedly interrogated by the FBI and local Internal Security agents before the hospital staff was allowed to treat her. Since the bullet that had pierced her throat had then become lodged in her left lung, she spent six days in agonizing pain, she said, before she was taken to surgery. After the bullet was removed, no antibiotics were administered and that led the wound to become infected. On November 11, 1950, not quite recovered from the surgery and by then running a fever from the infection, she was discharged from the hospital and taken to San Juan's district jail, La Princesa. There, she said, she would have died had it not been for the jail's physician who prescribed daily doses of antibiotics until her wound healed.[22]

The San Juan Jail and Its Challenges

When Doris arrived at La Princesa, she was placed in a small cell, which was already occupied by her comrades Carmín Pérez, Ruth Mary Reynolds, and Olga Isabel Viscal. A fifth occupant of that cell, Isabel Rosado Morales, arrested nearly two months later, would not join the group until the following January (1951). According to Doris and her cellmates, La Princesa, a prison built for men, was not equipped to handle female prisoners, much less female political prisoners. Thus, their arrival forced the warden to create a makeshift cell, by outfitting a small room (10'x 18') with two bunk beds and a cot on the second floor of the jail. The only way to access the makeshift cell, they explained, was through an adjacent room, previously used as a classroom, and thus known as "la escuelita." One major problem with the makeshift cell was that it lacked a bathroom. To get access to the only bathroom on that floor, they had to summon a guard and wait until he or she "found the time" to escort them.[23]

Adjacent to the makeshift cell there was a closet-sized alcove they called "la alacena" or pantry. The alcove could only be accessed through an interior door, constructed of wood and mesh wire. That door, when left open, was the only source of ventilation for the cell because the small barred window in the room had been sealed shut, shortly after they arrived. The window in the cell was shut, explained Ruth Reynolds, after

Olga Viscal and Carmín Pérez were caught shouting greetings from the window to Doris' mother, who was out on the sidewalk. (For details about this incident and its repercussions, see the section devoted to Carmín Pérez in this book.) Keeping the mesh door open, Reynolds explained, became not only a source of ventilation, but a means of communication between the occupant of the alcove and the others in the adjacent room. They generally accomplished that feat by pushing little notes through the wire mesh when the guard was distracted. The first of their comrades to occupy the alcove, they said, was Blanca Canales and the second was Ruth Mary Reynolds.[24]

Conditions in La Princesa were difficult for all of them, but proved "nearly fatal for Doris, whose health was so delicate," noted Isabel Rosado. She speculated that in Doris' case the authorities "might have wanted to let her die rather than to help her to recover." Asked, "Why did you think that?" She replied, "Because Doris came from a family that was deeply involved in the revolution. Her brother Elio [Torresola] led the revolutionary troops in Jayuya on October 30 (1950) and her other brother Griselio led the 'demonstration' in Washington [D.C.]" two days later. Curiously, both Isabel Rosado and Carmín Pérez often referred to the Nationalist assault on Blair House (November 1, 1950) as a demonstration.[25]

Trials, Absolution and Conviction

The first trial in which Albizu Campos and his co-defendants (Doris Torresola, Carmen María (Carmín) Pérez, and Juan José Muñoz Matos) were processed began on February 7, 1951 and set a pattern for the rest of the proceedings. For example, all indictments, except those related to Law #53 (the Gag Rule enacted in June 1948) were tried first, in separate proceedings, while those pertaining to Law #53, involving conspiracy against the established order, were tried last. The violations of Law #53 were always defined as "felonies" and carried excessive bails of $25,000, though that sum was generally reduced upon appeal. Conviction of just one violation of Law #53 also carried a potential prison sentence of one to ten years.[26]

Doris was indicted on four counts, as follows: a) two violations of the Law of Explosives ("possession and illegal use of incendiary bombs");

b) one "attack with intent to commit murder;" and c) one violation of Law #53. She was not charged with "possession of a firearm," even though one witness testified having seen her shooting a pistol from Albizu's place on October 30. She was absolved on three of the four counts, when her defense demonstrated that her accusers (nearly two dozen police officers) had been "unable to establish where Doris had been standing when she allegedly threw the incendiary bombs at them," or where they, "the intended victims, stood when she allegedly tried to assassinate them." Absolution on three counts meant that she was spared several years of imprisonment since the "attack with intent to murder" could mean a prison sentence of one to five years, and the two violations of the Law of Explosives (Law #67) could lead to sentences of one to two years each.[27]

Yet absolution from those crimes did not mean she would be released from jail, for she still had the biggest case (one violation of Law #53) pending, for which she hadn't been able to post bail, which was initially set at $25,000 but later reduced to $15,000 upon appeal. Thus, in March 1951, she was transferred from La Princesa to the Women's Wing of Arecibo's District jail, where she was ordered to remain until her case came up for review. The proceedings in that case began on July 7 (1951) and lasted approximately twelve days. She was convicted of that charge (one violation of Law #53) and sentenced to a prison term of one to three years. Since the island didn't yet have a prison entirely devoted to women, she was sent back to serve her term at the Arecibo district jail. She remained there until August 23, 1953 when she was eventually released.[28]

Life in the Arecibo Prison

According to cellmates Isabel Rosado and Carmín Pérez, Doris was in extremely poor health when she arrived at the Arecibo jail in March 1951. "We were all shocked to see the state she was in when the warden brought her to our cell," exclaimed Isabel Rosado. "We noticed that she had lost much weight and that she appeared nervous and disoriented." Concerned for her, Isabel and the others asked the warden to leave her in their care, even though their cells were crowded with the four already there. The warden agreed to their request and sent in a cot for the fifth occupant. (Carmín Pérez said she volunteered to take the cot that was placed next to the toilet.) Over the next few days, Doris recounted the hardships she had endured at La Princesa. She said she had been subjected to "cruel experiments" when she was left alone in La Princesa. The experiments, she continued, involved "low-level electric shocks, exposure to a constant humming noise, and the sound of diabolical voices," which asked her to say things that she knew "weren't true and never in (her) best interest." The "electric shocks," she explained, were applied while she was trying to sleep or rest, and were at times so strong that they jolted (her) out of bed." She compared the "humming noise," to that of "a motor of an old refrigerator." The "voices," she clarified, "were the worst because they made me feel like I was losing my mind." The effort it took "to focus my mind and control my actions," she added, left her "dazed and exhausted." The curious thing, she recalled, was that just when she thought she might be losing her mind, the experiments would cease, and she would feel normal again. But then the cycle would be repeated again and again. (It should be noted that Albizu Campos and Ruth Reynolds, also registered similar complaints about having been exposed to "evil experiments" while they were held at La Princesa.)[29]

Although none of their claims was ever acknowledged by the Puerto Rican government, it is now fairly well known that human experiments were conducted in many state penitentiaries under the United States flag until the late 1970s. According to a major study ordered by President Bill Clinton (and published by Oxford University Press in 1996), "the practice of using prisoners for drug testing, irradiation, and mind control exercises was widespread" in various state penitentiaries. The report also highlights the point that this practice remained unregulated for nearly three decades (1940s-1970s) before the House of Representatives, motivated by an expose published in the journal *Atlantic Monthly*, ordered an investigation and issued the first set of regulations in 1976. The report also states that many of the human experiments conducted within state prisons, "Were carried out by military medical teams and were partly or fully funded by federal agencies, with little or no oversight from the U.S. government."[30]

Though Puerto Rico's prisons were not included in the federal investigation, the omission does not necessarily mean that they did not engage in the practice of human experimentation with prisoners. The mounting complaints from Pedro Albizu Campos, Doris Torresola and Ruth Reynolds, as well as the cases discussed by Heriberto Marín in his book *Eran Ellos*, tend to suggest that in at least two of the island's prisons a few inmates were subjected to human experiments. Marín, who spent nine years in the state penitentiary in Río Piedras (for his participation in the uprising of 1950) contends that he repeatedly saw American military medical teams in that institution trying to entice prisoners to volunteer for drug testing. He never volunteered, he said, but knew of others who did. The saddest case, he reports, involved a World War II veteran, "who in his mistaken belief that army doctors would never hurt him," took part in one of the drug-testing experiments and died as a result. The irony of this situation, Marín explained, was that prisoners who volunteered for the experiments "were generally paid in cartons of cigarettes."[31]

At the Arecibo prison, where Doris arrived in March 1951, apparently no such experiments were attempted and she was gradually able to heal, due in part to the tender care imparted by her cellmates. As her gunshot wound healed, and the memory of the "experiments" suffered at La Princesa faded, she gained weight and regained her sense of humor, according to Carmín Pérez. And though conditions in the Arecibo prison were far from ideal, Doris seemed to accept them without complaint. Her cellmates, on the other hand, complained about many things. First on the list was the fact that they were locked-up twenty-three hours a day in the confinement cells (calabozos), which had been designed for short stays for violators of prison rules and regulations. The fact that these cells were tucked away on the top floor of the Women's Wing kept them isolated from the rest of the prison population. They were also not able to receive visitors. The problem, according to the warden, was that the prison was overcrowded, and given his orders "to keep Nationalists women away from the common prisoners," he had been forced to improvise by outfitting the two confinement cells with two bunk beds and a cot in order to accommodate them.[32]

Being locked up twenty-three hours a day, Rosado said, was "an unnecessary punishment." The only break in that schedule, she added, "occurred at 3:00 in the afternoon when we were let out for one hour to exercise and shower." Since the rooms were also dark, she said, they had to keep the light on at all times. The other problem, according to Ruth Reynolds, was that the space was so small "that we could barely move about without bumping into one another or into the bunk beds." Boredom was the biggest problem, Carmín Pérez exclaimed, since there was nothing to do other than write letters or talk to each other during the hours they were awake. They saw no one for months, except the occasional visit from their lawyers, which meant they could not adequately prepare for their upcoming trials, Reynolds added.[33]

During the first two weeks she spent in the Arecibo jail, Reynolds said that the only persons she saw, besides the warden and guards, were "two FBI agents, who came bearing offers of a shorter or a suspended sentence, if she chose to collaborate with the authorities against Albizu Campos and other leading Nationalists." Since she opted not to collaborate, they stopped coming to see her and she was sent back to the "calabozo" to await the review of her case. She would remain in that prison, though not always in isolation, for 19 months before she was tried, convicted and later released on bail, pending the resolution of her appeal.[34]

Poor food and rat infestation were two other major issues Doris and her comrades encountered at the Arecibo prison. According to Ruth Reynolds, the food served to inmates in Puerto Rico's prisons "was hardly adequate to sustain life," and definitely not "nutritious enough to ensure health." The daily fare, she explained, consisted of "black coffee and bread for breakfast, and rice, beans and more bread for lunch and dinner." The rice, Carmín Pérez clarified, "was never fully cooked, and the beans were hardly ever more than a watery mess, without the least bit of flavor." The few times pig's feet were added for flavor, she said, "the meat had worms." (After her first stint in jail, she became a vegetarian.)

The exceptions to the "monotonous daily diet," Carmín Pérez recalled, "were Good Fridays, when salted codfish and root vegetables were served, and during the Christmas season when local citizens brought special foods, such as 'arroz con gandules' (rice with pigeon peas) roasted pork and 'pasteles' (a savory dish shaped like a Mexican tamale but made from ground root vegetables, instead of corn meal, and stuffed with stewed chicken or pork)." Salads were never served, they were told, because the ingredients were perishable and the prison was understaffed as well as underfunded. As a result, even those who had the funds to purchase the extra foods they had been approved had to rely on the warden's wife to shop for them once a week. To prevent spoilage from week to week, Reynolds said, they ordered only a few eggs at a time and purchased mostly powdered milk, crackers, canned meats and other items they could keep safely stored in their rooms. (For more details about Reynolds' battle to get access to better food, see the section devoted to her in this book.)[35]

The only times they ate fresh fruits was when Carmín Pérez' father brought or sent them from his farm in Lares, according to Isabel Rosado. Viscal and Torresola's relatives, she added, often brought them powder milk, crackers, and sweets when they visited. Since her own relatives lived far away from Arecibo, they visited less often, though her sister Adela often sent her guava paste and papaya chunks in syrup, which she shared with the others. "The important thing, she explained, was that we all shared whatever treats we had."[36]

The worst part about those tiny cells, Rosado said, was the mice infestation. At first, they tried to discourage the "critters from scurrying over our bodies by keeping the light bulb on all night." But the light made it difficult to sleep and they could still hear the mice scurrying around and making noise. After several sleepless nights, the warden sent them a mousetrap, and in one night, Rosado said, "we caught more than twenty rats and mice." Killing the critters helped, she agreed, but the experience left them "exhausted and disgusted." The mice infestation in the Arecibo jail was so serious, according to Angelina Torresola, (who spent six months there in 1954) "that one would see them crawling all over the plates where the food would be served later."[37]

Torresola's Second Arrest, 1954

At the time of her release, in August 1953, Doris Torresola had little reason to suspect that she would be sent back to prison less than seven months later. The event that led to her second arrest and new incarceration was unleashed on March 1, 1954 when four Nationalists from New York, led by Dolores (Lolita) Lebrón launched an armed attack on the United States Congress. After completing her first sentence, Doris returned to her sister's home until September 1953, when Albizu Campos was released from prison due to ill health. Afraid he might die in jail and become a martyr to his followers, the Governor had Albizu released on a conditional pardon. As it was explained later, his release rested on the premise that he would be sent back to prison if he violated any of the terms stipulated by the Governor. Never one to accept conditions, especially those issued by his rival, Albizu took advantage of a press interview in which he was asked to comment on the attack on Congress. According to the journalist Teófilo Maldonado, Albizu described the attack as "an act of sublime heroism." The comment provoked the Governor to revoke his pardon and order Albizu's arrest, apparently ignoring the fact that by this act, he was violating the separation of powers stipulated by the newly adopted Commonwealth constitution.[38]

On the morning of March 6, 1954, when dozens of policemen arrived at the corner of Sol and Cruz Streets with orders to arrest Albizu Campos, they were met with a shower of bullets. His caretakers (Torresola, Pérez, Rosado, and Rivera Sotomayor) had sworn they would rather die fighting than allow Albizu to be taken back to prison because they feared a new incarceration would kill their leader. Asked whether Albizu had also been shooting that day, Carmín Pérez replied: "We were all shooting!" When the same question was posed to Isabel Rosado in a separate interview, she replied, "No, no, he didn't shoot; he couldn't do anything; he was too ill." She added that during the siege she and the others "had laid Albizu on the floor, to protect him from the gases from the bombs the police were throwing into the apartment." Such disparate recollections from two of the participants in the shootout make it difficult to ascertain what role, if any, Albizu played during the events the day (March 6) of his arrest.[39]

Rosado and Pérez agreed, however, that the battle with the police lasted approximately two hours and that no one in their group was wounded. They agreed also that after their initial response they had to scale back their defense because they were running short of bullets. Sensing that this might be case, the police threw tear gas bombs into the apartment, Chief Roig said, in order to "coax them to surrender." Within minutes after the bombs landed in the residence, Pérez said, she and Rivera Sotomayor walked out to warn the journalists and passersby that Albizu, Rosado and Torresola were unconscious and could not walk down on their own. The two, she said, were nabbed by the police and placed under arrest as soon as they reached the ground floor. "Don Pedro," Pérez recalled, "was carried out, slumped over the shoulders of Dudley Osborne."(Details about Osborne actions are included in the section devoted to Carmen Maria Pérez and will not be repeated here.) Doris Torresola and Isabel Rosado, according to one press account, were "carried out still unconscious by some of the police officers." Yet according to a police report, "the two walked out of the building without assistance." Rivera Sotomayor, a journalist reported, was beaten to a pulp by several policemen.[40]

For her actions on March 6, 1954, Doris Torresola was indicted on three counts: a) one violation of Law #53, as amended in 1950; b) illegal possession of a firearm; and c) attack with intent to commit murder. The most serious of three counts was the one violation of Law #53, the act of "belonging to" the Nationalist Party. Since December 1950, when that law was last amended, the Nationalist Party had been reclassified by the local authorities "as a subversive group whose known intent is to over-throw the established government by force and violence."(It should be noted that after July 25, 1952, when Puerto Rico officially became a self-governing territory, it had obtained the autonomy it needed to resolve all matters of internal security, except in cases involving Communists, which were still subject to the federal Smith Act.) Any offense against the newly amended Law #53, such as "belonging to any subversive group or organization" carried a bail of $25,000 and a sentence, if convicted, of one to ten years in prison. The charge of "illegal possession of a firearm," called for a set bail of $5,000 and a prison sentence, if con-victed, of one to two years, while the charge of "attack with intent to murder," called for a set bail of $5,000 and a prison sentence, if convicted of one to five years.[41]

New Trials: Three Convictions

Since most of the Nationalists arrested in 1950 were still serving their prison sentences, the authorities found only thirty-eight suspects they could arrest in 1954 in connection with the attack on Congress. Most of the thirty-eight were arrested on one or more charges of conspiracy, based on the (1950) amendments to Law #53. In the proceedings that followed, all violations of Law #53 were addressed first, but far away from San Juan. The task in that case was left to the District Court of Arecibo and its presiding judge Rafael Padró Parés, even though most of the acts for which the defendants were accused did not take place in his jurisdiction. The first trial, held in the Arecibo's District Court, began on December 14, 1954 and ended on February 7, 1955. In that instance, Doris and thirteen co-defendants, five of them women, were convicted on a variety of charges, including an attack on the island's police. Already known for his hostile attitude toward the Nationalists, Judge Padró Parés provided ample latitude to the prosecutors, and little flexibility to the defense, as he had done four years earlier in other Nationalist cases. Dissatisfied with the process, the defense appealed the convictions, on grounds "that the Court had acted inappropriately regarding the rules of evidence and failed to properly instruct the jury." As a result of multiple appeals, sentencing for Doris Torresola and her comrades was postponed until May 1955, when the appeals process was completed.[42]

In the meantime, Doris and her comrades were taken to the women's facility, the so-called Escuela Industrial Para Mujeres, which had opened in Vega Alta, Puerto Rico in 1954. Their appeals were denied and sentencing proceeded on May 31, 1955. That day Judge Padró Parés sentenced Doris Torresola and four of her comrades to prison terms of seven to ten years each for their violations of Law #53. The sixth member of that group, Doris' sister Angelina Torresola de Platet, was sentenced to a shorter term of three to seven years. Doris, however, still had two other cases pending review at San Juan's District Court.[43]

Between May 2 and June 17, 1955, Doris was tried in San Juan on two counts: a) "attack with intent to commit murder," in which three undercover agents claimed they had been wounded; and b) "possession of an unregistered firearm." She was convicted on both counts. For the first count, she was sentenced to a prison term of one to five years and for the second to a term of one to two years. Although the defense tried valiantly to challenge the statements of the undercover agents on the first count, it did not succeed. There was little the defense could do about the second charge because she had in fact fired an unregistered gun. All told, by summer's end (1955), Doris Torresola had been sentenced to three prison terms, ranging from a minimum of nine years to a maximum of seventeen years.[44]

Mental Illness: Release from Prison

Doris' mental health deteriorated rapidly in the Vega Alta prison, according to her niece, Ana María Platet (Angelina Torresola's daughter). She told researcher Janet Martínez, that the director of the Vega Alta prison had told the family that she had to place Doris in isolation several times because of "her growing erratic behavior." Platet said also that she and her mother (Angelina) had already noticed that Doris often said "strange things and behaved oddly." They suspected that the changes in behavior she exhibited might be due "to the drugs she was administered in prison for her asthmatic condition." And years later they discovered that "thorazine" one of the medications regularly prescribed to Doris for her asthmatic condition, was "an antipsychotic drug, known for its effects on the nervous system." The same drug, they also learned, "might provoke asthmatic attacks in patients with chronic respiratory disorders."[45]

As her mental condition worsened, and since the prison was not equipped to handle cases of mental illness, Angelina and her family began a campaign to get Doris released so that she could be sent for psychiatric treatment. Part of their campaign, Platet said, included direct appeals to the Governor Luis Muñoz Marín to pardon Doris. Their efforts coincided with the militant actions of several progressive groups, which were demanding that the government release the Nationalist prisoners still incarcerated, she added. The groups based their demands on the fact that the law for which the Nationalists had been convicted (Law #53) had been abolished years earlier (1957). Whether because of the group's demands or because the Governor no longer considered Doris a threat to his government, he granted Doris Torresola "an unconditional pardon" and she was released on September 8, 1961 from the Vega Alta prison.[46]

With the family's consent, she was taken directly from the Vega Alta prison to the Psychiatric Hospital in Río Piedras, her sister said, and would spend the next year in that facility before she was considered well enough to be released into her sister's care. Thus, on October 12, 1962, Doris was taken to Angelina's home, where other relatives also lived. The small home she owned with her husband Alfredo Platet was located in Puerto Nuevo, a suburb of San Juan.[47]

Though officially pardoned, Doris was kept under strict surveillance by local I.S. agents and the FBI office in San Juan. According to the latter, she was "considered the Nationalist movement's best hope so long as Albizu remained in prison." The FBI reported also that the last time Doris had been let out of prison in August 1954 she had begun collecting funds in order to purchase gunpowder, which she intended to use to blow up a hole in a prison wall in order to allow Albizu and other leaders to escape. They said they had received information that she had also been planning an attack on the FBI office in San Juan, which was supposed to coincide with the visit to the island (September 1954) of several U.S. Congressmen.[48]

But despite the agents' continuous fears, in 1962, Doris was no longer the threat she might have been in 1954. Although even then, her sister claimed, she had spent most of her days caring for Albizu Campos, writing letters to comrades still in prison, attending mass and visiting cemeteries in honor of fallen comrades. In her spare time, Angelina added, she was busy sewing and knitting children's clothing in an attempt to earn a living. After she was released from the Psychiatric Hospital, and especially after Albizu Campos died (April 1965), she was too ill to continue with the political work she had done before. Albizu Campos' death, her sister said, led Doris into great periods of depression. The family, she explained, did its best "to keep her safe, but could not protect her from her sorrows."[49]

Not yet recovered from the loss of Albizu's death, in 1971 she was faced with the death of Doña Rosalina, the family matriarch. Her mother's death, said Angelina, "threw Doris into total despair" and a year later she tried to take her life by ingesting a combination of pills. She was found in time and survived the attempt, her niece said, but then sank into a severe depression. Then on February 10, 1972, when the family least expected it because she had met a fellow Nationalist who loved her and wanted to marry her, she poured gasoline on herself and lit her body on fire. This time no one was home to rescue her and she perished in the flames, according to her brother-in-law Alfredo Platet, who discovered the tragedy. She was buried the next day in the Jayuya cemetery, next to her parents and her brother Griselio. Her other brother, Elio, would be buried next to them only three years later.[50]

Since Doris' passing, many admirers have tried to make sense of her tragic death. Perhaps, Janet Martínez suggests, her death was already foreshadowed in the poem she wrote to Albizu Campos in April 1956, in honor of his birthday, titled "Luz del Deber," which reads, in Spanish, as follows:

Por el camino tortuoso de la vida	Along the tortuous road of life
iban caminando	four shadows were
cuatro sombras	walking
en busca de luz.	in search of light.
Una antorcha aparece lejana	A distant torch appears
pero con meta segura.	but with a solid aim.
Las cuatro sombras avanzan	The four shadows approach

con pasos alados
vanse acercando a la antorcha
para beber de su luz.

La sed de la sombra menor
fue tanta
que estalló en oclusión de luces
besó a las sombras hermanas
y se volvió al infinito.

Los demás esperan.

with winged steps
they draw close to the torch
to drink of its light.

The thirst of the smaller shadow
was so intense
that it burst into flames
kissed the sister shadows
and returned to the infinite.

The rest await.[51]

7. Olga Isabel Viscal Garriga (1929–1995)

Preface

According to dossier #692 of the Puerto Rican Police Department, Olga Isabel Viscal Garriga was born in Brooklyn, New York, May 5, 1929. She was twenty-one years old when she was summoned (November 1, 1950) by District Attorney Alma Delgado to appear as a potential "witness" in the investigation that had just begun regarding the 1950 Nationalist uprising.[1] She was then a college student, still living with her parents in Puerto Nuevo, a suburb of San Juan, Puerto Rico. She was ordered to appear for questioning at the Asilo de Indigentes, one of the makeshift detention centers set up in Santurce, Puerto Rico in order to accommodate the hundreds of detainees who had begun spilling out of other facilities. The District Attorney's order made it explicit that she would be charged with contempt if she failed to appear on the day assigned. She arrived on November 5, 1950, and was assigned to Angel Viera Martínez, one of seven district attorneys entrusted with the task of deciding which of the hundreds of persons detained island-wide should be charged in connection with the uprising.[2]

Background Leading to her Arrest

Viscal already had a growing surveillance file, dating back to April 1948, when she took part in a strike against the University of Puerto Rico. That deed had caused her to be expelled by the school administration in October 1948, and had brought her to the attention of the Police's Internal Security (I.S.) division. For example, during the summer of 1948, one of the I.S. agents trailing her reported that she had become a member of the Nationalist Party and was often seen visiting Pedro Albizu Campos

at the Nationalist Club (Party Headquarters) in San Juan. Others reported later that she met regularly
with well-known Nationalist leaders
in San Juan, Hato Rey and Río
Piedras. Then on October 27, 1948,
I.S. agent Lieutenant Jorge Camacho
Torres wrote that during the strike
at the university, Olga Viscal had
been observed "coming out of the
Café Universitario in the company
of Rafael Viera Medina," though he
failed to note the importance of the
sighting. He reported instead that
her participation in the strike had
"caused her to be fined $25," which
she had paid on January 19, 1949 at
the Municipal Court of Río Piedras.
"She caused herself that fine," he
said obviously amused, "when she
declared herself guilty of exploding
firecrackers during the strike before she was even accused." He added
that the prosecuting attorneys in that instance were José C. Aponte and
Guillermo A. Gil, two of the seven who would later play a major role in
sending nearly two hundred Nationalists to prison on charges related to
the 1950 uprising.[3]

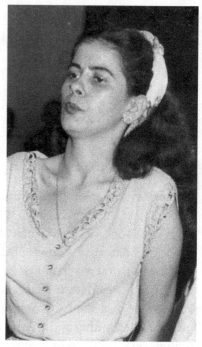

Olga Viscal, circa the day of her arrest.
November 5, 1950.

From 1948 onward, Olga Viscal was closely watched. Occasionally,
reports of her activities made their way up from the Chief of Police's desk
to the office of the Governor. In one of those reports she was merely
identified as Irma Viscal's sister, apparently because the latter had lived
temporarily in Albizu's home in San Juan and was known to be dating a
fellow Nationalist. According to Lieutenant Andrés Ramos Fernández,
by the summer of 1948, both sisters had "progressed from affiliates to
members of the Nationalist Party." On June 6, 1949, he also reported
that he had observed Olga Viscal entering the Nationalist Club in San
Juan at four in the afternoon and leaving two and half hours later. Apparently, the length of her visit was indicative of her commitment to the
Nationalist Party. In October 1950, days before the uprising, Detective

Luis W. Lynn reported that Olga Viscal had not only been a frequent visitor of Albizu Campos but had often been seen "in the company of Doris Torresola and other leading Nationalists."[4]

Given the widespread surveillance under which Albizu Campos and other Nationalist leaders operated, it is not surprising that news of Olga and Irma's activities would soon reach their parents. A great supporter of the government in power, their father, Francisco Viscal Bravo, was "distraught" to learn the news about his daughters' associations with the Nationalist Party and tried to put an end to their "misguided behavior" at once. According to one of Irma's accounts after she agreed to collaborate with the authorities, he gave them an ultimatum. "It did not work," she said, "because I found a job and took Olga to live with me at a rooming house in Río Piedras." But then she lost the job and the two of them stayed a few days at Juanita González Bouillerce's home and from there went to Albizu's home in search of shelter. For reasons that are not altogether clear, Albizu Campos delegated "the girls housing problem" to the Party's military commander, Raimundo Díaz Pacheco. According to what Díaz Pacheco's wife, Saturnina Ramos, told the prosecution, her husband "came home with the Viscal girls sometime in mid-December of 1949," expecting her to look after them.[5]

They stayed in their home for a while, she said, "without causing any problems at first, but then "Irma began disobeying our rules, coming in late almost every night" and 'Ray' (Raimundo) asked her to move out. "Olga was okay at first," Saturnina said. "She stayed close to the house and went to bed early because she shared a room with my sixty-year old aunt." But by April 1950, she had asked Olga to move out when she realized that she "had fallen in love with my husband." Asked where did Olga go after she evicted her? She replied, "Probably back to her parents' home."[6]

Was Olga in fact in love with Raimundo Díaz Pacheco, as his wife suspected? According to a testimony submitted by thirty-two year old Carmen Belén Sosa de Rodríguez, a female detective assigned to oversee Viscal and other Nationalist women held at San Juan's Police Headquarters, Viscal was in love with Díaz Pacheco and "was hoping to marry him after the revolution triumphed." She said Viscal had confided this and many other secrets during the period she oversaw her detention. For example, Viscal had said that, "she blamed herself for Raimundo's death [which occurred during the attack of La Fortaleza, the Governor's residence] because she had often told him she wouldn't marry him until the Republic became a reality." And she "seemed to have convinced herself," Detective Sosa said, "that this was the reason, why Ray had rushed to launch the attack."[7]

Ostensibly she had also told Detective Sosa that Ray had invited her to take part in the attack on La Fortaleza, "but had changed his mind ten minutes later" when she said she would need to go and change the blouse she was wearing for a white one. Why was a change of blouse necessary? She had replied, "Because I wanted to die dressed in black and white, the colors of the Nationalist Party." She had also said, the Detective claimed, that she had learned to shoot at Isla de Cabras [across the San Juan Bay] and that the target had been a picture of Governor Luis Muñoz Marín. She had added that since the strike at the University of Puerto Rico she had been "carrying a pistol in a secret compartment of her purse." Ostensibly, she had also said that she had helped Raimundo (Díaz Pacheco) make bombs during the time she had lived at his home and had often accompanied him on his military training missions, including one to the U.S. military base in Salinas, Puerto Rico. She added that, one month prior to the uprising she and Ray had delivered firearms and bombs to various places throughout the island. She also disclosed that "Ray had $30,000 for the revolution but had used part of the money to buy her a ring, a watch and a gold chain." Lastly, she ostensibly told Detective Sosa that everything she had told her could be "verified in the diaries" she and Ray kept at his home. When asked to comment on Detective Sosa's testimony, Viscal dismissed it as "a bunch of lies" and Díaz Pacheco's widow, Saturnina Ramos, told the prosecution that there had never been any diaries and that "Olga has a great imagination and demands a lot of attention."[8]

Approximately six weeks after Detective Sosa rendered her written report (December 21, 1950) another nearly identical account was submitted by National Guardsman José Enrique Tizol Bouret. The twenty-six year old artillery officer said that on November 5, 1950 he had been asked to report to work at San Juan's Police headquarters and had been surprised to see Olga Viscal among the detainees. Since she had been his classmate at the University of Puerto Rico, he had "stopped to say hello and chat a bit with her." He claimed that she was "surprisingly forthcoming about the reasons why she thought she was being detained" and proceeded to describe to him a few of the activities in which she had been involved. For example, she had said "that in August (1950) she had gone with Díaz Pacheco to a U.S. military base in Salinas, Puerto Rico, where they were scheduled to meet with a National Guard's officer, but that he did not show. She would not disclose the officer's name, he said, despite his entreaties. The rest of his account was very similar to the one provided by Detective Sosa, except that he added that Viscal had told him that "the only leader the Nationalists recognized was Pedro Albizu Campos, not Raimundo Díaz Pacheco." And she also mentioned that she had been looking for work and had recently applied at "Pan American Airways, the U.S. Post Office, and the U.S. Artillery Academy." Viscal also dismissed Tizol Bouret's statements as "outright lies."[9]

Why was Olga Viscal Arrested?

According to District Attorney Angel Viera Martínez, he ordered her to be detained "because she lied during the (his) interrogation." A review of their exchange, which took place on November 5, 1950, indicates that Viscal often offered more information than the question called for, and that Viera Martínez had more details about her activities than he let on. After verifying her name, home address, name of parents and siblings, he asked whether she was or had ever been a member of the Nationalist Party. She admitted she had joined the Party in 1948 and confirmed the fact that she knew Doris Torresola and Juanita González Bouillerce but added that she knew González Bouillerce simply as "a neighbor." The unsolicited explanation was a lie, noted the interrogator because he already knew from the I.S. surveillance reports that Viscal and González Bouillerce were more than neighbors. In fact, during the summer of 1948, the two of them had founded a chapter of Las Hijas de la Libertad (the female chapter of the Nationalist Party) in Río Piedras. He knew also that they had gone to bring the news of their accomplishment to Albizu Campos while he was staying at Blanca Canales's home in Coabey, Jayuya. Through other surveillance records, he knew that Viscal and González Bouillerce had often attended poetry recitals in an effort to recruit new members and raise funds for the Nationalist Party. The two of them, the same reports indicated, met regularly in what they believed were secret meetings at homes of other Nationalists in Hato Rey and Río Piedras. He chose not to mention any of this, but simply directed the line of inquiry to other areas. Many questions later, he asked her whether she knew Carmen María Pérez. She claimed she did not, which he knew not to be true because she had frequently visited Albizu Campos and Pérez was almost always there. [10]

He let that reply go unchallenged and instead asked her: "Why did you go to New York earlier this year?" She replied, "Because I wanted to enroll in a summer course at City College." Unconvinced by the explanation, he posed a few more probing questions, and several minutes later she admitted that she had "never enrolled in any course at City College." Feigning interest in what she was saying, he asked, "Why didn't you enroll in the course?" To which she replied, "Because I didn't have the money." He continued: "Is that why you returned home in June?" She explained that she returned home "because of family issues" and that her parents "had paid for the ticket when they learned that I was ill." He probed, "Was that because you were nervous in New York?" She agreed, "Yes, because I had an accident on the plane on the way to New York, and one day while I was staying at my aunt's house I tried to kill myself by jumping out of a window." Unmoved by her attempt to elicit sympathy, he asked the question he was really after: "Do you know Oscar Collazo and Griselio Torresola, the men who tried to kill President Truman?" (He seemed to be trying to determine whether she had been the person who could have taken such an order from Albizu Campos to the two attackers.) She said she did not. Without any apparent evidence to the contrary, he guided her back to an area explored earlier: "Why didn't you return home until June?" he asked again. "Because I did not have the money and had to wait so that I could buy the ticket on the installment plan." (Moments earlier she had said that her parents had paid for her return ticket.) He did not challenge her on that point either, but simply asked her to describe her whereabouts the day prior to the uprising. [11]

"Where were you on Sunday, October 29?" he inquired. "At home," she replied. But then rather than wait for a follow-up question, she proceeded to tell him an elaborate story as to why she was home that day and every Sunday before that. Unimpressed by her long explanation, he asked her to recount her actions, from Sunday October 29 up to that day (November 5). She complied as best as nerves allowed, given that he kept interrupting her. He would let her go on for a while and when she appeared to be telling the truth, he skipped over to another area of inquiry. After hours of this game, he asked her to write down the names and addresses of every person she had stayed with, visited, or talked to during her stay in New York between March and June 1950. He appeared to be looking for a thread that might connect her to the November 1, 1950 attack on Blair House. When it became apparent that she had nothing to contribute in that regard, he ended the session and ordered that she be detained at Police Headquarters in Puerta de Tierra until further notice. In reality, the interrogation in her case was a formality because he had the authority to hold her once she admitted she was a member of the Puerto Rican Nationalist Party, a group that days before had attempted to overthrow the island's government by force and violence.[12]

Since no direct evidence was found to connect Olga Viscal with the violent acts of October 30, 1950, she was charged with one violation of Puerto Rico's Sedition Act, Law #53 and sent to San Juan's District Jail, La Princesa to await review of her case. On December 29, 1950 she was indicted and assigned bail of $25,000, the standard sum for violations of Law #53. (Generally, the excessive sum was appealed, but we found no evidence that this was done in her case.) Since no one came forward to post bail for her, she was transferred to the Women's Wing of Arecibo's District jail to await trial. She remained there for another fifteen months, even though a colonial law (theoretically) guaranteed every accused the right to a "speedy trial" within six months of his or her arrest or to be released until the case came to trial.[13]

Prison Life for Olga Viscal

By all accounts Viscal's life in prison was a challenge for her, as well for those who held her captive. According to several letters in her file, Viscal was brought back to La Princesa at least twice during the next year and a half. The first time, one letter said, occurred on February 7, 1951, when she was summoned as one of the witnesses in Albizu Campos's trial. The second took place on May 5, 1952 when she was summoned for her upcoming trial. Everywhere she went, according to the wardens in San Juan and Arecibo, she did her best to test their patience with her incessant complaints about her health and demands for special medical attention. For example, on February 13, 1951, six days after she was brought back to La Princesa, the warden Juan S. Bravo received an urgent call from the Interim Superintendent of Prisons, Félix Rodríguez Higgins, requesting a report and Viscal's medical files because she had complained to a reporter that she had contracted tuberculosis in jail.[14]

In a detailed letter, Bravo explained to the Superintendent that Viscal had been complaining of ill health ever since she arrived at La Princesa on February 7. In fact, "the very evening she arrived she had asked the nurse on duty (Benjamín Figueroa) to inject her with 'streptomycin,' a medication she had brought with her from Arecibo." The nurse explained that he was not authorized to dispense any medication without Dr. Hazim's consent and suggested that she wait until morning and speak with him. The nurse left the warden a report, which he reviewed the following morning and which led him to ask Dr. Hazim to visit Olga Viscal in her cell. According to the physician, she told him she had suffered two "hemoptysis attacks" at the Arecibo prison and that was the reason she had asked for the injection. The doctor, the warden said, authorized the injection, but also recommended that he send her to be tested for tuberculosis at the San Juan District Hospital. That was done on February 9, 1951, according to the results he enclosed. He said the Hospital's leading physician, Dr. Velázquez, had indicated that a saliva test had been administered, which proved negative. But that the same physician had ordered a chest x-ray, scheduled for February 13. But one day before the x-ray was taken, the local daily El Imparcial published an article, claiming "Viscal is suffering from tuberculosis." In order to counter that story, Viscal's medical reports were apparently leaked to the rival newspaper, El Mundo, which reported a few days later, "Viscal does not suffer from Tuberculosis." The debate over Viscal's ill health was just getting started.[15]

According to another report sent to the Attorney General by the warden of the Arecibo jail, J. González Lebrón, on October 5, 1951, Olga Viscal was still complaining of "symptoms of hemoptysis." He, too, gave a detailed account of the steps the attending physician Dr. Cadilla had taken to address Viscal's medical complaints. The doctor, he said, had initially performed "the standard saliva test," but when this proved negative he had her sent to Arecibo's District Hospital for a chest x-ray. The results of the x-ray (which he enclosed), he had been told, "showed no lesions in her lungs or any other signs" that she suffered from tuberculosis. But since Viscal remained unconvinced, he said, her family was now demanding that she be examined by a pulmonary specialist. And since he could not authorize the expense without the Attorney General's consent, he was forwarding their request to the Department of Justice.[16]

Curiously, in a separate letter he (González Lebrón) wrote to the Chief Prosecutor, José C. Aponte, he confided that in his opinion "the cause of Viscal's malady is not hemoptysis, as she claims, but hysteria." He explained that, "from the first moment she arrived in this institution she has had several attacks of hysteria during which she has bitten her tongue to give the impression that she has hemoptysis." He added that, as far as he could tell, "She does this and other neurotic things so we keep her in the hospital, which is her way to avoid prison chores." In another letter he wrote to the Attorney General, this time in response to a telephone call he had received from that office, he admitted that, "in fact another inmate did slap Olga Viscal." He attributed the incident to "Viscal's constant whining (majaderías) and her lack of respect for others." In his opinion, "she fully deserved that slap." He complained further that, Olga Viscal and her comrades "want to live like royalty in a prison that lacks basic comforts." And he added that during the time they were in isolation, which is what they'd prefer, they spent their day in bed, slept late until 10:00 in the morning, and had their breakfast, lunch, and dinner brought in, while now they have to get up at 5:30 in the morning like the rest, and have to line up for their meals." He said he hoped to correct that behavior "once they are sentenced and we can put them to work a little harder." (It is possible that the warden, who was generally considered a kind person, might have been trying to appear tough to impress his superiors.)[17]

Two years later (September 1953), Olga Viscal's health claims continued, and her family was again visiting the press to complain that she had not yet been seen by a specialist. After a meeting with the journalist (Teófilo Maldonado) who filed the story, the Secretary of Justice instructed the Attorney General to send the state penitentiary's pulmonary specialist, Dr. José Soto Ramos, to the Arecibo prison to examine Olga Viscal and render a report. Two days later (September 18, 1953), Dr. Soto Ramos wrote that he had visited Olga Viscal in prison but that despite his best efforts she had refused to let him examine her. Thanks to the cooperation of Dr. Cadilla, who supplied him with all Viscal's medical records since she entered the prison and the x-ray plaques and medical records made available by the District Hospital, he had "found no evidence to suggest that Miss Viscal has, or has ever had, tuberculosis."[18]

Yet the question whether Viscal had tuberculosis was never adequately resolved. Interestingly, three months after her second medical report was issued regarding her state of health, Viscal wrote to Isabel Rosado (May 11, 1952) saying she was "in perfect health and excellent spirits." Curious about this apparent contradiction, I asked two of her former cellmates to comment about the question of Viscal's health. Their reply was: "Olga's illness was due to nerves." Asked if she was mentally ill, they said: "No, she just had little patience with cowards and fools; she was a very brave woman." Yet another cellmate said that she thought Viscal was "young and immature."[19]

Whether because of "nerves, courage, or immaturity," the fact remains that Viscal attracted a lot of press coverage during her trial, which began on May 5, 1952. The journalists appeared to love the spectacle she made every time she challenged Judge Julio Suárez Garriga and the prosecutors. At the onset of her trial she told Judge Suárez, "I will not accept legal representation because I do not recognize the authority of this colonial court or its representatives." Delighted with the logic of her arguments, some supporters (including Albizu Campos) applauded what she said as it was eagerly reported by journalists on the scene. According to various press accounts, she called the witnesses who testified against her "cowards, liars, and slaves" and dismissed their statements as "outright lies." She repeatedly called policemen, prosecutors, and other members of the court "liars, slaves, puppets, and stooges of the empire." On more than one occasion she reportedly defied Judge Suárez who threatened to cite her for contempt; "go ahead and do it because I do not care." He obliged, the journalists said, and cited her for contempt a total of thirty-one times over the course of the proceedings, which meant she would have to serve a minimum of 930 days in prison, even if she was absolved of the crime for which she was being tried. Scandalized by the "insolence of this young woman," something never before seen in Puerto Rico, the local dailies published her every remark.[20]

For the most part, the articles filed by the journalists were accompanied by photos of Olga Viscal out of her seat "gesturing and yelling at her accusers and members of the court." A few of the articles also offered detailed descriptions of the outfits she wore to court, and how she looked on a given day. (In general, she looked strikingly beautiful.) Other reports focused on her demeanor, explaining to the readers when she was "serene, listening intently to the proceedings," or when she was "furious and ready to pounce on her accusers." They described how often she fixed her hair or put on lipstick when the proceedings had "begun to bore her." The press, according to one account, "treated her as a celebrity and she responded in kind." She seemed to be enjoying her notoriety. Apparently, none of her antics amused the judge, the prosecutors, or the jury, for she was convicted as charged (of one violation of Law #53) on May 12, 1952. Two days later Judge Suárez Garriga sentenced her to a prison term of one to ten years for that crime. In addition, she would have to serve 930 days (nearly three years) for the thirty-one contempt citations she had earned during the proceedings.[21]

Three of Viscal's comrades defined her actions as "signs of courage and valor." Carmín Pérez and Isabel Rosado, for instance, chuckled as they recounted how Olga Viscal "had stood up to the colonial stooges" during the trial. They said they admired her "because she always told the truth as she saw it." Her friend and once collaborator, Juanita González Bouillerce told me during another interview, "Olga Viscal was a genuine human being; a woman of great courage, who was totally devoted to the cause of Puerto Rico's independence." More recently, a professor friend called her "the conscience of the Nationalist Party." She suggested that Viscal "was not always liked because she could be harshly irreverent with those who failed to live up to the ideals of Albizu Campos."[22]

That irreverence, according to the warden of Arecibo, was the cause of many of her problems in prison. In one of his letters to Chief Prosecutor, José C. Aponte, he indicated that his staff had grown tired of Viscal's complaints. He said, "she is forever writing negative things about me, the guards, and everything in this institution to her friends and relatives." Perhaps, he suggested, Aponte might want to investigate the soldiers Fausto Rosas and William Sánchez with whom Viscal often communicated. He sent Aponte a few letters he had intercepted from the soldiers. The censor at the Department of Justice apparently did not agree with his suggestion and returned the letters with the standard phrase scribbled along the margin "dele curso," let it through. Whenever a letter to or from Viscal was deemed important it was copied and added to her file. For example, on June 12, 1951, she wrote to the Attorney General, requesting a "speedy trial as soon as possible," or failing that, a transfer to "any solitary confinement cell anywhere" so long as "I am removed from this jail (Arecibo) and its unhealthy environment." Her petitions were ignored, and she was neither removed from the Arecibo jail nor given a speedy trial.[23]

In another letter she wrote to Isabel Rosado the day before her trial ended (May 11, 1952), she confided that if the jury ruled against her (which she hoped it would not), "I would need my faith in the Divine Providence and my firm political convictions … [to] fortify me and keep me strong." Apparently, by this time her life in the Arecibo prison had become intolerable. Still hoping the jury might absolve her, she promised to remain "firmly committed to the ideals of independence." But, as indicated, she was convicted and sent back to the Arecibo prison she had come to hate.[24]

Life Again in the Women's Wing

Once sentenced, Viscal was sent to live among the common prisoners in the open gallery where conditions were a lot harsher than they had been in solitary confinement. Less than a year later (April 1953), she was reported to the warden by a guard, who accused her of "trying to smuggle out documents." According to the investigation that followed, Viscal had attempted to send home "a batch of certification papers" she had received two months earlier from the University of Puerto Rico. The papers, which had been sent to her by one of the Deans at the University, were far from incriminating evidence, for they simply listed the courses she had attended, the total number of credits earned, grades received, and number of years accredited to her by the institution. The cover letter accompanying the records indicated that she had completed less than three years of study (1945-46; 1946-47; 1947-48) because of her suspension in October 1948. But since the suspension had been deemed "temporary," the Dean assured her that she would be able to resume her studies at any time. The "certification papers" intercepted by the guard were forwarded to the Department of Justice with a note from the warden. The note did not say whether Viscal had been punished for the offense. (The standard punishment for violations of prison rules was a few days in solitary confinement, which Viscal would have welcomed, according to her letter to the Attorney General.)[25]

During the same month (April 1953), another guard reported that Viscal had stopped her to inquire whether she had "access to the list of the Nationalist prisoners slated to be pardoned by the Governor." No mention of punishment was reported. The third disciplinary case occurred in September 1953, a few months before she was transferred to the newly built women's prison, the Escuela Industrial Para Mujeres, in Vega Alta, Puerto Rico. According to a letter from the new warden of Arecibo (the one before died on the job), Viscal had been accused of "trying to recruit an inmate who was about to be released to join the Nationalist Party and become her representative in the eastern town of Fajardo." That incident was considered sufficiently alarming to be reported to the Governor and the FBI office in San Juan. It is not clear whether the former inmate offered this information voluntarily, or whether she was coaxed by the warden of Arecibo or the ever-eager undercover agents of the division of Internal Security. Again, no mention was made of the punishment she might have received.[26]

Viscal at Vega Alta's Women's Prison

I found very few details about Olga Viscal's conduct after she was transferred (1954) to the Vega Alta prison, the Escuela Industrial Para Mujeres. Even the precise date of her arrival at that prison is hard to pinpoint because the information provided by the prison logs is contradictory. According to the prison log "Record de Ingresadas y Egresadas," which tracked the internal movements of inmates, Viscal was sent there from Arecibo on September 15, 1954 and was assigned the number F-33. Yet the log that tracked the prisoners' correspondence, "Correspondencia de Confinadas: Recibida" recorded that Viscal had received mail in that prison on May 5, 1954. Without any way to reconcile the discrepancy, one suspects that she could have been transferred to the Vega Alta prison soon after it opened.[27]

By years' end in 1954, according to El Imparcial, Viscal had written to the Governor, Luis Muñoz Marín "requesting clemency," explaining that she was "ill and wished to return to the University of Puerto Rico to complete her studies." In her request, the article said, she promised "to renounce her old ways and devote herself completely to her studies if she were released." Her letter was received by the Acting Governor, Roberto Sánchez Vilella, who agreed to have her paroled, provided that she "renounced her ideals publicly and promised to abstain from all Nationalist activities in the future." Apparently, she agreed to the conditions and she was released from prison on August 9, 1955 in time to register for classes at the University of Puerto that fall. But, as with all parolees, she was required to meet periodically with a member of the Parole Board. By all accounts, she completed her college degree and graduated with a major in Political Science.[28]

According to an FBI report filed in the spring of 1956, by February Viscal had grown tired of her meetings with the President of the Parole Board and had again written to Governor Luis Muñoz Marín "to solicit a full pardon." According to the informant who supplied the news, she was getting anxious because she had not received a reply from Governor Muñoz. As it turned out, she did not have to wait long because on August 7, 1957, the Puerto Rican legislature abolished Law #53, and she and a few others were "fully pardoned" by the Governor. In Viscal's case, however, the pardon was finalized a month later in September (1957).[29]

Life as a Free Woman

After a hiatus of nearly three years, she was again quoted by the press, after she ran afoul of the Nationalist Party leadership in 1960. Apparently, she had rejoined the Nationalist Party soon after she was pardoned and had been sent to Cuba to represent it at the First Latin American Youth Conference held in Havana. Once in Havana, she ostensibly got into an argument with the "old Party representatives" (Albizu's estranged wife Laura Meneses and her partner Juan Juarbe Juarbe) and that caused her to fall out of favor with the Party leaders back home. Her supporters would later argue that the discord had been provoked by the "rigidity of the old guard" while her detractors maintained that Viscal's "lack of discipline and tendency to ignore orders" had caused the rift. Exactly what happened in Havana is hard to know, given the self-serving accounts aired in the San Juan press by the different factions.[30]

According to Party officials, Viscal had not followed orders and had stayed in Cuba beyond the time period they had authorized. Viscal, on the other hand, argued that she had stayed in Cuba because she "was doing an effective job representing the ideals of independence," unlike the "old representatives who had allied themselves with the Communist regime (of Fidel Castro) and had thus betrayed the ideals of the Nationalist Party." She insisted that her effectiveness had "aroused the ire" of the 'old' Party delegates, "who out of spite and envy" had denounced her to the Cuban government "as a Yankee spy." Their intrigues, she claimed, was the reason Ernesto "Che" Guevara had withheld her passport until she left Cuba. (It is not clear whether the Party leaders in Puerto Rico intervened to get out her out of Cuba.)[31]

By May 6, 1962, she was quoted by *Bohemia Libre Puertorriqueña* (a right-wing Cuban publication) as having said that "Juarbe and Meneses had tried to discredit her to cover their own lackluster performance." Incensed by the troubles they had "caused her," she retaliated by accusing them of "living off the ideals of nationalism." She described Laura Meneses as "a cynical, heartless woman who lived well in Cuba, thanks to the sacrifices of her beleaguered husband, Pedro Albizu Campos." She questioned "Juarbe's political convictions, given that he had fled during the Party's hour of need." She accused other independence leaders of many sins. As might be expected, her rants in the press did little to endear her with Nationalist Party leaders. The clash escalated, and in April 1962, she said, she had to "call the police to protect her from death threats." The irony that she had to depend on the police (which she once called slaves and stooges of the imperial system) was not lost on the reporters who years earlier had treated her as a celebrity.[32]

Apparently, life in Olga Viscal's case was never free of drama. According to a glowing reminiscence published by reporter Eneid Routé in the *San Juan Star* (July 1995), Viscal had resumed her work with the Nationalist Party when she caught up with her in February of 1991. She met Viscal by chance, she said, during a street protest in San Juan, after not seeing her for nearly thirty years. Routé said she was amazed to see how little Olga had changed: she was "still elegantly dressed," wore "her long black hair and [had the] straight back demeanor of a warrior." Before they parted, she said, Viscal invited her to a Nationalist assembly slated to take place in Arecibo the following March. She agreed to attend "though with some trepidation because of the group's history," she said. But once again she was surprised "to find Olga addressing a packed gallery of revered old timers in her inimitable outspoken and brilliant style." In the audience, she said, were none other than Juan Jaca Hernández, Rafael Cancel Miranda, Oscar Collazo, Isabel Freyre, Francisco Matos Paoli, and Albizu Campos's granddaughter, Rosa Albizu Meneses.[33]

Their chance encounter in February 1991, Routé explained, "signaled a new beginning of a life-enhancing experience for me," which grew over the next four years into a deep friendship [with Olga]. That friendship, she said, in turn helped her "to sharpen my sense of justice, freedom, and responsibility." She described Viscal as a "highly analytical [person] who never wavered from her principles," as was the case with Pedro Albizu Campos. "Like him," she said, "Viscal was unafraid to question herself" or others. "She spoke openly," Routé said, "about the Puerto Rican society, its paragons, prophets, and parasites." Her "single-minded beliefs and mysticism," she told Routé, had at times been mistaken for "madness" by strangers and even acquaintances. "But she didn't care," she had said, "because she was utterly convinced" that Puerto Rico would one day be free and then would create a "virtuous, authentic individual."[34]

They remained close friends, Routé explained, until June 1995 when death (from cancer) claimed Olga's life. She was sixty-six years old.[35]

More recently Professor Marta Sánchez Olmedo, another close friend of Olga Viscal, described her as "one of Albizu Campos' best disciples; one who gave her all to the struggle of independence." Albizu, she said, had recognized Olga's valiant spirit and had paid her a great tribute when he heard the reasons why she refused legal representation during her trial. In that instance he had exclaimed, "I bow before the logic of her arguments. This young woman, at twenty-one years of age, is the incarnate dignity of the motherland."[36]

At the end of her life, Routé suggests, that Olga Viscal, like Albizu Campos, went to her grave fully convinced that "true Nationalists do not fear death because nationalism transcends death." When Olga Viscal died, on June 1, 1995, she left behind three adult children and a complex legacy of bravery, controversy, and mystery.[37]

Part III

Nationalist Women Imprisoned in the United States, 1950, 1954

1. Rosa Cortés Collazo (1904–1988)

Preface

Rosa Cortés Collazo was arrested twice in New York City during the 1950s for her political ideals. The first time was in connection with her husband's attempt to kill President Truman at Blair House, his temporary residence. After a night of interrogation by the FBI in Lower Manhattan, she was sent to the Women's House of Detention in the West Village on charges of conspiring with her husband Oscar Collazo. The judge assigned to review her case released her on December 23, 1950 on grounds of insufficient evidence (while her husband was sentenced to death by a federal court in Washington, D.C., though his sentence was commuted to life in prison two years later.) Rosa was arrested again in early March 1954, accused of conspiring with the four Nationalists who attacked the United States Congress. This time she was convicted of one violation of the Smith Act and sentenced to a prison term of six years, which she served at the Federal Reformatory for Women, in Alderson, West Virginia. A few years after her release from prison, she moved permanently to Puerto Rico, where she continued her work on behalf of Puerto Rico's independence and joined numerous other causes, including the release of Nationalists still imprisoned. She lived long enough to see her beloved husband Oscar released from prison after serving twenty-nine years in

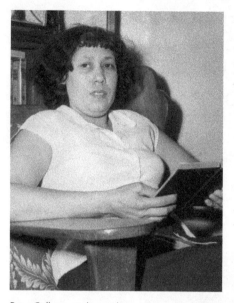

Rosa Collazo reading at home in New York City, circa 1950.

various federal penitentiaries. She was honored numerous times by her comrades and supporters before she died at age eighty-four.

Childhood and Adolescence

Rosa Cortés Fernández, better known in New York as Rosa Collazo, was born in Ponce, Puerto Rico, on August 26, 1904. Her parents Ramón Cortés Cordero and Juana Fernández Mercado moved the family to barrio Maní, Mayagüez, where Rosa spent her formative years under the guidance of her mother. Her father left the family to join the United States Merchant Marine when Rosa was still a child. She would not see him again until she was in her twenties. To feed, clothe, and keep her in school, Rosa's mother made many sacrifices. Rosa recounts a touching story in which her mother sold the living-room furniture in order to secure a seat for her in middle school, and pay for her schoolbooks and clothes. After she ran out of things to sell, Rosa said, Doña Juana sent her to Ponce to live with relatives so that she could finish high school.[1]

By the time Rosa reached her teens she had endured grinding poverty, survived an earthquake and the accompanying tidal wave that nearly destroyed the lowlands of Mayagüez in 1918. A year later she also witnessed the devastation of "the great fire" which consumed many of the city's major buildings and left dozens of charred bodies in its wake. She recalled she was in school the day the earthquake struck and left a few of her classmates crushed under the crumbled walls. She escaped unhurt, thanks in part to an alert principal who ushered her and others out of the school grounds as soon as the major tremors subsided. Her mother came looking for her and took her to Monte Carmelo (Cerro del Cólera), the safest place in the city.[2]

They had only minutes to spare before the sea, which had already retreated, would come roaring back and flood the area. She learned later
that people she saw on the beach catching fish stranded on the sand had
perished when the tidal wave hit the area. When they returned home
they found their own possessions had been destroyed. The chickens, pig,
and goat had drowned, and their food had washed away. The worst part
about the earthquake, she recalled, "was sleeping out in the open or in
the wagons of the cargo train because the earth kept shaking for more
than a month."[3]

Her time in Ponce, she said, "was the easiest time of my life because
my aunt and uncle were very kind" and provided for her until she finished high school. After graduation, she took a nurse's aide course and
quickly found work in the field, but the meager pay and grueling work
left her wondering what else she might do with her life. Fortunately, just
then her father wrote, inviting her to join him in New York. By then he
had left the Merchant Marine and found work in the train tracks in Manhattan. Full of hope for a new life, in July 1925, she boarded the ocean
liner "Nuevo Coamo" headed for New York. Six days later she had
moved into a cramped apartment in East Harlem, a city neighborhood
already known as El Barrio.[4]

Rosa's Life in New York City

Affordable housing in El Barrio, she said, was in short supply and many
Puerto Rican families had to share apartments. Her father was sharing a
three-bedroom, cold water flat with her godparents, for which the rent
was $16 a month. Rosa was given the spare bedroom. Barely heated in
winter, the room was stifling hot in the summer. Toilet facilities were
down the hallway and had to be shared with other tenants. Bathing was
done in a tub in the kitchen hardly ever "more than three times a week."
She disliked the apartment and longed to move to a better one, but discriminatory policies and the low wages they earned, she said, forced
them to remain in place. (Men in her household, she said, earned between $12 and $15 a week and the women between $8 and $10.) Thus,
until the 1940s, her family and many other Hispanics were confined to
a small geographic area that spanned from 98th to 125th Streets and from
Second to Lexington Avenue. Over time, she said, she grew fond of the

neighborhood "because it was still safe and tranquil."[5]

Though she had a high school diploma and rudimentary nursing skills, she couldn't find a job she liked and had to settle for factory work, starting at $8 a week. From those wages, she paid $2 a week for her room and sent another $2 to her mother. The remaining $4 she kept for travel, food and other expenses. A subway ride, she recalled, cost ten cents each way, while a dress could be purchased for $3 and a coat for $5. Eager to improve her skills and move to a better job, she enrolled in a secretarial course soon after she moved to East Harlem. Yet the good job never materialized, and she continued to work in factories for the rest of her working life.[6]

At age twenty-two (1926), she met and married Justo Mercado, a native of San Germán, Puerto Rico. Together they had two daughters: Rosa Iris (known as Iris) and Lydia. Their marriage ended in divorce. A single parent by 1929, Rosa was hard-pressed to find a better-paying job just as the United States was plunging into the Great Depression. She was fortunate, she said, to find work as a metal polisher at the Majestic Specialty Company, earning $12 a week. But with no one left at home to care for her daughters, she was forced to leave them all day in a Catholic nursery until she returned home in the evenings.[7]

Surviving the Great Depression, she explained, was a great struggle because her wages remained low. Desperate for higher wages, she joined her coworkers in a series of protests and work stoppages in 1934 in hopes they could establish a labor union to represent their interests at Majestic. After three months on the picket line Rosa's finances were totally depleted and she could no longer afford to send her daughters to the Catholic nursery. "There were times," she wrote, "when I had to choose between buying food for the family and paying the rent." Her parents helped, she added. Her mother moved from Puerto Rico to take care of the girls, while her father either paid the rent or bought groceries for the family. Yet there were times when food became so scarce that all she and her mother could do "was stand in line at the Salvation Army, to get free coffee and doughnuts." The one thing she would never do, she said, "was to take handouts from the government."[8]

The labor struggle at Majestic dragged on for nearly four years and many of her coworkers were arrested, some more than once. Her first arrest, she said, occurred in 1938, the same year the Company finally agreed to grant a wage increase. Her wages, she recalled, more than doubled to $28 a week. That sum finally allowed her to rent an apartment on her own, to buy clothes for herself and her daughters and to attain the minor comforts she had done without for years.[9]

But by the end of 1938, the workers' hard-won gains were threatened, as the owners of Majestic announced that they were moving the plant to Connecticut. Only those willing to relocate could keep their jobs. What should Rosa do? Uproot her family or let go of a job that finally paid her a living wage? What if her mother insisted on returning to Puerto Rico, as she wished? In the end, mother and daughter reached a compromise: her mother would remain in New York for the short term and continue to care for the girls, and Rosa would take the job in Connecticut but return to East Harlem every weekend.[10]

By the time Rosa followed her job to Connecticut, she had numerous civic and political obligations. She had joined the Club Caborrojeño, an organization that was beginning to challenge the various forms of discrimination Puerto Ricans faced daily in New York City. She joined the Club, she said, "Because after a decade in New York, I had grown tired of the daily abuse and needed to do something to address the rage that was growing within me." The Club Caborrojeño, like so many others founded by many Puerto Ricans in New York, explained Virginia Sánchez-Korrol, sought to provide a safe place for Puerto Ricans to meet, air complaints, exchange information about jobs and schools, and celebrate holidays and special occasions. Over time, Rosa said, the Club Caborrojeño also became politically active and began supporting politicians who promised to help the community. One individual who would never disappoint them, and thus received the Club's support for many years, was Congressman Vito Marcantonio.[11]

Rosa's work with the Club Caborrojeño gradually exposed her to the tensions of colonial politics in Puerto Rico. She explains: "In late March 1937, news reached the Club that the Puerto Rican police, on orders of the appointed American governor, had shot and killed nineteen unarmed Nationalists and wounded more than 150 others while they were attempting to hold a parade in Ponce." The marchers, many of them women and children were "massacred," (according to a subsequent investigation led by the American Civil Liberties Union). Incensed by the "great injustice," she said, the Club's leaders led thousands of compatriots and supporters in a demonstration through the streets of East Harlem.[12]

In 1936, Rosa also joined the Club Obrero Español, a Spanish organization that, like the Club Caborrojeño, sought to mobilize its compatriots to challenge the discriminatory policies they faced daily in New York City. Its members also raised funds for the Republicans fighting against the Fascist forces of General Francisco Franco in Spain.[13]

As Rosa's visibility in El Barrio grew, she was contacted by a member of the Puerto Rican Nationalist Party, a Puerto Rican coworker at Majestic. He brought her literature about the Nationalist movement and later introduced her to the Junta leaders in New York City. She recalled that by the time she joined the New York chapter, in 1936, the Nationalists had lost a space they rented at 112th Street and Lexington Avenue and were holding meetings at Juan Cárcel's (also known as Juan Cancel) printing shop. At Cárcel's shop, she would later meet two men who would change the course of her life. The first was Carlos Vélez Rieckehoff, president of the New York Nationalist Junta, who swore her into the Nationalist Party. The second was Oscar Collazo, a Nationalist who had returned from Puerto Rico in 1939 and who would become her second husband within the year.[14]

Work with the Nationalists: Meeting Albizu Campos

Thus, by the time Rosa went to work in Connecticut, she had been spending much of her spare time at Cárcel's shop, engaging in various political activities. While she and Oscar worked together on last minute details for the upcoming celebration of El Grito de Lares (September 1939), he said he discovered how much the two of them had in common. Since he was at the time "separated" from his wife, he began "to escort Rosa home." Soon their walks "turned into dates" and in August 1940 they made "the decision to marry." Oscar then brought his young daughter, Carmen Zoraida (generally called Zoraida, or Zori) to live with them. Rosa's daughters also lived with them and in time grew so fond of Oscar that they chose the Collazo surname as their own. (Their own family surname was Mercado.)[15]

Oscar found a job at the Majestic Company in Connecticut and he and Rosa commuted back and forth to East Harlem every week. One of Oscar's relatives agreed to care for "the girls" and that allowed Rosa's mother (Doña Juana) to return to Puerto Rico, as she wished. Living in

Connecticut, however, made it difficult for Oscar to do his political work in New York City, so he returned to East Harlem within the year. Rosa stayed behind a while longer until Oscar found a new job and then convinced her to leave hers. He told her he needed her help to reorganize the New York Nationalist chapter, which had fallen on hard times after its major leaders in Puerto Rico were sent to prison on charges of conspiracy to overthrow the United States government in Puerto Rico. A few key supporters were also sentenced to prison for evading the United States military draft. All of them were then shipped to federal penitentiaries, most often in Atlanta, Georgia and Tallahassee, Florida.[16]

After Rosa left her job, Oscar moved the family to 173 Brook Avenue in the eastern section of the Bronx, once a thriving Jewish neighborhood but which by the early 1940s was becoming a Latino enclave. Rosa soon became Oscar's right hand in his political work. During the next decade the couple's lives revolved around Oscar's work, their daughters, and their political obligations. By 1941, Rosa recalled, Oscar presided over a Bronx chapter of the New York Nationalist Junta he had organized, while she helped to recruit members, schedule meetings, and organize fundraising events for the chapter and the Nationalist Party in Puerto Rico. Within the space of two years, Oscar said, their apartment became a place of refuge for many of the Nationalists being released from federal prison. Both of them, but mostly Rosa, helped these comrades to find jobs, a place to stay, or a place to live, according to Oscar.[17]

One of those who left prison in need of help, although he never actually lived with them, was the Party's maximum leader, Pedro Albizu Campos. Released from the Atlanta Penitentiary in 1943, Albizu was in very poor health and had to be hospitalized soon after he arrived in New York. He would spend the next two years (1943-1945) confined to a room in Columbus Hospital, thanks in part to the intervention and ongoing support of Congressman Vito Marcantonio. Rosa and Oscar helped Albizu by serving as couriers between him and his followers in the Bronx, Brooklyn, and Manhattan. When Albizu left Columbus Hospital in 1945, he went to live temporarily at Juan Alamo's home, which coincidentally was located in the same building where the Collazos lived. There, according to Lydia Collazo, she and Rosa spent many hours helping to care for Albizu, whose health still remained precarious.[18]

In 1946, as Albizu's health improved, he moved to Lower Manhattan, according to Ruth Reynolds. Although the Collazo women saw much less of Albizu after he moved from the Bronx, they continued to receive updates from Oscar who met him regularly, according to Rosa. She said the two men became so close during Albizu's sojourn in New York that when he left for Puerto Rico in 1947, Oscar followed him. Oscar's plans, she explained, were to find a job in San Juan and then build a house for the family on a lot one of his sisters owned in Santurce. He found work as a translator for the news daily *El Imparcial*, but could not proceed to build the house, according to his daughter Zoraida, because his sister, also named Zoraida, "did not approve of Rosa and did not want her so close by."[19]

The Nationalists Attack Blair House: Rosa is Arrested

Unable to move his family to Puerto Rico, Oscar returned to New York and continued to devote his spare time to the Nationalist Junta, until November 1, 1950 when he was arrested for his failed attempt to kill President Truman. Oscar's actions that November created havoc for his wife and daughters, according to various press accounts. Rosa and the Collazo "girls" were detained late that afternoon and taken for interrogation to the FBI headquarters on Foley Square in Lower Manhattan.[20]

Rosa said she had been home "preparing dinner for the girls when the apartment building was surrounded by reporters, policemen, and about twenty Secret Service agents." The agents, reported Carmine Motto, Chief of the New York Secret Service sent to arrest them, arrived last on the scene, but quickly ordered the police to clear the area and cordon off the apartment building. He said he also ordered several of his agents to search the Collazo apartment. He hoped he could find evidence that could connect the women to the plot to assassinate the President, carried out that afternoon by Oscar Collazo and Griselio Torresola. But since not all the Collazo women were home when he arrived, Motto said, he chose to wait, so he could "take them downtown all at once."[21]

Fifteen-year old Zoraida had come home from school earlier that afternoon but was out on an errand for Rosa when she "learned the horrible news" from a reporter from the Spanish daily, *La Prensa*. She said he tracked her to the grocery store where she had gone to buy meat for the evening's meal. He asked her to comment on the story "that Oscar had been killed in Washington during the assault on Blair House." She yelled at him "that is totally absurd because my dad is in Puerto Rico." Stung by what he had said, she "ran home to ask Rosa." But when she reached the entrance to the apartment building where they lived, she saw "Rosa on the steps, surrounded by reporters, policemen, and nosy neighbors." Not knowing what else to do, she ran upstairs to her room and began looking through her things, "in search of a photo small enough to hide in my bobby socks, in case the police seized my stuff."[22]

She was still looking through her things "when the Secret Service agents entered the apartment with Rosa in tow and ordered the two to sit in the living room where they could keep an eye on them. Meanwhile several agents "began searching the bedrooms, bathroom, kitchen, and even the fire escape," she said. She was hungry but was "not allowed to move from the living room, to get anything to eat or drink, or even to use the bathroom." When her stepsisters returned home from work hours later, Chief Motto said he took them all away, but left a few of his men behind to guard the apartment.[23]

At Foley Square, the four women were interrogated in separate rooms for most of the night, Zoraida said. Rosa's daughters were released around dawn, she noted, but she was detained "until close to morning." Why were you detained longer than your stepsisters? I asked. "Perhaps," she replied, "because being Oscar's daughter and the youngest of the family, the agents thought they might intimidate me into revealing something they could use against my dad." She told them all she knew, which was "that Oscar had gone to Puerto Rico." She claimed during our interview that she "knew nothing that could have incriminated anyone," not even her stepmother, whom she said, she "disliked intensely." She added that while she was in the interrogation room she saw Griselio Torresola's "common-law wife, Carmen Dolores Otero (known as Carmen Torresola) as she was brought in for interrogation."[24]

According to Lydia's recollections, when she and her sisters returned home the next morning (November 2), "the apartment was in shambles." She explained, "The bed sheets were all crumpled, and every chest drawer in the bedrooms had been left open. Worst of all our food was gone." She concluded that the agents left to guard their place "ate our food and slept in our beds." Yet she was "thankful that a young agent had heeded her instructions and fed the cat and walked her dog. "The irony of it," she said, chuckling, "was that the young agent had more compassion for my pets than for me."[25]

The Women's House of Detention

For Rosa and Carmen Torresola, the interrogation at the FBI office did not go well. Accused of collaborating with their spouses in the plot to assassinate President Truman, they were sent to the Women's House of Detention in Greenwich Village the next morning. They were kept in that holding jail for nearly two months, until their case was reviewed because neither one had the resources to post bail, which had been set at $50,000 each. Rosa explained, "when we were brought to the Women's House of Detention, the morning of November 2, we were sleep-deprived, hungry, and thirsty." For Carmen, the ordeal had been much worse, she said, because she was pregnant at the time. She also had spent much of the night worrying about the little daughter she had left behind when she was arrested. She was also grieving for her dead husband.[26]

Though Rosa had worries of her own, she took comfort in the fact that her daughters were old enough (they were then in their early twenties) to fend for themselves until she returned home. Lydia Collazo recalled that she and her sister Iris "had managed" during the two months Rosa was imprisoned because of the kindness of a Jewish grocer who allowed them to buy foods on credit. She added that "some Nationalists would also come by once a week and leave us a few dollars in a sealed envelope." They shared those dollars with their mother. In another interview, Zoraida said that after Rosa was imprisoned she was removed from the Collazo apartment by one of Oscar's sisters who felt that she was "too young to be left in the care of Rosa's daughters."[27]

In her memoir, Rosa said that "life in the Women's House of Detention was a pure horror." She described the "food as inedible," so she used the funds her daughters brought her "to buy milk, juice, and cake at the commissary." At first, she said, she had eaten the oatmeal served at breakfast, but then stopped when she discovered that the "black lumps" in the bowl were "mice droppings rather than cinnamon." After that, she said, she settled for "toast and 'what passed for coffee' in that place." Lunch and dinner were "always the same: red kidney beans (to which hot dogs were occasionally added), bread, and coffee." The only time chicken, mashed potatoes, and salad were served, she said, was when important figures were expected to visit.[28]

The Women's House of Detention, she wrote, "was famous for its corruption and cruelty." That made "some women so angry one time that they set fire to their beds," she said. "One had to stay alert not to be wounded in that place." Boredom was another major problem, which she and Carmen tried to combat by knitting and taking walks around the enclosed roof deck during recess.[29]

In regards to the registration process, she said, "after the routine exams and enema, I was taken to a cell." Two other detainees brought in around the same time as Carmen and Rosa left more explicit accounts of the way the House of Detention welcomed the new inmates. According to labor activist Elizabeth Gurley Flynn, every prisoner brought to the House of Detention "was fingerprinted and registered by the admitting guard." Next, she was "taken to a room where she was asked to strip off her street clothes, which were then shoved into a bag," where they were expected to remain until she was let out. After that, added Miriam Moskowitz (who also spent time in that jail in the 1950s), the newcomer was subjected "to a body search in which every orifice of her body was poked and prodded, (on the pretext) that the she might be hiding drugs." Next, she was ordered to "lie down on a metal table for the routine pelvic examination and enema." After the routine exam was completed the prisoner was instructed to shower, "before she was issued a uniform." Once newly clothed, she was led to a storage room, where she was handed "a thin mattress, a blanket, sheets, and a pillow case." Carrying all that gear on her arms, "the newcomer was led to a cellblock upstairs, where another guard escorted her to her assigned cell." That last guard kept watch until the newcomer made her bed. Once in the cell, the detainee was left alone with absolutely nothing to do, except wait until she was released on bail, or summoned by the judge appointed to the case, Rosa explained. All were allowed visitors and meetings with their lawyers, if they had them. Neither Rosa nor Carmen had funds to hire legal representation or post bail, so they remained behind bars until December 1950 when they were released.[30]

What Rosa remembered best about that jail in New York was the noise, which made it nearly impossible for her to sleep during the first few nights she was there. Again, Gurley Flynn and Moskowitz explain the noise was in part due to the location of the jail, which lay on a busy thoroughfare, at the corner of Greenwich and Avenue of the Americas, in Greenwich Village. "The area," according to Moskowitz, "was known for the many businesses which stayed open late at night; their flashing neon signs a painful reminder of the free world [one] had left behind." The loud exchanges of patrons and the happy banter of passersby, said Gurley Flynn, contributed to the hubbub which kept the newcomers awake.[31]

In Rosa's case, she remembered being jolted awake by screams coming from the floor below. Neighboring cellmates, who slept through the night, explained the following morning that those came from "the newly admitted drug addicts." They yelled, they said, because they were enraged because they were "forced to sleep on the bare floor until they adjusted." According to Rosa, "the poor women were hosed down and then left shivering in their own wet mess if they complained." She described the Women's House of Detention as "hell on earth."[32]

The one pleasant memory she recalled from her time there was meeting Ethel Rosenberg. Ethel, she said, was a "sweet-natured woman" who sometimes sang to help ease the fear young women felt when they first came in. Ethel, she remembered, "nearly went mad with grief when she learned that her two sons had been removed from her mother's house by New York's Department of Social Services," after she and Julius were indicted. Yet despite her grief and legal problems, "Ethel always found time to counsel me and others not to lose faith in the American justice system," Rosa added. "She would try to cheer me up," saying Oscar would not be executed. "Ironically," Rosa said sadly, "the same justice system in which she placed so much faith had her and Julius executed a few years later."[33]

Rosa is Set Free

On December 23, 1950 Rosa and Carmen Torresola were released from the House of Detention when the judge assigned to review their case ruled that the prosecution had failed to make its case. Once free, Rosa joined the Pro-Oscar Collazo Defense Committee, founded during her absence by Luisa Quintero and other New York Latino leaders. The immediate goal of the Committee, she recalled, was to get Oscar's death sentence commuted. With the help of her daughters and many supporters from different corners of the world, the Committee gathered about 100,000 signatures in less than two years, she said. After he received the first 50,000 signatures, President Truman signed an order (July 24, 1952) commuting Oscar's death sentence to one of life in prison.[34]

Coincidentally, the next day (July 25, 1952), the island would be celebrating its new status as the Commonwealth of Puerto Rico, the Estado Libre Asociado (ELA). Part of that day's ceremony included flying the Puerto Rican flag (for which many Nationalists had been arrested) along-side the American flag from every public building in Puerto Rico. Through that act the local rulers intended to dispel the image that the island was a colony of the United States, as it had been during the pre-vious fifty-four years. For Oscar and his nuclear family, to have his life spared on the day that their beloved flag was being usurped by the same government that still kept so many of his comrades in jail was "a bitter-sweet pill to swallow," according to his daughter, Zoraida.[35]

During the two years Oscar remained in prison in Washington, D.C., Rosa visited him once a week, but after his death sentence was com-muted and he was transferred to the federal penitentiary in Atlanta, Georgia, and later to Leavenworth, Kansas, she could only visit once or twice a year because she either had to work or lacked the funds to un-dertake the journey. Though finding a job and keeping it was always a challenge, with the FBI on her heels, she managed to rebuild her life, help her daughters, and continue to work with other Nationalists in New York.[36]

The Nationalist Attack on Congress: Rosa is Arrested Again

On March 1, 1954 four Nationalists from New York City attacked the United States Congress, and Rosa's life unraveled once again. She was at work the day Dolores (Lolita) Lebrón and three male companions en-tered the Visitor's Gallery of the House of Representatives and sprayed the place with bullets, wounding five congressmen. She guessed that it would be a matter of hours before the Secret Service agents came to arrest her, for she was at this time "Secretary of the Women's Section and Treas-urer of the New York Nationalist Junta." To her surprise, five days passed before three Secret Servicemen arrived with orders to take her to the FBI office "downtown" for questioning. After the interrogation she was sent to the Women's House of Detention. Before the agents arrived, she said, she had time to remove many documents which could have been used incriminate her or others in the Party. But she still had in her possession $300 in cash she had collected in fees and donations from members and supporters. Fearing the agents might pocket the money, she asked them to record the existence of the funds, so she could reclaim them when she was released later. It is not clear whether she ever recovered the funds.[37]

Unlike the arrest of 1950, this time she was held for nearly seven months before her case came up for review. According to an article in the *New York Times*, Rosa was one of ninety-one Nationalists who were subpoenaed by three Federal Grand Juries, which began hearing depositions on March 8, 1954. Most of the detainees in this case were released, but Rosa was among the thirteen who were indicted, convicted, and sentenced to prison. Originally the indicted group consisted of seventeen (including the four attackers of Congress) and all were expected to be tried at once. But then four in the group, including Lolita Lebrón's brother, Gonzalo Lebrón, chose to collaborate with the prosecution (first in New York and later in Puerto Rico) and they were tried separately the following spring. The four collaborators (all members of the Nationalist Junta in Chicago) were later rewarded with reduced or suspended sentences. Of the thirteen tried and convicted for violations of the Smith Act, three were women (Lolita Lebrón, Rosa Collazo, and Carmen Torresola). Two of them were well known to the FBI.[38]

In Rosa's case specifically, the FBI office in New York City had recently received a report from the Internal Security (I.S.) division in Puerto Rico, stating that she had last visited Pedro Albizu Campos in February 1954. Rosa, like many other Nationalists in Puerto Rico, had a police file or *carpeta* (#11989). She was closely trailed by local I.S. agents and watched by their informants during that visit to the island in 1954. In fact, her dossier was regularly updated until the day she died more than thirty years later.[39]

In addition to sharing their surveillance reports with various intelligence-gathering agencies in the United States, the Puerto Rican I.S. also reported their findings to the office of the local governor. Thus, it is not surprising that on April 19, 1954, Police Chief Salvador T. Roig reported to Governor Luis Muñoz Marín that Mr. Courtney E. Owens, a member of the "House (Velde) Committee on Un-American Activities," had visited his office on March 5, 1954, to request access to the Department's files on stateside Puerto Rican Nationalists. He said he gave Mr. Owens access to 108 dossiers as well as an office in which to review them. But to his surprise Mr. Owens had chosen only "eleven files" none of which included "Rosa Collazo's or Ruth Reynolds' files."[40]

In her memoirs, Rosa wrote she had in fact visited Albizu in February 1954 because she had wanted to see for herself "the physical state he was in after all he had endured in prison." She was "appalled," she said, "to find him bedridden and with so many parts of his body charred due to the radiation experiments." She made no mention of what they discussed that day or repeated any instructions he might have given. Yet an informant who worked close to her in the Nationalist Junta reported to the FBI that Rosa was the person who brought the news of Lolita Lebrón's appointment to replace Julio Pinto Gandía for the position of Nationalist Party Delegate for the United States. The informant (believed to be Raymond Sánchez Sorrel) also said that Rosa "was probably the messenger who brought Albizu's orders for the attack on the United States Congress."[41]

Yet in an interview Lolita Lebrón granted shortly after she was released from prison in 1979, all she admitted was that she had followed the "leaders' orders." She did not specify which leaders had given the order for the attack on Congress or reveal who brought it. Her brother Gonzalo Lebrón (head of the Nationalist Junta of Chicago until May 1954) testified the following November that "Albizu must have been the leader who gave the order because nothing of that magnitude would ever take place without his approval." It is possible that Gonzalo Lebrón was trying to protect his sister by shifting the blame for the attack on Congress to Albizu Campos. In another portion of the testimony he gave to the Puerto Rican Police on November 6, 1954, he said that the two persons who brought him the news about the "need to attack key places within the United States" were Albizu's legal counsel Juan Hernández Vallé and Isabel Rosado Morales.[42]

But before the contents of Gonzalo Lebrón's testimonies became known, the FBI insisted that Rosa Collazo was the one who brought the orders for the attack on Congress. Hence, it is not surprising that Rosa as well as Carmen Torresola were indicted on charges of conspiring with the attackers, a violation of the Smith Act. They were convicted and sentenced to prison for their crime. Carmen Torresola was sentenced to four years while Lolita Lebrón and Rosa Collazo were each sentenced to six years. All three women were then sent to serve their terms at the Federal Reformatory for Women in Alderson, West Virginia.[43]

Life at the Alderson Prison

The trip from New York City to Alderson, West Virginia, according to Rosa Collazo, took approximately twelve hours by rail, from seven in the evening to seven the following morning. She and Carmen Torresola, she recalled, were placed together in a train cabin that contained four beds. One of the beds was occupied by a female guard escorting them while a male guard in the group occupied a bed in the adjoining cabin, Rosa said.[44]

The admission process at Alderson prison, according to Gurley Flynn and Moskowitz, also sent there, involved not only the "standard welcoming routine of strip and search for drugs, enema, and shower," but several other indignities. Gurley Flynn explained that a new prisoner at Alderson "had to be 'deloused' either by having their hair washed with a 'delousing shampoo,' or 'doused with DDT,' a chemical she was not allowed to wash off for the next forty-eight hours." In addition to the delousing, any new piece of clothing the newcomer brought was "submerged in a vat of cold water," a method the guards used "to erase any secret writing the article might contain." Once the admission process was completed, the newcomer was "locked up in an isolation cell for three consecutive weeks," in what was known as an "adjustment period" or "the quarantine." During this period, the inmate had her meals, which generally consisted of black coffee and peanut butter sandwiches, sent to her cell.[45]

Both Rosa and Carmen apparently survived the quarantine period fairly intact compared to others who were so weakened by the experience they had to be hospitalized when they were let out. What Rosa liked least about the quarantine, she said, was "the lack of contact with other human beings for so many days." To combat the loneliness and boredom that crept in, she said, she knitted for days on end. Apparently Carmen did the same since she later sold the items she had knitted during this period in the prison shop. The cash generated by those sales, Rosa explained, was used to purchase toiletries and food supplements at the commissary.[46]

She recalled that the cottage (#16) where she did her quarantine had a bed, a toilet, and a metal chest of drawers anchored to one wall. No mirrors were allowed in any part of the prison, she said, for fear they could be turned into weapons by the inmates. Luckily, her isolation cell had a window, though heavily screened and barred, which allowed her to listen to the birds that congregated in the backyard. Occasionally, she fantasized about what she would do and say when she rejoined Carmen and Lolita or when she met Blanca Canales, "the heroine of the Jayuya uprising." It took four weeks before she saw all of them at a Sunday Mass. With guards overseeing the religious service, she said, they barely had enough time to exchange greetings and tell each other the number of the cottage in which they lived. Since the prison had placed them far from one another, they agreed that the best way to keep in touch was to attend Sunday Mass and find a way to coordinate their trips to the commissary.[47]

There was no cell available when Rosa finished her quarantine, so she was sent to the open gallery, "with twenty other noisy inmates." By then Rosa was nearly fifty-one years old and hated noise. Worse than the noise, she said, was the "verbal abuse and sexual advances" she had to contend with in that place, a hurdle she apparently had not encountered in the New York prison. She said she dreaded the nights in the open gallery because that was when the bullies often went on their "rampage of immoral behavior." This was also the time when "fights and love quarrels broke out." Fearing that she might be hurt if she fell asleep, she said, she stayed up reading or knitting. But even that strategy proved unsuccessful because then some of the women began accusing her of "acting aloof and superior." She decided to appeal to the bullies' sense of compassion, explaining that she "did not feel superior" but was simply trying not to run afoul of the guards because she was "a political prisoner." Aware that compassion might not last, she tried to appease the bullies by sharing her toiletries and buying them cigarettes at the commissary. Though the latter strategies gradually paid off, she was delighted when she was assigned to a private cell a month later.[48]

In addition, she was thankful to be assigned to the sewing room where she would later reunite with Carmen and Lolita. Her job in the sewing room, she recalled, was to retrofit the dresses and coats of the inmates scheduled to be released. Blanca Canales, she learned later, was working in the weaving room, making curtains and decorative table runners for the prison. Lolita, the most talented seamstress among them, had at first been sent to do maintenance work. When she fell ill from the strain of the hard work, Rosa said she wrote to Conrad Lynn (Lolita's lawyer) and asked him to intercede. Apparently, he appealed her case because she was then transferred to the sewing room, where she soon dazzled every-one with the beautiful hats and embroidered garments she made for the women who were returning home.[49]

Among the women she met at Alderson were: Elizabeth Gurley Flynn and her comrades Alice Garnet and Claudia Jones also convicted of hav-ing violated the Smith Act. Gurley Flynn, she said, moved to the Soviet Union soon after she was released from Alderson and died there a few years later. She recalled attending a memorial organized on her behalf by her friends in New York. Claudia Jones, a native of Trinidad, a self-avowed Communist and a close friend of Gurley Flynn, was deported to London shortly after she arrived in Alderson, Rosa said. In London, ac-cording to her biographer, Carol Boyce Davis, Jones published a news-paper and became a leading figure within the Pan-African-Caribbean independence movements. Jones died in London in 1964 while Alice Garnet, according to Rosa, died in New York City a few years after her release from Alderson prison.[50]

Of the Puerto Rican group at Alderson, Rosa was the third to be re-leased from prison. Blanca Canales left first in 1956. She was transferred to the women's prison in Vega Alta, Puerto Rico, to begin serving a life sentence for a murder she had not committed. Carmen Torresola finished her four-year sentence shortly after Blanca left and returned to New York City. When it came Rosa's turn to leave, she said, she was sad to leave Lolita, even though by then (1959) Lolita had learned to cope with the harshness of prison life. Her devotion to her faith, her altar, her creative sewing, and her poetry, Rosa explained, would help Lolita to survive the daily strains of the long sentence ahead. (Lolita spent another twenty years at Alderson after Rosa left.)[51]

Life as a Free Woman

Rosa returned to the Bronx, in 1959, eager to find paid employment and resume her political work. Yet both tasks would prove difficult at first because she left prison with serious health issues that required immedi-ate medical attention. She had to have an ovarian tumor removed, as soon as she returned to the Bronx. Without a job or medical insurance, she lacked the means to pay for the surgery and became a charity case at Lebanon Hospital in the Bronx. She said the experience was "painful and traumatic," because she was not given sufficient anesthesia and woke up while the doctors were still stitching the wound. Shortly after that ordeal she had to undergo another surgery, this time to remove a salivary gland that had become infected.[52]

Not quite recovered from the second surgery, she had to fly to Puerto Rico, to attend to her mother who had fallen ill and had been taken to the Mayagüez public hospital. She booked a flight though she "could barely walk" and had to be hospitalized soon after she landed in Puerto Rico. Fortunately, she said, she was taken to the Aguadilla municipal hospital, where the attending physician was a recent immigrant from Cuba who was not yet familiar with her political history. Because of that fortuitous situation, she said, he not only admitted her, but treated her rather well during her stay at the hospital. He told her she had an "infection from the last surgery" and he would need to reopen and clean the wound before he could administer antibiotics to let it heal. She recalled that during the week she was at the hospital, the doctor would "come by daily to practice the few English words he knew." She credits him for saving her life even though that surgery left her face partially paralyzed. Her main complaint about the Aguadilla hospital, she said, was the food, a meager fare of coffee and bread for breakfast, and rice and beans for lunch and dinner (a diet similar to the one fed to inmates in the island's prisons.)[53]

Once released from the Aguadilla hospital she spent a week recovering at her mother's place before she flew back to the Bronx to resume her life. She lived in the same neighborhood until 1968 when she moved permanently to Puerto Rico. She worked at various jobs during the next decade and took time out to visit Oscar in Leavenworth, Kansas. In addition to her work with the Nationalist Chapter in New York, she also collaborated with various civic and political groups. In 1965, for example, she marched in front of the United Nations to protest the United States invasion of the Dominican Republic. In the early 1960s, she tried to make contact with Fidel Castro when he came to the United Nations. She was unsuccessful, she explained, even though she had followed Castro to the Hotel Teresa in Harlem. She was luckier and "thrilled" beyond words, when she met Ernesto "Che" Guevara years later when he came to speak at the United Nations.[54]

In 1968 Rosa was sixty-four years old and looking forward to retirement. After forty-four years in New York, she felt it was time to return to Puerto Rico to spend time with her aging mother. She was also tired of menial jobs and ready to leave that struggle behind. The neighborhood where she had lived for nearly three decades had deteriorated and she no longer felt safe. By then her oldest daughter Iris was happily married and her youngest, Lydia, a single parent, had said she was willing join her so that she could raise her only son in Puerto Rico. There wasn't any reason to tarry, so she moved temporarily with her mother while she looked for a home for her entire family. Lydia arrived in 1969 and with the help of Iris and her husband Rosa purchased a house in Levittown, a suburb of Cataño, a municipality across the San Juan Bay. Once they settled into the new house they brought Rosa's mother (Doña Juana) to live with them. Having her mother and grandmother at home was a relief for Lydia who needed care for her son while she went out to work and study.[55]

For Rosa, who did not drive, the move to Cataño made sense, for it allowed her to commute by ferry to meet friends and comrades and attend political meetings and rallies. One who always seemed ready to drive Rosa to political events was Blanca Canales, her old pal from the Alderson prison days. (Canales was pardoned and released from prison in August 1967.) Rosa's health continued to be a challenge and during the 1970s she had to undergo treatment for breast cancer. Yet despite her declining health, she continued to do political work and to advocate for the release of Nationalists prisoners. In addition, she joined the Vieques' struggle to oust the U.S. Navy from its soil. In 1976, she began writing her memoirs.[56]

Oscar Collazo is Released from Prison

On September 8, 1979, Rosa felt her prayers had been answered when she learned the news that Oscar Collazo would be one of the four Nationalist prisoners to be released two days later on a pardon issued by President Jimmy Carter. Andrés Figueroa Cordero, one of the four who attacked the United States Congress in 1954, had been released the previous year because he was dying of cancer. The news of the "heroes" impending release, Rosa said, threw their supporters in San Juan, Chicago, and New York into a gleeful uproar and rushed preparations to welcome them back to freedom.[57]

She and a few friends met that evening in San Juan to plan their own welcoming reception for the four. By dawn, they had agreed to travel to the United States to be the first to greet their "heroes" as they were released. Though elated by the news and the plans discussed by her friends, she was also mortified by the fact that she did not have the funds to fly to Kansas to escort Oscar home. A comrade who noticed her distress, offered to pay her expenses, while another went to search for a coat she could use. Her daughter Lydia packed a bag for her. Too excited to sleep, Rosa spent the rest of the night at a friend's house near the airport, thinking of the joy ahead once Oscar was again at her side. In that state of heightened expectation she arrived in Leavenworth, Kansas on September 9 eager to welcome Oscar back into her life.[58]

The morning Oscar was released (September 10) fifty persons, including friends, relatives and several journalists stood outside the Leavenworth penitentiary ready to greet him, according to Rosa. A few in the group were waving a huge Puerto Rican flag and shouting "Viva Puerto Rico Libre." After an impromptu news conference outside the prison, the group flew to St. Louis, Missouri, where they were scheduled to meet Irving Flores and Rafael Cancel Miranda, also pardoned, before proceeding to Chicago's O'Hare airport, where Lolita Lebrón would join them for a joint press conference and several public appearances in the city's Puerto Rican neighborhood, according to Miñi Seijo, who covered the event for the newsweekly *Claridad*.[59]

After the press conference at O'Hare, the four were escorted to a sumptuous dinner given in their honor by friends and Nationalist leaders in Chicago. They were then driven to The First Congregationalist Church in the Puerto Rican neighborhood, where Reverend José Torres, whose son was then being tried for political crimes, welcomed them, according to Rosa. "The church was so packed with well-wishers," she said, "that thousands had to wait outside." After basking in their compatriots' love, and answering many of their questions, the four were finally allowed to get some rest at the various homes which had invited them. Rosa and Oscar, for example, were taken to the Pastor's home. Much too excited to sleep, Rosa said, she spent the night relishing the joy of the day's events.[60]

"Clinging" to her beloved Oscar, she said she followed "the four to New York City, where thousands more, including (her) daughter Iris, lined the streets of El Barrio, the Bronx, and Lower Manhattan in their eagerness to welcome them." Rather than disappoint anyone, the four opted to split up, two of them (Oscar and Lolita) went to the United Nations where the Cuban delegation had organized a press conference and the other two (Irving and Rafael) went to an event organized by Nationalist comrades. Rosa, who followed Oscar and Lolita to the United Nations, recalled feeling proud of the way they handled the tough questions they were asked by unsympathetic reporters. She lamented not having a tape recorder to record the exchanges. (Miñi Seijo, who covered the event for the newsweekly, *Claridad,* left a vivid account of the exchanges.) That evening, after another festive dinner, the four and their entourage were received at the Church of Saint Paul in East Harlem by its pastor, Antonio Stevens Arroyo.[61]

The following day (September 12, 1979), the four and their entourage flew to San Juan, Puerto Rico. During the flight they were again asked many questions by the reporters on board. Rosa was particularly moved by the reply Oscar gave to a reporter, who asked him: "Why did you marry Rosa?" He replied, "Because she is a Nationalist of high moral standards, faithful to her ideals ... and who as an ex-political prisoner understands our sacrifice."[62]

She said she was also proud of Lolita, who "distributed copies of 'La Borinqueña' (the island's national anthem) to all on board and led the singing when they landed in San Juan's airport." Again, she was happily surprised to see so many thousands lining Avenida Baldorioty de Castro (the road connecting the airport to Old San Juan) and hundreds more already waiting at the Old City's tiny cemetery when they arrived in the afternoon to pay homage to their late leader Pedro Albizu Campos. She marveled at "how eager they all were to shake hands with the 'four patriots' who had so valiantly fought for the island's independence." She, too, "felt enormously grateful for what they had done, and began praying silently by Albizu's tomb that his prediction would come true." He had told her many times, "Puerto Rico's independence will follow shortly after my death." In 1979, Albizu had been dead a little more than fourteen years. Rosa was in poor health and nearing her seventy-fifth birthday.[63]

The evening of September 12 Oscar, Rosa and several others were treated to another welcoming dinner at a friend's home. Rosa sat next to Oscar, as she had done since the morning of his release, patiently waiting for the moment when she could take him 'home' to Cataño. But before the dinner ended, he made a telephone call and then announced that he would be staying with his daughter Zoraida from then on. "Stunned and heartbroken by the unexpected news," Rosa returned home alone and "would not see Oscar again for another year and a half." When he finally "deemed to return" to her, she told him, "It's too late. We will never again live as husband and wife." They remained friends, she said, and always comrades, for they continued to share the same political beliefs that had brought them together forty years earlier. They met often at Party activities and joined forces with various progressive groups endeavoring to bring social justice to the downtrodden in Puerto Rico and elsewhere. They also never stopped supporting the beleaguered Nationalist Party.[64]

On September 16, 1984, a group of friends and supporters held a reception in honor of Rosa and other Nationalist women who had given their lives to the struggle of Puerto Rico's independence. The activity, which was held at Colegio de Abogados de Puerto Rico (Puerto Rico's Bar Association) in San Juan, also celebrated Rosa's 80th birthday. Through the night friends and comrades offered testimonies of her devotion to the cause of Puerto Rico's freedom during fifty years of struggle. One of the many heart-felt tributes of that evening was the one pronounced by her husband Oscar Collazo.[65]

Rosa died on May 3, 1988, three months short of her eighty-fourth birthday. She died as she had lived, totally committed to the ideals of Puerto Rican independence. During the last twenty years of her life, she had lived in relative peace, in her beloved homeland, surrounded by her loving family, devoted friends and loyal comrades.[66] She was survived by her daughters Iris and Lydia, her grandson Carlos, and her great granddaughter Karla. Her husband Oscar Collazo died in February 1994 six years after she did.

2. Dolores (Lolita) Lebrón Soto
(1919–2010)

Preface

Dolores (Lolita) Lebrón is probably the best-known Puerto Rican Nationalist woman of the twentieth century. She rose to world attention on March 1, 1954, for her leading role in the attack on the House of Representatives of the United States Congress. She told the arresting authorities and the reporters who questioned her that she was "responsible" for planning and launching the attack that left five congressmen wounded. She didn't waver from that story of self-claimed responsibility during the twenty-five years she spent in a federal prison in West Virginia. Others, including her brother Gonzalo Lebrón, who turned state witness for the prosecution shortly after his arrest, would tell a slightly different story.

In September 1979, Lolita and two of her companions were released from prison on a presidential pardon granted by President Jimmy Carter. Andrés Figueroa Cordero, Lolita's third companion in the 1954 shooting, had been released months earlier because he was dying of cancer. Also released on the same day was Oscar Collazo, another Puerto Rican Nationalist who had been serving a life sentence in Leavenworth, Kansas for his attack of Blair House on November 1, 1950. After a heroes' welcome by thousands of admirers and fellow Nationalists in Chicago and New York City, the four pardoned by President Carter returned to Puerto Rico to live out the rest of their lives.

The following account provides a short profile of Lolita's life before and after her signature act of 1954. It explores the motivations that led her to join the Puerto Rican Nationalist Party in New York City in 1947 and the effects her decisions had on her life and the lives of her family. While her attack on Congress brought her instant worldwide recognition, it also brought her a long prison sentence of fifty-six years. She served twenty-five years of her sentence at the federal women's prison in Alderson, West Virginia before she was pardoned and released in 1979.

Lolita Lebrón getting arrested in Washington, D.C. March 1, 1954.

As she told journalist Federico Ribes Tovar during her first known interview in 1974, the worst part about her imprisonment was "being isolated from my family, my comrades, and my friends." Despite the loving recognition she enjoyed after her release, she said, that when she first went to prison she felt that everyone seemed to have forgotten her.[1]

Coming of Age in Lares, Puerto Rico

Dolores (Lolita) Lebrón Soto was born in barrio Pezuelas, in the western municipality of Lares, Puerto Rico, on November 19, 1919. Her father, Gonzalo Lebrón Bernal, worked at first as a day laborer in the coffee farms in the region, but at some point during Lolita's childhood he was promoted to the job of foreman, according to his great granddaughter, Irene Vilar. Lolita's mother, Rafaela Soto Luciano, stayed home to care for the couple's children.[2]

In her 1974 interview, Lolita recalled her childhood as "if it were a dream." She described a time when she contracted pneumonia during early childhood and had to be treated by the local pharmacist because the town did not have a doctor. As a result of that illness, she said, her respiratory system became compromised and she was no longer able to run or climb rocks and trees, as she had done earlier. The forced inactivity, she said, made her "an observant, dreamy child," two qualities that would help her later when she became a poet. She recalled "falling in love with nature, my homeland and my people at an early age." She remembered the sense of awe she felt the very first time she saw the sea.[3]

She began school at age six, and distinctly recalled being led there by her first-grade teacher, a boarder in her home. While she was still in elementary school, the family moved to barrio Mirasol, Lares, where her father took a job as foreman in a coffee hacienda. She graduated sixth grade from the Mariana Bracetti Elementary School and confessed leaving the place without knowing who Mariana Bracetti was or what role her hometown (Lares) had played in the uprising of 1868. It seems that she learned about the importance of both much later when she joined the Nationalist Party Junta in New York. Bracetti, as most independence advocates know, sewed the revolutionary flag for the first Puerto Rican Republic proclaimed in Lares (September 23, 1868).[4]

When Lolita Lebrón completed the sixth grade her father agreed to send her to middle school in another barrio of Lares, even though the decision entailed a financial sacrifice for him, as he would have to pay for her transportation to and from school. She graduated eighth grade (1933) in the midst of the Great Economic Depression, a crisis that solidified the island's poverty after thirty-five years of exploitative colonial policies. In addition to the man-made economic woes, the island was suffering the devastating effects of two major hurricanes (1928 and 1932), which left hundreds of people dead and over two hundred thousand homeless. Yet despite his own economic hardships, Lolita's father found a way to send her to study fashion in San Juan. He seemed intent on giving his daughter a chance for a better life than he had known.

His plans, however, came crashing down when he was diagnosed with advanced tuberculosis. She was asked to return home, to help care for him in order to shield her mother and younger siblings from his illness. Lolita told her interviewer that her father had succumbed to the dreadful disease because "of the lack of timely medical attention." No longer able to work during the last stages of his illness, her father not only "lost his job, but the humble house the hacienda provided for the family." Her family, she said, would have been homeless had it not been for a kind uncle who gave them shelter until her brothers, Agustín and Julio, were able to find work and a place to live for the family.[5]

Though her father had never been more than a nominal Catholic, he did an extraordinary thing just before he died. According to Lolita, he arranged to marry his wife Rafaela Soto in the Catholic Church in town and to have all of their children baptized. He and Rafaela had married years earlier in a Protestant Church, but that was, Lolita said, because the town priest had not been available the day they had chosen to marry. This time, however, her father arranged for the priest to perform the two ceremonies on the same day. Regrettably, Lolita said, her father died the following day. He was just forty-two years old and, Lolita not quite eighteen the year he died (1937), according to his great granddaughter, Irene Vilar. After his death, his sons found work and moved the family to a farm in Castañer, Lares.[6]

Lolita was a beautiful girl who drew the attention of one young man in town. "Being young and inexperienced," she said, she soon had her heart broken. In 1933, at age fourteen, she was courted by eighteen-year-old Francisco Matos Paoli, a suitor well above her social station. Ostensibly, he became quite smitten by her beauty and began to write her love poems and impassioned letters. She fell madly in love with the young bard and spent her days daydreaming about him. As rumors of their budding romance spread through the sleepy town, his family became alarmed and sent him off to school in San Juan. The move soon had the desired effect, and before long he had stopped writing to her altogether.[7]

Heart-broken but still hopeful, she dreamt of seeing him at least one more time. Perhaps, she thought, he would come running to see her the minute he learned that she, too, had come to San Juan. It did not happen. In fact, she would not hear from Matos Paoli again until after she was sentenced to prison in 1954. By then Matos Paoli had become a well-known college professor and respected poet. He had also married the fiery Nationalist Isabel Freyre. Like Lolita, he had joined the Nationalists Party and had spent time in prison, on charges of having conspired with Albizu Campos and others to depose the United States government in Puerto Rico by force and violence. After Lolita was sentenced to prison for her role in the attack on Congress, Matos Paoli would again write poems to her in which he celebrated their earlier love.[8]

At eighteen, Lolita had blossomed into a beautiful young woman and her home town crowned her "Queen of the Flowers of May," in the annual celebration of its patron saint, the Virgin Mary. That distinction soon caught the attention of her brothers' boss in Castañer, the agronomist Francisco (Paco) Méndez, a well-educated man, with a degree from Columbia University. He had recently been sent to the area to administer a government farm. Lolita's family thought he was a "good catch" and encouraged the love affair, according to what she told her interviewer.[9]

Deprived of "my father's guidance," she said, she fell in love once again and this time got into bigger trouble than just a broken heart. After a year of courtship, she moved in with Paco Méndez to a place in San Juan, which had been rented and furnished for her by her cousin, Luis Sotomayor. As Sotomayor told Irene Vilar in an interview years later, "Don Paco" had given him money to set Lolita up in a modest place in barrio Obrero (a working-class neighborhood) in Santurce because by then "Lolita was already pregnant." He added that the romance between Lolita and Don Paco ended about a month after she gave birth to Gladys Mirna (Irene Vilar's mother) because Lolita had "a bad temper" and did not like being left alone in San Juan so she opted to return home to Lares. Her "quasi-husband," as Vilar called him, "wouldn't acknowledge the child though he occasionally sent a check for her."[10]

With two additional mouths to feed, the Lebrón family's economic hardships multiplied, and Lolita, ashamed and heart-broken, chose to leave town and leave her daughter in the care of her mother in Lares. She set out on April, 1941 in hopes of finding work which would allow her to support herself and her child and help her widowed mother who still had young children of her own to raise.[11]

For a woman of rural Puerto Rico in the 1940s the best place to find work was New York City. "With great sadness in her heart," she asked her brother Agustín to take her to the San Juan port. He left her there, she said, with the mildly reassuring words: "If you don't like it, you can always come back." She was not yet twenty-one years old when she boarded the "Coamo" headed for New York, where she arrived on April 28, 1941.[12]

Lolita in Manhattan: Joining the Nationalist Party

Upon her arrival in New York City, in the spring of 1940, she moved into a relative's home in one of the overcrowded tenements typically occupied by Puerto Ricans in East Harlem. Though she knew little English and lacked employment experience, she had good sewing skills and soon found employment in the garment industry. The problem, she told her interviewer, was not finding work, but keeping the jobs she found because she hated "the appalling working conditions" and the shabby fashion in which she and her fellow workers were treated. The unfair labor practices and rampant discrimination, she added, "provoked my rebellious nature."[13]

At some point during that first year she tried her luck in Chicago. "But that city wasn't any better," so she returned to New York, where, she "soon met and married a man whose name I'd rather forget," she said. She divorced him after a few years but took custody of their son Félix. After that failed romance, she resolved "to avoid all future romantic entanglements, and devote myself to a bigger love: the liberation of Puerto Rico."[14]

Then in 1948 she took Félix to Puerto Rico and left him in Lares with her mother. Coincidentally, 1948 was the first time she saw her daughter since she had left her behind eight years earlier, according to Irene Vilar. Why did Lolita leave her son in Lares? According to what she told her interviewer, her life had become "very difficult and there were nights I went to bed hungry." Her sister Aurea Lebrón, many years younger than Lolita, speculated that she had left her son in Lares because "she was already deeply involved with the Nationalists in New York City." Her cousin, Luis Sotomayor concurred, stating that by the time Lolita left Félix in Lares she "had divorced her husband Anderson Pérez and was deeply involved with the 'damned [Nationalist] Party'." He makes it clear that neither he nor Lolita's ex-husband (a friend of his) had wanted anything to do with the Nationalist Party.[15]

Lolita Lebrón explained to her interviewer that she had begun attending Nationalist Junta meetings in Manhattan in 1946, when "my son was a bit grown," but had not joined the Nationalist Party officially or taken its oath until 1947. She said she was brought to the Junta meetings by a neighbor, Doña Mercedes Villanueva. The latter was one of dozens of

Puerto Rican women in New York City who were either members or affiliates of the Nationalist Party during the 1940s, according to researcher Sandra Morales Blanes.[16]

Why did Lolita join the Nationalist Party? She did not initially provide a precise answer when the question was posed to her by Ribes Tovar. Instead, she recited a long list of grievances she had observed or experienced since she landed in New York many years earlier. She said she had grown tired of the daily humiliations she experienced and felt badly that she and her compatriots had had to leave their homeland in search of work, only to land in a place that did not want them. It pained her also to see the "disintegration of the Puerto Rican families as women had to go to work in order to remedy the poverty of their households." She added that she was especially bothered by "the oppression of Puerto Rican women, who in addition to caring for their homes and families had to go out to work and then come home to put up with difficult husbands." Joining the Nationalist Party appealed to Lolita because of its promises. Its leaders claimed that a free Puerto Rico "would not have to export its poor," because there would be work for everyone at home. The free homeland the Nationalists envisioned would also create "a just society in which women, children and the poor would be able to thrive."[17]

In another portion of the interview, she said, she joined the Nationalist Party because she was "ready to be faithful to God, to my homeland, and to Don Pedro Albizu Campos, all at once." And though she was already "tired of the lies of men," she believed Albizu Campos was "the perfect man one could love unconditionally, the way one loves Christ." She joined the Party, she added, because "I loved my homeland as one loves God [and] could love Albizu Campos as God's incarnation on earth. I was ready to follow him without questioning his orders." Asked by the interviewer, "Did you meet Albizu Campos while he was in New York?" "No," she replied, but that "did not deter me from my path. I did not need to see him or speak to him face-to-face or listen to any of his speeches to know what he meant."[18]

Was she aware that Albizu's religious conversion to the Catholic Faith occurred during his student days at Harvard University? She does not say. Her remarks only suggest that she shared his religious beliefs in the Catholic faith. Like many in his camp, she considered Catholicism an essential part of the Puerto Rican identity. It is not clear whether Albizu saw the Catholic religion as a rallying cause in the struggle for liberation against the Protestant faith being spread by the American colonizers. That is something he probably had learned from the Irish nationalists he came in contact with, according to his friend and colleague Juan Antonio Corretjer. Lolita also believed that the island's Catholic Church would guide them to create the compassionate, just society "God had intended." And though she would have preferred to have the Nationalists achieve their goal via peaceful means, her leaders had learned from history "that armed struggle could not be discarded when the enemy insisted on blocking the path to freedom."[19]

By the time Lolita took the Nationalist oath in New York City in 1947, she also shared with Albizu Campos and others the ideal of "self-sacrifice." She explained that she admired Albizu Campos "because he had sacrificed himself for his homeland." First, he had "sacrificed a potentially profitable career as a lawyer by devoting himself to the cause of Puerto Rico's liberation." That in turn had cost him his personal freedom, his health, and eventually his life, she said. He had lived "a life of poverty and persecution," for his commitment to the struggle, yet he never once abandoned the idea of freeing his people or betrayed his ideals," she added. That selfless devotion, in her view, made Albizu Campos "a man of integrity, a model for the 'new man' the island needed if it intended to forge ahead as a free land." Only with such a man, she believed, would her people be inclined "to change the present oppressive conditions and allow the poor to prosper." In the new society Lolita envisioned, women would be helped to advance economically and politically. "What about Albizu's wife, Laura Meneses de Albizu?" She replied that she admired her also, "Because she had sacrificed her career, left her homeland (Perú), and followed Albizu to Puerto Rico, where all they had known was poverty and persecution."[20]

Which of her expressed beliefs led her to undertake the suicidal mission of March 1, 1954 is hard to say. Was it the ideal of self-sacrifice, as her granddaughter suggests? Was she trying to follow the path of the martyred saints of Christianity? Or was she trying to prove herself to Pedro Albizu Campos, a man who had sacrificed himself and who might have reminded her of her late father? One can only speculate. She was indeed a religious woman who loved Jesus Christ for his own sacrifice on behalf of humanity. She had also been socialized by her family to place the welfare of others above her own, as she makes evident when she left school to care for her sick father. Additionally, she came of age during an era when Puerto Rican women were trained to defer to men, and those above one's social station. For Lolita, and the other Nationalist women, Albizu Campos was a remarkable man, not only because he recognized their political worth but because he offered them a place in history if they joined him in the 'sacred struggle of liberation.' They said they understood what he meant when he stated: "La Patria es valor y sacrificio" and stood ready to meet the challenge. Yet when the time approached to make the ultimate sacrifice Lolita was among the few who offered to lay down her life for her homeland. By that act, explained Irene Vilar, [Lolita] "stripped herself of all womanhood … [and became] a martyr for the liberation of Puerto Rico." Yet one wonders whether martyrdom was her only motivation.[21]

Lolita's Road to Congress

Lolita's work with the Nationalist Junta in New York enabled her to rise to positions of leadership within a few years. Between 1947, the date she joined the Party officially, and February 1954, when she was appointed Party Delegate for the United States, she had served as General Secretary and Vice-President of the New York Junta. She said she "felt honored because the latter position had never before been occupied by a woman." She accepted the assignment and all the responsibility it entailed because she believed in the Nationalist cause. Her main concern, she recalled, was displacing her comrade Julio Pinto Gandía, but then learned that he had been assigned the important task of lobbying members of the United Nations' General Assembly on behalf of Puerto Rico's independence. That task had previously been performed by Party Observer Thelma Mielke until the post was revoked under pressure by the United States.[22]

Mielke's role at the United Nations represented the Nationalists' latest attempt to achieve liberation for Puerto Rico through peaceful means. Earlier, they had tried to win adherents to the cause of independence via the ballot, but after their defeat at the polls in 1932, Albizu Campos advised his followers to prepare in case armed struggle became necessary. (As indicated in the Introduction to this book, four Nationalists were killed by the police in 1935, and that in turn led two Nationalists to kill the island's Chief of Police, Francis E. Riggs. Following the Chief's death, Albizu and seven of his closest aides were tried on seditious charges and sentenced to prison terms of six to ten years, which they served in Atlanta, Georgia.) The Nationalists' retaliatory strategy led the colonial forces to increase surveillance of the group and to arrest Party followers and sympathizers for minor infractions.[23]

Upon Albizu's return to Puerto Rico in December of 1947, he followed a two-pronged approach to the liberation struggle. On the one hand he continued trying to enlist support at the United Nations, and on the other he began to prepare for the eventuality of armed struggle. Since the United States continued to block the Nationalists' efforts to get the United Nations involved in Puerto Rico's case, Albizu Campos ordered his followers to take up arms because they "were left no choice." The result was the Nationalist uprising of October 30, 1950 and the subsequent attempt (two days later) by Oscar Collazo and Griselio Torresola to kill President Truman at Blair House.[24]

In the meantime, other Puerto Rican groups had also been pressuring the United States to reform the island's colonial status. As indicated earlier, the United States government had promised to review the island's case after World War II ended. By the late 1940s, as the demands for reforms grew louder, and the Nationalists sought to embarrass the United States at international meetings held at the United Nations. Leaders in Washington, D.C. decided to work with Luis Muñoz Marín and other Popular Democratic Party (PDP) leaders who had already retreated from their earlier position in support of independence. Between 1947 and 1952, the leaders of the PDP with the help of their allies in Washington, D.C. hammered out a deal that would permit Puerto Rico a measure of "self-rule" while keeping it within the framework of the United States government. The new formula would become known worldwide as the Commonwealth of Puerto Rico and among the islanders as the Estado Libre Asociado. (For details about the meaning of the reforms achieved, see the introductory chapter in this book.)[25]

It was against the "effrontery" legitimized by the United Nations in November 1953, when it relieved the United States of the obligation of having to submit yearly reports on Puerto Rico, that Lolita Lebrón and her three male companions chose (or were ordered by Albizu Campos) to launch an attack on the United States Congress (March 1, 1954). According to what Lolita Lebrón told an interviewer twenty years later, she had targeted the Congress because that "was the body that robbed our people of our 'God-given right' to rule our own destiny."[26]

Who Gave the Orders: Who Brought Them?

Though Lolita Lebrón and her companions claimed responsibility for the attack on Congress, the judicial authorities in Puerto Rico and New York insisted that Albizu Campos had given the orders. After her release from prison, twenty-five years later, Lolita merely said that she had "followed my leaders' orders." She did not disclose which leaders had given the orders or who brought them to New York. She also did not explain the contents of the orders. [27]

Yet when her brother Gonzalo Lebrón was arrested in Chicago as a co-conspirator in the plot to attack the Congress, he told the Puerto Rican Police during a three-part interrogation (November 17-December 2, 1954) what he had already told the prosecution in New York, that "plans to attack key places in the United States" had been discussed as early as September (1953) during a Labor Day picnic at Bear Mountain, New York. He said he had been "summoned to that meeting by the representative of the Nationalist Junta of New York." The revelations Gonzalo Lebrón made during his various testimonies were the subject of a thirteen-page confidential letter sent to Governor Muñoz Marín, on December 2, 1954 by the Chief of Police Salvador T. Roig. According to Roig's letter, Gonzalo Lebrón had disclosed that the first person to introduce the idea of attacking "key places in the United States" had been Albizu's legal counsel, Juan Hernández Vallé.[28]

Chief Roig's letter also said that Gonzalo Lebrón had testified that while many Nationalists attended the Labor Day picnic the only ones present at the meeting, in addition to himself and Hernández Vallé, were Julio Pinto Gandía, representing the New York Junta, and Jorge Luis Jiménez, then vice-president of the Chicago Junta. He and Jiménez, he claimed, attended the Bear Mountain meeting because Hernández Vallé was considered the "Acting Chief of the Nationalist Party" while Albizu was in prison. (A gubernatorial pardon allowed Albizu Campos to be released from prison on September 30, 1953.) Gonzalo Lebrón explained that no women had attended the Bear Mountain meeting, and no one else overheard the discussion the four men were having because they had taken the precaution to "go off to chat at a considerable distance from the others."[29]

He claimed that Henández Vallé had also told them that Party leaders in Puerto Rico were planning "a new uprising, to coincide with the state-side attacks." It had been made clear that the attacks were to be carried out by the Juntas of New York and Chicago. The details of the attacks, however, had been left to the discretion of the stateside leaders. The new uprising, he had assured them, would "have the support of 300 to 400 'independentistas' (members of the Partido Independentista Puertor-riqueño PIP), provided the fight continued for more than a week." He had said that he personally would orchestrate a prison outbreak, to "facilitate the escape of the imprisoned leaders." Lebrón, Chief Roig continued, had left the meeting under the impression that "killing President Eisenhower, during his upcoming fishing trip to Colorado," was one of the acts being considered. (That allegation was later included in several FBI reports as evidence of the "Nationalists' terroristic plans to harm the United States government.")[30]

Gonzalo Lebrón also said that he had rejected Hernández Vallé's plan outright, claiming that "my men would not fight in the United States." But since he "did not wish to appear uncooperative, he had offered to send twelve trained, armed men" from the Chicago Junta "to fight in the upcoming revolution in Puerto Rico." In exchange, he had asked for the title of military commander for himself. He added that Pinto Gandía had also raised objections to the stateside plan, but had ultimately agreed to send funds and weapons for the new uprising in Puerto Rico. Ostensibly, Hernández Vallé had not pressed the issue about their participation and had settled instead for the help he was offered. Yet before the meeting ended, he had asked for "twenty short-wave radios" which he claimed the rebels would need "when they went to the mountains to train." He had told them that once the revolution began, the rebels would seize control of two radio stations in western Puerto Rico and use them "to spread the news of the new revolution." He said also that Hernández Vallé had instructed them to send the funds, men and war material they had promised for the revolution through his office in Old San Juan. Lastly, he had asked Lebrón to dispatch his "trained men, two at a time, in order not to arouse suspicion."[31]

Chief Roig's letter also stated that Lebrón and Jorge Luis Jiménez returned to Chicago to report the outcome of the Bear Mountain meeting to their Junta, and since no one objected to the plan of joining the rebels in Puerto Rico, Lebrón had proceeded to send the first two armed, trained men to San Juan as promised. Weeks later when Lebrón learned that Albizu Campos had been released from prison, he had organized a parade in his honor in Chicago. He also disclosed that among the persons who attended that parade was Ruth Mary Reynolds, who presumably had stopped in Chicago while in transit to a Pacifist Conference.[32]

The second person to bring Lebrón orders for the stateside attacks, he said, was Isabel Rosado Morales, who traveled to New York from Puerto Rico at the end of October 1953. He said that he first met Rosado after he was summoned to New York, on the pretext that Lolita was ill, by the newly elected Junta president, Francisco Ortiz Medina. He knew that "illness was a ruse the Nationalists used whenever they wished to escape the Secret Service's radar." But since his sister had moved, and he did not have her new address, he went directly to Ortiz Medina's home, and there, to his surprise, he found Lolita in the company of a woman he had never seen! The stranger, whom he later learned was Isabel Rosado Morales, had told him that she had "orders for him from the Party leaders." She suggested they had to speak privately so he took her to a restaurant he knew at 125th Street in Manhattan. On the way there, he said, she handed him a piece of paper, signed by Albizu Campos, which ordered him "to stop sending men to Puerto Rico, and to obey Party orders, which I presumed were those brought by Hernández Vallé to the Bear Mountain meeting a month earlier." Albizu's message also ordered him "to recall the two men he had sent to Puerto Rico" (one of whom was believed to be an FBI informant).[33]

Lebrón also disclosed that during his meeting with Isabel Rosado she had instructed him to relay the leaders' orders to Juan Bernardo Lebrón (no relation to Gonzalo or his sister Lolita). He said that he tried "to make Rosado understand that his men would not fight in the U.S.," but she had been adamant and reminded him that "Party orders had to be obeyed." She had even offered herself for one of the missions, saying: "I am ready to defend the homeland in Puerto Rico or in the United States."[34]

He added that he met with Isabel Rosado two days later, to explain that Juan Bernardo Lebrón would not obey the leader's orders because he thought they were "a crazy scheme." But she had surprised him by saying: "It no longer matters. Pinto Gandía has been persuaded to carry out the mission." (Lebrón's version of Pinto Gandía's role in the execution of the orders coincides with a revelation made by Rafael Cancel Miranda, one of Lolita's companions in the 1954 attack, during an interview he gave in August 2010 to the newsweekly *Claridad*.)[35]

Lebrón also said that after his meeting with Isabel Rosado he had returned home to Chicago and "forgotten about the matter" until February (1954) when his sister Lolita came to visit him. "She came," he explained, "to determine which of my men" could be entrusted with the missions outlined by the Party leaders. He claimed he had tried "to persuade her not to get involved in these schemes" because he believed that "she was being used." But since she insisted on speaking to his men personally, he "agreed to let her to speak to one of them, but only in his presence." After he and his chosen man "talked to her for what seemed a very long time," he left the meeting, thinking that she had been "dissuaded." Asked: "What had convinced him?" He replied: "The fact that at one point she admitted 'feeling confused' and also said that she "had already tended her resignation to Hernández Vallé." Then imagine his surprise when on March 2, 1954, he read that Lolita was one of the attackers of the United States Congress! Asked: Why were you surprised? He replied, "Because when I left Lolita in February (1954) I was under the impression that her role was circumscribed to selecting the men for the stateside missions."[36]

Three days after the attack on Congress (March 4, 1954), Gonzalo explained, he was summoned again to New York City by Francisco Ortiz Medina. When he arrived at Medina's house he was "asked to secure legal representation for Lolita and her companions because Julio Pinto Gandía and the other Junta leaders had gone into hiding." Claiming he had been worried about his sister, he went to the office of Conrad Lynn, an African-American, New York City lawyer who often defended the Nationalists. He said that while he was in New York, he learned that the authorities were looking for him, and he turned himself in with Attorney Conrad Lynn at his side. He said he was interrogated but released by one of three Grand Juries which had been set up in Manhattan to investigate the Nationalist attack. He claimed he had "admitted nothing the authorities didn't already know," namely that he was a leading member of the Nationalist Junta in Chicago. He said he was allowed to come and go freely until May 26, 1954 when he was arrested on charges of having conspired with the attackers. In the meantime, he said, he visited New York several times, in hopes of "uncovering the reason" why his sister had become one of the attackers. To that end, he said, he visited Rosa Collazo and Juan Bernardo Lebrón, but all they told him was that "the orders received in New York had called for a group of six attackers: three men and three women, but that at the very last moment Lolita had excused the other two women (no names given) and taken on the assignment herself." He said also he had not been able to discover who had brought the final orders. Yet according to the FBI, Rosa Collazo was the suspected messenger because she had visited Albizu Campos when she traveled to Puerto Rico in February (1954.)[37]

The Attack on Congress

Why did the Nationalists choose March 1, 1954 to launch the attack on Congress? According to what Lolita Lebrón told journalist Ribes Tovar in 1974, she chose the date to coincide with the opening of the Inter-American Conference in Caracas, Venezuela where Nationalist Party representatives were going to bring up the case of Puerto Rico. March, she added, was also the month the Nationalists paid homage to their fallen comrades in the Ponce Massacre of 1937. Beyond that she did not elaborate. She made no mention then of the fact that four months earlier (November 1953) their hopes for a negotiated solution to Puerto Rico's colonial dilemma had been dashed at the United Nations. (On that occasion the U.N.'s General Assembly had succumbed to pressure from the United States and approved Resolution 748 (VIII) 26 votes in favor, 16 against, 18 abstentions, which legitimized that nation's claims that it no longer needed to report on the political status of Puerto Rico because its people had exercised "self-determination" and had achieved "self-government." And the Puerto Rican people had also chosen to remain associated with the United States.)[38]

Following the General Assembly's vote, Albizu and others in his Party vowed to expose the new government of Puerto Rico for what it was: "a new form of colonialism disguised as self-government." Lolita Lebrón and her companions shared Albizu Campos' disillusionment at having the island's potential destiny blocked by the new colonial arrangement. But given that many of the fighters for independence remained in prison and the others were under close surveillance by the Secret Police and FBI agents on the island, a second uprising did not appear to be a viable option. What else could the enraged Nationalists do to register their opposition to the new status formula? Perhaps the best they could hope for was to implement the stateside plan of attack discussed five months earlier at Bear Mountain.

But since a few Junta leaders had shown reluctance to obey orders, perhaps it might not be a bad idea to give the assignment to a trusted woman. (Some say the orders were sent to Pinto Gandía and not to Lolita.) Regardless of who ultimately received the orders, the fact remains that Lolita Lebrón was the one who led three male companions to the seat of the United States government, the place they were least expected, despite the previous Nationalist attack against Blair House in 1950 by Oscar Collazo and Griselio Torresola.[39]

Was Lolita a reluctant participant, as her brother claimed, or did she volunteer for the job, as he was told later? Did she in fact have misgivings about the wisdom of the operation, as he also suggested? If she had any doubts, she did not allow them to deter her from the assigned mission. She always claimed she had been a willing participant. Did she undertake the mission to avenge her leader for the pain he had suffered in prison, as one of her interviewers suggest? Or did she have other motives? All we know is that a note found in her purse during her arrest said the attack on Congress had been undertaken "in order to break the veil of silence the United States had draped over [her] homeland." She also told her interviewer that the attack on Congress had served "to mitigate the guilt and pain I felt for having to abandon my children."[40]

Regardless of her motivations, it is a known fact that she led a team of three equally determined Nationalists to the "very heart" of the United States government to give their lives for their homeland. According to the arresting officers, she and her companions said they had "no regrets;" and felt "honored to have been selected for the mission." For her part, Lolita explained in her 1974 interview that the orders "originally called for three attacks," but she "reduced the number to one and chose the place that would have the greatest impact." When a reporter asked her if she had known who would be her assigned companions, she gave the names of three men arrested with her. No one asked her, and she did not volunteer, whether any other women had been selected for the mission, as her brother claimed during one of his depositions.[41]

In a book he self-published years later, Rafael Cancel Miranda wrote that he had initially been approached by Julio Pinto Gandía, a person he "respected greatly." He said he did what he did "because it was Pinto Gandía who asked me." Had it been anyone else, he explained, "I would have said, go somewhere else with that crazy scheme." But then, as if not wishing to detract from Lolita's role, he added, "Once the plan moved into action we followed Lolita's orders." (Pinto Gandía was apparently involved in the planning stages of the attack, even though Lolita later claimed responsibility "for everything," as she told the Washington Police when she was arrested.)[42]

Following his arrest, Cancel Miranda told the Washington, D.C. police that he had bought "four one-way (train) tickets" for himself and his companions. Asked, "why had he done that?" He replied: "Because no one in the group expected to come out alive from the mission." In an interview he did for *Claridad* in 2010 he said that, on March 1, 1954, he had "also packed a pistol for Lolita but that he had not given it to her until later that morning." Lolita agreed with his recollections, stating that he had given her the pistol when "we stopped at a coffee shop in Washington." No one asked, so we are left to wonder: Why didn't Cancel Miranda arm Lolita earlier? Was he following Party orders or was he afraid she might not want the weapon? Or was he playing the protector role so commonly assigned to Puerto Rican males? None of these questions were asked, so we are left to think that perhaps several of these forces might have been at play.[43]

What Lolita revealed about March 1, 1954 was that all of them had been unusually quiet during the train ride to Washington; "each preoccupied with 'his' own thoughts." In her case, she said, she had been thinking about her children and how they "would soon become orphans." But that once they reached the Capitol steps all their personal thoughts had vanished. Cancel Miranda remembered that when they reached the Capitol steps, he and the other two men had stopped to rest and take in the view but that Lolita had urged them to move along, saying, "It is time." Obviously still amused, he said, "Lolita seemed to be in a great hurry, so we followed her up the steps and entered the Capitol." There, they "went up to the House Gallery and took four seats, in the back row, on the right side of the room, and sat in them long enough to recite 'Our Father' and commend our souls to God." Then Lolita "gave the order and we all got up and began shooting."[44]

As five Congressmen fell wounded, a combined force of Capitol guards, alert congressmen, and House visitors tackled the attackers to the ground, disarming them. Lolita was escorted out first, Cancel Miranda recalled, while one of her companions was being kicked into submission. In the confusion that followed, Irving Flores Rodríguez slipped

out and made his way to the bus depot. The three apprehended companions were arrested and taken to police headquarters for questioning.
There, Lolita told her interrogators that she was "the leader of the attack
and the one responsible for everything." She added that she was "not
sorry" for what she had done, though she had not intended to hurt anyone and that was the reason she had "fired the shots at the ceiling."
Asked to explain, she replied: "Because I came to Washington to die, not
to kill." Cancel Miranda confirmed Lolita's account years later. He said,
"Lolita raised the Puerto Rican flag, cried out 'Freedom for Puerto Rico
now,' aimed at the ceiling, and waited to be killed."[45]

According to what the police disclosed to the press, "The attackers
had admitted their roles, but none had shown remorse." Flores, the attacker caught at the bus depot, had refused to say anything at all about
his companions and would only answer questions about his own role.
As for Lolita's motives, the police pointed to the note they had found in
her purse, which said as follows:

> Before God and the world my blood clamors for the independ-
> ence of Puerto Rico! I give my life for my homeland. This is a
> cry of victory in the struggle for independence, which for
> more than a half a century has sought to conquer the land that
> belongs to us.
>
> I declare that the United States of America has betrayed the
> sacred human principles by its continuous subjugation of my
> country, in violation of its rights to be a free nation, with its
> tortures of our apostle of independence Don Pedro Albizu
> Campos."(On the back of the note it said, 'I am responsible
> for everything.')[46]

Photographs of the attackers made the front cover of many newspapers
across the nation. *The New York Times*, for example, published a picture
of a well-dressed Lolita on the cover of its March 2, 1954 edition. The
leading story of that day described her as a 34-year old seamstress, whose
last residence had been at 315 West 94th Street. She was said to have been
carrying a Luger pistol, which required "the use of both hands in order
to fire it." That observation led one reporter to speculate that this was
"probably the reason why Mrs. Lebrón draped the Puerto Rican flag over

her shoulder during the attack." Another article stated that the attackers had "fired a total of 24 shots, a few of which had struck their targets and wounded five congressmen: three Democrats and two Republicans." The initial stories, described only two of Lolita's male companions: Rafael Cancel Miranda, a twenty-five year-old male, resident at 120 South, First Street, Brooklyn and Andrés Figueroa Cordero, twenty-nine, resident at 108 East, 103rd Street, Manhattan. Details about Irving Flores Rodriguez, twenty-seven, resident at 108 East 103rd Street, Manhattan appeared in subsequent articles because he was arrested later than his companions. One of the stories reported that Flores Rodríguez had also been carrying a .45 caliber pistol and "that like the others in the group he had shot with intent to kill."[47]

Indictments of Attackers and Other Suspects

On March 10, 1954 the four self-confessed attackers were indicted on ten counts each: five of them labeled "assaults with intent to kill" and five as "assaults with a deadly weapon." Unable to secure bail, which was set at $100,000 each, the four were remanded to jail to await a review of their case. Surprised that they were "still alive" when they "had come to die," the four initially showed little interest in their legal predicament, according to news accounts. Without funds with which to pay for legal representation, except for Lolita, whose brother had retained New York City counsel Conrad Lynn to represent her, the group accepted the public defenders assigned to them by Judge Alexander Holtzoff. The first hearing in their case took place on June 4, 1954, according to one news account.[48]

In the meantime, members of the FBI and the Secret Service combed the Puerto Rican neighborhoods of New York City and Chicago in search of clues that might lead to other conspirators. Along their path they spread the rumor that the attackers had ties to the Communists, "whose known intent is to destroy the United States government." They said also that the attack on Congress "was part of a much larger conspiracy," which among other things included "plans to kill the President and harm other top officials in the United States and Puerto Rico."[49]

Intent on stopping "the impending threats," the Secret Service of New York City and Chicago rounded up ninety-one Puerto Ricans they believed to have ties to the "seditious conspirators." (A similar operation was being carried out in Puerto Rico.) Of the ninety-one interrogated by three Grand Juries (set up in Manhattan to investigate the case), only seventeen were ultimately arraigned on charges of seditious conspiracy. Among them were the four attackers of Congress, even though they had already been tried and sentenced for their crimes by a court in Washington, D.C. All seventeen were indicted and scheduled for trial in the Federal Court for the Southern District of New York during the fall of 1954. But when four of the indicted chose to collaborate with the authorities, the initial number scheduled to go to trial was reduced to thirteen, and the four collaborators were rescheduled to be tried separately the following spring (1955). Lolita's brother, Gonzalo Lebrón, as stated earlier, was among the four who testified for the prosecution in New York and later in Puerto Rico. For his willingness to betray his comrades, including his own sister, he eventually received a six-year suspended sentence. The other three collaborators also escaped having to serve time in prison.[50]

In addition to the testimonies provided by Gonzalo Lebrón and others, the FBI and the Secret Service had been amassing information for many years on the leading Nationalists in Puerto Rico, New York, and Chicago. Generally, the secret agents received leads from paid informants, and infiltrated agents. The various intelligence agencies in Puerto Rico and the United States also generally exchanged information. One agent who proved useful to the New York trial of 1954 was Raymond Sánchez Sorrel, for he had infiltrated the Nationalist Junta of New York sometime in the early 1950s. He had earned the trust of the Junta members and had held the post of secretary for a time. According to what he testified during the 1954 trial, he had worked closely with Rosa Collazo and other leading Nationalists in New York.

Rosa Collazo's daughter, Lydia, recounted during an interview that [Sánchez] "Sorrel" had not only testified against her mother and other Junta members, but was probably the one who had supplied many of the photographs the Grand Juries used in March (1954) to identify and summon many Nationalists for interrogation. She explained, "The Grand Jury kept or dismissed a person depending on the photograph it had on hand. If the photograph placed a person at a Nationalist event, or in the company of some well-known Nationalist, he or she would be held, or called back for questioning." (She recalled that this was the way she had been summoned.) "Though in most cases," she said, "the suspects had to be released for lack of evidence." Lolita's cousin, Luis Sotomayor told Irene Vilar in an interview that he had been harassed by the FBI after Lolita was arrested even though he had never been a Nationalist. He explained that he was "probably targeted because I owned a bar that the Nationalists sometimes used to do fundraising." He mentioned also that among the Nationalists of the New York Junta he had often seen a man "taking photographs" of those who frequented his bar. Apparently, the man in question was Raymond Sánchez Sorrel.[51]

Reactions to the Attack on Congress

Though most journalists did their best to refrain from editorializing, a few could not resist the temptation to depict the attackers as "lunatics" and "terrorists." They also reminded their readers that the attackers had failed to show remorse and warned that there were many more like them. An article in *The Washington Evening Star* (March 2) portrayed Lolita as "a defiant woman" who had not only led the attackers but had said that she was "not afraid to have the law punish her." And though she had also said that she "did not shoot to kill," she had expressed "no regrets" and claimed instead that she had come to Washington "to demand the liberty of my country ... to call attention to the world ... to the terrible situation of Puerto Rico." She had also insisted that "only through such acts could Puerto Rico be heard." And while her companions also claimed they had "not come to kill, but to give their lives for their homeland, they had in fact wounded five congressmen."

Not willing to let the Nationalist acts detract from the good work his government had done to ingratiate itself with the United States, Governor Luis Muñoz Marín traveled to Washington, D.C. via New York, on March 2, 1954. His plan was to speak with various national leaders, visit the wounded congressmen, and make amends to the American people in the name of his own. (This was the second time in four years the Nationalists had forced Governor Luis Muñoz Marín to undertake such a delicate mission.) The Congress, the President, and the director of the FBI, J. Edgar Hoover, told him they were grateful for his visit and promptly reassured him that there were "no hard feelings." He in turn reassured them that the Nationalists were a "small group of lunatics, with little support among the good people of Puerto Rico." Privately, he also assured the director of the FBI that he would do everything in his power to eradicate the "lawless lunatics." Mr. Hoover had no reason to doubt the Governor's resolve because he had been on that path since 1948, when as president of the Puerto Rican Senate he had secured approval of a Gag Rule, officially known as Law #53. The law, which resembled the Smith Act enacted in the United States in 1940, intended to silence the Nationalists and intimidate members of the newly created independence party, Partido Independentista Puertorriqueño (PIP). (That Party had been established by disaffected members of the Popular Democratic Party) ousted by Muñoz Marín and others, who had already retreated from their earlier adherence to the cause of independence.) Invested as he was in Muñoz Marín's new mission, Mr. Hoover offered his support through the FBI office in San Juan. Energized by the warm reception he had received in Washington, D.C., Governor Muñoz returned to Puerto Rico eager to redouble his efforts to quash the Nationalists and keep independence advocates and other dissident groups in check.[52]

The Attackers' First Trial: Washington

By the time Lolita and her companions went to trial in Washington, D.C. on June 4, 1954, there was very little the defense, headed by F. Joseph Donohue, could do to ameliorate the impending prison sentences that were to befall them, for they had all confessed their crimes. When Lolita took the stand, she again restated her claim that she was "responsible for everything" regarding the attack on Congress. She justified her actions by stating, "after looking into my heart and into my mind ... I knew I had to make great sacrifices for my country. I did what I did for my country. I did not come to kill," which, as she had explained earlier, was the reason why she "shot at the ceiling." She also told the prosecutor, Leo A. Rover, and members of the Court, "I love you; I love the world; I love God." Andrés Figueroa Cordero and Irving Flores Rodriguez limited their remarks to admitting their roles but abstained from providing any other details about the mission. Rafael Cancel Miranda reportedly told the Court: "It was not my intent to hurt anyone and I am glad no one has died." And added: "As a human being, it does not please me to hurt another, but I am satisfied with what I have done."

Without much to go on, the defense offered to plead their case "on grounds of insanity," a defense all four "vehemently rejected." They told Donohue, Lolita and Cancel recalled, that "we wished to be judged as we are: 'freedom fighters' for our homeland."[53]

Prosecutor, Leo A. Rover (who four years earlier had defended Oscar Collazo after his attempted attack of Blair House) called several individuals to the stand, including a few congressmen and members of the police. At one point, he asked Police Lieutenant Lawrence A. Harnett to tell the Court what the four attackers had revealed when they were interrogated. Harnett basically repeated what he had already told the press, namely that "Mrs. Lebrón claimed to be the organizer and leader of the attack, and each of the men had admitted his role in the shooting." He said also that "not one of them had shown remorse or apologized for the crimes they had committed." He added that "Mrs. Lebrón said she was prepared to accept any punishment: 'a life sentence or the death sentence,' whichever was coming to her."[54]

In his summary of the case on June 16, 1954, the prosecutor reminded the jury that this attack was "one of the worst crimes ever perpetrated against the nation's capital." He added that the defendants had "obviously intended to kill, regardless of what the defense claimed." He urged the jury to disregard Mrs. Lebrón's "lies" when she said: "I love you; I love the world; I love God," because if that were the case she (and her companions) would have "used blanks, not live bullets that kill." To him the case was clear: "They came to kill." The best proof of that was that five congressmen were wounded. Given their crime, for which they had "shown no remorse," he believed each deserved the maximum penalty of 125 years.[55]

For its part, the defense limited itself to calling for a "non-guilty verdict," on grounds that the four were political activists who were fighting for freedom of their homeland. Judge Holtzoff rejected the motion and sent the jury (seven men and five women) to deliberate on the evidence at hand. In the verdict the jurors rendered, the male attackers were convicted on all ten charges, while Lolita was exempted of the charge "assault with intent to kill" because it was proven that she had shot at the ceiling.

Judge Holtzoff passed sentence on July 8, 1954. All three men were convicted on all ten charges and were sentenced to prison terms of twenty-five to seventy-five years. Lolita, absolved of one of the charges, was sentenced to a prison term of sixteen years and eight months to fifty years. After Judge Holtzoff passed sentence, he explained to the four that according to the laws of the District of Columbia, a prisoner was not eligible for parole until he or she had served a third of the maximum sentence. In Lolita's case that meant she would have to serve sixteen years and eight months of her fifty-year sentence before she became eligible. Yet neither she nor her companions appeared interested in the explanation because they "had no plans" to apply for parole. According to what Lolita said at the time, she would "gladly remain in prison for the rest of my days rather than apply for clemency from the United States government." Later, she clarified her position, stating that the only way she would agree to leave prison would be if she were granted an unconditional pardon. At the time of their sentencing in July 1954 the prospect of being granted an unconditional pardon seemed farfetched. In fact, what awaited her and her companions was a new trial in New York City, on charges of conspiracy to overthrow the United States government, a violation of the Smith Act. But before the day was over Lolita would receive another major blow.[56]

Lolita's Grief and Mystic Visions

Before Judge Holtzoff read Lolita's sentence, she had received terrible news. Her thirteen-year-old son Félix, whom she had left in Lares six years earlier (1948), was dead. Though he had died in April (1954) no one had thought to tell her until July 8, the very day she was to be sentenced. The person who told her, she said, was the guard who was escorting her to the Washington Court. She recalled that he had just blurted out: "Your son is dead, just like that, without any explanation or a word of comfort." The shock of the news, she said, was such that she "broke down in court." She "was so sad," she recalled, that she "could barely hear what the judge was saying" because all she could do was "pray and cry because I blamed myself for his death." Her breakdown, she explained, was not "due to the prison sentence," as reporters had claimed, "but because of what I had just heard about my son's death."[57]

That night when she was taken to her cell, she said, she had been given a newspaper in which she read that her son "had drowned." She was told later that she fainted and a guard had carried her to her cell. She stayed in bed, she remembered, "totally grief-stricken for four days."

Her grief was so intense, she said, that she "could not move, eat or sleep for days. But then a doctor gave me an injection which helped a little." Years later she confided to Irene Vilar that, it was during this period of intense grief that she had her "first [mystic] vision." She recalled that she had been praying to Jesus Christ for help, and he had appeared and comforted her. That "vision," she had said years earlier, "was what helped me to survive the pain and guilt I felt about my son's death." She had other "visions" later that she said helped her to understand "I had to remain strong so that I could carry out my divine mission on this earth." That mission required her "to warn others about the impending dangers of the atomic age, to work for world peace, and to unite her compatriots into a peaceful movement to achieve the liberation of Puerto Rico."[58]

Lolita's Second Trial: Her Life in Prison

During the fall of 1954 (between September and October) Lolita, her companions, and nine other Nationalists from New York City and Chicago were tried in New York, on charges of seditious conspiracy. As stated earlier, four of the original seventeen, including Lolita's brother Gonzalo Lebrón pled guilty to the charges but agreed to collaborate with the authorities, in hopes of receiving a leaner sentence. Of the remaining thirteen tried that fall, three were women: Lolita Lebrón, Rosa Collazo, and Carmen Dolores Otero de Torresola (known as Carmen Torresola because she was the widow of Griselio Torresola). Among the witnesses testifying for the prosecution were Gonzalo Lebrón, Raymond Sánchez Sorrel (who had infiltrated the Nationalist Junta in New York), Police Lieutenant Astol Calero, then Assistant Superintendent of the Puerto Rican Division of Internal Security, and the ex-Nationalist (from Arecibo, Puerto Rico) Guillermo Hernández Vega. The latter had testified several times against his comrades and against Pedro Albizu Campos in the trials that followed the 1950 Nationalist uprising in Puerto Rico. Though neither he nor Astol Calero had any direct evidence to contribute against those on trial in New York, their testimonies were accepted by the prosecution in an effort to show the Court the "ill intent and criminal practices" of Nationalists in general. In the end, all thirteen defendants were convicted as charged and sentenced to terms of four to six years imprisonment. In Lolita's case the new sentence added an extra six years (to be served consecutively) to the previous fifty-year sentence imposed in July by the Court in Washington. Rosa Collazo was similarly sentenced to six years while Carmen Torresola was sentenced to four years. All three women were shortly thereafter dispatched to serve their terms at the Federal Reformatory for Women in Alderson West Virginia.[59]

Prison life for all the three women was incredibly hard, but for Lolita Lebrón, the experience turned into "a terrible ordeal." According to what she told radio host Antonio Rodríguez of WAKQ (San Juan) in 1979, she was immediately separated from the rest of the prison population when she arrived at Alderson. The penal administration in that prison, she said, declared her "the most dangerous woman on the planet, the most inhuman" and warned other inmates to stay away from her. Obviously still stung by the experience she found it hard to provide details and merely told the radio host: "a lot was done to me in the United States." She added that during the interrogations "electronic radiation was applied." Years later, in the privacy of her own home, she confided to Irene Vilar that she had been "raped and tortured" in prison.[60]

Rosa Collazo, who also spent time in the same prison, recounted in her memoir that Lolita had been "mistreated" by the administration because she was considered "a terrorist." Lolita, she said, was even isolated from me and the other Puerto Rican comrades Blanca Canales, Carmen Torresola. She recalled that she often had heard rumors that Lolita "was kept shackled in her cell" on the pretext that "she was crazy" because of "her excessive devotion to the Catholic faith." She remembered that when assignments for work were distributed, Lolita had been assigned to do maintenance work, a task the guards generally reserved for the "toughest inmates" in that facility. The heavy work, she said, proved too hard for Lolita, who "was young and delicate," and she became ill. When that happened, Rosa said, she "snuck out a letter to Conrad Lynn," Lolita's counsel, and asked him to intercede. Apparently, he followed through because Lolita was later sent to work in the sewing room.[61]

Then in the fall of 1957, Rosa learned that Lolita had been sent to a psychiatric hospital in Washington, D.C., but she did not know why. More recently, Irene Vilar explained that Lolita said she was sent to St. Elizabeth after she had a vision in which God warned her about the dangers of the Atomic Age and she shared the message with President Eisenhower via a letter. After that incident, she told Vilar, "Two women came to escort me to the insane asylum, even though there was nothing wrong with me." She had said also that when she saw the two women enter her cell, she "knew that their visit wouldn't lead to anything good." She suggested that at St. Elizabeth she had been subjected to "electronic torture" and to "prove it" had shown Vilar the "scars" she still had from that time. Vilar subsequently learned from her father that Lolita had been at St. Elizabeth Hospital in 1957 because that was the year that he and his wife Gladys Mirna (Irene's mother) had visited her there.[62]

After that hospitalization, Lolita apparently learned to keep her 'visions' to herself and to become as inconspicuous as possible, according to Rosa Collazo. She recalled that by the time she (Rosa) was released in 1959, Lolita had been reintegrated into Alderson's prison life, though she still spent "most of her free time in her cell praying and taking care of her altar." During working hours, Rosa remembered that Lolita made "elaborate hats and retrofitted dresses" for the women going to be released. She was also assigned by the staff to "sew curtains and other items" the prison needed.[63]

After Rosa was released, Lolita spent another twenty years at the Alderson prison before she was granted a presidential pardon, as explained earlier. Although she had been eligible for parole since the early 1970s, she had refused to apply, on grounds that "as a freedom fighter" she had nothing to "apologize for and would never ask for clemency from a government that keeps my people enslaved." Besides, she wouldn't think of leaving prison unless her companions were also released. That rebellious stance would cost her not only many more years of imprisonment but much loneliness. Far away from friends and relatives, she received few sporadic visits during the years she remained in Alderson. Three years after she was imprisoned she received devastating news. For example, in December 1957 she learned that her beloved mother, whom she had not seen since 1948, had recently died of cancer. Only three years into her prison sentence, she was not allowed to attend her funeral, which was a big emotional blow for her. On the twenty-third anniversary of the attack on Congress (March 1, 1954), she learned that her only surviving offspring, Gladys Mirna, then just thirty-six years old, had died in San Juan. According to a police account, she died in a car accident. Her granddaughter, however, would claim later that her mother (Gladys Mirna) had "jumped to her death from a speeding car," following a marital quarrel.[64]

This time, according to several Puerto Rican newspapers, Lolita was given a two-day pass to attend her daughter's funeral. Irene Vilar, then six years old, remembered meeting her grandmother for the first time at Gladys Mirna's funeral. The death (or suicide) of Lolita's daughter traumatized them both, according to Vilar's account. She contends that when she visited Lolita in a San Juan suburb many years later she was still "so grief-stricken by her daughter's death that she couldn't even say her name and would only refer to her by her nickname, Tatita." The photographs taken the day of the funeral portray a sad but stoic Lolita, surrounded by thousands of well-wishers. Vilar claims that many of the persons present came to the funeral "to see and be seen by Lolita."[65]

A Movement to Free Lolita and Others

During the 1960s and '70s, various protest groups, some linked to the Independence Party (PIP) and others to the recently established Partido Socialista Puertorriqueño (PSP), organized marches, demonstrations and picket lines on the island and the United States, calling for the release of Lolita Lebrón and other Puerto Rican political prisoners still held in penal institutions in Puerto Rico and across the United States. To that end, they urged women, workers, and students groups on the island and abroad to write to the American President to request clemency for the imprisoned Nationalists. A few of these groups' representatives also attended international conferences where they urged sympathizers to pass resolutions, sign petitions, and/or write letters to the American President to request the release of Lolita Lebrón and others. According to the newsweekly *Claridad*, these efforts gradually bore fruit, and by January 26, 1976 delegates from one hundred thirty-five nations and seventy-five organizations had written to President Carter urging him to release the Puerto Rican political prisoners. Then on April 24, 1978, the local news daily *El Nuevo Día* reported that Fidel Castro's government had offered to exchange an American prisoner held in Cuba for Lolita Lebrón. Though that story was later denied by the Castro government, according to another edition of the same newspaper (June 27, 1978), Lolita was quoted as saying that she would reject any offer for her release, unless her companions were freed as well.

Though it is not altogether clear what motivated President Carter to pardon Lolita and her companions, the fact remains that they were granted an unconditional release on September 10, 1979. Some would argue that President Carter had yielded to growing pressures from the international community, while others preferred to believe that his clemency was motivated by the growing concern for human rights in United States.[66]

The four Puerto Ricans released in September 1979 were given a heroes' welcome by Nationalists and sympathizers of independence in Chicago, New York, and Puerto Rico, according to Miñi Seijo, a reporter for *Claridad*. Everywhere they went, she wrote, they were greeted by thousands of enthusiastic persons who lined the streets, church grounds, and the various airports waving Puerto Rican flags and chanting their names. Their arrival in San Juan (September 12, 1979) was also greeted by a huge crowd, which stretched from the airport to the cemetery in Old San Juan, where the four went to pay homage to their late leader Pedro Albizu Campos. Hundreds of those lining Avenida Baldorioty de Castro (the road that connects Isla Verde to San Juan) followed their caravan, chanting their names, Seijo wrote. Once at the cemetery, Rosa Collazo recalled, "many of those [following the caravan] lined up to kiss Lolita's hand and to welcome their 'heroes' back home."[67]

Life as a Free Woman: Back in Puerto Rico

At the press conference, organized by the Cuban Delegation at the United Nations the previous day, Lolita was asked how she felt about what she had done. "Would she do it again?" She replied, "We were left no choice." Then, apparently still unrepentant, she said that, if circumstances required it she would again "take up arms." Whatever she had done, she said, she had done for her homeland. Asked, "What are your plans when you get to Puerto Rico?" She replied: "To unify the various pro-independence groups so that together we can achieve the liberation of Puerto Rico."[68]

Yet by the time Lolita returned to Puerto Rico, nearly four decades after she left it in 1940, conditions had drastically changed. During the time she had been away the island's economy and society had been transformed, thanks in part to the changes introduced by the PDP government, and partly to the exigencies of the new industrialized economy. As indicated earlier, the PDP government had revamped the old infrastructure and educated a new generation of loyal citizens by virtue of increasing the number of schools and offering scholarships to the poor to attend colleges and other institutions of higher learning. It is estimated that between the 1940s and 1970 the government spent about a third of its annual budget on education. During that period also large portions of the rural residents had moved to urban areas or left the island for the United States. The internal migration had led to a proliferation of housing developments in order to accommodate the thousands of families who had moved closer to San Juan and other major cities in search of new opportunities. Lolita Lebrón, according to Irene Vilar, was among those who settled in one of these housing developments (in the municipality of Río Piedras) shortly after she returned to Puerto Rico.[69]

Many of those who had remained on the island, including three of Lolita's siblings had benefited from the social and economic changes of the post war period. The Lebrón Soto family, like thousands of others, had been uplifted from poverty within one generation. Lolita's younger sister Aurea and her brother Julio had become public school teachers while her older brother Agustín had started his own business. In the process they had apparently become supporters of the PDP government, according to a letter Aurea and Julio wrote to the governor in 1954. In the letter they indicated that they supported Gonzalo's actions and deplored what Lolita had done. They added that they wished to welcome Gonzalo home whenever he came to Puerto Rico [to testify against the Nationalists]. They also said they wished to spare their mother the bad news about Lolita's arrest in Washington.[70]

By 1979 the world of politics had also changed. Lolita found that an increasing number of voters who had benefited from the socioeconomic transformation had become convinced that the island's prosperity and their own well being were linked to the generosity and power of the United States. To insure the permanence of these gains, they joined the annexationist movement, renamed the Partido Nuevo Progresista (New Progressive Party, NPP), which wrested power in 1968 from the once entrenched PDP forces. The newly minted NPP rapidly began propagating the message that only by securing a permanent union with the United States would the islanders become first-class United States citizens and be allowed proper representation in Congress. Encouraged by the acceptance of Alaska and Hawaii into the American Union, the leaders of the NPP government renewed their campaign to pressure Congress to reconsider the case of Puerto Rico. Meanwhile, stunned by their loss of power, PDP leaders mobilized their forces around Rafael Hernández Colón and regained the governorship in 1972. His promise was to perfect the ELA and safeguard the Spanish language and culture. Since then the PDP has won and lost control of the governorship, the legislature, or both in various elections. To win, it had become necessary to seek the support of the independence advocates, who also feel threatened by the growing annexation movement.[71]

Meanwhile, the Nationalist Party had been reduced to "a shadow of its former self," and the independence movement had split into two camps: the older Partido Independentista Puertorriqueño (PIP) and a newly created Partido Socialista Puertorriqueño (PSP). Yet the combined forces of the two pro-independence camps drew less that ten percent of the electoral votes in the late 1970s. Also a fringe within the independence movement had become radicalized and joined or created various clandestine groups. On more than one occasion some of the clandestine groups destroyed federal and local government properties and/or targeted armed forces and naval personnel. As in the past, pro-independence and other dissident groups were placed under strict surveillance, this time by well-financed federal programs that operated under the umbrella of COINTELPRO. (Feminists, students, workers and other progressive groups were targeted by the enhanced counter-intelligence agencies, which included the local Secret Police, the National Guard, the FBI, the U.S. Navy, and others security programs designed to protect U.S. interests on the island.) These agencies, according to some recent studies, spent a great deal of time and energy creating and disseminating disinformation in order to feed existing animosities between the various political factions. It was into this fiercely divided political environment and sophisticated system of surveillance that Lolita entered in 1979 when she returned to her homeland.[72]

Though for the most part the population at large was ignorant of the counterintelligence practices, it could not escape the scandal that resulted from the entrapment and assassinations of two independence advocates by local undercover agents during the late 1970s. During the well-publicized (PDP-controlled) Senate hearing that followed the youths' assassination, a careless (or vengeful) undercover agent disclosed that the Police Department had thousands of Puerto Ricans under surveillance and kept their active dossiers or "carpetas" on file. According to a Civil Rights Commission investigation that followed the agent's disclosure, the practice of targeting individuals and groups for their political beliefs had been in place for at least fifty years. The agent's disclosure also mobilized House Representative David Noriega and a group of colleagues to sue the Puerto Rican government for having violated the civil and human rights of its citizens. The legal suit demanded that the targeting practice be stopped at once and the dossiers be placed under the protective custody of the Department of Justice until such time when they could be released to the aggrieved parties. After the protracted legal battle which lasted nearly a decade and the Civil Rights Commission's report came to light, the Supreme Court of Puerto Rico concluded that the government had in fact violated the civil and human rights of thousands of its citizens and ordered the Police Department to turn over the (un-redacted) dossiers to the Justice Department for safekeeping until they could be returned to those who requested them. It also ordered the Justice Department to devise a method by which the aggrieved parties could obtain their dossiers when they requested them. (The aggrieved parties had only six months to request their files.)[73]

Thus, it is not surprising that upon her return, Lolita would also be assigned a dossier or "carpeta" (#13,888) by the Puerto Rican Police Department. A revision of her dossier enabled researcher Ivonne Marín Burgos to compile a long list of the political and religious activities Lolita engaged in from the day she arrived in Puerto Rico to the day she died thirty-one years later. For the purpose of this work, a review of a few of those activities will suffice. For example, in September 1981, two years after her return, a local undercover agent reported that she had called a meeting of the various independence groups in hopes of consolidating them under a larger organization she named the "Comité Unidad Nacional Pedro Albizu Campos." The mission of the proposed Comité, she explained at the meeting, was "to unite all the different groups so that they can work together for the liberation of Puerto Rico." One of the Comité's major principles, the agent added, called for a boycott of colonial elections [just as Pedro Albizu Campos had done during the 1930s]. To that end, the Comité made clear: "We declare that the electoral process is the strong arm that sustains the power of the United States in our national territory and through which it reaffirms its colonial rule every four years. For those reasons we totally repudiate the electoral process as a means to achieve independence for our invaded nation."[74]

Less than a year later (April 18, 1982), at another meeting of the Comité, Lolita reportedly issued a statement in support of the "liberation movements of Puerto Rico, Latin America, and the World." At that meeting, she explained that the Comité would be sub-divided into three working groups or circles. The first of them, the agent reported, would be known as Círculo Cristiano, whose charge was to work towards the abolition of nuclear weapons. (We should recall that this was one of the missions God had assigned to Lolita during one of her "mystic visions" while she was imprisoned in Alderson, West Virginia.) The task of the second circle, called Círculo Cultural, was to promote Puerto Rican culture. The job of the third circle was to keep track of the group's finances and was therefore called Comité de Finanzas. The meeting, the agent claimed, did not go well and ultimately devolved into a heated argument when a woman in the audience challenged Lolita's assertion "that God will help us to liberate Puerto Rico." According to the same agent, Lolita's entreaties were rejected by the majority of the attendees, and that rejection derailed her call to unity. Another dossier entry, dated June 13, 1982, reported that Lolita had joined a meeting in Río Piedras, whose purpose was to create a Comité Contra las Armas Nucleares," or a Committee Against Nuclear Arms.[75]

Two years after the Río Piedras meeting (December 1984), she was photographed in front of the island's Capitol, as she took part in a demonstration in support of Nicaragua, organized by Bishop Antulio Parrilla Bonilla. During the 1980s and '90s she joined several religious and secular groups, which proposed or supported various progressive goals, ranging from a call for world peace to social programs intended to benefit the poor. She was also often photographed at political rallies in support of Puerto Rico's independence. Other times she was observed taking part in political or religious activities in honor of Nationalists who fell during the uprising of 1950 or were killed during the Ponce Massacre of 1937. Eighteen years after she returned to San Juan (April 1997), the news daily El Nuevo Día reported that Lolita Lebrón had been elected President of the Nationalist Party and that she had once again called for unity of all the pro-independence groups. She was quoted as follows: "As President of the Nationalist Party and even earlier, I had envisioned the unity of the people of Puerto Rico [in the struggle] for liberation, and as much as I desire it, and will work toward that goal—I will not stop—that does not mean I will succeed. But I will try and see if it is possible."[76]

Also that April (1997), the newsweekly *Claridad* reported that Lolita had participated in a hearing held by several U.S. Congressmen in the city of Mayagüez. At the hearing, Lolita was said to have petitioned the legislators "to amend the error of their forefathers and stop instilling fear of freedom among the Puerto Rican people." During her turn at the podium, she had also questioned the American legislators about the long prison sentences being served by her compatriots in American federal prisons and requested that they be released. She questioned them also about the nuclear arsenals the United States kept in Puerto Rico and insisted that these had to be removed. She also urged the Congressmen to join the Movement for World Peace. When Congressman George Miller interrupted to remind her that "her time was about to expire," she is reported to have responded angrily: "I will not permit anyone to shut me up when I'm defending the liberty of my country."[77]

Lolita Turns to Civil Disobedience

During the last years of her life, Lolita reportedly became involved in various acts of civil disobedience. For example, on May 4, 2000 she joined a group of pacifists led by Rubén Berríos Martínez, president of the Partido Independentista Puertorriqueño (PIP) in a struggle to push the United States Navy out of Vieques. A few years earlier, while Lolita was still incarcerated in Alderson, West Virginia, Berríos and many others had succeeded in pressuring the United States Navy to evacuate its troops from the island of Culebra after a five-year struggle (1970-1975). Berríos' role in the campaign to push the American Navy out of Vieques, where it controlled two thirds of the island's territory, began in the early 1980s. By 1983, the naval authorities had promised to protect the environment from the nuclear fallout of their maneuvers and to help the island to develop its languishing economy. It failed on both counts and conditions between the islanders and the Navy personnel gradually deteriorated. Frustrated by the unmet demands, some Viequenses resorted to sporadic picketing, marches, and demonstrations, many of which were covered by the more progressive members of the Puerto Rican media.[78]

When on April 19, 1999, security guard David Sanes Rodríguez lost his life as a result of one of the Navy's maneuvers, Berríos, his group, and dozens of sympathizers from various religious denominations, rallied to the support of the Viequenses, calling for justice in the name of the late Sanes Rodríguez. The Navy appealed its case to the municipal authorities, which proceeded to have the protestors arrested on charges of "trespassing on military property." Berríos was among the many persons arrested and later released after a short stint in jail. Instead of desisting from his plans, he led his followers to set up camp on a Vieques' beach, which he named Campamento Gilberto Concepción de Gracia, in honor of the PIP's founder. The immediate purpose of the camp, he declared, was to continue to pressure the Navy to stop conducting its maneuvers. The just cause of the Viequenses, Berríos' arrest, and the prolonged presence on the island of many political figures and entertainers began attracting representatives of the foreign media. Their reports in turn attracted hundreds of sympathizers from diverse political camps from Puerto Rico and the United States.[79]

Among those who rushed to join Berríos was eighty-one year old Lolita Lebrón, who arrived at the Vieques camp on May 4, 2000. As the protests escalated, dozens more were arrested and sentenced to jail on charges of trespassing on American military property. One of those arrested in June 2000 was Lolita Lebrón, though she was released without being charged. She continued to protest and the third time she was arrested (July 26, 2001) she was sentenced by Judge Aida Delgado to sixty days in prison, which were to be served in the newly built federal facility in Guaynabo, Puerto Rico. Sentencing Lolita backfired, for she used the opportunity to hold a press conference in which she accused the U.S. Navy "of committing genocide against the citizens of Vieques by poisoning the air and the sea with its maneuvers." The unwanted publicity was far from helpful to the Navy's image and the judicial authorities had her sentence overruled by another judge. The latter simply said: "It is time to stop judging this woman for her 1950s acts." She was released less than a month later. The Navy left Vieques, though the pollution it left behind continues to plague the environment.[80]

Honors, Death and Tributes

In September 2005, Lolita and several comrades were honored by friends and admirers, for their work in the struggle for the recovery of Vieques's homeland. The event was held at the Puerto Rican Bar Association (the

Colegio de Abogados) in San Juan. Among those who lauded Lolita's work was her old companion in the attack on Congress, Rafael Cancel Miranda, who though absent from the activity, sent a text to be read for the occasion. Parts of it read as follows:

> To speak about Lolita one has to find the right words because no word can be as eloquent as her life has been. To understand Lolita, of course, one has to love deeply, as do the women who jumped over the fence to challenge the Yankee Navy in defense of the people of Vieques.

> Only love understands love, since the spiritual motor which has always guided Lolita is love. I knew her before March 1, 1954, but it was that March first that I got to know her as a woman ready to sacrifice her all for her people.

> On that historic day Lolita went to sacrifice her life. I have said many times that I have never seen anyone so willing to give her life for her homeland as Lolita Lebrón.

> The Lolita you see today and that you met in Vieques is the same Lolita.[81]

Lolita Lebrón died on August 1, 2010 and was buried the next day in the Old San Juan cemetery, not far from her political mentor, Pedro Albizu Campos. She was nearly ninety-one years old. At the time of her death she had spent nearly two-thirds of her life, struggling for the liberation of her homeland. In the process she had 'found God' through her love of Jesus Christ. That love gradually changed the way she came to view her mission on earth and helped her to redirect her actions toward a pacifist path during the last two decades of her life. After the 1980s, she reportedly abandoned the idea of armed struggle in favor of pacifist means through which she claimed Puerto Rico's liberation would be achieved. In the end, her devotion to world peace and her participation in the pacifist struggle for a Navy-free Vieques earned her the love and admiration of many in Puerto Rico and the Americas. At last, she seemed to have found a peaceful formula through which to channel the work "God had assigned" her: to fight for social justice, world peace, and the liberation of her homeland.

Many dignitaries, including a few who clearly disagreed with her political views and often questioned her goals, took the podium to eulogize the "great woman she had been." Hundreds accompanied her coffin from the funeral home in Río Piedras to the Cathedral in Old San Juan and stayed on for the religious services performed by Monsignor Roberto González and Bishop Rubén González. Many of them also followed the funeral procession to the Old City's cemetery where she was finally laid to rest.

Upon learning of her death, her friend and comrade in the Vieques' struggle, Rubén Berríos, paid her a great tribute when he referred to Lolita as: "the most eternal of the women in our history. Her faith, actions, and sacrifice transmuted her into a patriotic mystic who irradiated light and love. We, her sons and daughters, are grateful and honor her for her dedication to [the struggle] for the liberation of our homeland. History will immortalize her, and future generations will pay homage."[82]

3. Carmen Dolores Otero de Torresola (1928–?)

Preface

Carmen Dolores Otero, a native of Mayagüez, was known in New York as Carmen Torresola after she became the common-law wife of Griselio Torresola. She was twenty-two years old when she was first arrested in Manhattan in connection with her husband's attempt to assassinate President Truman on November 1, 1950. She spent two months in the Women's House of Detention in Lower Manhattan before she was released on grounds that the prosecution had failed to make its case. She was arrested again in March 1954 on suspicion that she had conspired with Lolita Lebrón and others who attacked the United States Congress. This time she was convicted of violating the Smith Act and was sentenced to a prison term of four years, which she served at the Federal Reformatory for Women in Alderson, West Virginia. She later abandoned the struggle for independence and refused to speak of her earlier involvement with the Nationalists.

The First Arrest

According to Rosa Collazo, also arrested on conspiracy charges in November 1950, she and Carmen Torresola were interrogated by the FBI in Lower Manhattan the night of November 2. Both stood accused of collaborating with their husbands in the plot to assassinate President Truman. Carmen's husband, Griselio Torresola, was killed during the attack on Blair House by the White House Guard, and Collazo was severely wounded, though he survived. Griselio's death left Carmen a young widow, with a young daughter and another child on the way.

The night of the interrogation, according to Rosa Collazo, Carmen had a difficult night "because the interrogators refused to let her to use the bathroom even though she was pregnant." She also spent much of that night, Collazo said, "worrying about the little girl she had to leave behind when the agents came to arrest her." Fortunately, Carmen's mother had arrived in time to take the child. After an intense night of questioning, Collazo explained, they were both taken to the Women's House of Detention, in New York's West Village, the following morning.[1]

They remained in the House of Detention for nearly two months because neither of them had the funds to post the bail assigned to them by the court of $50,000 each. According to Collazo, the Women's House was "a horror." (For details about that jail's conditions, see the section devoted to Rosa Collazo in this book.)

Without funds to hire a lawyer, she said, they accepted the public defender assigned to them by the court and waited for their case to come up for review. To their relief, Collazo explained, they were both released on December 23, 1950, "on grounds that the prosecution had failed to make a persuasive case."[2]

According to Puerto Rico's undercover police, Carmen Torresola returned to Puerto Rico after her release from prison and stayed with her cousin, Julia Flores, in an apartment in Columbus Landing, a sector of Mayagüez. The I.S. also indicated that prior to her 1950 arrest, Carmen had lived with Griselio at 610 East 138th Street in New York. An earlier report by the FBI's SAC (Special Agent in Charge) in San Juan noted that Torresola had been overheard "complaining that NPPR leaders in New York no longer trusted her and did not advise her of pertinent developments."[3]

The Second Arrest

Despite her apparent distance from the Nationalist chapter in New York, Carmen Torresola was again arrested in March 1954 by New York's Secret Service, on charges of "conspiring" with Lolita Lebrón and others "in their plot to harm the United States government by force and violence," a violation of the Smith Act. She was again interrogated by the FBI office on Foley Square and then taken to the Women's House of Detention to await a review of her case.[4]

It is not clear whether she posted bail at this time. According to one press account, she was one of seventeen Puerto Rican Nationalists (from

New York and Chicago) who was indicted in March 1954 for having violated the Smith Act. She was one of the thirteen tried in the Federal Court for the Southern District of New York between the fall of 1954 and February 1955. Though she was convicted of conspiracy in the plot to attack Congress, she was sentenced to a shorter sentence of four years compared with the six-year sentences given to Rosa Collazo and Lolita Lebrón. (Lolita Lebrón, as indicated earlier, had already been sentenced to fifty years for nine other crimes by the Federal Court in Washington, D.C.) Once convicted, in February 1955, the three women were transferred by train from the Women's House of Detention in New York to the Federal Reformatory for Women in Alderson, West Virginia.[5]

Except for a few comments by Rosa Collazo, little is known about Carmen's prison experience and much less about what happened to her once she was released from prison, in part because she refused to grant interviews as other Nationalist women did. According to one account reported by Puerto Rico's Secret Police, Carmen Torresola remarried a short time after she left prison and then "apparently dropped out of the Nationalist Party." Then in 1978 reporter Miñi Seijo, who interviewed Carmen for an article on the late Griselio Torresola, noted that Carmen had been reluctant to say anything about her life. She had merely confirmed two facts Seijo already knew: that she had joined the Nationalist Party chapter in Mayagüez (in 1948) while she was still in high school and that the person who inducted her into the Party, "Julio Ramón del Río, had been a federal agent."[6]

About Griselio, she said that he was "a good-natured man and a caring father" who had helped her to care for their baby daughter. She confirmed also that she had returned to Mayagüez in February 1951 (as the Insular Security agents had reported) in order to give birth to the child she was carrying when she was arrested in 1950 and that she named the boy Griselio after his late father.[7]

Part IV

Brief Accounts of Other Women Arrested in Puerto Rico

1. Juana Mills Rosa

According to Puerto Rico's Internal Security (I.S.) agents, Juana Mills Rosa joined the Nationalist Party in 1934 and was often seen collecting funds at various events. She later moved to New York City where she apparently became a close friend of Pedro Albizu Campos while he lived there (1943-1947). After a few years in New York City, she returned to Puerto Rico during the late 1940s and took up residence in Villa Palmeras, a working class neighborhood in the municipality of Santurce. On April 16, 1949, I.S. agents again reported that Mills was "observed attending a celebration in honor of José de Diego in barrio Obrero," a region of Santurce. By 1950 she had been "observed attending two annual Nationalist Party meetings: one at the Ateneo Puertorriqueño in Old San Juan (1948); and one in the Teatro Navas" in Arecibo, Puerto Rico (1949). She had also attended two major Party celebrations: one in Lares, September 23, 1949; and one in Fajardo, October 26, 1950.[1]

Suspected of having supported the uprising of October 30, 1950, she was detained several days later, according to a summary of that case included in her 1954 police file. I found no further evidence of what happened to Mills Rosa in that instance and suspect that she was released, without being charged, as was the case with more than eight hundred of those detained following the October 30 uprising.[2]

Juana Mills Rosa was one of the Nationalist women detained at Police Headquarters in Puerta de Tierra, San Juan. November, 1950.

She was again arrested on March 6, 1954, following the Nationalist attack on Congress. She was one of the thirty-eight men and women (including a few Communists) detained that day in Puerto Rico on suspicion that they had conspired with the attackers, a violation of Puerto Rico's Sedition Act, Law #53. Among the Communists were two women (Consuelo Burgos de Saez and Jane Speed de Andreu) who, like most of their comrades, were released a few days later for lack of evidence. Mills, however, was charged with having violated Law #53 for the mere act of "belonging" to the Puerto Rican Nationalist Party, which had already been declared a "subversive organization whose known intent was to overthrow the government by force and violence." In that instance, bail was set at $25,000. Unable to post bail at the time, she was sent to the Women's Wing of Arecibo's District Jail to await a review of her case.[3]

According to the arresting officers, led by Lieutenant Manuel G. Urrutia, they arrived at Mills' residence, in Villa Palmeras, at 6:00 in the morning on March 6, 1954, as ordered by the Justice Department. They knocked on the door of her residence and Mills asked, "Who the hell is knocking on my door at this hour?" They replied: "The police, with orders for your arrest." To which she ostensibly responded: "If it is the police, go shit on your mothers and go to hell," statements, he said, she repeated twice. He proceeded with the arrest, ordering his officers to "take Mills to a nearby [police] car until she calms down." They took her out of her home "still wearing a nightgown," he explained, "because she was violent and tried to slap the officers." With her out of the way, he said, he had his men search the place. The officers took so many items from Mills' home that they stopped enumerating them after a while yet claimed they had labeled all of them so they could be returned to her later. "[4]

Mills remained at the Women's Wing of the Arecibo jail until June 10, 1954, when she was released on bail, which had been reduced to $10,000 upon appeal. In August, she wrote to the Justice Department, demanding the return of the items seized by the police. Most of them (162) were returned, according to a receipt she signed on September 23rd. But other items were kept as evidence to be used at her upcoming trial. Among the latter were: a few Nationalist flyers and pamphlets, various receipts of funds contributed by Party members and sympathizers, three letters mailed to her from New York City by the well-known Nationalist Ramón Medina Ramírez (also under arrest) and a Christmas card mailed to her in December 1953 by Party leader Pedro Albizu Campos. Missing from the lot, she claimed, were a wristwatch, a fountain pen, and a pair of glasses.[5]

She was tried, along with thirteen others (five of them women), in the District Court of Arecibo between mid-December 1954 and February 7, 1955. All the defendants in that case were convicted as charged and later sentenced to many years in prison. In Mills' case, she was convicted of two violations of Law #53 and sentenced to serve a term of seven-to-ten years in prison. Her defense counsel, Antonio Reyes Delgado, appealed the conviction on grounds that "her incarceration had been illegal." The paper trail stopped at that point and I was unable to determine whether her appeal failed or succeeded. [6]

Yet the fact that she was not listed among the Nationalist inmates sent to the women's prison (in Vega Alta) in 1955 suggests two possibilities: a) she might have remained in the Arecibo jail for the duration of her sentence; b) or she could have won her appeal and was released at some point thereafter. The fact that she was listed among those attending an activity of Acción Patriótica Puertorriqueña on March 11, 1960, indicates she had been released from jail. Three days later (March 14), according to another I.S. account, she was "seen visiting Attorney Luis Manuel O'Neill's office in Old San Juan in the company of Paulino Castro." They had gone there, an informant said, "to discuss plans for the construction of a monument the Nationalists planned to erect in honor of the Nationalists killed in Ponce." Another police report included in Emily Vélez de Vando's Papers indicates that Mills was one of seventy-four independence advocates who attended the March 21, 1962 commemoration of the Ponce Massacre.[7]

2. Juanita Ojeda Maldonado

Juanita Ojeda Maldonado was originally from Utuado, Puerto Rico and lived there at the time she was arrested in November 1950. According to her police file, she was questioned at the District Court of Arecibo and then sent to the Women's Wing of Arecibo's District jail. Her police file also states that she joined the Puerto Rican Nationalist Party in 1935, remained active during the decade Albizu was in jail in the United States, and had presided over the Utuado chapter in 1948. The agents who trailed her said they often saw her depositing flowers at the grave sites of comrades killed in the Ponce Massacre, saying masses for their souls,

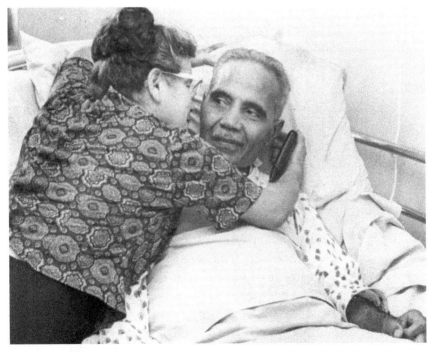

Juanita Ojeda visiting Albizu Campos at Presbyterian Hospital in Condado, San Juan, after she was released from prison.

or collecting funds for the monument the Nationalists planned to erect in their honor. They said that she had joined Albizu's inner circle as soon as he returned to Puerto Rico and had accompanied him to the rallies the Nationalists held in Manatí (June 11, 1948), Lares (September 1948, 1949, 1950), and other places.[8]

Though no evidence was found to link her to the attack in Utuado (1950), the prosecution charged her with two counts of violations of Law #53 (the fallback charge in such cases). She was convicted on both counts in September 1952 and sentenced to two prison terms: seven-to-thirteen months on the first count, and eight-to-thirteen months on the second. Both sentences were to be served concurrently. But since she had been in jail nearly two years already, she was released the very day the trial ended (September 16, 1952), according to documents in her file.[9]

She was free only a short time before she was arrested again in March 1954, following the Nationalist attack on Congress. She was detained on suspicion that she supported the attackers, which in the authorities' views meant she had violated the amended version of the island's Sedition Act, Law #53. She was again sent to the Women's Wing of Arecibo's District jail, even though she had moved her residence to Río Piedras (part of the San Juan metro) and should have been sent to San Juan's District jail, La Princesa. This time Ojeda was able to post bail (reduced from $25,000 to $14,000 upon appeal), and she was released pending a review of her case.[10]

The proceedings for Ojeda and thirteen others, as indicated elsewhere, were held in the District Court of Arecibo between December 14, 1954 and February 7, 1955. The fact that she was tried in Arecibo was an anomaly, given that her alleged crimes had been committed in San Juan, under whose jurisdiction she had lived for a few years. She was convicted, as were all her female comrades, and sentenced on May 31, 1955 to a prison term of seven-to-ten years. This time she was transferred to the Escuela Industrial Para Mujeres in Vega Alta, Puerto Rico, but apparently did not stay there very long before she was released. According to a report that appeared in Albizu Campos' FBI file, Ojeda was freed on bond in August 1955, pending resolution of an appeal. In January 1956, she was still free and was "seen delivering packages to the state penitentiary for Albizu Campos" and three months later was observed visiting Albizu at the Presbyterian Hospital.[11]

3. Ramona Padilla de Negrón

Ramona Padilla de Negrón, a native of Naranjito, Puerto Rico, was expecting a child the day her husband Antonio "Ñin" Negrón took to the mountains with nine other rebels, after having led them in an attack against the police station in their hometown. According to what Padilla told reporter Peggy Ann Bliss fifty years after the uprising, she was unaware of what her husband was doing or what could happen to her when she headed out to Corozal a few days later to buy a few things she needed for the baby. Someone in town, she said, must have recognized her and pointed her out to the police. She was arrested, she explained, in an attempt to force Ñin to surrender.[12]

After a night in a holding cell, she was taken to the Bayamón District Hospital, Ruiz Soler, for a vaginal exam. "The doctor," she said, "was a brute when he examined me; I guess he was looking for traces of my husband." After the exam, she recalled, "my shoes were so full of blood that they squished when I walked." From Bayamón she was transferred to San Juan, where she was sent to a makeshift holding center in Miramar because the other facilities were full. "They threw me in a padlocked room," she said, and since "I was sick of my own smell I had the doctor take pity on me and allow me to wash." But the stress of the incarceration and the violence of the vaginal exam sent her "into labor right there, in the holding cell." The worst part of the ordeal, she told Bliss, was that she "was so naïve" she had consented to a policeman's request: "to name the boy after him because he had been born during his watch." Not wishing to contradict him, she named her son Ernesto after the policeman.[13]

Apparently, Ramona's arrest proved effective because her rebel husband surrendered a few days later, and through this action enabled her and his newborn son to return home while he was taken off to jail. He was convicted and sentenced to prison for many years, though he was released after serving eight years. In any case, Ramona explained, Ñin was hardly ever around to help raise their five children because in the early days of their marriage he had been deployed to Germany to fight in the Second World War and after he was released from prison he went to Cuba, "to live the life of a revolutionary." He joined the Cuban army, she said, and stayed there about three years, "and when he came back to Naranjito he found himself another woman." Their lives would have been much harder, she told Bliss, had it not been for her in-laws who built her a house on their land and helped to care for the children. She also took a job at a factory in town making plastic flowers, which paid $6 a week. She continued to raise her children and in time, her son Ernesto became a lawyer. At the time of the interview (October 2000) he had a law practice in downtown Naranjito.[14]

Though neither Ramona nor her son seemed bitter about having been abandoned, they remembered Ñin (who died in 1990) with "mixed feelings." Ramona recalled the early days of their marriage, when she had "shared his ideals and feared for him." But then, she said, "I got tired and threw him out." Her son Ernesto, on the other hand, called his father "a hero" and seemed proud of the revolutionary legacy he had left him. At age seventy-seven, Ramona was still a strong woman, Bliss said, and was then caring for an invalid daughter-in-law.[15]

4. Angelina Torresola de Platet

Angelina Torresola was born in Jayuya, Puerto Rico, circa 1915 and died on September 7, 2015, at age one hundred. She was the oldest of four (Torresola Roura) siblings, all of whom became well-known Nationalists. Three of them took part in the violent events of 1950, as indicated earlier. Her brother Elio [Torresola] led the rebel troops of Jayuya the day the uprising began, and her sister Doris [Torresola] was wounded defending Albizu Campos when the San Juan police came to arrest him on October 30. Her youngest brother Griselio [Torresola] was killed in Washington (D.C.) on November 1, 1950 during his failed attempt to assassinate President Truman.[16]

Though her home was under constant surveillance, and she had a hefty police file, she was not arrested in connection with the uprising of 1950. According to local I.S. agents and the FBI men in San Juan, hers was the place where "Nationalist leaders often meet and relatives congregate." And according to the FBI censors in Pittsburgh, Pennsylvania (where her letters to her Blanca Canales were read, copied and translated into English) she and her husband, Alfredo Platet Canales, were great supporters of Albizu Campos and the cause of Puerto Rican independence. Her husband Alfredo was detained in 1950 but soon released for lack of evidence.[17]

Torresola de Platet was first arrested on March 8, 1954 on grounds that she had violated Law #53. The officers carrying out the arrest said she had not resisted but merely expressed concern about having to leave her elderly mother and her young children. They said also that they took her directly to the Women's Wing of the Arecibo's District Jail as ordered by the Justice Department. According to her case file, she remained in the Arecibo jail about six months before she was released on bail.[18]

She was one of the fourteen (including six women) who were tried in the District Court of Arecibo, between December 14, 1954 and February 7, 1955. Like them, she was convicted, but only of one violation of Law #53 and sentenced to a prison term of three to seven years. After sentencing, on May 31, 1955, she was remanded to the Escuela Industrial Para Mujeres in Vega Alta, Puerto Rico. According to a prison log, she stayed there only one day before she was released on bail, pending resolution of her appeal.[19]

Once released, she continued to support her siblings and other incarcerated comrades by writing, visiting, or sending care packages, according to her friend Heriberto Marín and various police accounts. A devout Catholic like many other Puerto Rican Nationalists, Angelina went to Church often to say masses for her fallen comrades or to pray for her imprisoned siblings and for Don Pedro's health. The Vega Alta prison logs indicate that she visited her sister Doris regularly. She also cared for Doris after she was released from prison. (Doris became mentally ill during her second stint in prison.) With the aid of her husband Alfredo Platet, Angelina provided a loving home for her aging mother Doña Rosalina Roura and for sister-in-law Delia Rivera and her son Elio Ariel Torresola.[20]

According to local I.S. agents and FBI men in San Juan, Angelina never stopped working for the cause of independence. She was often "seen with Juanita Ojeda, Carmen María Pérez, and Isabel Rosado raising funds to pay the Nationalist headquarters' rent during the years Albizu Campos remained in jail." Other times, reported Heriberto Marín, Angelina bought toiletries and other items for a few of the men while they were imprisoned. Referring to the generosity of the Platet Torresola couple, Ruth Reynolds said admiringly, "There are many ways to be a good revolutionary." (For more details about Angelina, see the letters quoted in the section devoted to her cousin Blanca Canales in this book.)[21]

A notice placed on Facebook by her friend and comrade Heriberto Marín reported that Angelina Torresola de Platet died on September 7, 2015. He lamented that she had left this earth before the Jayuyan Committee (ten of them women) had a chance to honor her revolutionary work and her birthday at the upcoming 65th anniversary of the Nationalist uprising. Though puzzling, I found no other mention in the press of the passing of this revolutionary woman.[22]

5. Monserrate Valle de López

Monserrate Valle was married to the Nationalist commander of Arecibo Tomás López de Victoria. Though she too was a Nationalist, according to Isabel Rosado, who shared a prison cell with her in Arecibo, there was never any proof that she had participated in the plot leading to the attack on the police station of that city. She was arrested in early November (1950) and sent to the District Jail of Arecibo on suspicion that she "probably had collaborated with her husband in the Nationalist plot to unseat the island's government." But when that charge could not be sustained, the prosecution charged her with one violation of Law #53, which, if proven, could result in a jail sentence of one to ten years. [23]

After questioning at the District Court of Arecibo, she was sent to the Women's Wing of that District's jail to await a review of her case. She was housed in the prison's open gallery, where she encountered two other Nationalists from the region: Juanita Ojeda Maldonado from Utuado and Leonides Díaz Díaz from Arecibo. In the same prison, she would later meet five other Nationalist women sent there from San Juan's District jail, La Princesa, between February and March 1951. The latter, however, were confined to two tiny rooms on the third floor of the jail, in part because the authorities had ordered the warden to keep them away from the general prison population until further notice. According to Ruth Mary Reynolds (one of the five confined to the third floor), the open gallery was so overcrowded that "some inmates had to sleep on the floor because there wasn't enough space to accommodate the cots needed."[24]

Since Valle's husband was also arrested after the attack on the Arecibo police station, she was forced to leave their two little girls in the care of friends (Juan Alamo and his wife Germana Bilbao) in Bayamón, Puerto Rico. She was worried about the girls and desperate to return home to care for them, according to Isabel Rosado. But the wheels of justice turned slowly in her case, and she was kept in detention for nearly two years before her case was brought to trial. In the meantime, Rosado said, Valle did her best to help others, especially the Nationalist comrades on the third floor. According to Ruth Reynolds, the women Valle, Díaz, and Ojeda had been a great help to her to her and Doris Torresola. One of them (she did not reveal which) helped them to smuggle out the testimonies they wrote in the Arecibo jail about the prison experiments they had suffered in 1951 during the time they spent in La Princesa.[25]

In 1952, Valle was brought to trial and absolved by a jury, while her husband was convicted and sentenced to more than 480 years. Apparently scarred by the experience, she vanished into anonymity after she was released from prison.

Conclusion

In the introductory chapter to this book, I offered an overview of Puerto Rico's history in order to explain how different sectors of the island's political elite challenged Spain's colonial rule during the nineteen century and later opposed the government implanted by the United States after 1898. The idea was to demonstrate how different political factions also struggled amongst themselves in their quest to take control of the island's government. By the 1860s, for instance, the Creole leadership was subdivided into two ideological groups: one that favored reforms while remaining within the framework of the Spanish empire; and another that wanted to liberate the island from Spain. The latter failed to achieve its goal but exerted enough pressure to predispose Spain to grant the island a few political reforms. The reformists, first known as Liberals and then as Autonomists, benefitted from the rebels' pressure and from the Spanish-American War and in 1897 they wrested a charter from Spain that granted Puerto Rico autonomy.

A similar pattern of resistance played out in Puerto Rico against the United States during the first half of the twentieth century except that during this period a third political faction emerged during the first five years of the United States' occupation. At first, the majority of the island's leaders favored making Puerto Rico a state of the American Union, but when that appeared unlikely because of Congress' reluctance, many of the leaders retreated to their earlier positions: the majority reverted to seeking reforms in search of self-government; a minority continued to push for independence; and a third group insisted on the idea of annexing the island to the American Union at a later time.

The political scene became further complicated by the emergence of an organized labor force, which joined different factions for a time and eventually formed its own political organization, the Socialist Party. There was much political wavering over the first forty years of the twentieth century as the various groups split and regrouped though their goals remained essentially the same.

Nationalists lined up, with National Guardsmen pointing rifes at them, at the National Guard head-quarters in Puerta de Tierra, San Juan.

Two major world wars and other international issues helped to shape the local leaders' attitudes and to pressure the United States into making adjustments to the colonial formula it had initially implanted in Puerto Rico following the end of the Spanish-American War. As in the previous century, the reformists (first called Unionists, then Liberals, and later Populares, or members of the Popular Democratic Party, PDP) pressured the United States to grant reforms, while a radicalized liberation movement took up arms in 1950 in an attempt to reach power. The combined forces of the two groups and mounting pressures from the world beyond gradually pushed the United States to find common cause with the reformists, the Populares, and to grant the island a measure of self-government in 1952. (The extent of power the United States yielded to Puerto Rico continues to be a subject of debate to this day.)

It is within this political framework that the imprisonment of the Nationalist women discussed in this book need to be understood, for they were actors in a political drama that dated back to the nineteenth century. Their actions, like those of their comrades, were part of a two-pronged struggle to liberate the island from colonial rule and from the reformists (Populares) in power, whom they described as "stooges of imperialism." For their part, the Populares, recent arrivals to the seat of power, described their challengers as "a bunch of lunatics" and vowed to crush them. In this mission, they were helped by several sectors of the United States government. Thus, in one week in November 1950, the newly elected PDP administration detained more than one thousand Nationalists and other supporters of independence, even when most of them had to be released a week and half later for lack of evidence on which to charge them. Then on March 6, 1954, the PDP government arrested another thirty-eight dissidents on suspicion that they had conspired with the four Nationalists who attacked the U.S. Congress. About half of these also had to be released for lack of evidence.

Such were the judicial excesses of the PDP administration that a Civil Rights Committee (established by Governor Luis Muñoz Marín in February 1956) concluded after fourteen months of work that "the government had [in fact] violated the civil and human rights of a portion of the island's citizenry." Thus, the Committee recommended that the government "pay compensation to those whose civil rights it had violated." It also recommended that the government "establish a Civil Rights Commission in order to safeguard against similar abuses in the future." It recommended "abolishing the Sedition Act (Law #53) which had led to the civil rights violations." Additionally, it called for the "abolition of the Internal Security division," which had carried out the persecution of the Nationalists and other independence advocates with the help of the Justice Department.

It was within this contentious environment that eleven of the twelve women detained in Puerto Rico during the 1950s were indicted on seditious charges (some twice in less than five years) while three were arrested in the United States on similar charges.

Most of those arrested in Puerto Rico and all three arrested in the United States during the 1950s were unable to post bail and had to remain in jail for months before they were brought to trial. The three indicted in the United States in 1954 were convicted and sentenced to prison terms ranging from four to fifty-six years. Nine of the eleven processed in Puerto Rico were sentenced to excessive prison terms. Only two of the eleven processed in Puerto Rico were absolved of their charges by a jury but after they had spent nearly two years in jail.

Both Leonides Díaz and Blanca Canales were denied bail and later sentenced to life in prison. Díaz, a fifty-year-old housewife from Arecibo, was convicted of eleven crimes she had not committed and given a prison sentence of 496 years. It took her seven years to win her freedom upon appeal. Blanca Canales, a forty-four year old social worker from Jayuya, was sentenced to life in prison for crimes she had not committed. Accused of killing a town's policeman, she was ultimately convicted on the allegation that she "had been the brain behind the insurrection that led to death and destruction" in her hometown. Accused also of having participated in the destruction of the U.S. Post Office in town, she was convicted and sentenced by the U.S. Federal Court in San Juan to a ten-year prison term. Though that sentence was reduced upon appeal, she served five and half years in Alderson, West Virginia before she was returned to Puerto Rico to begin serving her lifetime sentence. She won her freedom in August 1967, in part because the Sedition Act (Law #53), which had led to her arrest and incarceration, had been abolished ten years earlier (August 1957). (The abolition of Law #53 was in part due to the fact that the United States had repealed the Smith Act in 1956 and partly to the reality that a group of Puerto Rican lawyers challenged the constitutionality of the island's Sedition Act before the island's Supreme Court the following year.)

According to the journalists who covered the trials in which the women were convicted, the proceedings were rarely impartial. Though two of the women accused (Monserrate Valle and Carmen María Pérez) were absolved of their charges by a jury, it was only in 1952 after they spent nearly two years in jail. Pérez was arrested again in March 1954 in connection with her role in a shootout with the police. This time she was released on bail until her case came to trial. She was subsequently convicted of three criminal charges and sentenced to seventeen years in prison.

Ramona Padilla, a housewife and mother of four young children, was detained in 1950 in order to coax her husband, Antonio "Ñin" Negrón to surrender. She was held in a padlocked cell for more than a week. She gave birth in that cell before she was released. (To her dismay, she complied with a suggestion of the policeman on duty that she name her son after him because the boy was born during his watch.)

Ruth M. Reynolds, the lone North American in the group, was accused of two violations of Law #53 and kept in solitary confinement for many months before her case was brought to trial. She was absolved of one count and convicted of the other for which she was sentenced to a prison term of two-to-six years. She spent nineteen months in prison before her counsel got her released on bail. Her sentence was later revoked upon appeal by the Puerto Rican Supreme Court.

Juana Mills Rosa, a working class, black Puerto Rican woman from San Juan, was dragged out of her home still in her nightgown the morning of March 6, 1954 by the officers sent to arrest her. They later explained their deed, saying "she was out of control and needed to be subdued." They then carted off her belongings "as evidence that she was a dangerous Nationalist." Mills Rosa was later released on bail until her case came to trial. She was then convicted and sentenced to a prison term of seven to ten years. Her conviction was appealed and she eventually regained her freedom.

All of the women suffered a great deal in jail. Isabel Rosado, for instance, described in several interviews the many "horrors" she witnessed in one of the prisons where she had been held. She said that inmates were often held for many days in "dark confinement holes," without access to toilet facilities or running water "until they learned to obey prison rules." Ruth Reynolds and Doris Torresola left written indictments of the "tortures" they personally suffered in the San Juan District jail, La Princesa.

Rosa Collazo described the "horrific" conditions she witnessed at the Women's House of Detention in Lower Manhattan, where she, Lolita Lebrón, and Carmen Torresola spent time before they were sent to the Women's Reformatory in Alderson, West Virginia. In the latter, she said, Lolita Lebrón was often kept "shackled in her cell" because the guards thought she was "insane" because of her "excessively religious behavior."

Lolita later told her granddaughter Irene Vilar that she had been "sexually abused in prison" and subjected to "electric shocks" at a hospital for the insane in Washington, D.C.

What else did these women share in common besides their prison experience? According to their accounts, they all believed in Puerto Rico's right to be independent. They believed that Pedro Albizu Campos (the Nationalist Party's maximum leader) was a remarkable man who treated them as equals in the liberation struggle. They considered him the best-qualified leader to liberate Puerto Rico and bring about the changes the island needed. For those reasons they had sworn the Party's oath and pledged to give their lives and fortunes to the quest for their homeland's liberation. Most were religious women who viewed their faith as part of their cultural identity.

Notwithstanding their political beliefs, at the time they were arrested in 1950, only one of them had taken up arms against the colonial government. Four did so in 1954, for they claimed that their imprisonment had only reinforced their determination to continue the liberation struggle.

The women also differed in various ways from each other and the public in general. Most were better educated than the majority of women in their societies. Ruth Reynolds, for example, had an M.A. in English from an Illinois university while two of her Puerto Rican comrades had graduate degrees in Social Work as well as teaching licenses from the University of Puerto Rico. Another had completed more than two years of courses also at the same university. Four had high school diplomas, two had finished eighth grade, and only two had not gone past the third grade. Most were white and two were black.

They also differed in age. The oldest among them was nearing fifty years of age and the youngest was only twenty. (No age information was found on four of the convicted.) Eight were single and five were married. Two had been married previously, but one had divorced while the other had been left by her husband. One was a young widow.

Five had children (some young enough to need their care). One was held in the same prison where her husband and their two sons were imprisoned on criminal charges similar to hers. Another learned that her teen-age son had drowned the day she was being sentenced in 1954. Twenty-three years later she would also learn that her thirty-six year old daughter had perished in a car accident. Before joining the Nationalist

Party, another woman had witnessed the death of her two daughters from malnutrition.

The majority left prison with a variety of ailments, due in part to the poor prison diet and the lack of prompt medical attention. Many suffered from weak hearts and/or diabetes. A few died later of cancer or diabetic complications. One went mad during her second imprisonment and committed suicide nine years after her release from a psychiatric hospital.

Life after prison was also very difficult for all of the women. Upon their release, some were too old to look for work. The younger ones generally had trouble finding work due to their prison record. The few who found jobs were often fired after the Secret Service or the FBI "visited" their employers. Every one of them was kept under strict surveillance until they died.

Yet through it all, the great majority remained faithful to their political ideals and often rejoined the Nationalist Party or other independence groups. They marched for world peace, supported prison reform, protested against nuclear arms proliferation, demonstrated against the United States Navy's occupation of the islands of Vieques and Culebra, joined labor and students' protests, and called for the release of the Puerto Rican political prisoners still held in the United States.

Despite great odds, all of these women remained resilient. They were admired and also loved. Many were honored by comrades and supporters. A few were eulogized in death, even by those who disagreed with their politics, for in time they were recognized as heroines of the homeland.

A Note about Sources

Mastering the facts included in the introduction to this book took me more than three decades of teaching dozens of courses on Puerto Rico, the Caribbean, and Latin America. During a period of three years I also taught an introductory course on the history of the United States. Hence, the judgments and generalizations I venture here cannot be explained by simply adding an endnote here and there, though I also do that for the benefit of the reader. The data needed for each of the biographical essays included in this book was painstakingly compiled from a variety of primary sources over a period of four years. In a few cases, I had the opportunity to interview several of the women who had been imprisoned, their cellmates, or relatives who were still alive when I began the project. In other cases, I culled information from interviews they had granted to various journalists over the years.

In every case, I tested the accuracy of the stories I read or heard by reviewing multiple sources and checking the details provided at different times by the narrators. Occasionally, I uncovered errors or inconsistencies in their stories, even when these were recounted by the same person. To document the process that led to the women's imprisonment and eventual release from prison, I reviewed dozens of newspaper articles reported as the events unfolded, conscious of the fact that some journalists were less impartial than others. For the official view, I examined hundreds of government documents, including arrest orders, police reports, letters and memoranda sent to or from the office of the governor. In addition, I examined dozens of police and FBI profiles of the individuals I was studying and other Nationalists, compiled long before they were arrested. In many cases, the police files were accompanied by photos of the person profiled. I also read numerous reports issued by the warden and guards of the Arecibo district jail and the Vega Alta women's prison. For information about conditions in the district jails of San Juan and Arecibo, I relied on the testimonies of women who had spent time in both institutions. For details about the New York House of Detention and the Federal Women's Reformatory in Alderson, West Virginia, I relied on the "Memoirs" of Rosa Collazo, and the personal accounts of Elizabeth Gurley Flynn and Miriam Moskowitz, all of whom spent time in those facilities during the time Lolita Lebrón, Carmen Dolores Otero de Torresola, and Blanca Canales were imprisoned there.

In the case of Ruth Mary Reynolds, I spent many weeks during two separate summers reading through the extensive collection, "The Ruth M. Reynolds Papers," she donated to the Archives of the Centro for Puerto Rican Studies at Hunter College in Manhattan, which contains, among other documents, the dossier (#1340) the Puerto Rican police kept on her. I was particularly grateful for the transcripts of the one hundred and twelve hours of interviews she granted to Blanca Vázquez at the Centro. They contain very useful information not only about Reynolds' life and actions on behalf of the Nationalist Party and its cause but also about other Americans (some friends of Reynolds) who supported Puerto Rico's right to be independent. It also contains copies of speeches Reynolds gave on behalf of Puerto Rico or Albizu Campos and articles she wrote on these topics. The collection is a veritable gold mine of information.

The information for the biographical essay on Dominga de la Cruz was extracted from three extensive interviews, an account she wrote in 1976 during her short visit to Puerto Rico, and several letters she wrote to her comrade Juan Antonio Corretjer. The interviews cited were conducted between 1976 and 1978 in Puerto Rico and Havana, Cuba. The longest of these was the one conducted by journalist Margaret Randall, who later published portions of the transcript in a book she wrote (in Spanish) on Dominga de la Cruz. Recently, she authorized me to use the information in that book for the purpose of my work.

Though this study relies most heavily on primary sources, there were a few secondary sources that also proved extremely useful. In terms of Puerto Rico's Sedition Act, Law #53, I could not have managed without Ivonne Acosta's seminal work *La Mordaza: Puerto Rico, 1948-1957* or without the speeches of Albizu Campos she compiled and published. For the overall details about the 1950 uprising, I relied on Miñi Seijo's *La Insurrección Nacionalista en Puerto Rico, 1950* as well as on the numerous interviews she conducted with many participants of the uprising after they were released from prison. For details about the Nationalists' attacks of Blair House and later the United States Congress I relied almost exclusively on newspaper coverage of those events. For details about the conditions of the New York House of Detention and the Federal Women's Reformatory in Alderson, West Virginia I depended on the works of Elizabeth Gurley Flynn, *My Life as a Political Prisoner* and Miriam Moskowitz, *Phantom Spies, Phantom Justice.* (For the precise details about the sources I cite throughout this book, see the notes included at the end of each biographical essay.)

Notes

Introduction

1. Miñi Seijo Bruno, *La insurrección nacionalista en Puerto Rico, 1950* (Río Piedras: Editorial Edil, 1997).
2. Pedro Aponte Vázquez, *El ataque a la Fortaleza* (San Juan: Publicaciones René, 2007).
3. The list of forty-one women came from various sources; the most accessible is contained in the appendix in Ché Paralitici's book, *Sentencia Impuesta: 100 Años de encarcelamientos por la independencia de Puerto Rico* (San Juan: Ediciones Puerto, 2004).
4. For specific references about Oscar Collazo and Griselio Torresola's attack of Blair House and how their actions impacted their families, see the newspaper coverage I cite in the section devoted to Rosa Collazo in this book.
5. For details about the Nationalists' attack on Congress, see the newspaper coverage I cite in the section devoted to Lolita Lebrón in this book.
6. The data about the arrests that followed the 1954 Nationalist attack was gathered from multiple government documents I found at the Archivo General de Puerto Rico (AGPR), Fondo: Departamento de Justicia, Serie: Nacionalistas, Tarea: 90-29. (For more details, see the notes on each of the biographical essays in this book.)
7. I spent many years teaching numerous courses on Puerto Rican, Latin American, and Caribbean history. Over a period of three years, I also taught U.S. history. I have also spent years doing primary research on various Puerto Rican topics and published the following books: *Puerto Rico's Revolt for Independence: El Grito de Lares* (Boulder: Westview Press, 1984); *El Grito de Lares: Sus causas y sus hombres* (Río Piedras: Ediciones Huracán, 1984); *Puerto Rico: An Interpretive History From Pre-Columbian Times to 1900* (Princeton: Markus Wiener, 1998), and co-edited with Kal Wagenheim; *The Puerto Ricans: A Documentary History* (Princeton: Markus Wiener, 2013). For an overview of five hundred years of Puerto Rican history, see Francisco Scarano, *Puerto Rico: Cinco siglos de historia* (Bogotá: McGraw Hill Interamericana, 1993). For an overview of Puerto Rico's twentieth century history, see César J. Ayala and Rafael Bernabe, *Puerto Rico in the American Century: A History Since 1898* (Chapel Hill: University of North Carolina Press, 2007).
8. The transformation of the Puerto Rican economy and society during the nineteenth century was due in part to new imperial policies, which facilitated the arrival of thousands of foreign migrants. I researched the coffee economy of the western region of Puerto Rico for my book on "El Grito de Lares" (1868). For details about the groups who settled in Puerto Rico during the nineteenth century, see Estela Cifre de Loubriel, *La formación del pueblo puertorriqueño: La contribución de los catalanes, baleáricos, y valencianos* (San Juan: Instituto de Cultura Puertorriqueña, 1975); see also Pedro Juan Hernández, "Los inmigrantes italianos de Puerto Rico, durante el siglo XIX," *Anales de Investigación Histórica*, vol. III, no. 2 (1976); for a general study of Puerto Rico within the Caribbean context, see Arturo Morales Carrión's book, *Puerto Rico and the Non-Hispanic Caribbean* (San Juan: University of Puerto Rico Press, 1971).
9. Ibid. For details about the sugar plantations in nineteenth century Ponce, see Francisco Scarano, "Inmigración y estructura de clases: Los hacendados de Ponce, 1815–1845," in Scarano, *Inmigración y clases sociales en el Puerto Rico del siglo XIX* (Río Piedras: Ediciones

Huracán, 1981); see also his seminal book on the subject, *Sugar and Slavery in Puerto Rico: The Plantation Economy of Ponce, 1800–1850* (Madison: University of Wisconsin Press, 1984).

10. Ibid. For the conditions under which the laboring classes toiled in the coffee region, see the following books by Fernando Picó: *Registro general de jornaleros (Utuado, Puerto Rico, 1848–1850)* (Río Piedras: Ediciones Huracán, 1976); *Libertad y servidumbre en el Puerto Rico del siglo XIX* (Huracán, 1979); *Amargo Café* (Huracán, 1981). See also Salvador Brau, "Las Clases Jornaleras de Puerto Rico," in *Ensayos: Disquisiciones Sociológicas* (Río Piedras: Editorial Edil, 1972). During my teaching days, I discovered that the fastest way to get undergraduate students to understand the economic and social disparities that existed in Puerto Rico's coffee region was to have them read Manuel Zeno Gandía's novel, *La Charca* (San Juan: Instituto de Cultura, 1966). The novel was translated into English as *The Pond* by Kal Wagenheim and later published by Markus Wiener.

11. For details about the social tensions in the coffee region during the 1860s, see Jiménez de Wagenheim, *El Grito de Lares: Sus causas y sus hombres*; also Laird Bergad, "Hacia el Grito de Lares: Café, Estratificación Social y Conflictos de Clase, 1828–1868," in Francisco A. Scarano, ed., *Inmigración y clases sociales en el Puerto Rico del siglo XIX* (Río Piedras, Ediciones Huracán, 1981). Also Picó, *Amargo Café*; Zeno Gandía's, *La Charca*.

12. There are numerous books on the history of Latin America and its battles for independence. The one cited here is by John Lynchs, *The Spanish-American Revolutions, 1808–1826* (New York: W.W. Norton, 1973); for details about the Spanish reforms that led to the first steps in revamping Puerto Rico's agrarian economy, see Luis E. González Vales, "Towards a Plantation Society," in Arturo Morales Carrión, ed., *Puerto Rico: A Political and Cultural History* (New York: W.W. Norton, 1983).

13. Picó, Brau, Zeno Gandía, in works cited.

14. For details, see Jiménez de Wagenheim, *Puerto Rico's Revolt for Independence;* also Ada Suárez Díaz, *El Doctor Ramón Emeterio Betances: Su vida y su obra* (San Juan: Talleres Gráficos Inter Americanos, 1970); María Luisa Torre del Alba, "Testamentos en Lares, 1849–1899," in *Anales de investigación histórica*, vol. III, no. 2 (1976), Juan Antonio Corretjer, "The Day Puerto Rico Became a Nation," *The San Juan Star Sunday Magazine*, September 22, 1968 (reprinted in Wagenheim and Jiménez de Wagenheim, *The Puerto Ricans: A Documentary History*), p. 71.

15. Ibid.

16. Ibid.

17. There are numerous treatises about Puerto Rico's political history. For details, see the pioneer works of historian L. Cruz Monclova, which he summarized in "The Puerto Rican Political Movement in the 19th Century," for the United States-Puerto Rico Commission, in preparation for the Puerto Rican plebiscite of 1967. It was published as part of the Commission's Status Report (Washington, D.C.: Government Printing Office, 1966). See also F. Bayron Toro, *Elecciones y Partidos Políticos en Puerto Rico* (San Juan: Isla, 2000); and for a critical version of the populist centrist parties, see Luis Nieves Falcón, *Un siglo de represión política en Puerto Rico: 1898–1998* (San Juan: Ediciones Puerto, 2009).

18. The United States conducted various studies of its new possession. One of the earliest was William Dinwiddie's study *Puerto Rico: Its Conditions and Possibilities* (New York and London: Harper and Brothers, 1899).

19. For details about the U.S. invasion of Puerto Rico, see the following documents in Wagenheim and Jiménez de Wagenheim, *The Puerto Ricans: A Documentary History*, "The Autonomist Concept," p. 84; "Seize San Juan," p. 102; "Our Flag Is Raised in Puerto Rico," p. 106; "To the Inhabitants of Porto [sic] Rico," p. 109; and "Diary of the War," p. 113.

20. Ibid. The role and motivation of the Puerto Ricans who took up arms since the Lares uprising are still debated. For details about two such moments in the island's history, see the works of Juan Manuel Delgado, *El levantamiento de Ciales* (Guasábara, 1980), and Mariano Negrón Portillo, *Cuadrillas anexionistas y revueltas campesinas en Puerto Rico, 1898–1899*

(Río Piedras: Centro de Estudios Sociales: Universidad de Puerto Rico, 1987). The well-known historian Fernando Picó has argued that the "partidas sediciosas" were "settling old scores" with the Spaniards.

21. For details about the economic role of slavery in Puerto Rico's sugar industry (in Ponce) during the nineteenth century, see Francisco Scarano, *Sugar and Slavery*. For other details about the role of slavery in the sugar industry, see Luis A. Figueroa, *Sugar, Slavery, and Freedom in Nineteenth-Century Puerto Rico* (Chapel Hill: University of North Carolina Press, 2005).

22. Cruz Monclova, "The Puerto Rican Political Movement . . . " For details about Spain's political development during the latter part of the nineteen century, see Melchor Fernández Almagro, *Historia política de la España contemporánea, 1868–1885* (Madrid: Editorial Alianza, 1969).

23. For Betances' role in Puerto Rico's struggle for independence, see Suárez, *El Doctor Ramón Emeterio Betances*; also Carlos N. Carreras, *Betances: El Antillano Proscrito* (San Juan: Editorial Club de la Prensa, 1961); Juan Manuel Delgado, "El Levantamiento . . . "; Negrón Portillo, "Cuadrillas . . . ."

24. Wagenheim and Jiménez de Wagenheim, *A Documentary History*, see the following documents: "Puerto Rico as a Permanent Possession," p. 94, "Seize San Juan," p. 102, and "Our Flag Is Raised," p. 106. See also "To the Inhabitants of Porto Rico," p. 109.

25. For details about the individuals who were imprisoned by American colonial rulers, see Ché Paralitici, *Sentencia Impuesta: 100 Años de encarcelamientos por la independencia de Puerto Rico* (San Juan: Ediciones Puerto, 2004). For details about the colonial economy implanted by the United States, see James Dietz, *Economic History of Puerto Rico: Institutional Change and Capitalist Development* (Princeton: Princeton University Press, 1986). For the changing strategies adopted by local leaders since the 1970s, see Dietz, *Puerto Rico: Negotiating Development and Change* (Boulder: Lynne Reinner, 2003).

26. Most historical accounts of Puerto Rico provide information about the devastation caused by the various hurricanes from 1899 to the end of the twentieth century.

27. For comments about the Puerto Ricans in Hawaii, see Iris López, "Borinkis and Chop Suey: Puerto Rican Identity in Hawaii, 1900 to 2000," in Carmen T. Whalen and Victor Vázquez, eds., *The Puerto Rican Diaspora: Historical Perspectives* (Philadelphia, Temple University Press, 2005), pp. 43–67.

28. The reference about Puerto Ricans in Cuba is cited by José A. Cobas and Jorge Duany, *Cubans in Puerto Rico: Ethnic Economy and Cultural Identity* (Gainesville: University of Florida Press, 1997).

29. For a discussion about the first three decades of American colonial rule in Puerto Rico, see Pedro A. Cabán, *Constructing a Colonial People: Puerto Rico and the United States, 1898–1932* (Boulder: Westview Press, 1999).

30. The point about the federal court system was clarified by Attorney Irma Alicia Rodríguez. For details about the role of this court in the incarceration of Pedro Albizu Campos and other Nationalists, including Blanca Canales, see other sections of this book. For details about the incarceration of the men who evaded the military draft, see the works of Ché Paralitici.

31. The point about the spread of the Protestant religions was made by Blanca Canales in an interview she granted to journalist Peggy Ann Bliss. For details, see the section devoted to Canales in this book.

32. The acquisition of new territories by the United States in 1898 led to a series of legal cases (known collectively as the "Insular Cases"). In respect to Puerto Rico, the Congress' definition of Puerto Rico as an "unincorporated territory" was upheld by the Supreme Court in 1901. The creation of the Commonwealth of Puerto Rico in 1952 attempted to challenge that definition, but met with resistance from the U.S. Congress, which claimed it had not yielded any of its "plenary powers." The fact that federal legislation applies in Puerto Rico (unless Congress determines otherwise) led Albizu Campos and many others to claim that

Puerto Rico remains a colony, despite the vote by the United Nations in 1953.

33. Cabán, *Constructing a Colonial People.*

34. Cabán, ibid. See also Angel Quintero Rivera, *Conflictos de clase y política en Puerto Rico* (Río Piedras: Ediciones Huracán, 1976). Some of Quintero Rivera's arguments were later challenged. For details, see Rafael Bernabe, *Respuestas al colonialismo en la política puertorriqueña, 1899–1929* (Río Piedras: Ediciones Huracán, 1996).

35. For details about the island's labor movement and its political struggles, see Angel Quintero Rivera, *La lucha obrera en Puerto Rico: Antología de grandes documentos en la historia obrera puertorriqueña* (Río Piedras: CEREP, 1971). For its link to the AFL, see Carlos Sanabria, "Samuel Gompers and the American Federation of Labor in Puerto Rico," *Centro* 17, no. 1 (Spring 2005), pp. 141–61.

36. In Wagenheim and Jiménez de Wagenheim, *A Documentary History*, see the following documents: "An Idle Dream," p. 141, "The Future of my Country," p. 142, and "Treachery and Disenchantment," p. 153.

37. The requirement to have Puerto Ricans serve in the U.S. armed forces was included in the Jones Act of 1917 and was enforced while the draft lasted. For details about Puerto Ricans in the U.S. armed forces, see the various publications of Ché Paralitici. He has devoted many years to documenting this topic. For details about the Jones Act and the type of U.S. citizenship it extended to Puerto Ricans, see José A. Cabranes, *Citizenship and the American Empire: Notes on the Legislative History of the United States Citizenship of Puerto Ricans* (New Haven: Yale University Press, 1979).

38. For details about the annexionist trend in Puerto Rico, see Edgardo Meléndez, *Puerto Rico's Statehood Movement* (Westport, Conn.: Greenwood Press, 1988). See also Aarón Gamaliel Ramos, ed., *Las ideas anexionistas en Puerto Rico bajo la dominación norteamericana* (Río Piedras: Ediciones Huracán, 1987).

39. For details about the suffrage movement in Puerto Rico, see María Barceló Miller, *La lucha por el sufragio femenino en Puerto Rico, 1896–1935* (Río Piedras: Ediciones Huracán-Centro de Investigaciones Sociales, 1997). For the voting rights struggle of working-class women, see Yamila Azize, *La mujer en la lucha* (Río Piedras: Editorial Cultural, 1985). For details about anarchist Luisa Capetillo, see Norma Valle Ferrer, *Luisa Capetillo* (Río Piedras: Editorial Cultural, 1990). See also Julio Ramos, ed., *Amor y anarquía: Los escritos de Luisa Capetillo* (Río Piedras: Huracán, 1992).

40. For a detailed biography of Pedro Albizu Campos, see Marisa Rosado, *Las llamas de la aurora: Acercamiento a una biografía de Pedro Albizu Campos* (San Juan: Author's Edition, 1998); for the text of Alibizu's speeches, see Ivonne Acosta, *La palabra como delito: Los discursos por los que condenaron a Pedro Albizu Campos 1948–1950* (San Juan: Editorial Cultural, 1993).

41. Rosado, Interview, 1998.

42. Rosado, ibid. For details about the rise of Albizu Campos and the Nationalist movement he led, see Wagenheim and Jiménez de Wagenheim, *The Puerto Ricans: A Documentary History*, Part VII, and Cesar Andreu Iglesias, "The Conscience of his People," *El Imparcial* (San Juan), April 14, 1965, p. 30 (translated by Kal Wagenheim and reprinted in *The Puerto Ricans: A Documentary History*, pp. 260–62).

43. The author lived through the "peaceful revolution" ushered in by the Popular Democratic Party government and witnessed firsthand many of social and economic reforms. During the 1950s she was one of the many rural children who benefited from the government-subsidized education, the bookmobile, and medical services provided to the poor by the PDP administration. In her home, as in many homes in her neighborhood, Luis Muñoz Marín's photograph was displayed on the living-room wall and his pamphlets were read at night. There are numerous scholarly studies on the deeds of the PDP that the reader can access. For the rise of Albizu Campos and his political significance, see, in addition to Rosado, ibid., the following documents in Wagenheim and Jiménez de Wagenheim, *A Documentary History*, "The Rise of Albizu Campos," p. 185; "Rebellion in Puerto Rico,"

p. 192; "Violence and Nationalism," p. 198.

44. Rosado, Interview, 1998.

45. Ibid.

46. Ibid.

47. Ibid. For details about the political repression practiced by the PDP administration, see Acosta, *La Mordaza*; for references about the ACLU's role in the investigation of the Ponce Massacre, see the section devoted to Dominga de la Cruz in this book.

48. Ibid.

49. The Chardón Plan and the economic incentives offered by the PDP government to prospective foreign investors have been studied a great deal. For an introductory review, see James Dietz, *Economic History of Puerto Rico*; also Ayala and Bernabe, *The American Century*, chap. 9.

50. The Puerto Rican Migration to the United States has been covered by many, including various works by the Center for Puerto Rican Studies at Hunter College. For a few documents on the subject, see Wagenheim and Jiménez de Wagenheim, *The Puerto Ricans*, Part IX: "Exodus," pp. 263–318.

51. James Dietz, *Puerto Rico: Negotiating Change*; also Dietz, *Economic History of Puerto Rico*.

52. Ayala and Bernabe, *The American Century*, chap. 9.

53. For details about the shifting policies of the PDP, see Carlos Zapata Oliveras, *Nuevos caminos hacia viejos objetivos: Estados Unidos y el establecimiento del Estado Libre Asociado de Puerto Rico, 1945–1953* (Río Piedras: Comisión Puertorriqueña del Quinto Centenario, 1991).

54. For contrasting views on the programs of the PDP, see Thomas Mathews, *Puerto Rican Politics and the New Deal* (Gainesville: University of Florida Press, 1969), and Emilio Pantojas-García, "Puerto Rican Populism Revisited: The PDP During the 1940s," *Journal of Latin American Studies* 21, no. 3 (October 1989), pp. 521–57.

55. Zapata Oliveras; *Nuevos Caminos*; also Pantojas-García, "Puerto Rican Populism Revisited."

56. For a detailed study of the Gag Rule (Law #53) and its pernicious effects (1948–1957), see Ivonne Acosta's book *La Mordaza*; see also her own summary of that work, in English, titled "The Smith Act Goes to San Juan: La Mordaza, 1948–1957," in Ramón Bosque-Pérez and José Javier Colón Morera, eds., *Puerto Rico Under Colonial Rule: Political Persecution and the Quest for Human Rights* (Albany: State University of New York Press, 2006), pp. 59–66.

57. The information about Albizu Campos' efforts at the United Nations is known by a select few, namely those interested in the topic of Puerto Rican independence. For the details offered here I relied on Sandra Morales Blanes, "La participación de la mujer en el Partido Nacionalista de Puerto Rico (PNPR) en Puerto Rico y Estados Unidos vista a través de la carpetas del negociado Federal de Investigaciones (FBI), 1941–1951," a master's thesis she presented to the Centro de Estudios Avanzados de Puerto Rico y el Caribe, San Juan, 2013.

58. According to information provided by Lolita Lebrón, after Thelma Mielke lost the Observer's post at the United Nations, Albizu Campos assigned Julio Pinto Gandía to continue lobbying members of the General Assembly, and she was appointed to replace Pinto Gandía in his previous role, Nationalist Party Delegate for the United States.

59. For details about Albizu's revolutionary plan, see Blanca Canales' testimony, which is cited in detail in the section devoted to her in this book.

60. For the actions of Muñoz Marín and the responses by President Truman, see Zapata Oliveras, *Nuevos caminos*; also Pantojas-García, "Puerto Rican Populism Revisited."

61. The terms provided by Public Law 600 were debated at length by the architects of the Commonwealth government and by its critics and political rivals. For details, see Zapata Oliveras, ibid., Pantojas Garcia, ibid. See also newspaper coverage by *El Mundo* and *El Imparcial* during the last weeks of July 1952 and November 1953. For a brief summary of the process, see Ayala and Bernabe, *The American Century*, chaps. 7 and 8.

62. Details of the preparations for the official recognition of the Estado Libre Asociado (ELA)

government (July 25, 1952) were covered by the island's major dailies (*El Mundo* and *El Imparcial*). See the coverage of July 26, 1952. For a version of the darker side of the history of the PDP government in connection to the Nationalists, see José Javier Colón Morera, "Puerto Rico: The Puzzle of Human Rights and Self-Determination," in Bosque-Pérez and Colón Morera, *Puerto Rico under Colonial Rule* (New York: State University of New York Press, 2006), pp. 83–102.

63. Zapata Oliveras, *Nuevos caminos*.

64. Since the 1960s, Cuba's representatives at the United Nations have adhered to Fidel Castro's interpretation that Puerto Rico remains a "scented colony" (*una colonia perfumada*). They have also supported the idea of revisiting Puerto Rico's case with the General Assembly. During the 1960s, when Puerto Rico's economy seemed healthy and the PDP leaders had not yet lost control of the electorate to the annexationist forces, they continued to stand by their earlier interpretation that Puerto Rico's colonial status had ended in 1952 when the ELA government was implanted. After the oil crisis of the 1970s pushed the island's economy into a downward spiral, ex-governor Rafael Hernández Colón came around to Cuba's and his political foes' interpretation that Puerto Rico was still a colony. Thus, he came to agree with the views of Albizu Campos, Rubén Berríos (leader of the Partido Independentista Puertorriqueño (PIP), Juan Mari Bras (leader of the Partido Socialista Puertorriqueño), and other advocates of independence. This had also been the position of the leadership of the statehood movement. The Nationalists and others used the colonial argument to justify the need for independence, and the annexationists used it to propagate the notion that statehood is the better option.

Part I: Dominga de la Cruz Becerril Rescues the Flag

1. The biography of Dominga de la Cruz presented here was essentially extracted from three interviews she granted between 1976 and 1978, plus an account she wrote about the Ponce Massacre during her short stay in Puerto Rico in 1976. The first of the interviews, titled "Entrevista a Dominga de la Cruz: Miren la Bandera," was conducted by Julia Mirabal and published, *Romances* in Havana, Cuba, in March 1976. The text of that interview was reprinted in San Juan by *Claridad, En Rojo Section*, March 26, 1976, pp. 5–6. The second interview, titled "Entrevista de Dominga de la Cruz," was conducted by Miñi Seijo and then published by *Claridad, En Rojo Section*, July 10, 1976, pp. 22–24. De la Cruz' own account, titled "Relato de la Masacre de Ponce," was first published in *Correo de la Quincena*, March 1977, and reprinted by *Claridad*, March 21–27, 1997, pp. 20–21. The longest interview with Dominga de la Cruz was conducted by Margaret Randall in Havana, Cuba, circa 1978. She later published the text of that interview as part of a biographical essay she titled *El pueblo no sólo es testigo: La historia de Dominga* (Río Piedras: Ediciones Huracán, 1979). Randall granted me permission to translate the text of her interview from Spanish to English and make use of it for the purpose of my project. I also had access to several letters Dominga de la Cruz wrote to her comrade Juan Antonio Correjter between 1963 and 1974. Also useful was an article by Cacimar Cruz, titled "Dulces Labios y Dominga Cruz," posted online, which I retrieved from http://lists.indymedia.org/pipermail/cmi-pr/2006-March/0322-gs.html. For details of how De la Cruz was remembered, I relied on the eulogy by Jacinto Rivera Pérez (President of the Nationalist Party), titled "Muere Heroína Puertorriqueña: Dominga de la Cruz Becerril." In this, Rivera Pérez basically recounts the political deeds of De la Cruz.

2. Randall, *El pueblo no solo es testigo*, pp. 18–19; she told Seijo during their interview in 1976 the names of her father: Domingo Clarillo de la Cruz; mother: Catalina Becerril; and godmother: Isabel Mota de Ramery.

3. Randall, *El pueblo no solo es testigo*, pp. 20–23; Seijo, Interview, pp. 3–; for details about the garment industry in Mayagüez (known in Puerto Rico as the needle industry), see

María del Carmen Baerga, ed., *Género y Trabajo: La industria de la Aguja en Puerto Rico y el Caribe Hispánico* (San Juan: Editorial de la Universidad de Puerto Rico, 1995. Chapters 2, 3, and 4 helped me to understand the lives of the garment workers in Puerto Rico during the first three decades of the twentieth century.

4. In Baerga, see Luisa Hernández Angueira, "El trabajo a domicilio femenino y la industria de la aguja en Puerto Rico, 1914–1940." Also Randall, p. 24.

5. De la Cruz makes references to the deaths of her daughters in several interviews, as well as in a letter she wrote from Havana, Cuba, on April 30, 1963, to her comrade Juan Antonio Corretjer. See also Randall, p. 26; Mirabal, Interview, March 1976; Seijo, Interview, July 1976. In the letter to Corretjer, she briefly described the treatment the Cuban state offered to its women and children and compared that to her experience in Puerto Rico during the 1930s. She said, " I see how the Socialist State helps the mothers to keep their children safe and healthy and I think about mine and how I watched them die in my arms for lack of money to buy food or pay for a good doctor." (Copies of her letters to Corretjer were accessed at the Corretjer Library in Ciales, Puerto Rico.)

6. Seijo, Interview, 1976; Randall, pp. 26–30.

7. Ibid. Randall, p. 34.

8. Randall, pp. 35–36.

9. Ibid. pp. 3–37; for details about the breakup of the Mayagüez Nationalist chapter, see Marisa Rosado's biography, Pedro Albizu Campos. The one cited here is her revised edition, *Pedro Albizu Campos: Las llamas de la Aurora, un acercamiento a su biografía* (San Juan, Puerto Rico: Author's Edition, 1998).

10. Randall, p. 37; also Seijo, Interview, 1976.

11. According to José Manuel Dávila's essay, "Metamorfosis: De las Hijas de la Libertad al Cuerpo de Enfermeras," the association called "Las Hijas de la Libertad" was founded in March of 1932 in Caguas, Puerto Rico, by a group of sixty-two Nationalist students from Central High School. The group's president was Lamia Azize Mawad. He said the Nationalist Party not only welcomed the new association but urged it to branch out to other high schools across the island. The major goals of the new association, reported *El Imparcial*, in "Se forma en Caguas la Asociación 'Hijas de la Libertad'" (March 9, 1932, p. 7) were as follows: to restore the Republic of Puerto Rico; to defend the prestige and honor of the homeland; to inculcate the ideals of and love for the homeland among the young; and to spread the Nationalist ideals and values among women. The Nationalist women's roles, explained María Barceló Miller, were "basically extensions of the traditional ones women already occupied in the society, except that this time they were being asked to perform them in the name of the homeland." Apparently, some of the women wanted to play more than the traditional roles and founded the "Junta de Damas Nacionalistas". According to another news report published in *El Imparcial*, July 28, 1932, "the purpose of the new association was to encourage women to 'fulfill the Nationalist oath they had sworn,' and be prepared to fight and die if necessary in defense of the homeland." The Junta women proclaimed they were "ready to take on the same burden as the Cadets of the Republic and to show their determination, they adopted a variation of the Cadets' uniform and wore this to public functions." The uniform, according to the same report, consisted of a black skirt, white shirt, black tie, and a black beret. They wore a black cross on the left sleeve of the shirts and two miniature machetes on the beret. José Manuel Dávila explains that the uniform designed by the Junta de Damas was adopted by the members of Las Hijas de la Libertad. Some of those women were said to have also trained in the use of firearms.

12. The reasons that led De la Cruz to take the Nationalist Party oath are described most eloquently in her interview with Randall, pp. 41–42 and in her interview with Julia Mirabal in Havana, Cuba, cited.

13. For a detailed account of what happened in Ponce on March 21, 1937, see Dominga de la Cruz' account, titled, "Relato de la Masacre de Ponce," which she wrote in March 1976 while she was visiting Puerto Rico, reprinted in *Claridad*, March 21–27, 1997; see also

what she told Randall, pp. 45–46; Seijo, Interview; Mirabal, Interview.

14. Ibid. See also Randall, p. 50.

15. Ibid. See also Randall, p. 51.

16. Ibid. See also Randall, p. 52. During her interview with Seijo, she said the owner of the house where she took cover was Don Mario Mercado. She did not give the name of Mercado's wife.

17. De la Cruz' account, in *Claridad*, March 21–27, 1997; Randall, p. 52.

18. Ibid. See also Randall, p. 52.

19. Ibid. See also Randall, p. 53.

20. Ibid. According to the Hays Commission Report, "19 unarmed Nationalists were killed and more than 150 were wounded by island's police force on March 21, 1937." After an extensive investigation, the commissioners concluded that the Ponce incident had been "a massacre." For details, see Arthur Garfield Hays' account published in *The Nation* (June 5, 1937). A reprint of his account, "Defending Justice in Puerto Rico," is reprinted in Kal Wagenheim and Olga Jiménez de Wagenheim, eds., *The Puerto Ricans: A Documentary History*, (Princeton: Markus Wiener Publishers, 2013), pp. 199–201.

21. Hays Report.

22. De la Cruz' account in *Claridad*, 1997; Randall, p. 65.

23. De la Cruz' account; Seijo, Interview; Randall, p. 71.

24. Seijo, Interview; Mirabal, Interview.

25. Ibid. See also Randall, p. 79;

26. In a letter she wrote to J.A. Corretjer from Moscow, dated July 21, 1963, she describes the tender way she was treated by everyone she met in Moscow. She said she had been invited to speak at the Women's International Conference at the Kremlin and that her paper would be published by the journal *Soviet Women*. In one of her interviews, she said she had denounced America's colonialism of Puerto Rico and the "forced sterilization" practiced by the local government on Puerto Rican women. (The latter topic has been quite controversial, with members of the Left arguing that it was part of a plot to reduce the island's birth rate and that it was done without the women's consent. The topic merits an objective investigation.)

27. Mirabal, Interview; Seijo, Interview; Randall, p. 102.

28. Cacimar Cruz, "Dulces Labios y Dominga de la Cruz." Also Jacinto Rivera Pérez, "Muere Heroína Puertorriqueña . . ."

Part II: Nationalist Women Imprisoned in Puerto Rico, 1950, 1954

1. Blanca Canales Torresola

1. The information about Blanca Canales provided here is based on numerous archival documents and newspaper accounts of the Nationalist uprising of 1950. It is also based in part on Canales' testimony, titled: *La Constitución es la Revolución*, published in Spanish by El Comité de Estudios del Congreso Hostosiano (San Juan, Puerto Rico, 1997). The past director of the Instituto de Estudios Hostosiano, Professor Vivian Quiles-Calderín, granted me permission to translate Canales' testimony and use it for this project. I thank her for the authorization, which was made possible with the help of Professor Felix Ojeda Reyes.

2. According to the introduction in Canales' testimony, a professor friend had offered to write her biography, but she declined, saying she would prefer to write her own story. I have borrowed extensively from Canales' story for the reconstruction of the events that culminated in the attack on Jayuya on October 30, 1950. In the first part of my account, I merely summarize what she said and thought during that fateful weekend. For the latter parts of

my account, I relied on newspaper articles, FBI and police reports, letters written to her by her cousin Angelina Torresola de Platet, prison reports by guards, and the director of the Vega Alta women's prison. For her experience in the Alderson prison, I relied on the book of her jail mate, Elizabeth Gurley Flynn, *My Life as a Political Prisoner: The Alderson Story* (New York: New World Paperbacks, 1972). The book I used is a reprint of the 1963 edition, pp. 23–115.

3. Ibid.

4. Ibid.

5. Ibid. It should be noted that General Valero Bernabé, a native of Fajardo, had fought with the revolutionary forces of Simón Bolívar in Latin America's War of Independence. According to an oral account Ruth Mary Reynolds recorded with Blanca Vázquez at Centro de Estudios Puertorriqueños, at Hunter College, she had overheard a conversation between the agents who planned to assassinate Albizu Campos while she was seated behind them at a restaurant in Old San Juan. She said that she notified Albizu and then attended the event on October 26, 1950. On the way back to San Juan, around one in the morning, she and three others had been detained and taken to police headquarters for questioning. (For details on the Reynolds case, see the section devoted to her in this book.)

6. *El Mundo*, Nov. 2, 1950, "Imputan a Líder Nacionalista la Muerte del Policía Camacho," p. 5.

7. For details, see chapter 8 in Miñi Seijo's book, *La insurrección Nacionalista en Puerto Rico, 1950* (Río Piedras: Editorial Edil, 1989).

8. According to one press account, more than 300 men under the command of Elio Torresola surrendered in Jayuya on Nov. 2, 1950. See *El Mundo*, Nov. 3, 1950, "Nacionalistas se Rinden en Masa," pp. 1, 16, *El Mundo*, November 4, 1950, "Pueblo Jayuya Trató de Atacar: Elio Torresola," pp. 1, 16.

9. The charges levied against Blanca Canales, Elio Torresola, and other Jayuyans were listed in various articles published by *El Mundo*: Nov. 1, 1950, "Revoltosos Queman 14 Edificios en Jayuya," pp. 1,16; also "Saña Destructora Hace de Jayuya Pueblo Fantasma," p. 6; *El Mundo*, Nov. 2, 1950, "Imputan a Líder Nacionalista la Muerte del Policía Camacho," p. 5; also "Acusan de Asesinato a Blanca Canales: Desolación y Destitución en el Pueblo de Jayuya," p. 5.

10. Ibid. Details about La Princesa and the tiny cubicle where Canales was housed were provided by Ruth Reynolds, Isabel Rosado, and Carmen María Pérez in several interviews (listed throughout this book).

11. *El Mundo*, Nov. 29, 1950, "Acusan Nacionalistas: Comparecen a la Corte Federal," pp. 1, 16.

12. Ibid.

13. The case of Canales' dismissal was reported by *El Mundo*, Nov. 30, 1950, "Geigel Ordena la Destitución de Blanca Canales Torresola, p. 18. According to various surveillance reports filed by the Puerto Rican police, dismissal or threats of dismissal from jobs were used against supporters of Puerto Rican independence during the 1940s and 1950s. Teachers and other government employees were particularly vulnerable, according to those reports.

14. *El Mundo*, Nov. 10, 1950, "Demanda Contra Canales," p. 15.

15. A copy of the Secretary of Justice's letter is found in AGPR, Fondo: Departamento de Justicia, Serie: Correspondencia al Gobernador, Tarea 90-29, Caja 16, Item 3(a). See also *El Mundo*, Dec. 5, 1950, "Acusan a Ocho Nacionalistas Violar Ley #53," pp. 1, 14; *El Mundo*, Jan. 9, 1951, "Cuarenta Nacionalistas Acusados en Arecibo," pp. 1, 10.

16. *El Mundo*, Feb. 21, 1951, "Alegan Blanca Canales Estuvo en Tiroteo al Cuartel," pp. 1, 12

17. Ibid. Also *El Mundo*, Feb. 22, 1951, "Testigo Relata Drama Anterior: Fuego Jayuya; also *El Imparcial*, Feb. 22, 1951, "Testigo Declara que Blanca Canales Pedía Quemar Todo," pp. 1, 2, 31.

18. *El Imparcial*, Feb. 23, 1951,"Testigo del Fiscal Declara Blanca Canales Salió Antes del Fuego Correo," pp. 2, 35.

19. Ibid. Also *El Imparcial*, Feb. 23, 1951, "Caso Rebeldes de Jayuya Quedará Cerrado Hoy," pp. 2, 35.

20. *El Imparcial*, Feb. 27, 1951, "Termina Presentación de Prueba Caso Canales," pp. 2, 31.

21. *El Imparcial*, Feb. 28, 1951, "Declaran Culpables Rebeldes," pp. 2, 22; also *El Mundo*, Feb. 28, 1951, "Nacionalistas de Jayuya Encaran Penas de 35 Años," p. 3.

22. *El Mundo*, April 10, 1951, "Ocho Nacionalistas Cumplirán Pena Federal Entre Seis y Once Años," pp. 1, 14.

23. *El Mundo*, ibid. *El Imparcial*, April 22, 1951, "Pide Anulación de una Pena a Blanca Canales," p. 2. To review text of Canales' letter, see *El Imparcial*, June 29, 1951, pp. 3, 35.

24. *El Imparcial*, April 30, 1951, "Juzgan Hoy Rebeldes Jayuya: Corte de Arecibo," pp. 2, 46: Also *El Imparcial*, May 1, 1951, "Juzgan 31 Personas por Revuelta Jayuya," pp. 2, 27. Also see *El Imparcial*, May 4, 1951, "Blanca Canales se Niega a Juicio por Separado," pp. 3, 29.

25. Details surrounding the requests for separate trials were reported by *El Imparcial*, May 2, 1951, "Defensa Rebeldes Alega Ley es Inconstitucional," pp. 2, 31. Also see *El Mundo*, May 2, 1951, "Se Espera Empiece Juicio Nacionalistas," p. 5.

26. Ibid.

27. *El Imparcial*, May 5, 1951, "Constituye Jurado en Caso Nacionalista," p. 7.

28. *El Imparcial*, May 6, 1951, "Temen que Blanca Canales Burle Penas Suicidándose," pp. 5, 31; also *El Imparcial*, May 8, 1951, "Niegan Blanca Canales Piense Quitarse la Vida," p. 35; The Secretary of Justice summoned Teófilo Maldonado to his office to explain the basis for his column. For details, see AGPR, Fondo: Departamento de Justicia, Serie: Nacionalistas, Tarea 90-29, Caja 16, Item 3a.

29. Raúl Torresola was also Doris Torresola's uncle. In 1948 he was sent by Doris' mother to accompany her while she lived in Albizu's home. Apparently, he had returned to Jayuya before the uprising of 1950 and had gone to live at Blanca Canales' home and was thus considered a key witness by the prosecution. After both his nieces were sent to jail, in part because of his testimonies, the family still forgave him. For details of what he said at Blanca's trial, see *El Imparcial*, May 9, 1951, "Tio Inculpa a Blanca: Relata Plan de la Revuelta," pp. 1, 2, 39.

30. Luis Quiles' testimony was reported in the above article, "Tio Inculpa a Blanca."

31. The firefighter who searched the ashes of Jayuya's police station was one of the more than 100 witnesses called by the prosecution, according to reporters at the court during the duration of the Arecibo trial. For details about the biased fashion in which the trial was conducted, see *El Imparcial*'s reporting between May 5 and May 12, 1951. The specifics of what the firefighter reported appear in *El Imparcial*, May 11, 1951, "Sucesos del 30 de Octubre: Relatan Como Fue Incendiado el Cuartel Policía de Jayuya," pp. 1, 2, 47.

32. Attorney Hernández Vallé repeatedly objected to the "unprofessional actions" of the prosecution. He also questioned the biased attitude of Judge Padró Parés, who admitted irrelevant evidence to the case. On more than one occasion, he and other members of the defense team had to remind the court that Blanca Canales and her co-defendants had already been tried for their alleged participation in the destruction of the Jayuya post office. For details about the heated exchanges, see *El Imparcial*, May 11, 1951 "Sucesos del 30 de Octubre . . . "

33. *El Mundo*, May 12, 1951, "Hallan Culpables en Arecibo," p. 16; also *El Imparcial*, May 12, 1951, "Veintiún Nacionalistas Culpables de Asesinato," pp. 3, 50.

34. *El Imparcial*, May 11, 1951, "Sucesos del 30 de Octubre . . . "; also *El Mundo*, May 22, 1951, "Sentencian a Cadena Perpetua a Veintiún Nacionalistas en Arecibo," pp. 1, 14.

35. *El Mundo*, May 12, 1951, "Hallan Culpables en Arecibo," p. 16; also *El Imparcial*, May 22, 1951, "Sentencian a Cadena Perpetua a Veintiún Nacionalistas en Arecibo," pp. 1, 14; The text of Canales' letter to Hernández Vallé was published by *El Imparcial*, June 29, 1951, pp. 3, 35.

36. Gurley Flynn, *The Alderson Story*, pp. 23–115.

37. Ibid., p. 111.

38. Ibid., pp. 111-13.

39. Ibid., p. 140.

40. Ibid.

41. For a full version of the poem, see Carole Boyce Davies, *The Political Life of Black Commu-nist Claudia Jones: Left of Karl Marx* (Durham and London: Duke University Press, 2007), pp. 110-11.

....

[Part of the poem reads as follows:]
It seems I knew you long before our common ties—of conscious choice
Threw under single skies, those like us
Who, fused by our mold
Became their targets, as of old

....

Oh wondrous Spanish sister
Long-locked from all your care
Listen—while I tell you what you strain to hear
And beckon all from far and near

We swear that we will never rest
Until they hear not plea
But sainted sacrifice to
A small nation free

....

42. Gurley Flynn, *The Alderson Story*, pp. 125-127.

43. Ibid.

44. Ibid.

45. Thousands of declassified FBI documents related to the Nationalist Party were released by the FBI Office in Washington, D.C., to three Puerto Rican archival repositories, thanks to the efforts of Congressman José Serrano. The documents cited here were reviewed at the Capitol Library of the Puerto Rican Legislature in San Juan, Puerto Rico. Each citation henceforth will provide the form of identification by which the PR Capitol Library archived the documents under the heading "Carpetas del FBI," Serie: Nacionalistas. The files are grouped by numbered Sub-Series, volume, and numbered documents as indicated below.

46. PR Capitol Library, Fondo: "Carpetas del FBI," Serie: Nacionalistas (FBI Files), Sub-Serie: 29, vol. 36, Doc. 100-3-4958.

47. PR Capitol Library, "Carpetas del FBI," Nacionalistas, Sub-Serie 29, vol. 37, Doc. 100-3-5184.

48. PR Capitol Library, "Carpetas del FBI," Nacionalistas, Sub-Serie 33, vol. 41, Doc. 100-3-5772.

49. PR Capitol Library, "Carpetas del FBI," Nacionalistas, Sub-Serie 29, vol. 37, Doc. 100-3-5183.

50. PR Capitol Library, "Carpetas del FBI," Nacionalistas, Sub-Serie 33, vol. 41, Doc. 100-3-5772.

51. Lydia Peña de Planas apparently had to submit quarterly reports to the penal authorities in San Juan. I found two of those reports in the prison files I reviewed. The one cited here dated Feb. 11, 1958, is found in AGPR, Fondo: Escuela Industrial Para Mujeres, Tarea 60-A-19, Caja 20.

52. In an earlier report submitted by Lydia Peña de Planas, dated June 7, 1954 (shortly after she was appointed in May), she discusses the many actions she took in order to reform the prison functions. This report and others submitted by the guards are archived at AGPR, Fondo: Escuela Industrial, Tarea 60-A-19, Cajas 20, 21.

53. Ibid. According to a few guards' reports, they encountered many challenges, which affected their lives as well as those of the inmates. For details, see the various reports found in

AGPR, Escuela Industrial Para Mujeres, Tarea 60-A-19, Cajas 4, 5, 21.

54. Ibid.

55. Information derived from the guards' reports of the tasks the Nationalist women performed during their time in that prison.

56. Interviews with Isabel Rosado Morales and Carmen María Pérez in April 1998.

57. Details provided by two guards' reports.

58. Rosado, Interview, April 17, 1998.

59. Rosado, Interview, ibid. Rosado told that story to a few journalists. The most recent version was reprinted by *Claridad* shortly after Rosado died. For details, refer to the section on Rosado in this book.

60. Interview with Pérez, April 1998.

61. "Relación de Castigos de la Junta de Disciplina: Informe de Feb. 12, 1959," Escuela Industrial Para Mujeres, AGPR, Tarea 60-A-19, Caja 24.

62. "Libro de Visitantes," Escuela Industrial Para Mujeres in AGPR, Tarea 60-A-19, Caja 1.

63. "Libro de Visitantes." Also "Libro de Paquetes Recibidos, 1956-1958," Escuela Industrial Para Mujeres in AGPR, Tarea 60-A-19, Caja 1, Libro #3.

64. AGPR, Serie: Nacionalistas, Tarea 90-29, Caja 4, Item 3.

65. *El Mundo*, Aug. 24, 1967, "RSV (Roberto Sánchez Vilella) Da Indulto a Blanca Canales," p. 1.

66. Peggy Ann Bliss, *The San Juan Star*, Aug. 29, 1993, "Blanca Canales Still Carrying Ammunition of Independence," p. 3.

67. Ibid.

68. Ibid.

69. Bliss, *The San Juan Star*, Aug. 29, 1993, "A Home with a Spirit," p. 5.

70. Ibid.

71. Ibid.

72. Author's interview with Lydia Collazo, April 1998. A copy of Canales' letter to Rosa Collazo is found among the Oscar Collazo Papers, donated by Lydia Collazo to the Colección Puertorriqueña, University of Puerto Rico. The papers were not yet catalogued when I reviewed them.

73. For details about the Arecibo celebration in honor of Leonides Díaz, Canales, and five other women, see Cándida Cotto's article in *Claridad, En Rojo Section*, June 3-9, 1985, p. 12.

74. See Miñi Seijo, *Claridad, En Rojo Section*, "Carlos Irizarry: Mártir de la Revolución," Oct. 25, 1975, pp. 5-7.

75. Miñi Seijo, *Claridad, En Rojo Section*, "Raimundo," Oct. 31, 1980, pp. 1, 4, 8.

76. *El Mundo*, "Puerto Rico Ilustrado," Oct. 28, 1990.

77. Bliss, "Blanca Canales . . . ," Aug. 23, 1993; Jean Zwickle's account appears in "Peacehost," an online publication.

78. Details offered by Marisa Rosado a few days after Canales' death, in her article, "Blanca Canales: Bisografía de una Patriota," *Claridad, En Rojo Section*, August 2–8, 1996, pp. 16, 17.

2. Leonides Díaz Díaz

1. The details about Leonides Díaz and her family were compiled from various sources, including the "Hojas Personales" filed on her behalf by the staff at the Escuela Industrial para Mujeres, Vega Alta's women's prison. A portion of that prison's records (boxes 1-25) are available at the Archivo General de Puerto Rico (AGPR), Fondo Departamento de Justicia, Sub-Fondo: Escuela Industrial para Mujeres, Vega Alta, Puerto Rico, Tarea 60-A-19. The details offered in this instance came from Caja 6. Other information cited throughout the text came from other documents labeled "Expediente de Confinadas," found in Cajas 4, 9. The Vega Alta prison source will be cited herewith as AGPR, Escuela Industrial, Tarea

60-A-19, followed by the appropriate box number.

2. The comments were based on my conversations with Isabel Rosado Morales in April 1998. The comments made by Ricardo and Angel Ramón Díaz were published by the news weekly *Claridad*'s *En Rojo Section*, October 25, 1975, pp. 9–10.

3. Details found in AGPR, Escuela Industrial, Tarea 60-A19, "Hojas Personales," Cajas 6, 9; and "Libro de Apuntes de Visitantes," October 2, 1955—June 7, 1957, Caja 4.

4. AGPR, Departamento de Justicia, Serie: Nacionalistas, Tarea 90-29, "Tribunal Superior de Puerto Rico, Sala de Arecibo, Caja 3, Folder 2; see also AGPR, Escuela Industrial, Tarea 60-A-19, Cajas 4, 6, 9.

5. AGPR, ibid. For details about the (Arecibo) trial of April 1951, see *El Imparcial*, "Hoy Continúa el Caso de los 13 Nacionalistas," April 18, 1951, pp. 1, 12; also "Defensa Anuncia no Presentará Testigos en el Caso de Arecibo," April 19, 1951, pp. 1, 2, 12.

6. Details of Díaz's case, including the appeals filed on her behalf, and her eventual release from prison in 1957 are found in AGPR, Nacionalistas, Tarea 90-29 "Tribunal Superior de Puerto Rico, Sala de Arecibo, Caja 3, Folder 2; also in AGPR, Escuela Industrial, Tarea 60-A-19, Cajas 4, 6, 9. Also see *El Imparcial*, "Corte de Arecibo Halla Culpable Nacionalistas," April 23, 1951, pp. 1, 12.

7. AGPR, ibid. The trial was covered in detail by *El Imparcial* during the last two weeks of April 1951; see articles cited earlier for the extensive remarks made by Hernández Vega.

8. *El Imparcial*, ibid.

9. Details about Hernández Vega's reappearance as a witness in the New York 1954 Nationalist trial were reported by the FBI-New York Office on September 10, 1954. The report, which forms part of the declassified FBI files, was released to the Puerto Rican Legislature and can be read at the Capitol Library, Fondo: "Carpetas del FBI," Series: Nacionalistas, Sub-Series 39, vol. 47, Doc. 100-3-6278.

10. In addition to Leonides Díaz and her husband and their two sons, there were nine others convicted at the same time (April 1951) in Arecibo. They were: Leonides' brother Bernardo Díaz, her nephew Ismael Díaz Matos, plus friends and neighbors: Juan Jaca Hernández, Carlos M. Castro Ríos, Tomás López de Victoria, Rafael Molina Centeno, Manuel Méndez Gandía, Carlos Feliciano, and Justo Guzmán Serrano. Please note that Monserrate Valle (López de Victoria's wife) also held in the Arecibo jail between 1950 and 1952 was not part of the group tried in April 1951. According to historian Ivonne Acosta, Valle was tried the following year (August 1952) for violations of Law #53. According to the evidence I found, Valle was absolved during that trial and released from prison. (For details, see the section devoted to her in this book.) Details about Leonides' convictions and sentences were found in AGPR, Departamento de Justicia, Fondo: Nacionalistas, Tarea 90-29, Caja 3. References about her life in the Vega Alta prison were found in AGPR, Escuela Industrial, Tarea 60-A-19, "Expediente de Confinada," Caja 6.

11. Acosta, *La Mordaza*, 1989, pp. 194–99. *El Mundo*, July 12, 1957, p. 2.

12. Details provided by Isabel Rosado and Carmín Pérez during their interviews in April 1998.

13. The details about the women who interacted with Leonides Díaz in prison were compiled by the author from a variety of sources.

14. Rosado and Pérez, Interviews, April 1998.

15. Ruth Reynolds, Interviews, Tape 37, Box 46, Centro Archives, Hunter College.

16. Pérez and Rosado, Interviews, April, 1998.

17. According to the data gathered by the staff at the Vega Alta prison, Leonides Díaz listed Spiritualism as her religion. I found no evidence that she had conducted séances in that prison, as she had done in the Arecibo jail, according to Ruth Reynolds. The religious preferences of the Vega Alta inmates were recorded in "Hojas Personales," which are found in AGPR, Escuela Industrial, Tarea 60-A-19, Caja 4.

18. Escuela Industrial, ibid, Caja 6, Informes, Guardias de Turno.

19. AGPR, Escuela Industrial, ibid, Caja 9, "Informes de Movimiento Diario . . . "

20. For details about the impact of the Supreme Court's decision and Amadeo's and Lynn's

efforts to get help from the ACLU in calling for an investigation of the legal abuses in Puerto Rico, see Acosta, *La Mordaza*, 1989, chap. 6.

21. Acosta, ibid. Also Reynolds, Interview transcript, Tape 47, Sides B and C, in "The Ruth Reynolds Papers," Centro Archives. They shed much light on the topic of Amadeo, Lynn, and the ACLU.

22. Ibid.

23. The information on the case *Pennsylvania v. Nelson* was retrieved from Wikipedia. According to its entry, "The case Pennsylvania v. Nelson-350 U.S. 497 (1956), argued November 15-16, 1955, decided April 2, 1956, refers to the respondent Steve Nelson, an acknowledged member of the Communist Party (USA) who was convicted in the Court of Quarter Sessions of Allegheny County, Pennsylvania of a violation of that state's Sedition Act and sentenced to imprisonment for twenty years and to pay a fine of $10,000 and the costs of prosecution in the sum of $13,000." Pennsylvania's superior court affirmed the conviction but the state's Supreme Court decided the case on the issue that "the federal law supersedes the Pennsylvania Sedition Act."

24. The applicability of federal laws in Puerto Rico is well known to scholars of Puerto Rican history. For example, until the 1970s, the federal minimum wage law did not apply in Puerto Rico. That has now changed. Meanwhile, federal laws on expenditure on health care and education apply partially, and on a case-by-case basis, depending what Congress approves.

25. Although the Smith Act was applicable in Puerto Rico in 1950, while the island remained "a colony," it was not enforced in the case of the Nationalist uprising. Perhaps because, at the time, the United States was in the midst of negotiating with the recently elected PDP administration a plan for self-government in order to change its image around the world, just as other empires were divesting themselves of their possessions. But since the Smith Act had been enacted to protect the United States (and its possessions) from internal threats, namely from Communist and other "subversive groups," it was applied to a handful of Communists in Puerto Rico in 1954, following the attack on Congress by four Puerto Rican Nationalists. It was also applied to Puerto Rican Nationalists in New York City and Chicago.

26. I am interpreting from a transcript of the speech the governor gave in January 1956, included in the documents that make up Tomo I, *Informes de la Comisión de Derechos Civiles del Estado Libre Asociado de Puerto Rico*, (Años 1950–1968), Orford, N.H.: Equity Publishing, 1973, p. xi, and pp. 85-97. (Copies of various Commission Reports were donated to me by Attorney Irma Alicia Rodríguez.)

27. Ibid, pp. 97–98. For an illuminating discussion of the violations of the Nationalists' civil and human rights following the events of the 1950s, refer to the extensive report prepared by Professor David M. Helfeld for the Office of the Governor, later published under the heading "Discrimination for Political Beliefs and Associations," *Revista del Colegio de Abogados de Puerto Rico* vol. 25 (Nov. 1964), pp. 5–276. The report includes an impressive set of testimonials from important government figures. See, for example, the letter sent by the ex-Attorney General, Vicente Geigel Polanco to Dr. Helfeld at the Civil Rights Committee, July 2, 1958, in ibid, pp. 218–21. A copy of the Helfeld publication was obtained thanks to the efforts of University of Puerto Rico Professor Norma Rodríguez Roldán.

28. Cited by Acosta, *La Mordaza*, 1989, chap. 6; also *El Imparcial*, July 20 and August 8, 1957.

29. The legal questions raised by Santos P. Amadeo and his colleagues were cited by Acosta, in *La Mordaza*, pp. 199–200.

30. The touching description of Leonides Díaz's first visit to her husband at the state penitentiary in July 1957 was described by Heriberto Marín in a self-published book, *Eran Ellos*, 2000 edition, p. 70.

31. Ibid.

32. Reminiscences of Leonides' sons, quoted in the *Claridad* interview of October 25, 1975, pp. 8–10.

3. Carmen María Pérez González

1. Much of the biographical information about Carmen María (Carmín) Pérez cited throughout this essay was culled from an extensive interview I conducted with her on April 21, 1998. Details of her political work, arrests, trials, and imprisonments were compiled from a variety of sources, including her own account, newspaper articles, Department of Justice notices, legal motions, and appeals introduced by the defense, prison records, Internal Security (I.S.) surveillance reports, and declassified FBI files on the Puerto Rican Nationalist Party, which are now archived at the Puerto Rican Legislative Library in San Juan's Capitol building, under the heading "Carpetas del FBI." Pérez's comments, corroborations, and/or denials of the various claims made by the undercover police were discussed during our interview.

2. Pérez, Interview April 21, 1998.

3. Interview, Ibid. See also portions of the transcript of Gonzalo Lebrón's November 17, 1954 testimony included in a letter sent by Marco A. Rigau (Aide to the Governor) to the Secretary of Justice, José Trias Monge on November 22, 1954. According to that document, Lebrón gave the San Juan police an extensive account of how and when he joined the Nationalist Party (1949) and the leaders he met in Puerto Rico, including Pedro Albizu Campos and his attorney Juan Hernández Vallé. For details, see AGPR, Fondo: Departamento de Justicia, Serie: Nacionalistas, "Cartas: Oficina del Gobernador," Tarea 90-29, Caja 8.

4. Pérez, Interview, April 21, 1998.

5. Interview, ibid. According to one I.S. report, Albizu's personal secretary in December 1948 was Isolina Rondón, a resident of Río Piedras. She was listed as one of the fourteen women who accompanied Albizu Campos to the Party's Annual Assembly, held at the Ateneo Puertorriqueño, December 19, 1948. The other thirteen listed were: Doris Torresola Roura, Ruth M. Reynolds, Isabel Rosado Morales, Dilia Rivera de Torresola (Elio Torresola's wife), Ana Maria Campos (Albizu's haf-sister who came from Ponce), Maria Martínez (a friend of Ana María Campos, from Ponce), Laura Medina Maisonave, Irma Viscal (Olga Viscal's sister), Lola Dumey, Laura Meneses de Albizu, Rosita Albizu Meneses, Juanita Ojeda (who came from Utuado), and Veneranda Rivera de Avila (from San Juan). Details in AGPR, Departamento de Justicia; Serie: Nacionalistas, Tarea 90-29, Caja 10, Item 24.

6. Interview, ibid.

7. Interview, ibid. For details about her activities, according to the Internal Security (I.S.) agents, see AGPR, Justicia, Nacionalistas, Tarea 90-29, Cajas: 8, 10. See also the reports submitted by FBI Special Agent in Charge (SAC) in San Juan, Jack West, July 7, 1948, in Capitol Library, "Carpetas del FBI," Sub-Serie 10, Doc. 100-3-1822 and Feb. 16, 1950, Doc. 100-3-2044.

8. Interview, ibid.

9. Interview, ibid. A photograph published in El Imparcial, December 19, 1948, shows Ruth M. Reynolds, Isabel Rosado, and Isolina Rondón seated next to Albizu Campos at the presidential table during the Party's annual assembly, held at the Ateneo Puertorriqueño. Articles in the local dailies were often translated into English and attached to reports sent by the FBI agents in San Juan to the main office in Washington. Copies were often sent to the FBI offices in New York and Chicago. For example, on July 7, 1948, SAC Jack West reported that various women had been working closely with Pedro Albizu Campos since he returned to Puerto Rico in December 1947. In his February 16, 1950, report, for example, he included a copy of a letter Juanita González Bouillerce had written to Albizu Campos on December 7, 1948, in which she told him that she had founded and presided over the Río Piedras Women's Board (of the NPPR). She named Olga Isabel Viscal as the group's secretary. In Capitol Library, "Carpetas del FBI." Sub-Serie: 10, Doc. 100-3-2044.

10. Interview, ibid.

11. Interview, ibid.

12. Interview, ibid.

13. Interview, ibid.

14. Interview, ibid. Doris Torresola offered a similar rendition of the events of October 30, 1950, in her written testimony (August 1953). For details, see the section devoted to her in this book.

15. Interview, ibid.

16. Interview, ibid. In an interview I conducted with Juanita González Bouillerce in 1998, she said that she had gone to the Nationalist Club the day of the uprising and Don Pedro had sent her away, cautioning that she might be arrested. Carmín Pérez recalled seeing González Bouillerce at the Puerta de Tierra police station. She said she had been "detained, but not charged, apparently because she was intimidated and she talked." I found no evidence to substantiate or reject Pérez's claim.

17. Interview, ibid. The slapping incident was brought to my attention by Isabel Rosado. It was also mentioned by Ruth Reynolds in one of the interviews she granted Blanca Vázuez of Centro de Estudios Puertorriqueños, which form part of the "Ruth Reynolds Papers," archived at Centro Archives, Hunter College, Manhattan. For details, see Box 2, "Political Prisoners," Folder 6.

18. Pérez, Interview, ibid.

19 Interview, ibid. For the letter sent by the Arecibo warden, J. Gonzáez Lebrón, to Special Prosecutor José C. Aponte at the Department of Justice, see AGPR, Nacionalistas, Tarea 90-29, Caja 16, Item 16.

20. Pérez, Interview, ibid.

21. Pérez, Interview, ibid. Also Isabel Rosado told similar stories about Leonides Díaz, her mother, and members of her family.

22. Interview, ibid. For details about the case of Leonides Díaz, see the section devoted to her in this book.

23. Interview, ibid. Isabel Rosado did not feel the revolution had failed "since the spirit of independence is still alive."

24. Interview, ibid. The question about Albizu's role that afternoon noticeably upset her, which was probably the reason she felt the need to justify his inaction.

25. I found no record of the poet's detention. But since 1,006 Puerto Ricans were detained during the first week of November 1950, it is very likely that a lot more women were arrested than I was able to document. The news daily El Imparcial in its Sunday section "El Diario Ilustrado" of November 5, 1950, pp. 6–7 displayed a photograph of three women (Digna Marín Pagán, Concepción Pérez viuda de Padilla, and Catalina Mesire de Jordán) as they were taken to the Arecibo jail, and for whom I found no records.

26. Conclusion based on the summary accounts published by El Imparcial during its coverage of the second trial, July, 20, 1952, pp. 3, 5.

27. Interview, ibid. For details of the irregularities practiced by the Arecibo Court during Pérez and Torresola's trial, see the articles published in El Imparcial, July 8, p. 2; July 9, p. 2; July 11, p. 6; July 17, p. 8; July 19, pp. 5, 6; July 23, p. 3.

28. El Imparcial, ibid. The story about her father's role was told by three individuals, who wished to remain anonymous. It was also mentioned by her ex-comrade in arms, Jose Rivera Sotomayor in the testimony he published in Claridad, En Rojo Section, April 11–17, 2002, p. 21.

29. Interview, ibid.

30. Interview, ibid.

31. Interview, ibid. Also El Imparcial published several articles on Olga Viscal, who had claimed that she had contracted tuberculosis in jail. For details, see the section devoted to Viscal in this book.

32. Interview, ibid. The question was motivated by a story told by Isabel Rosado about inmates who were often taken out of prison for the night by some guards.

33. Interview, ibid. Also El Mundo and El Imparcial reported on October 1, 1953, the governor's pardon of Albizu Campos.

34. Reports of Pérez's activities by local I.S. agents and FBI men resumed as soon as she was

released from jail. For details, see AGPR, Departamento de Justicia, Nacionalistas, Tarea 90-29, Caja 8, Item 14 and Caja 19, Item 1, which describe in detail the many Party activities she ostensibly attended or organized between July 1952 and March 1954. Similarly, the FBI office in San Juan offered numerous reports, and some were listed as part of Albizu Campos' FBI File No. 105-11898, Section X. The references to Carmín Pérez are found on pp. 123, 132, 134, and 149 of that section. The specific information about Pérez's attempt to purchase a firearm was also reported in a Quarterly Report submitted by the FBI SAC San Juan, dated November 14, 1953 (covering the period August 1 to October 31), in Capitol Library, "Carpetas del FBI," Sub-Serie 32, vol. 39, Doc. 100-3-4951.

35. Capitol Library, "Carpetas del FBI," ibid. Also see I.S. Bulletin #79, dated February 15, 1954, which describes her activities, in AGPR, Nacionalistas, Tarea 90-29, Caja 8, Item 14.

36. See "Informe del Teniente Astol Calero," March 6, 1954, in AGPR, Nacionalistas, Tarea 90-29, Caja 2, Item 32. In addition, see FBI SAC San Juan, Quarterly Report of March 10, 1954, which offers details about the activities of Albizu's companions between November 1, 1953, and March 6, 1954. In Capitol Library, "Carpetas del FBI," Sub-Serie 32, vol. 39, Doc. 100-3-5416.

37. FBI SAC San Juan, Richard Godfrey, "Report to File," dated March 5, 1954, and a follow-up Radiogram he sent to his superior in Washington, Assistant Director Belmont. In Capitol Library, "Carpetas del FBI," Sub-Serie 32, vol. 39, Doc. 100-3-5470.

38. Ibid.

39. Pérez, Interview, ibid.

40. For details about the arresting mission, see Chief Roig's report to the governor, March 11, 1954, in AGPR, Justicia, Nacionalistas, Tarea 90-29, Caja 8, also Informe del Teniente Calero, cited earlier. It seems that the information reported by Chief Roig was based on the field notes submitted by Lieutenant Astol Calero, the person in charge of the police officers sent to arrest Albizu Campos and his companions. Thirty of the men assigned were said to be detectives supervised by Captain Benigno Soto, head of the I.S. Division. Also present was Dudley Osborne, who, according to police protocol, should not have been taken on the arresting mission and the reason why Chief Roig went out of his way to explain his usefulness.

41. Interview, ibid. For details about Rivera Sotomayor's injuries, see El Imparcial, March 7, 1954.

42. Interview, ibid. Details about her "propensity to slap people" and the claim that she possessed a .38 caliber pistol for which she was carrying eleven bullets were reported on March 8, 1954, to Captain Soto by policemen Epifanio Bonet, Santos Mercado, and Regino Nieves. See AGPR, Justicia, Nacionalistas, Tarea 90-29, Caja 2, Item 32, and Caja 24, Item 16.

43. See Chief Roig's report of March 11, 1954, cited. Also see El Imparcial, "Policías Declaran Perseguían a Líderes Nacionalistas," Dec. 29, 1954, p. 10. For details about Pérez's arrest and charges, see AGPR, Justicia, Nacionalistas, Tarea 90-29, Caja 2, Items, 24 and 32, Caja 24, Item 16.

44. Pérez, Interview, ibid.

45. Ibid. Also Chief Roig's report, March 11, 1954, cited.

46. Chief Roig's report, ibid.

47. For details of Pérez's arrest and charges in 1954, see AGPR, Justicia, Nacionalistas, Tarea 90-29, Caja 2, Items 24 and 32, and Caja 24, Item 16.

48. Ibid.

49. Speculations reported by Isabel Rosado, Carmín Pérez, and others.

50. For details about the Arecibo trial, see the coverage provided by El Imparcial, beginning December 7, 1954, through February 11, 1955. On Dec. 7, 1954, see "Allanamientos Fueron Ilegales," p. 12; Dec. 8, 1954, "Policías Niegan Abofetearon a Uno de los Acusados," in that same newspaper's "El Diario Ilustrado" Dec. 9, 1954, "Fiscales Cierran Caso Nacionalistas," pp. 2, 12; Dec. 11, 1954 "Caso Nacionalistas: Defensa Alega Policía Dio Golpes

a Acusado," pp. 5, 23; and "En Arecibo: Citan Nuevos Jurados Casos Nacionalistas," p. 18; Dec. 13, 1954, "Continúa Proceso Contra Nacionalistas en Corte de Arecibo." p. 7; Dec. 14, 1954, "Defensa Alega Puerto Rico No Tiene Soberanía," p. 16; Dec.16, 1954, "Impugnan Declaración del Teniente Calero," pp. 16, 53; Dec. 29, 1954, "Policías Declaran Perseguían a Líderes Nacionalistas, p. 10; January 9, 1955, "Admiten en Evidencia Armas Ocupadas en la Residencia de Albizu," p. 7.

51. El Imparcial, Jan. 12, 1955, "Defensa se Opone Fiscal Compare Balas Ocupadas a los Acusados," p. 12; Jan. 17, 1955, "Termina Prueba en Caso Nacionalistas," p. 7; Jan. 19, 1955, Acusan a Nacionalistas de Falta de Valentía," p. 6; Jan. 26, 1955, "Aplazan Nuevamente Juicio Nacionalistas, p. 6; Feb. 3, 1955, "Defensa Critica la Acción de los Fiscales," p. 7. Details about the "speedy conviction" and the reaction by the audience are covered in El Imparcial, Feb. 8, p. 3.

52. El Imparcial, Feb. 9, 1955, "Juicio Arecibo: Culpables Catorce Nacionalistas," p. 3; also February 9, "Culpables Nacionalistas en Corte de Arecibo," pp. 1, 3. Also El Imparcial, Feb. 11, 1955 offered a list of the convicted plus various photographs of four of the convicted (Doris Torresola, Carmen María Pérez, Isabel Rosado, and José Rivera Sotomayor) on p. 12. Also El Imparcial, Feb. 11, 1955, "Señalan Juicio de Nacionalistas," p. 12; Feb. 11, 1955, "Piden Se Posponga Lectura de Sentencia," p. 12; also in El Imparcial, Feb. 14, 1955, "Aplazan Sentencia a los 14 Nacionalistas," p. 5.

53. El Imparcial, May 1, 1955, "Procesan Lunes a 4 Nacionalistas Por Tiroteo Casa Albizu," p. 2; May 3, 1955, "Comienza Juicio Por Tiroteo Frente a Casa Albizu Campos," p. 18; also May 6, 1955, "Identifican Afiliación Política de Acusados Prejuicio Ante el Jurado," p. 1; May 8, 1955, "Teniente Policía No Sabe Quien lo Hirió," p. 5; May 10, 1955, "Fiscales Terminan Su Prueba Contra Acusados," p. 12; May 11, 1955, "Gelpí Impugna Legalidad de Órdenes de Arresto a Nacionalistas," pp. 12, 25; May 13, 1955, "Jurado Delibera en Caso Nacionalistas," pp. 14, 35.

54. El Imparcial, May 13, 1955, "Jurado Delibera en Caso Nacionalistas," pp. 14, 35. Judge Suárez Correa instructed the jury to take into account that the crimes of attempted murder and possession of a firearm were also violations of Law #53. Defense Attorney Gelpí argued that the accused had already been tried and convicted for the violations of Law #53; El Imparcial, May 14, Pedirán Nuevo Juicio Para los Nacionalistas," p. 5; also May 17, "Aplazan Sentencia a 4 Nacionalistas, pp. 1, 2. Also El Imparcial, May 31, 1955, "Isabel Rosado Pide le Dicten Sentencia," p. 14.

55. Pérez, Interview, ibid. Also in El Imparcial, June 23, 1955, "Gestionan Apelación de Líderes Nacionalistas," p. 5; and June 18, 1955, "De Uno A Quince Años de Presidio a 4 Nacionalistas," p. 27 (The one who received the longest sentence from Judge Padró Parés in Arecibo was José Rivera Sotomayor.). See also in AGPR, Departamento de Justicia, Serie: Nacionalistas, Tarea 90-29, Caja 20, Item 13f; Caja 21, Item 2j, and Caja 24, Item 16.

56. For details about Carmín Pérez's job assignments in the Vega Alta prison, see AGPR, Departamento de Justicia, Serie: Escuela Industrial Para Mujeres, Tarea 60-A-19, Caja 6 (Cartapacios). Also in Caja 4, "Libro de Visitantes," which details the number of visits the inmates received, who came to see them, and what they brought to the inmates they visited.

57. For details, see AGPR, Departamento de Justicia, Serie: Escuela Industrial Para Mujeres, Tarea 60-A-19, Caja 6, "Informes de Disciplina," Turno: 6:00 a.m. a 2 p.m., Area: Seguridad Maxima, Guardia de Turno, Sra. Salazar.

58. For the accusation and resolution of the case brought against Pérez by Guard Otero, see AGPR, Escuela Industrial Para Mujeres, Tarea 60-A-19, Caja 6, "Informes de Disciplina."

59. Pérez, Interview, ibid. Law #53 was abolished by the Puerto Rican Legislature in August 1957 at the request of Governor Luis Muñoz Marín. By then the Nationalist Party had been dealt a hard blow as most of its leaders were in jail.

60. Pedro Albizu Campos died on April 21, 1965. He had been pardoned a second time by the governor, this time just weeks before he was to die. Doris Torresola was driven insane

in prison, according to her family. Apparently, the cause of her malady was a drug called "thorazine," prescribed for her asthmatic condition. She committed suicide a few years after Albizu Campos died. Isabel Rosado went on to live until the age of 107.

61. Details about Pérez's activities were summarized in various articles published at the time of her death in 2003. The information about the COINTELPRO programs in Puerto Rico was gleaned from Luis Nieves Falcón, *Un Siglo de represión política en Puerto Rico, 1898-1998*. (San Juan: Ediciones Puerto, 2009).

62. Pérez, interview, ibid. Details about her work at the Puerto Rican Bar were provided in Cándida Cotto's article "Un Emotivo Adiós a Carmín," published in *Claridad, En Rojo Section*, April 11–17, 2003, p. 7.

63. The references to her "humility, generosity, and shyness" were mentioned by those who eulogized her at her death. The same traits came across during our interview, as she was often reluctant to take credit for some of the deeds she had done. A copy of the speech in which he celebrated the "Tres Heroínas" in Humacao was published in *Claridad*, June 13–19, 1997.

64. *El Nuevo Día*, Saturday, April 5, 2003, p. 44: See also Rivera Sotomayor's unedited testimony, published in *Claridad, En Rojo Section*, April 11–17, p. 21.

65. The comments of the various mourners were compiled under the heading "Palabras Sobre Carmín Pérez," in *Claridad, En Rojo Section*, April 11–17, 2003, p. 32.

66. Ibid. See also Alida Millán Ferrer, "Hasta Siempre Comandante Pérez," in *Claridad, En Rojo Section*, April 11–17, 2003, p. 3.

67. Cotto, "Un Emotivo Adiós . . . "

4. Ruth Mary Reynolds

1. Much of the information cited throughout this book about Ruth Reynolds' birthplace, early life, and education was gleaned from a series of tape-recorded interviews she granted to Blanca Vázquez at El Centro de Estudios Puertorriqueños at Hunter College, Manhattan (between 1985–1986). The details about her family and early childhood correspond to Tape 1 (dated Aug. 26, 1985). In that interview, she said that her first memory of social injustice occurred when she was eleven years old, and she noticed the Sioux Indians, the previous owners of the land, had been relegated to the edges of town during the celebrations of 1927. Yet that same day, she said, she gained great respect for her father, who told her the truth about the way the Indians were mistreated instead of hiding the facts from her, and then took her to meet the Indian chief, Yellow Robe.

2. Ibid., Reynolds, Tape 1.

3. Ibid., Reynolds, Tapes 2 and 3 (dated June 11, 1985). She described her salary in that job as $810 a year, of which she paid $7 a month for a room and $40 a month to various restaurants in town for her meals. The school budget was so tight, she explained, that she and the other teacher were paid in "warrants" which they cashed at a ten percent discount in the town's general store.

4. Ibid., Tape 4 (June 21, 1985).

5. Ibid., Tape 5 (June 21, 1985).

6. Ibid., Tape 5. Hipólito Cotto Reyes, she said, was the minister of a Baptist Church located at 114th or 116th St. in East Harlem but had grown up near the Ponce Playa and knew a great deal about the Ponce Massacre.

7. Ibid., Tape 5. She recalled that Albizu had gone to visit both brothers at their churches when he was released from the hospital in order to show his gratitude for their visits and prayers. She added that Albizu was a Catholic and generally attended Sunday Mass at the Catholic Church on 14th Street, whose name she couldn't remember.

8. Ibid.

9. Reynolds, Tape 7 (June 26, 1985).

10. Ibid.

11. Reynolds, Tape 31 (August 26, 1985).

12. Ibid., see also Jean Zwickel, "Doña Ruth Reynolds," a tribute posted online in June 1993 by a friend and fellow Pacifist. For details, see http://www.peacehost.net/whitestar/voice/eng-ruthreynolds.html.

13. Reynolds, Tape 31; for details of police and FBI surveillance, see Ruth Reynolds' Carpeta #1340 created by the Puerto Rican Police's Internal Security division. She was one of thousands of suspected dissidents indexed by the local secret police. It has generally been said that surveillance of dissidents in Puerto Rico began in the 1930s, but more recent studies have shown that the practice is as old as colonialism itself. Reynolds was able to retrieve her carpeta thanks to a protracted legal battle that was won in the late 1990s by Attorney David Noriega and other PIP members. Their legal triumph pushed the local Justice Department to seize the index files from the Police Department and hold them for safekeeping until they could be returned to the persons who requested them. Unfortunately, they had to request them within a narrow timeframe. For details about that legal battle and the government's attempts to block the various injunctions, see Ramón Bosque-Pérez, "The Political Persecution Against Puerto Ricans in the Twentieth Century," in the book he co-edited with José Colón Morera, *Puerto Rico Under Colonial Rule: Political Persecution and the Quest for Human Rights* (New York: State University of New York Press, 2006), 13-47. Reynolds' Carpeta (#1340) is included in "The Ruth Reynolds Papers," at the Centro de Estudios Puertorriqueños Archives, Hunter College, Manhattan. Her carpeta (#1340) is found in Box 48. The details cited were taken from Doc. 000303.

14. Ibid.

15. Reynolds, Carpeta #1340, Doc. 000303.

16. Ibid.

17. Reynolds, Carpeta #1340, Doc. 000302. See also I. S. Memorandum #919. According to Rosa Collazo, Carlos Vélez Rieckehoff headed the New York City chapter of the Nationalist Party in the 1930s and inducted her into the Party.

18. "The Ruth Reynolds Letter," was circulated by members of the Ruth Reynolds Defense Committee, which her friends organized in NYC in 1951. The letter from Reynolds was printed on the reverse side of an appeal form sent out to request funds for her defense. Both documents form part of "The Ruth Reynolds Papers," Centro Archives, Hunter College, Box 1, Folder 01.

19. For a summary of the charges levied against Reynolds, see the "Memorandum" sent by Special District Attorney José C. Aponte to Víctor Gutiérrez Franqui, May 1951, in AGPR, Fondo: Departamento de Justicia, Serie: Nacionalistas, Tarea 90-20, Caja 16, Item 20g.

20. In addition to "The Ruth Reynolds Letter" in which she provides rich details about her arrest and imprisonment, see Reynolds, Tape 47B. Newspaper accounts of the Nationalists' arrests were published in *El Mundo*, "Veinte Líderes Nacionalistas Encarcelados," Nov. 7, 1950, pp. 1, 12. According to that article, Ruth was kept away from the other five women at police headquarters in Puerta de Tierra. It said also that she had been arrested on the rumor that she "had been seen in front of Fortaleza" (the governor's mansion) the day the Nationalists attacked his residence.

21. "The Ruth Reynolds Letter," Centro Archives, Box 1, Folder 01. See also in AGPR, Fondo: Departamento de Justicia, Serie: "Law Violations," a document in English, dated Dec. 29, 1950, in Tarea: 642.4, Caja 2236; see also Reynolds, Tape 47 B and José C. Aponte's Memorandum to Gutiérrez Franqui, in AGPR, Justicia, Nacionalistas, Tarea 90-29, Caja 16, Item 20g.

22. Reynolds, Tape 47 B. For details about the incident that led the warden to shut the window, see the section devoted to Carmen María Pérez in this book.

23. Reynolds, Tape 47 B. Regarding the staff in Arecibo prison, Reynolds said: "I had no feeling that they disliked me or any of the political prisoners. They were just people who had a job and wanted to keep it . . . they had a general sense of human kindness."

24. Reynolds' complaints about the Puerto Rican prisons were reported to various groups and

their letters made their way back to the governor of Puerto Rico. For details, see AGPR, Fondo: Oficina del Gobernador, "Cartas al Gobernador," Tarea 96-20, Caja 531.

25. Details reported by Ruth Reynolds in a (six-page) written testimony she smuggled out of the Arecibo jail sometime in the fall of 1951. She revised and updated the document (June 30, 1952) shortly after she was released from prison. The complete version is found in "The Ruth Reynolds Papers," Centro de Archives, Hunter College. Box 16, Folder 01.

26. Ibid.

27. Ibid.

28. Emry's "bizarre" behavior was also described by Isabel Rosado and Carmen María Pérez. Both concur with Reynolds' assessment but said that Emry was "a guinea pig" for the prison experiments that were later practiced on Doris, Ruth, and Albizu Campos. See Reynolds' Testimony, June 30, 1952, in Centro Archives, Box 16, Folder 01.

29. Reynolds, Testimony (June 20, 1952), Centro Archives, Box 16, Folder 01.

30. Ibid.

31. Ibid.

32. Ibid.

33. Ibid.

34. Ibid.

35. Ibid.

36. Viscal's Testimony in AGPR, Nacionalistas, Tarea 90-29, Caja 19, Item 2d. For details of the trial, see AGPR, Tarea 90-29, Caja 7, Item 2. See also Reynolds, Carpeta #1340, Doc. #000284.

37. For details about Reynolds' case, see the summary: "Enjuiciados y Declarados Culpables," AGPR, Fondo: Justicia, Nacionalistas, Tarea 90-29, Caja 8, Item 15b.

38. Details of Reynolds' trial are found in AGPR, Nacionalistas, Tarea 90-29, Caja 7, Item 2.

39. See "Confidential Memorandum" (I.S. #25459) issued by Captain J.W. Hernández, June 23, 1959. The three who posted Reynolds' bail on June 21, 1952, were: Caguas resident: Félix Rodríguez (Carpeta #6624); Santurce resident, Ramón Vicente (Carpeta #4517); and Ciales resident, Santiago Ruiz (Carpeta #7196). The document appears in Reynolds' Carpeta #1340, Doc. 000267.

40. According to Reynolds, the cell in Arecibo had a window up high "with bars through which we could see a little light in the daytime, not a very comfortable spot." She recalled that the warden had been relieved when she told him she spoke Spanish. Over time she noticed that in his mind he divided the inmates into two categories: "street women" for whom he had little regard and "the other women." The Nationalists fell in the latter category and were treated with respect. Yet she felt that there were numerous cases of women with great intelligence and talent who had gone into prostitution because of poverty and lack of opportunity. She also found some women who had been jailed for performing abortions on themselves or others. Reynolds, Tape 47, side B.

41. A copy of the Secretary of Justice's reply to Congressman John S. Wood in December 1950 appears in in AGPR, Fondo: Oficina del Gobernador, Serie: Cartas al Gobernador, Tarea 96-20, Caja 531. The charges against Reynolds, cited in English, were found in AGPR, Departamento de Justicia, "Law Violations," Tarea 642.4, Caja 2236. A more detailed account of Reynolds' indictment was provided by Special Prosecutor José C. Aponte's "Memorandum" of May 1951.

42. A copy of the letter from Longstreth to Oscar Chapman appears in AGPR, "Cartas al Gobernador," Tarea 96-20, Caja 531.

43. The report issued by Interim Superintendent of Prisons Rafael N. Rodríguez to the Interim Attorney General, Federico Tilén, on November 5, 1951, appears in AGPR, Fondo: Oficina del Gobernador, Tarea: 642.4, Caja 16.

44. Ibid.

45. Reynolds's, Tape 47, sides B and C.

46. Ibid., Tape 47 C. A "Confidential Memorandum" (I.S. #26459) issued by Internal Security

Superintendent Capt. J. W. Hernández, June 23, 1959, states that the Ciales businessman who posted part of Reynolds' bail was Santiago Ruiz (Carpeta #7196). See Reynolds' Carpeta #1340, Doc. 000267.

47. "Doña Ruth Reynolds," a tribute posted online in June 1993 by a friend and fellow Pacifist, Jean Zwickel. See http://www.peacehost.net/whitestar/voice/eng-ruthreynolds.html.

48. Ibid.

49. The 1954 attack on Congress is documented in the section devoted to Lolita Lebrón. The FBI's harassment and the anecdote about the Jewish employer who refused to fire her in 1954 are described in Reynolds, Tape 47, side C.

50. Reynolds, Tape 47, side C.

51. Ibid. Details of her comrades' arrests were provided by The New York Times as well as El Mundo and El Imparcial among others during the first ten days of March 1954. (See the multiple sources cited in the sections devoted to Rosa Collazo and Lolita Lebrón in this book.)

52. Gonzalo Lebrón collaborated extensively with the New York City and Puerto Rican authorities. For excerpts of his accounts, see the section on Lolita Lebrón in this book.

53. For details as to how Reynolds' lawyers formulated their appeal to the Puerto Rican Supreme Court, see El Mundo, "Ataque a Ley 53: Solicitan Revoquen Condena a la Reynolds," July 18, 1953. For the outcome of their appeal, see The New York Times and El Mundo on November 19, 1954. For Reynold's tart comments about the ACLU, see "The Ruth Reynolds Papers," Centro de Estudios Puertorriqueños Archives, Box 12, Folder 01. For a summary of Reynolds' case, see AGPR, Nacionalistas, Tarea 90-29, Caja 3, Item 13, which specifies that Reynolds' sentence was "revoked" on Nov. 17, 1954.

54. Ibid. According to the local press, the Puerto Rican Supreme Court also absolved Rafael Burgos Fuentes and Rafael López Vázquez, on November 17, 1954. They, like Reynolds, had been convicted of violating Art. 1, Sec. 1 of Law #53. For details, see El Imparcial, "Supremo Absuelve a Tres Nacionalistas," Nov. 19, 1954, pp. 5, 38; also in El Mundo, "Fallo Exonera a Otros Dos Nacionalistas," Nov. 19, 1954, pp. 1, 27. (The news clippings from El Imparcial were included in Reynolds' Carpeta #1340, Documents No. 000217 and 000219.)

55. A "Memorandum" sent by Police Lieutenant Astol Calero (Dec. 30, 1954) to the Chief of Internal Security, Captain Benigno Soto, said that Torresola sent the money order on Dec. 15, 1954, from Arecibo, Puerto Rico. The agents at the airport said Reynolds arrived in San Juan on December 26, 1954. For details, see Docs. Nos. 000205 and 000211 in Reynolds' Carpeta, Centro Archives, Box 48, Folder 03.

56. According to El Imparcial, Oct. 11, 1955, Reynolds was petitioning President Eisenhower to intercede with Puerto Rico's governor to permit Pedro Albizu Campos to be removed from prison and sent to a hospital. Details appear in Albizu Campos' FBI File, Number 105-11898, Section 14, p. 32. The Pacifists led by Ruth Reynolds from Guánica to San Juan (Dec. 26-31, 1958) were: Ruth Miller, Valerie Aldrich, Ralph Templin, Seymour Eichel, Arthur Harvey, Wally Nelson, Gayle Isens, and Albert Uhrie. I.S. agents reported that the group spent the night of Dec. 25th at the Castañer Hospital in Adjuntas and arrived in Guánica at 7:30 a.m. on Dec. 26, where they were interviewed by El Imparcial. They marched from Guánica across the mountains to Yauco, where they spent the night at Sonia Roig's Hotel, on Betances St., #10. The march was followed by a demonstration at eleven U.S. military bases on Jan. 1st, 1959. They visited Juanita Ojeda's home on Jan. 2 and Leonides Díaz on Jan. 3. On Jan. 6, 1958 Ojeda visited Albizu Campos at the Presbyterian Hospital, presumably to report what had transpired during the Pacifists' visit. For details, see I.S. "Confidential Memorandum," Jan. 21, 1959, Doc. #000151, in Reynolds' Carpeta #1340. On the morning of August 26, 1963, Ruth Reynolds and Ruth Miller picketed the island's superior court (at Stop 18) calling for Albizu Campos' release. In the afternoon they picketed the Vega Alta prison, calling for the release of the Nationalist women. On Aug. 27, Reynolds visited Albizu Campos. See El Imparcial, "Grupo Norteamericano Pide

Libertad de Albizu Campos," Aug. 27, 1963.

57. Ruth Reynolds, "The Funeral of Don Pedro Albizu Campos," published in *Peacemaker*, May 1965, pp. 5-6; a typewritten copy of the original (dated May 12, 1965) is found at the Centro Archives, "The Ruth Reynolds Papers," Box 12, Folder 02. (Among the government officials who came to pay his respects, Reynolds said, was Vicente Géigel Polanco, the man who had signed the order of Don Pedro's arrest. This man, she told her interviewer, had dared to attend a Christmas dinner given at the Arecibo prison while she and her comrades were there and they boycotted the affair, even though his wife came to their cell to urge them to attend. She said she was not happy to see him filing by Don Pedro's coffin these many years later.

58. Reynolds, "The Funeral of Don Pedro Albizu Campos," ibid.

59. Details based on Jean Zwickel, "Doña Ruth Reynolds," cited.

60. See biographical sketch prepared by the staff of Centro de Estudios Puertorriqueños included in her collection. See also comments by Rosa Meneses Albizu, in *Claridad, En Rojo Section*, Dec. 29, 1989, to Jan. 4, 1990, pp. 17–24.

61. Anecdote recounted by Jacinto García Pérez in his tribute to Reynolds, *Claridad, En Rojo Section*, Dec. 29, 1989 to Jan. 4, 1990, pp. 17-24.

62. Isabel Rosado, in *Claridad*, ibid.

63. Oscar Collazo, in *Claridad*, ibid.

64. Lolita Lebrón's comments, in *Claridad*, ibid.

5. Isabel Rosado Morales

1. The information about Isabel Rosado cited throughout this essay was extracted from multiple sources. Key among these was an extensive interview I conducted with Isabel Rosado on April, 17, 1998. Other details were culled from Rosado's self-published account, *Mis Testimonios* (San Juan, Puerto Rico, 1972). For details about her arrests, surveillance, incarceration, and trials, I relied on Justice Department and Police records archived at the Archivo General de Puerto Rico. In other instances, I relied on newspaper articles written at the time, and on FBI reports submitted at various times before and after her two arrests. Also valuable were the various speeches given in her honor and the interviews she granted over time. The articles and speeches related to her death were sent to me by Professor María Canino.

2. Ibid.

3. Ibid. The details about her social worker's license are found in AGPR, Fondo: Departamento de Justicia, Serie: Nacionalistas, Tarea: 90-29, Caja 25, Item 1. The file contains a copy of a certification letter sent by the Board of Examiners of Social Workers, which states: "This is to certify that the Board of Examiners of Social Workers issued Permanent License No. 363 to Isabel Rosado Morales on April 12, 1950. By virtue of this license (she) is authorized to practice as a social worker in the Island of Puerto Rico. Said license has never been revoked" [asserted the Assistant Director of the Examining Board on April 18, 1950]. That fact would change after Rosado was convicted (of one violation of Law #53) in April 1952.

4. Rosado, Interview, April 17, 1998. The accounts of her arrests were covered by the press or told by her to journalists after the fact. See, for example, Miñi Seijo, "Isabel Rosado: Ejemplo de Valor y Sacrificio," *Claridad, En Rojo Section*, June 8-14, 1979, pp. 1-3. Also useful was Marisa Rosado's biographical sketch of Isabel Rosado, *Claridad, En Rojo Section*, March 8-14, 1996, reproduced without a title by *Biekesí* (Revista del Comité de Trabajo en Apoyo a Vieques, CTAV) shortly after Rosado's death in January 2015.

5. For details of the Ponce Massacre, see the section devoted to Dominga de la Cruz.

6. Rosado, Interview, ibid.

7. Ibid. The details of Albizu Campos' conviction and imprisonment in 1936 are well known. Those interested in his life and deeds would profit from reading Marisa Rosado's book,

Pedro Albizu Campos: Acercamiento a su biografía, cited.

8. Numerous Internal Security (I.S.) reports issued by Puerto Rico's secret police are found in AGPR, Fondo: Departamento de Justicia, Serie: Nacionalistas, Tarea 90-29. The ones cited here correspond to Caja 19, Items 1, 8; and Caja 20, Item 13f.

9. AGPR, Tarea 90-29, Caja 19, Items 1, 8, and Caja 20, Item 13f. Also see Rosado, Interview, ibid.

10. Rosado, Interview, ibid. Also in AGPR, see Tarea 90-29, Cajas 19, 20, Ibid.

11. For an enlightening discussion of Law #53, see Ivonne Acosta, *La Mordaza* (San Juan, Puerto Rico: Editorial Edil, 1989). The forms used by the police to carry out their arrests generally described the "infractions" to Law #53 for which the person was being arrested. Those detained following the uprising, but prior to December 20, 1950, were held under the parameters of the old Law #53 enacted in June 1948, while those detained after December 20 were charged under the parameters of the amended Law #53, which made it a crime to be a member of any group considered subversive by the authorities.

12. In February 1956, Governor Luis Muñoz Marín established a Civil Rights Committee and charged it to investigate the actions of his administration in connection with the uprising of 1950. The findings submitted by the Committee in 1957 made it clear that the civil and human rights of Puerto Rico's citizenry had been violated. One of the Committee's recommendations was to establish a permanent Civil Rights Commission to guard against such practices in the future. The recommendation was not implemented until 1965, according to a historical summary provided in the Commission's first published account, *Informes de la Comisión de los Derechos Civiles del Estado Libre Asociado de Puerto Rico* (Orford, N.H.: Equity Publishing Corporation, 1972).

13. Rosado, Interview, ibid. Also useful were various official documents pertaining to her arrest, especially those located at AGPR, Fondo: Departamento de Justicia, Serie: Nacionalistas, Tarea 90-29, Caja 19, Item 8, and Caja 20, Item 13f.

14. Rosado, Interview, ibid.

15. Ibid.

16. Ibid.

17. Ibid. Also *Mis Testimonios*, pp. 14–15. For the warden's reports on the Nationalists, see AGPR, Tarea 90-29, Caja 16. Item 16, Caja 19, Item 2c.

18. Ibid. For Pérez's views, see the section devoted to her in this book.

19. Rosado, Interview, ibid. Also in AGPR, Fondo: Departamento de Justicia, Serie: Nacionalistas, Tarea 90-29, Caja 9, Item 33, and Caja 3, Items 1 and 2 (Resúmenes del Caso de Isabel Rosado, 1950).

20. Rosado, Interview, ibid. Also in AGPR, Serie: Nacionalistas, Tarea 90-29, Caja 10, Item 1. Puerto Rican I.S. agents reported that she had attended various Nationalist or other "subversive" activities between April 1953 and March 6, 1954. The prosecutors used the I.S. reports to establish that Rosado (and others arrested in 1954) were enemies of the government who continued to violate the laws of the land and should be incarcerated.

21. Rosado, Interview, ibid. In the introduction to *Mis Testimonios* she thanks Paulino Castro for helping her to obtain that job.

22. Rosado, Interview, ibid. The stories Rosado told about Doña María Díaz have also been attributed to other Puerto Rican women who engaged in the struggle for Puerto Rico's independence.

23. For details about the Nationalist attack of the U.S. Congress, and sources cited in that regard, see the section devoted to Lolita Lebrón, included in this book. Albizu Campos and his companions' arrests in March 1954 were amply covered by the San Juan dailies, *El Mundo* and *El Imparcial* (March 2–7, 1954). Also useful was a report sent by Police Chief Salvardor T. Roig to Governor Luis Muñoz Marín, dated March 11, 1954. The document forms part of the collection of letters to the governor, labeled "Miscelanea: Correspondencia al Gobernador, 1950–1954," located in AGPR, Fondo: Departamento de Justicia, Serie: Nacionalistas, Tarea 90-29, Caja 8, Item 15 b.

24. For decades the FBI office in San Juan submitted a variety of reports to its headquarters in Washington, D.C., on the island's dissidents (Nationalists, Communists, independence advocates, labor leaders, and militant students). The reports were generally based on information supplied by the island's Division of Internal Security (I.S.) attached to the Police Department and by the FBI's own informants. The sources cited here form part of the declassified FBI files that are now archived at the Puerto Rican Legislative Library, at the Capitol in San Juan, under the heading "Carpetas del FBI," The one cited here regarding the agent's meeting with the governor on March 5, 1954, was labeled a "Radiogram" and sent under the heading "Very Urgent" to Assistant Director Belmont. It forms part of Sub-Serie: 31, vol. 39, Doc. 100-3-5399. The same information was included in a "Quarterly Report" for the period November 1, 1953 to March 6, 1954, which is part of Sub-Serie 31, vol. 39, Doc. 100-3.5416. For details about Isabel Rosado, provided by Police Captain Benigno Soto of I.S. to SAC San Juan, see "Weekly Intelligence Summary for Puerto Rico and the Virgin Islands," dated February 17, 1954, Sub-Serie 32, vol. 40, Doc. 100-3-5421, in which it was reported that she had been seen selling tickets for an upcoming dance in Río Grande to raise funds for the Nationalist Party. A translation of another I.S. Bulletin, dated March 10, 1954, which was attached to the SAC San Juan's report, described Isabel Rosado as a native of Ceiba, Puerto Rico, height: 5 feet 6 inches tall, weight: 140 pounds, resident of San Juan. It accuses her of firing against the police on the morning of March 6, 1954. For details, see "Carpetas del FBI," Sub-Serie: 32, vol. 40, Doc. 1003-5482. An earlier FBI report sent by the SAC San Juan on November 2, 1953, reported that Isabel Rosado had accompanied Antonio Moya Vélez to La Princesa jail to pick up a refrigerator and a fan left there by Pedro Albizu Campos when he was pardoned and released [in September 1953]. For details, see "Carpetas del FBI," Sub-Serie 29, vol. 37, Doc. 100-3-5008. Also valuable was a Quarterly Report for the period Aug. 1–Oct. 31, 1953, which placed Isabel Rosado in N.Y.C. in October 1953 and suggests that she was the person who brought Albizu Campos' order for the attack on Congress to Nationalist leaders Julio Pinto Gandía, and Lolita and Gonzalo Lebrón. (Gonzalo Lebrón corroborated the FBI's suspicions after he was arrested.) According to a "Memorandum" sent by I.S. to SAC San Juan, Rosado had been observed visiting Albizu Campos (September 30, 1953) shortly before she went to New York, ostensibly, to meet with Pinto Gandía and Lolita Lebrón. See "Carpetas del FBI," Sub-Serie 28, vol. 36, Doc. 100-3-4951.

25. FBI Files, ibid.

26. For details about Gonzalo Lebrón, see section devoted to Lolita Lebrón in this book.

27. FBI Files, ibid.

28. Chief Roig's report to Governor Luis Muñoz Marín, March 11, 1954, cited earlier.

29. Rosado, Interview, ibid. Pérez, Interview, April 21, 1998.

30. Pérez, Interview, ibid. Also Roig's report to Governor Muñoz Marín, March 11, 1954.

31. Rosado, Interview, Ibid. Details of Rosado's arrest, charges, and the sum of her bail in 1954 are scattered in various boxes in AGPR, Serie: Nacionalistas, Tarea 90-29, Caja 2, Item 15, Caja 8, Item 10; Caja 9, Item 33; Caja 21, Item 2d and 2k; Caja 25, Item 1.

32. The Nationalists tried in Arecibo's district court in 1954 received much tougher sentences than those tried in San Juan's district court. The question why Rosado and her co-defendants were tried outside the jurisdiction where they were arrested has never been adequately explained.

33. Rosado's complaints of the Vega Alta prison have appeared in various writings, including her self-published Mis Testimonios, pp. 30–36, and during the interview she granted me, April 17, 1998. For details about the flooding of the cell block in Maximum Security, see the reports submitted by guards Sra. Esquilín and Sra. Ithier, dated September 29, 1957. According to the initial report submitted by Sra. Soto, on September 26, 1957, Conrada Osuna [another mentally ill inmate] sang all night, which made Genoveva Flores angry and led her to stuff the toilet and flood the area. For their accounts, see "Informes de Supervisión: Rutina del Turno" [Edificio de Psiquiatría, Puesto 3] for the cited dates, which

are found in AGPR, Departamento de Justicia, Escuela Industrial Para Mujeres, Tarea 60-A-19, Caja 5.

34. Rosado, Interview, ibid. *Mis Testimonios*, pp. 30–36.

35. See the details provided by the prison guards in their "Informes de Supervisión: Rutina del Turno," Sección Máxima Custodia [Edificio de Psiquiatría, Puesto 3], Tarea 60-A-19, Caja 5.

36 Rosado, *Mis Testimonios*, pp. 37–38. Speculation based on the actions of Governor Roberto Sánchez Vilella during his one-term administration (1964–1968).

37 Rosado, Interview, ibid. Also details she gave to Miñi Seijo in an extensive interview. See "Isabel Rosado: Ejemplo de Valor y Sacrificio," *Claridad, En Rojo Section*, June 8–14, 1979, pp. 1–3.

38. Seijo, ibid. Details about her participation in other groups besides the Nationalist Party were reported by Marisa Rosado in a biographical sketch of Isabel which was originally published in *Claridad, En Rojo Section*, March 8–14, 1996, reprinted and circulated at the time of Isabel's death by *Biekesí* (Revista del Comité de Trabajo en Apoyo a Vieques, CTAV).

39. Seijo, ibid. Rosado, ibid.

40. Seijo, Ibid. Rosado, Ibid.

41. Details of how others viewed her were culled from speeches given in her honor. For example, see Cándida Cotto's account of an event, titled "Las Madres de la Patria," held in barrio Santana, Arecibo, in honor of Isabel Rosado and the late Leonides Díaz, among others. Cotto's account was published in *Claridad*, June 7–13, 1985, p. 12. See also Alejandro Torres' account, titled "Tres Heroínas de la Independencia: Tres Mujeres de la Libertad," in *Claridad, En Rojo Section*, June 13–19, 1997, p. 19.

42. Details provided by filmmaker Melissa Montero and others who visited Rosado at the nursing home. Montero has been working on a film of Rosado's life and has documented much of her political work. Rutgers Professor María Josefa Canino visited Rosado occasionally during the last years of her life.

43. Details of Rosado's death and comments posted by her admirers appeared in *Primera Hora*, Jan. 14, 2015, p. 20 and *El Nuevo Dia*, Jan. 14, 2015 (information recovered online (*http://elnuevodia.com*). Details of her funeral arrangements, religious service, and speakers selected to give the eulogies were tweeted on Jan. 14, 2015, by the Comité Isabel Rosado (Indice Puerto Rico.com and Claridad.com). Comments by politicians and civil servants were tweeted and/or cited by the press. Mark Viverito's comments, for example, were cited by New York's *Daily News*, Jan. 15, 2015, p. 20.

44. For a moving account of the funeral procession to the Ceiba cemetery, see Nydia Bauzá's article, "Honras Entre el Llanto y la Alegría," *Primera Hora*, Jan. 16, 2015, p. 8. The coverage includes photographs and an apt description of the mourners' actions: "One of the most emotional moments occurred when the funeral procession stopped at the humble house . . . where she had lived, on Escolástico López, in the center of town. They took the coffin inside and laid it in the living room, while outside, the 'pleneros' improvised songs about the transcendental figure who had been a teacher and social worker." (This is an approximate translation of Bauzá's well-crafted comments.)

45. The selected quotations from Rafael Cancel Miranda, Alicia Rodríguez, and Senator María de Lourdes Santiago, among others were reported by Bauzá, ibid. On January 24, 2015, Rosado was honored also by the Colegio de Profesionales de Trabajo Social (CPTS) in a radio program titled "Vida y Legado de Isabel Rosado Morales," organized by Nélida Rosario and Rosa Figueroa Sánchez and led by Francine Sánchez Marcano. One of the guests at that event was Rafael Cancel Miranda. (The pamphlet describing the event was mailed to me by Professor María Canino.)

6. Doris Torresola Roura

1. The biographical sketch of Doris Torresola presented here is based on a variety of sources, including several testimonies: two written by Doris Torresola and three others by her cell mates. It is based also on numerous interviews provided by friends and relatives of Doris. It is also based on contemporary newspaper accounts of such topics as the Nationalist uprising of 1950, the trials, the 1954 attack on Congress, and the events it unleashed. Surveillance reports from Puerto Rico's Internal Security Division and reports from the FBI Office in San Juan helped to corroborate the dates of many of her activities. Select secondary sources helped to fill some gaps in the chronology of events. Among these, the most valuable were the self-published testimonies of Heriberto Marín: *Coabey: El Valle Heróico* (1995) and *Eran Ellos* (2000); also the unpublished master's thesis by Janet Martínez González, which she submitted in 2011 to El Centro de Estudios Avanzados de Puerto Rico y el Caribe (CEA), titled "La Participación de la Mujer en la Lucha Nacionalista: Doris Torresola Roura." I relied on Martínez to establish the chronology of Doris' life and on a few of her interviews to flesh out some details about Doris' family life, birth date, and place of origin (discussed on pp. 139–40). Also helpful in terms of details about the Torresola brothers and their friends was the work of Stephen Hunter and John Bainbridge Jr., *American Gunfight: The Plot to Kill Harry Truman—and the Shoot-out That Stopped It* (New York: Simon & Schuster, 2005) p. 209.

2. Janet Martínez' interviews with Angelina Torresola de Platet, April 4, 2008, and the brothers Rodríguez Orama, April 5, 2008, cited throughout her work. The details cited here are from p. 142.

3. Ibid.

4. Ibid. Marín, 1995, pp. 13–14; Martínez, ibid.

5. Rodríguez Orama, Interview, cited in Martínez, p. 144; Angelina Torresola, Interview by Hunter and Bainbridge, *American Gunfight*, pp. 207–9; Interviews conducted by Vionette G. Negretti and cited in her self-published work, *Tiempos Revueltos* (Bogotá, Colombia: Author's Edition, 2008), p. 108.

6. Joint Interview of the Rodríguez Orama brothers, cited in Martínez, "La Participación de la Mujer," pp. 144–45.

7. Martínez, ibid, p. 147; Marín, *Coabey: Valle Heroico*, pp. 57–58; Negretti, *Tiempos Revueltos*, p. 108. It should be noted that after Puerto Ricans were granted American citizenship in 1917, all eligible adult males were conscripted into the U.S. Armed Forces. That obligation continued for as long as the military draft remained in effect. Those who resisted were accused of draft evasion and often sentenced to serve their sentences in U.S. federal prisons. For details about the many Puerto Ricans who went to prison because of draft evasion, see José (Ché) Paraliticis multiple works on the subject. The one cited here is *Sentencia Impuesta: 100 Años de encarcelamiento por la independencia de Puerto Rico* (San Juan, Puerto Rico: Ediciones Puerto Histórico, 2004).

8. Martínez, ibid. It should be noted that Doris Torresola was sent to prison twice: for three years in 1950, for violations of Law #53, and again in 1954, for conspiring against the government in the Nationalist Attack on Congress. This time she was sentenced to seventeen years in prison.

9. See Archivo General de Puerto Rico (AGPR), Fondo: Departamento de Justicia, Serie: Nacionalistas, Tarea 90-29, Caja 21, Item 3.

10. Angelina Torresolas's interview was cited in Hunter and Bainbridge, *American Gunfight*, p. 209; see also Blanca Canales' 1967 testimony included in the section to her in this book. Canales' testimony was originally published in Spanish as "La Constitución es la Revolución" (San Juan, Puerto Rico: Congreso Nacional Hostosiano, 1997).

11. Canales, Testimony, ibid.

12. Ibid.

13. Marín, *Eran Ellos*, p. 65.

14. Angelina Torresola, Interview, cited by Martínez, p. 164.
15. Carmen María Pérez, Interview, April 21, 1998. It has been said that Carmín Pérez was still in high school when she skipped classes to be with Albizu. She told me that by then she had graduated from high school and was enrolled in secretarial courses at a vocational college.
16. Ibid.
17. Isabel Rosado, Interview, April 17, 1998.
18. Copies of the Internal Security Division reports, most of which were shared with the FBI Office in San Juan, are available in AGPR, Fondo: Departamento de Justicia, Serie: Nacionalistas, Tarea 90-29, Cajas 5, 8, 21, 25. Details about the creation and evolution of the Nurses Corps are discussed in the section devoted to Dominga de la Cruz Becerril in this book. The comments by Isabel Rosado were made during her interview, April 17, 1998.
19. Irma Viscal's testimony appears in AGPR, Fondo: Departamento de Justicia, Serie: Nacionalistas, Tarea 90-29, Caja 19, Item 2d.
20. Carmín Pérez, Interview, ibid. See also the various police reports kept in AGPR, Fondo: Departamento de Justicia, Serie: Nacionalistas, Caja 5, Items 32–37.
21. Ibid.
22. Details offered in the second testimony that Doris Torresola wrote on August 29, 1953, six days after she left the Arecibo prison. An earlier, shorter version of this account—written on November 8, 1951—shortly after she was convicted—forms part of "The Ruth Reynolds Papers" and is archived at the Centro de Estudios Puertorriqueños Archives at Hunter College, Manhattan. For details, see Box 2, Folder 6.
23. Details of the configuration of the cell and the ordeals the Nationalist women endured during the months they remained in La Princesa were provided by Ruth Reynolds and Doris Torresola in the written testimonies they left behind, now archived as part of "The Ruth Reynolds Papers," Centro Archives, Hunter College, Manhattan, See Box 16, Section: "Political Prisoners," Folders 6–12.
24. Details provided by Carmín Pérez and Isabel Rosado during their conversations with the author. Pérez and Torresola's accounts were also published in Havana, Cuba, in 1952 by Juan Juarbe Juarbe.
25. Isabel Rosado and Carmín Pérez, Interviews, cited earlier.
26. For details about the indictments against Albizu Campos and his co-defendants, see the official records in AGPR, Serie: Nacionalistas, Tarea 90-29, Caja 5, Items: 30-32. Other details were culled from the news coverage of El Imparcial, Feb. 11, 1951, p. 34; Feb. 16, 1951, pp. 3, 35.
27. AGPR, ibid, Tarea 90-29, Caja 25, Item 14. The prison sentences and bail sums were described in Albizu Campos' FBI File No. 105-11898, Section X, pp. 37–38. The file can be accessed online.
28. Details of Torresola's trial were reported in El Imparcial, July 8, 11, 19, 1951.
29. Information gathered from several testimonies and the oral accounts provided by Isabel Rosado and Carmín Pérez during their interviews. Also helpful was Ruth Reynolds' account of June 30, 1952, which is archived with "The Ruth Reynolds Papers" at Centro Archives, Hunter College, Manhattan.
30. See the study edited by Dan Gudman, The Human Radiation Experiments: Final Report of the President's Advisory Committee (President Clinton) (New York: Oxford University Press, 1996); see also Jessica Mitford's exposé of the practice of human experimentation in U.S. prisons, published by Atlantic Monthly (Jan. 1973); also helpful was Edward Marrey's report: "American Nuclear Guinea Pigs: Three Decades of Radiation Experiments on U.S. Citizens," U.S. House of Representatives Committee on Energy and Commerce, Sub-Committee on Energy, Conservation and Power (Nov. 1986) ACHRE, Number CON-050594-A-1. The cited 1996 presidential report makes the point that the regulations enacted in 1976 had a loophole which allowed the military and other medical teams, some financed by big pharmaceuticals, to skirt the new regulations by simply asking the "volunteer pris-

oner" to sign an "informed consent form."

31. Marín, *Eran Ellos*, pp. 72–73.

32. Carmín Pérez and Isabel Rosado, Interviews, and Ruth Reynolds' testimony, all cited earlier.

33. Ibid.

34. Reynolds, Testimony, ibid.

35. Carmín Pérez, Interview.

36. Isabel Rosado, Interview.

37. Observation related by Angelina Torresola in her interview with Janet Martínez, "La Participación de la Mujer," p. 210.

38. Reports of the attack on Congress were published in numerous newspapers in the United States. In Puerto Rico, *El Mundo* and *El Imparcial* offered extensive coverage in early March 1954. For other sources, see the section on Lolita Lebrón in this book.

39. Accounts provided by Pérez and Rosado, Interviews, cited earlier.

40. Photographs of Rivera Sotomayor appeared in *El Imparcial*, March 9, 1954; for details about the siege of Albizu's place and the arrests that followed, see coverage in *El Imparcial* and *El Mundo*, March 7–9, 1954. For Chief Roig's comments about Osborne, see AGPR, Departamento de Justicia, Serie: Nacionalistas, Tarea 90-29, Caja 25, Item 5.

41. Details about Doris' indictment on the various counts appear in AGPR, ibid, Caja 25, Item 5.

42. The tensions between Judge Padró and the women's defense were reported by *El Mundo* and *El Imparcial* on December 15, 1954 (the day after the trial began), and February 9, 1955 (the day after Doris Torresola and thirteen others were convicted), and also February 14, 1955, which described the reasons why the judge had to postpone sentencing.

43. For details regarding Doris' sentencing and subsequent appeals, see AGPR, Nacionalistas, Tarea 90-20, Caja 21, Item 2k, also Caja 25, Item 5. See also José Paralitici, *Sentencia Impuesta*.

44. AGPR, Nacionalistas, Tarea 90-29, Caja 21, Item 2k; also *El Imparcial*, May 3-6, 1955, also June 18, 1955.

45. Interviews of Ana María Platet and her mother, Angelina Torresola, by Janet Martínez, cited in her work, pp. 218, 230; The Federal Drug Administration warned "that 'Thorazine' should be used with caution in patients with chronic respiratory disorders, such as severe asthma," according to what Platet told Martínez, p. 198.

46. Information on Doris' release and time spent in the Psychiatric Hospital was cited by Martínez, "La Participación de la Mujer," p. 231.

47. The home address of the Platet Torresola family was listed in the orders for the arrests of the two sisters: Doris and Angelina Torresola. Details of those arrests appear in their files at AGPR, Nacionalistas, Tarea 90-29, Cajas 21, and 25.

48. The continued surveillance by the FBI was reported by Martínez, "La Participación de la Mujer," pp. 232–33.

49. Ibid.

50. Details of Doris' tragic death were reported by the local dailies: *El Imparcial, El Nuevo Día,* and *El Mundo*, February 11, 1972. The weekly *Claridad* carried an article plus two poems that were written in her honor: one of them by Edwin Reyes and the other by Francisco Matos Paoli. For details, see the issue of March 5, 1972, p. 23. Many more poems were written later in Doris' honor.

51. Poem cited by Martínez. (The English translation of Torresola's poem is my own and is meant only as an approximation since poetry is not my area of expertise.)

7. Olga Isabel Viscal Garriga

1. The information about Viscal was culled from various sources starting with police documents located at the Archivo General de Puerto Rico (AGPR), Fondo: Departamento de Justicia, Serie: Nacionalistas, Tarea 90-29, Caja 1, Tomo 2, folio 111 y 111 vuelto. In the government files I also found surveillance reports, notices of her arrest, the transcript of the interrogation conducted by D.A. Angel Viera Martínez, and copies of letters exchanged between the wardens of Arecibo and San Juan prisons and their superiors. There are copies of Viscal's father's and sister's depositions as well as numerous reports the undercover police shared with the FBI office in San Juan. There were copies of Olga's letters to various government officials as well as newspaper clippings detailing her antics during her trial. There were also articles describing her troubles with the Nationalist Party after she was readmitted to that Party.

2. AGPR, ibid. Nacionalista, Tarea 90-29, Caja 19, Items 2d, 2g.

3. AGPR, ibid. Caja 19, Item 2e, "Informes de la Policía, 1948–1950."

4. AGPR, ibid. Caja 19, Item 2e, "Informes de la Policía, 1948–1950."

5. AGPR, ibid. Caja 19, Items 2d, 2e. See "Testimonios de Francisco Viscal Bravo y de Irma Viscal," Nov. 9, 1950; see also "Declaración de Saturnina Ramos de Díaz Pacheco," May 2, 1952.

6. AGPR. ibid. Caja 19, Item 2e, "Declaración de Saturnina Ramos."

7. AGPR, ibid. Caja 19, Item 2d, "Declaración jurada de la Detective Carmen Belén Sosa de Rodríguez" Nov. 9, 1950.

8. AGPR, Tarea 90-29, Caja 19, Item 2d, ibid. "Declaración de la Detective Sosa." See also details reported by El Imparcial, May 5–14, 1952.

9. AGPR, ibid. Caja 19, Item 2d, "Declaración de José Enrique Tizol Bouret," Dec. 21, 1950; also see the coverage in El Imparcial and El Mundo, May 5–14, 1952.

10. AGPR, Tarea 90-29, Caja 19, Item 2d, "El Pueblo vs. Olga Isabel Viscal Garriga," Interrogación, Nov. 5, 1950. See also the Testimony given by Irma Viscal (Nov. 9, 1950) in which she said that Juanita González Bouillerce created a chapter of the Women's Junta and took Olga and Irma to her home and from there to Blanca Canales' home to meet Albizu Campos ("Creó una sub-junta de mujeres y nos reunió a Olga y a mí en su casa y nos llevó a Jayuya conocer a don Pedro Albizu Campos que vivía en casa de Blanca Canales.")

11. Interrogación de Olga Viscal, Nov. 5, 1950, in AGPR, ibid, p. 10.

12. Interrogación de Olga Viscal, ibid.

13. AGPR, Nacionalistas, Tarea 90-29, Caja 19, Items 2f, 2g, "El Pueblo vs. Olga Isabel Viscal Garriga"; see also "Fijación de Fianza."

14. AGPR, Nacionalistas, Tarea 90-29, Caja 16, Item 16, Warden González-Lebrón's report to Victor Gutiérrez Franqui, Feb. 12, 1951.

15. AGPR, Caja 16, Item 16, Juan S. Bravo's report to Rodríguez Higgins, Feb. 13, 1951; see also the Medical Report submitted by Dr. Velázquez, San Juan District Hospital, Feb. 9, 1951, and El Mundo, Feb. 26, 1951, p. 3 "Srta. Olga Viscal no padece de tuberculosis: Examen de Tisis fue negativo."

16. AGPR, Nacionalistas, Tarea 90-29, Caja 19, Item 2c; Carta de J. González Lebrón a José C. Aponte, Oct. 5, 1951.

17. AGPR, ibid, Caja 19, Item 2c, Informe de J. González Lebrón, Oct. 16, 1951, in which he enclosed various letters Olga Viscal had written to the soldier Fausto Rosas Rivera and a note in which he complained about Olga Viscal and Doris Torresola and the "nonsense they continue to write."

18. AGPR, Tarea 90-29, Caja 16, Item 16, contains a great deal of correspondence regarding the health claims of Olga Viscal. See also the report sent by Dr. Soto Ramos to the Department of Justice and another sent by the new warden of the Arecibo prison, Sept. 16, 1953.

19. AGPR, Tarea 90-29, Caja 16, Item 16. Comments made to the author in 1998 by Isabel Rosado and Carmen María Pérez. The comment made by Ruth Reynolds appears in an

oral interview tape-recorded by Blanca Vázquez at Centro de Estudios Puertorriqueños, Centro Archives, Hunter College, Manhattan.

20. For details of Olga Viscal's unusual behavior in court during her trial, see the extensive coverage of *El Imparcial* and *El Mundo,* May 6–14, 1952.

21. For details about the daily drama, see the press coverage cited. See also AGPR, Tarea 90-29, Caja 3, Items 1, 13, "Resumen del Caso de Olga Viscal Garriga;" the details of her sentence are in AGPR, Tarea 90-29, Caja 19, Items 2b and 2g;

22. Rosado and Pérez, Interviews, April 1998.

23. AGPR, Tarea 90-29, Caja 16, Item 4a contains a copy of the letter Olga Viscal sent to Víctor Gutiérrez Franqui, June 6, 1951.

24. AGPR, Tarea 90-29, Caja 19, Item 2c. The file contains copies of letters intercepted by the new Arecibo warden, Balbino González, which he forwarded to José C. Aponte on Sept. 28, 1953. One was from the soldier William Sánchez and another from Angelina Torresola de Platet.

25. AGPR, ibid. Tarea 90-29, Caja 19, Item 2c, "Copias de Certificación enviadas por la Universidad de Puerto Rico" were forwarded by the warden of Arecibo to the Department of Justice.

26. AGPR, ibid. Caja 19, Item 2 c, "Informe de la Guardia Rosa A. Quesada al alcaide (warden) de Arecibo.

27. AGPR, Sub-fondo: "Escuela Industrial Para Mujeres," Tarea 60-A-19, Caja 9, "Record de Ingresadas y Egresadas." Her assigned number was F-33. Another prison log labeled "Correspondencia de Confinadas Recibida," May 5, 1954, lists Olga Viscal among the recipients of mail that day.

28. AGPR, Tarea 90-29, Caja 19, Item 2b. For details about the governor's pardon, see the undated police report (circa March 1961) that appears in AGPR, ibid. Caja 2, Item 23. See also the press account in *El Imparcial,* Aug. 11, 1955, which claims that Olga had written to the governor soliciting a full pardon.

29. The FBI report sent from San Juan dated March 8, 1956, alleges that Viscal's appeal letter to the governor was sent in December 1955. For the full story, see the Puerto Rican Capitol Library, "Carpetas del FBI," Serie: Nacionalistas, Sub-Serie 54, vol. 60, Document 100-3-7758.

30. In *El Mundo,* see the following articles: "Olga Viscal Deja Partido: Acusa Líderes de Vivir del Ideal Nacionalista," April 12, 1962, p. 3; "Partido Nacionalista Rechaza la Acusación que Hizo Olga Viscal," April 12, 1962, p. 9; also "Olga Viscal es amenazada de muerte por desconocido," April 14, 1962.

31. Ibid.

32. For a complete account of Viscal's accusations, see "Los falsos nacionalistas le están haciendo el juego al comunismo," *Bohemia Libre Puertorriqueña,* May 6, 1962, pp. A8, A9, A31 A32 (an English translation of the article was filed by the FBI and can be read at the Puerto Rican Capitol Library, "Carpetas del FBI," Serie: Nacionalistas, Sub-Serie 54, vol. 60, Document 105-93124-73. See Rafael Gil de la Madrid, "Que es lo que se traen con Olga Viscal? (article reprinted from *El Diario, La Prensa,* in *Bohemia Libre Puertorriqueña,* ibid. pp. A 4, A 5.

33. "La Bravisima Hija de la Patria," by Eneid Routée, in *The San Juan Star,* July 2, 1995, p. 20.

34. Ibid.

35. Ibid.

36. "La Invicta Olga," by Marta Sánchez Olmedo, in *Claridad,* July 28–Aug. 3, 1995, p. 28.

37. Olga Viscal's death notice was published in *El Nuevo Dia,* June 2, 1995, p. 170.

Part III: Nationalist Women Imprisoned in the United States, 1950, 1954

1. Rosa Cortés Collazo

1. The account of Rosa Collazo's life and role in the Nationalist Party provided here is based on several sources, including two tape-recorded interviews I conducted with her daughter Lydia Collazo and stepdaughter Carmen Zoraida Collazo (Oscar's daughter); Rosa's own reminiscences in "Memorias de Rosa Collazo", published after her death by Lydia; a "Semblanza de Rosa Collazo" (describing some aspects of her life and her political work), presented by her husband Oscar Collazo at her 80th birthday celebration at the Puerto Rican Bar Association in San Juan, September 16, 1984. It is based also on the surveillance files kept by the Puerto Rican Division of Internal Security and select declassified FBI files dispatched from New York and San Juan about her role in the Nationalist Party, and numerous contemporary newspaper articles published in San Juan and New York following the Nationalist attacks of Blair House (November 1950) and on Congress (March 1954). Both attacks led to Rosa's imprisonment. A few secondary sources helped to fill some gaps. The details about Rosa's childhood discussed above were extracted from her *Memorias*, pp. 7-8, 16.
2. Memorias, ibid. pp. 11–12.
3. Ibid. p. 13.
4. Ibid. pp. 16–17.
5. Ibid. pp. 17–18.
6. Ibid. pp. 18, 19, 22.
7. Information extracted from Lydia Collazo's interview with the author, April 18, 1998, and Oscar Collazo's "Semblanza de Rosa Collazo," Sept. 16, 1984.
8. *Memorias*, ibid. pp. 20, 22.
9. Ibid.
10. Ibid.
11. *Memorias*, p. 19; also in "Semblanza de Rosa Collazo." See also Virginia Sánchez Korrol, *From Colonia to Community: The History of Puerto Ricans in New York City, 1917–1948* (Westport, Conn.: Greenwood Press, 1983).
12. *Memorias*, pp. 20–23.
13. Oscar Collazo's "Semblanza de Rosa Collazo."
14. Ibid.
15. Ibid.
16. *Memorias*, pp. 24–25; also Oscar Collazo's "Semblanza de Rosa Collazo."
17. For details about the incarceration of Puerto Ricans for draft evasion, see José (Ché) Paralitici's works on the subject. For an English account of this subject, see "Imprisonment and Colonial Domination, 1898–1958," in Ramón Bosque-Pérez and José Javier Colón-Moreira, eds., *Puerto Rico Under Colonial Rule: Political Persecution and the Quest for Human Rights* (New York: State University of New York Press, 2006), pp. 67–80. For a more detailed account of the same topic (in Spanish), see *Sentencia impuesta:100 años de encarcelamiento por la Independencia de Puerto Rico* (San Juan, Puerto Rico: Ediciones Puerto, 2004), pp. 25–59.
18. *Memorias*, pp. 25, 30; "Semblanza de Rosa Collazo."
19. Ibid.
20. *Memorias*, ibid: Also see author's interview with Carmen Zoraida Collazo, May 6, 1998.
21. *Memorias*, pp. 27, 29, 32, 33; see also Stephen Hunter and John Bainbridge Jr.'s fast-paced account of the attack on Blair House, *American Gunfight: The Plot to Kill Harry Truman— and the Shoot-out that Stopped It* (New York: Simon & Schuster, 2005); see the numerous articles published by the *New York Times* and *Washington Evening Star*, many of which were translated into Spanish by Puerto Rico's dailies *El Imparcial* and *El Mundo*. For exam-

ple, *El Mundo*, Nov. 2, 1950, carried two important articles: "Boricuas Tirotean," p. 7, and "Un Crimen Contra Puerto Rico," pp. 1, 12; and on Nov. 3, 1950, "El Objetivo Era Asesinar el Presidente," pp. 1, 12; see also "Prensa de Estados Unidos Refleja Espanto ante Atentado al Presidente," p. 24. The articles cited in this essay were emailed to me by research assistants Nahomi Galindo and Raúl Romero Torres, both graduate students.

22. *Memorias*, p. 35; Zoraida Collazo, Interview, May 6, 1998; for details of what he found at the Collazo home that afternoon, see the account of Chief Detective Carmine J. Motto, "They Weren't Wild About Harry," in his memoir, *A Generation of U.S. Secret Service Adventures: In Crime's Way* (Boca Raton, New York: CRC Press, 2000), pp. 85–87.

23. Zoraida Collazo, Interview, May 6, 1998.

24. Ibid.

25. Zoraida Collazo and Lydia Collazo, Interviews; also Chief Detective Motto's entry, "They Weren't Wild About Harry . . . "

26. Lydia Collazo, Interview, ibid.; Rosa Collazo, *Memorias*, p. 38.

27. Lydia Collazo, Interview; *Memorias*, p. 38. See also "Acusaciones por el Atentado," *El Mundo*, Nov. 5, 1950, pp. 1, 16; and "Nombran Abogado para Oscar Collazo," pp. 1, 3.

28. Collazo, *Memoria*, p. 39; also Lydia and Zoraida Collazo, Interviews; also article in *El Mundo*, Nov. 3, 1950, "Perito Analiza el Caso Boricua en N.Y." p. 2; and "El Presidente Vió el Tiroteo desde Ventana," (a translation of the *Washington Evening Star*'s November 3, 1950, editorial).

29. *Memorias*, pp. 39, 76; also in *El Mundo*, "Acusaciones por el Atentado," Nov. 5, 1950, pp. 1, 16; and in the same newspaper, "Nombran Abogado para Oscar Collazo," pp. 1, 3.

30. *Memorias*, pp. 39, 41, 76–78; for details of the entry process at New York's Women's House of Detention, see Elizabeth Gurley Flynn, *My Life as a Political Prisoner*, (New York: New World Paperbacks, 2nd ed., 1972), pp. 15–23; see also Miriam Moskowitz, *Phantom Spies: Phantom Justice: How I Survived McCarthyism* (New York: Banim and Bannigan, 2010), pp. 18–20.

31. *Memorias*, pp. 39, 77; Moskowitz, pp. 18–20.

32. *Memorias*, pp. 41–42.

33. *Memorias*, ibid.

34. *Memorias*, ibid.

35. Zoraido Collazo, Interview, ibid.

36. *Memorias*, pp. 42, 46; also Lydia Collazo, Interview, ibid.

37. Accounts and photographs of the four attackers of Congress appeared on the cover of the *New York Times*, March 2, 1954, "Five Congressmen Shot in House by 3 Puerto Rican Nationalists: Bullets Spray from Gallery," pp. 1, 15; also "Capitol Assassins Resistant of Plea," pp. 1, 9. Related stories were reported in Puerto Rico by *El Mundo*, from March 2–13, 1954.

38. *Memorias*, p. 74; also in the *New York Times*, March 2, 1954, "Gunplay Incidents Rare in Capitol," p. 16; also in the same newspaper, March 9, 1954, "91 Nationalists Rounded Up Here," pp. 1, 2.

39. By the early 1990s, approximately 125,000 individuals and organizations in Puerto Rico had been indexed and assigned dossiers or *carpetas* by the island's Internal Security division. Copies of many police reports were placed under the protection of the island's Department of Justice and can now be reviewed at the Archivo General de Puerto Rico (AGPR), Fondo: Departamento de Justicia, Serie: Nacionalistas, Tarea 90-29. The ones cited here were found in Caja 5, Items 7–18 and Items 31–38. Ruth M. Reynolds dossier, #1340, retrieved in the 1990s from the Puerto Rican Department of Justice, is now part of "The Ruth M. Reynolds Papers" at Centro de Estudios Puertorriqueños Archives, Hunter College, Manhattan. It is found in Box 48 of the Reynolds Collection. For details about the many Puerto Rican women tailed by the FBI, see Sandra Morales Blanes, "La Participación de la Mujer en el Partido Nacionalista de Puerto Rico (PNPR) en Puerto Rico y Estados Unidos a través de las Carpetas del FBI, 1941–1951." The work is an unpublished master's thesis she presented to the Centro de Estudios Avanzados de Puerto Rico y el

Caribe, 2013. Chapter 2 proved very useful in placing Rosa Collazo and others at different activities in New York.

40. The Roig letter cited is part of a large body of correspondence between the island's Police Chief and the Governor's Office. Their correspondence can be read at AGPR, Departamento de Justicia, Serie: Nacionalistas, Tarea 90-29, Caja 8, Items 8, 14, 15, which includes Report #79 in "Informes de la Policía: Nacionalistas, 1951–1954." For details about Governor Luis Muñoz Marín's visit to Washington, D. C., following the attack on Congress, and his promise to help the Velde Committee's investigation, see C.P. Russell, "Four Are Indicted in House Shooting," the New York Times, March 3, 1954, p. 10.

41. Rosa Collazo, Memorias, ibid. Details of Rosa's activities in February 1954 were reported by the Internal Security in Puerto Rico to the various intelligence-gathering agencies in Washington, New York, and Chicago. See police reports at AGPR, Fondo: Oficina del Gobernador, Serie: Nacionalistas, Tarea 90-29, Caja 4, pp. 15–34 and 175–76.

42. For references to Lolita Lebrón and her multiple interviews, see the section devoted to her in this book; for details of Gonzalo Lebrón's depositions, see section on Lolita Lebrón; for details about the arrests, see the New York Times, March 2, 1954, "Eisenhower Target for Fanatics," pp. 9, 17; also the New York Times, March 4, 1954, "Four Are Indicted in House Shooting Plot: Plans Bared," pp. 1, 10.

43. Rosa Collazo described the prison sentences, Memorias, pp. 78–79.

44. Ibid.

45. Gurley Flynn, My Life as a Political Prisoner, pp. 24–29; Moskowitz, Phantom Spies: Phantom Justice: How I Survived McCarthyism, pp. 151–65: Memorias, p. 79.

46. Memorias, pp. 79–81.

47. Memorias, ibid.

48. Memorias, ibid.

49. Memorias, ibid.

50. Memorias, p. 82; Gurley Flynn, My Life as a Political Prisoner. Details of the life and works of Claudia Jones are excellently portrayed by Carol Boyce Davies in her book, Left of Karl Marx: The Political Life of Black Communist Claudia Jones (Durham and London: Duke University Press, 2007).

51. Memorias, pp. 81, 83. Lolita Lebrón was released on a presidential pardon after serving twenty-five years of a fifty-six-year sentence.

52. Memorias, pp. 84–85.

53. Memorias, pp. 86-87. The daily diet served in Puerto Rico's prisons during the 1950s was the subject of some discussion in the interviews I conducted with Isabel Rosado Morales and Carmen María Pérez, April 1998.

54. Memorias, pp. 93–96.

55. Memorias, pp. 96–100, 103, 108.

56. Memorias, pp. 111–12. The details about Canales' release from prison were reported by El Mundo, Aug. 24, 1967, "RSV da indulto a Blanca Canales," p. 1; see also the section devoted to Blanca Canales included in this book.

57. Memorias, pp. 111–12.

58. Memorias, ibid.

59. Miñi Seijo's report on the welcoming reception and press conferences following the Nationalists' release in September 1979. Her account was published by the news weekly Claridad, En Rojo Section, (Sept. 28–Oct. 4, 1979), pp. 6–9.

60. Memorias, p. 112; Seijo, Claridad, ibid.

61. Memorias, ibid: Part of Seijo's report includes the remarks made by Oscar Collazo and Lolita Lebrón at the United Nations. (Rafael Cancel Miranda and Irving Flores were not cited in Seijo's article because they went to a meeting organized by Nationalist comrades in another area of Manhattan.)

62. Memorias, p. 118.

63. Memorias, pp. 119–22.

64. Ibid.
65. "Semblanza of Rosa Collazo," given by Oscar Collazo in honor of Rosa's 80th birthday at the Puerto Rican Bar Association in San Juan, Sept. 16, 1984, quoted throughout this study.
66. Details provided by Lydia Collazo.

2. Dolores (Lolita) Lebrón Soto

1. The biographical sketch of Lolita Lebrón presented here is based on a wide array of sources, most of them written in Spanish and which I translated for the benefit of the reader. Many details of her life and political trajectory were culled from interviews she granted at various times, especially those she gave at O'Hare Airport in Chicago and at the United Nations right after her release from prison in September 1979. Other details were obtained from newspaper articles written about her from 1979 to 2010, especially those written by Miñi Seijo for the news weekly *Claridad*. FBI files and surveillance reports compiled by the Puerto Rican Police provide dates and topics of the meetings she attended. The recollections of Rosa Collazo and Rafael Cancel Miranda helped to place Lolita's politics in historical context. One scholarly work which proved useful in tracking the last twenty years of Lolita's life was Ivonne Marín Burgos' master's thesis, "Lolita Lebrón: De la Lucha Armada a la Desobediencia Civil," a project she presented to the Centro de Estudios Avanzados de Puerto Rico y el Caribe, San Juan, Puerto Rico, in 2012. Details of Lebrón's early life were gleaned from an oral interview she granted to journalist Francisco Ribes Tovar in 1974 that he published as *Lolita Lebrón: La prisionera* (New York: Plus Ultra Educational Publishers, 1974). For a more intimate view of Lolita and her family, I turned to the memoir published by Lolita's granddaughter, Irene Vilar, titled *The Ladies' Gallery: A Memoir of Family Secrets* (New York: Vintage Books, 1996). Speeches made in Lebrón's honor at the Colegio de Abogados de Puerto Rico in 2005 and the eulogies that followed her death in 2010 helped me to understand her life within the context of Puerto Rican history.
2. Irene Vilar, *The Ladies' Gallery*, p. 67.
3. Ribes Tovar, *Lolita Lebrón: La Prisionera*, p. 23.
4. Ribes Tovar, ibid. p. 69; for details about the Lares Revolt of 1868, see also Olga Jiménez de Wagenheim, *El Grito de Lares: Sus causas y sus hombres* (San Juan, Puerto Rico: Ediciones Huracán, 1984).
5. Ribes Tovar, ibid. p. 72; Vilar, *The Ladies' Gallery*, p. 70. Ribes Tovar, p. 39.
6. Ribes Tovar, p. 39
7. Details about their brief romance appear in Ribes Tovar, pp. 44, 58–59.
8. The data about Matos Paoli's arrest and imprisonment appeared in *El Imparcial*, Nov. 2–13, 1950. A short biographical entry and photograph of his wife, Isabel Freyre de Matos Paoli, were part of the surveillance records kept by the Puerto Rican Police Department on the Nationalists and can be seen at AGPR, Fondo: Departamento de Justicia, Tarea 90-29, Caja 1.
9. Ribes Tovar, pp. 81–85.
10. The comments made by Lolita's cousin, Luis Sotomayor, were cited by Vilar in *The Ladies' Gallery*, pp. 103-8; the detail about the illegitimacy of Lolita's daughter was provided by Irene Vilar, ibid. p. 72.
11. Irene Vilar, p.72, op. cit. claims Lolita Lebrón left Lares for New York on March 18, 1941 aboard the Marine Tiger. Yet, Mr. Ariel Blondet, researcher of Passenger Lists of Vessels Traveling between Puerto Rico and New York, discovered that a Dolores Lebrón, born in Lares, age 21, left San Juan aboard the ship Coamo and arrived in New York on April 28, 1941. He lists as his source: Year: 1941, Arrival: New York, New York; Microfilm Serial: T 715, 1897-1957; Microfilm Roll: Roll 6541; Line 28, Page, 64.
12. *According to Mr. Blondet, the Marine Tiger did not take passengers from Puerto Rico to New York until June 24, 1946, when she sailed with 929 passengers on board, arriving on June 28.*
13. Details about Lolita's jobs were discussed during the 1974 interview she granted to Ribes

Tovar, pp. 86–93. and mentioned by her sister Aurea Lebrón in an interview with Ivonne Marín Burgos in 2012, which she cited in "Lolita Lebrón; De la Lucha Armada a la Desobediencia Civil," p. 131.

14. The problems of discrimination at work, the move to Chicago, and the marriage to Anderson Pérez were discussed by Lolita during her interview with Ribes Tovar, pp. 94–95.

15. Details about the son Lolita left in Lares were also discussed by her cousin Luis Sotomayor during his own interview with Irene Vilar, p. 108; and by her sister Aurea Lebrón in her interview with Marín Burgos, p. 148.

16. For a detailed discussion of the many Puerto Rican women who belonged to and/or supported the Nationalist Party in New York City and Chicago, see the unpublished master's thesis by Sandra Morales Blanes, titled "La participación de la mujer en el Partido Nacionalista de Puerto Rico (PNPR) en Puerto Rico y los Estados Unidos vista a través de las Carpetas del FBI, 1941–1951," which she presented to the Centro de Estudios Avanzados de Puerto Rico y el Caribe, May 2013. Chapter 2 of that thesis was very valuable in terms of signaling the roles played by Lolita Lebrón and other women in New York.

17. Comments Lolita made to Ribes Tovar, pp. 93–95, and 99–100.

18. Explanations Lolita gave at various times as to her decision to join the Nationalist Junta in New York and to follow the principles outlined by Pedro Albizu Campos. See a portion of an interview cited by researcher Ivonne Marín Burgos, p. 131. Details of Albizu's vision for Puerto Rico were gleaned from his speeches compiled and published by Ivonne Acosta: *La palabra como delito: Los discursos por los que condenaron a Pedro Albizu Campos, 1948–1950* (San Juan, Puerto Rico: Editorial Cultural, 2000). Two of his speeches were translated into English and are included in Wagenheim and Jiménez de Wagenheim, *The Puerto Ricans: A Documentary History*, pp. 185–92.

19. Ribes Tovar, pp. 100, 104; the Catholic conversion of Albizu Campos and the influence of the Irish Republican Army's philosophy on his views were discussed by Juan Antonio Corretjer in his eulogy of Albizu in 1965 and in a pamphlet he published in New York (World View Publishers, 1965) titled *Albizu Campos and the Ponce Massacre*, p. 10; for a concise discussion of the disruptive changes Puerto Ricans experienced in matters of religion during the first four decades of the twentieth century, as the American colonization took hold, see Nélida Agosto Cintrón, *Religión y cambio social en Puerto Rico, 1898-1940* (San Juan, Puerto Rico: Ediciones Huracán, 1996).

20. Lolita's admiration for Albizu's willingness to sacrifice his life was discussed in Ribes Tovar, pp. 104–12. The women I interviewed in 1998 also expressed a similar disposition to sacrifice their lives for their homeland. A good example of their commitment is described in Blanca Canales' 1967 testimony, "La Constitución es la Revolución." (See section devoted to her in this book.)

21. Vilar, p. 8; Lolita's devotion to the Catholic faith was well known. During her 1954 trial, she told the Washington, D.C. court that she had willingly sacrificed herself in order to let the world know about the enslavement of her homeland.

22. Remarks Lolita made to Ribes Tovar, pp. 112–16.

23. The information about Thelma Mielke was reported by Morales Blanes, pp. 125–27.

24. For details of Albizu's life and political evolution, see Marisa Rosado, *Las llamas de la aurora: acercamiento a una biografía de Pedro Albizu Campos* (San Juan: Author's Edition, 1998).

25. For a brief account of Puerto Rico's political goals and accomplishments during the 1940s and '50s, refer to Fernando Picó, *History of Puerto Rico: A Panorama of Its People* (Princeton: Markus Wiener Publishers, 2006), pp. 228–79; for the roles played by the PDP and the last American governor in Puerto Rico, Rexford G. Tugwell, see Tugwell, *The Art of Politics* (New York: Doubleday, 1958), pp. 36, 147–50. See also the work by César J. Ayala and Rafael Bernabe, *Puerto Rico en el siglo Americano: Su historia desde 1898* (San Juan, Puerto Rico: Ediciones Callejón, 2011). For an enlightened discussion of the political developments in the 1940s, see chap. 7 in that work.

26. According to the various comments the four attackers made to the press after they were released from prison in 1979, many of which were cited by Miñi Seijo.

27. Ibid.

28. The Roig letter, dated December 2, 1954, was forwarded by Marco A. Rigau (Aide to Governor Muñoz Marín) to the Secretary of Justice, José Trias Monge, on December 6, 1954. A note attached to the Roig letter stated that "this is the 3rd part" of Gonzalo Lebrón's testimony for he had already sent him the "2nd part," dated November 22, 1954. The document is found in AGPR, Fondo: Departamento de Justicia, Serie: Nacionalistas, Sub-Serie: "Cartas al Gobernador," Tarea 90-29, Caja 4, Item 13. To simplify, the reference will henceforth be cited as Roig's Dec. 2 Letter, followed by the page number.

29. Roig's Dec. 2 Letter, p. 1.

30. Ibid. p. 2.

31. Ibid. pp. 2, 3, 5.

32. Ibid. p. 6.

33. Ibid. pp. 6–7.

34. Ibid. pp. 9–10.

35. Ibid. pp. 10–11; see also Rafael Cancel Miranda's self-published book, Del Cimarrón a los Macheteros (San Juan, 2008), p. 21, and his interview in Claridad, Aug. 5–11, 2010, p. 7.

36. Roig' Dec. 2 Letter, pp. 11–12.

37. Roig's Dec. 2 Letter, p. 12.

38. For details about the United Nation's vote, see Ayala and Bernabe, pp. 246–48.

39. Conclusion based on the revelations made by Gonzalo Lebrón to the Puerto Rican police.

40. Comment Lolita made to Ribes Tovar, p. 93.

41. For the numerous remarks attributed to Lolita Lebrón, see the following articles in the New York Times: "Five Congressmen Shot in House by 3 Puerto Rican Nationalists: Bullets Spray from Gallery," March 2, 1954, p. 1; and "Shooting Blasted a Day of Routine," p. 2, and "Witness Describes Shooting, Capture," p. 3; also see the Washington Post, March 2, 1954, "I Love My Country," Lolita Lebrón's declaration, reprinted with permission in Wagenheim and Jiménez de Wagenheim, The Puerto Ricans: A Documentary History, pp. 238–41. See also articles about the attack and the attackers in San Juan's dailies, El Mundo and El Imparcial, March 2–13, 1954.

42. Cancel Miranda, Interview, Claridad, Aug. 5–11, 2010, p. 7; see also his self-published book, Del Cimarrón a los Macheteros, p. 25; refer to articles in the New York Times and Washington Post articles cited earlier.

43. "Witness Describes Shooting, Capture," New York Times, March 2, 1954, p. 3.

44. Ribes Tovar, p. 137; see also articles cited in note 41.

45. "Sidelight of Shooting," New York Times, March 2, 1954, p. 17; also see "I love My Country," in Wagenheim and Jiménez de Wagenheim, The Puerto Ricans: A Documentary History, pp. 238–41.

46. Cited by Ribes Tovar, p. 137; see also articles in the American press cited earlier.

47. Photographs accompanied the cover stories in the New York Times, El Mundo, and other dailies during the first week of March 1954.

48. "Four Are Indicted in House Shooting: Plots Bared," the New York Times, March 4, 1954, pp. 1, 10.

49. FBI's speculation in "Eisenhower Target for Fanatics Also," NYT, March 2, 1954, pp. 1, 17.

50. "91 Puerto Ricans Rounded Up Here," NYT, March 9, 1954, pp. 1, 21; also "Puerto Rican Fanatics Intended to Slay Ike," The New York Daily News, Sept. 14, 1954, p. 3.

51. Details offered by Lydia Collazo during our interview, April 18, 1998; also see Luis Sotomayor's comments in his interview with Irene Vilar, The Ladies' Gallery, pp. 103–8.

52. "Regrets Voiced by Muñoz Marín," the New York Times, March 2, 1954, p. 14; for an enlightened discussion of the enactment and effects of Puerto Rico's Sedition Act, Law #53, see Ivonne Acosta's treatise, La Mordaza: Puerto Rico, 1948–1957 (Río Piedras, Puerto Rico:

Editorial Edil, 1989); see also her equally well-argued case, "The Smith Act Goes to San Juan": La Mordaza, 1948–1957," in *Puerto Rico Under Colonial Rule: Political Persecution and the Quest for Human Rights*, ed. by Ramón Bosque-Pérez and José Javier Colón Morera, (Albany, New York: SUNY Press, 2006), pp. 59–66.

53. Details of Lolita Lebrón's defense offered by her lawyer, Conrad Lynn, during an interview he granted to Irene Vilar, pp. 95–96.

54. Details of the trial were provided by Lolita to Rives Tovar, pp. 179–90.

55. Ribes Tovar, p. 193.

56. Ibid.

57. Ibid.

58. For details about Lolita's "mystic" visions, see Ribes Tovar, p. 93. The topic of her son's death was discussed later, according to Vilar, pp. 259–63.

59. "Island Partisans Pictured at Trial," *New York Times*, Sept. 9, 1954, p. 18; also see "Revolt Trial Jury Told of D.C. Shooting," *Daily Mirror*, Sept. 9, 1954, and Ribes Tovar, pp. 177–81.

60. Lolita's comments about her ordeal in prison were extracted from the transcribed text of her (October 7, 1979) radio interview, cited by Marín Burgos, p. 153. The comments about her rape and torture in prison were cited by Vilar, p. 287.

61. According to Rosa Collazo's memoir.

62. Ibid. Also Vilar, pp. 258–68.

63. Collazo, ibid.

64. Lolita's refusal to apply for parole concurred with what other leaders of the Nationalist Party did or prescribed. She viewed herself as a political prisoner and was thus prepared to serve her sentence and said so to the court. See Vilar, p. 158.

65. The photographs of Lolita Lebrón captured by the Puerto Rican press show her surrounded by thousands of compatriots at her daughter's funeral. Stories about Gladys Mirna's funeral appeared in the local dailies *El Nuevo Día* and the *San Juan Star*, March 3, 1977.

66. News of Lolita's refusal to be released before her colleagues was reported by *El Nuevo Día* (April 24, 1978) and cited by Marín Burgos, pp. 158–59.

67. Reports of the long Puerto Rican campaign to get the Nationalists released from prison appeared in the *San Juan Star*, May 1, 1967, *El Nuevo Día*, July 23, 1975, and *Claridad*, Jan. 27, 1976.

68. The receptions and press conferences attended by the four in Chicago and New York City were covered by journalist Miñi Seijo for the news weekly *Claridad*. The reception they were given in Puerto Rico was covered also by *El Nuevo Día*, Sept. 13, 1979. For a touching account of the love with which the four were received at every turn, see the section on Rosa Collazo included in this book.

69. The socioeconomic changes Puerto Rico underwent between the 1940s and 1970s have been well studied by numerous scholars. What has been less well studied is the topic of the PDP government's abuse of power during the 1950s. The best accounts of this topic are contained in a pioneering work edited by Ramón Bosque Pérez and José Javier Colón Morera, titled *Puerto Rico Under Colonial Rule: Political Persecution and the Quest for Human Rights* (Albany, New York: State University Press, 2006). Bosque Pérez's overview of the issue, "Political Persecution against Puerto Rican Anti-Colonial Activists in the Twentieth Century," (pp. 13-37) is a must read for anyone unfamiliar with the topic of human rights violations in Puerto Rico. To better understand the extent of the violations of civil rights issues during that period, see the works included in Part I of the same cited book. Also a must read is the seminal study, though this is much harder to find, by David M. Helfeld, "Discrimination for Political Beliefs and Associations," published by the *Revista del Colegio de Abogados*, vol. 25, no. 1 (Nov. 1964), pp. 5-276. I secured a copy of Helfeld's work, thanks to the diligence of Professor Norma Rodríguez Roldán, who located the journal at the University of Puerto Rico's Law Library.

70. Information gleaned from many scholarly works. For a review at a glance, see the work of Fernando Picó, and the one by Ayala and Bernabe. The bookmobile provided books for

rural children in Puerto Rico (including the author of this book).

71. The NPP elections of 1968 and beyond were covered by the local press on a daily basis. For details about the evolution of the annexationist movement in Puerto Rico, see Edgardo Meléndez, *Puerto Rico's Statehood Movement* (Westport, Conn.: Greenwood Press, 1988).

72. For details about the FBI, its collaboration with the Puerto Rican police, and the tactics these agencies used against many Puerto Rican dissidents from the 1950s to 1971, see the pioneer work of Carmen Gautier Mayoral and Teresa Blanco Stahl, titled "Documentos Secretos del FBI, 1960–1971," in Ramón Bosque Pérez and José Javier Colón Morera, eds., *Las carpetas: Persecución política y derechos civiles en Puerto Rico* (Río Piedras, Puerto Rico: Centro para la Investigación y Promoción de los Derechos Civiles, 1997), pp. 255–97. For details about the lingering persecution since the 1970s, see the works included in Part II in Bosque Pérez and Colón Morera in: *Puerto Rico Under Colonial Rule*, pp. 83–149. For other details about the activities of COINTELPRO, see Luis Nieves Falcón, *Un siglo de represión política en Puerto Rico, 1898–1998* (San Juan: Ediciones Puerto, 2009).

73. Bosque Pérez, "Political Persecution . . .," in *Puerto Rico Under Colonial Rule*, pp. 13–37. The case was the subject of a Civil Rights Commission investigation. To review the documents later made public, see Comisión de Derechos Civiles. 1989. "Informe sobre discrimen y persecución por razones políticas: La práctica gubernamental de mantener listas, ficheros y expedientes de ciudadanos por razón de su ideología política" (CDC-028. San Juan: Comisión de Derechos Civiles, 1989).

74. Cited by Marín Burgos, p. 193.

75. Cited by Marín Burgos, p. 196.

76. Reported by *El Nuevo Día*, April 27, 1997.

77. Reported by *Claridad*, May 2–8, 1997, p. 5.

78. The participation of Rubén Berríos in the struggles of Culebra and Vieques against the U.S. Navy was reported by the Puerto Rican press at the time. For a scholarly account of Vieques' struggle against the U.S. Navy, see Katherine T. McCaffrey, *Military Power and Popular Protest: The U.S. Navy in Vieques, Puerto Rico* (New Brunswick, N.J.: Rutgers University Press, 2002).

79. Ibid. For a lengthier discussion of Lolita Lebrón's participation in the Vieques struggle, see Marín Burgos, pp. 212–15. The Navy's failure to clean up the island remains an environmental hazard.

80. Lolita Lebrón was one of several Puerto Rican women honored in September 2005 at the Puerto Rican Bar Association in San Juan. Marín Burgos, ibid.

81. The portion of Cancel Miranda's testimony included here was read at the honoring ceremony and later included in his book, *Del Cimarrón a los Macheteros*, p. 25.

82. Lolita Lebrón's death, funeral procession, and the tributes paid to her by many Puerto Rican leaders, including Rubén Berríos, were reported in *El Nuevo Día*, Aug. 2, 2010, p. 8.

3. Carmen Dolores Otero de Torresola

1. Photos of Carmen Torresola's arrest were published in San Juan by the news daily *El Mundo* on Nov. 4, 5, 6, 1950, pp. 1, 16. One of the photos (Nov. 6, p. 5) shows Torresola being escorted to the Women's House of Detention by Secret agent Albert Whitaker. The information published in San Juan was taken from the one filed by the United Press. According to an article in *El Mundo*, Nov. 4, Torresola was one of seven Nationalists who had been interrogated by a New York Grand Jury on Nov. 3. The charges against her were summarized by follow-up articles in *El Mundo* (Nov. 7, pp. 1, 3 and 5, 50). Rosa Collazo's comments about Torresola's incarceration appear in *Memorias de Rosa Collazo*, published after her death by her daughter Lydia Collazo (San Juan, Puerto Rico, 1993).

2. Collazo, *Memorias*, Ibid.

3. The I.S. report cited here was dated Feb. 22, 1954, and was sent to the FBI office in San Juan by I.S. director Capt. Benigno Soto and can be obtained in AGPR, Fondo: Departa-

mento de Justicia, Serie: Nacionalistas, Tarea 90-29, Caja 8, Item 14. The FBI's Quarterly Report can be read in Puerto Rico, Capitol Library, "Carpetas del FBI," Serie: Nacionalistas, Sub-Serie: 32, vol. 38, Doc. 100-3-5233.

4. Details of Torresola's second arrest were summarized in an article in *El Imparcial*, Dec. 3, 1954, p. 14. A copy of her indictment (for subversive activities) can be obtained in AGPR, Departamento de Justicia, Nacionalistas, Tarea 90-29, Caja 11, Item 11. Details about the Alderson prison are provided in the sections devoted to Rosa Collazo and Blanca Canales in this book.

5. Collazo, *Memorias*, ibid.

6. See I.S. report by Capt. Benigno Soto, Feb. 22, 1954; Miñi Seijo, Interview with Carmen Dolores Otero Cruz de Avilés published in *Claridad, En Rojo Section*, June 2–8, 1978, p. 4.

7. Miñi Seijo, Interview with Carmen Dolores Otero, ibid.

Part IV: Brief Accounts of Other Women Arrested in Puerto Rico

1. Details about Mills Rosa were culled from various sources. The data about her 1950 arrest was reported as part of a summary of her second arrest in March 1954 and can be found in AGPR, Fondo: Departamento de Justicia, Serie: Nacionalistas, Tarea 90-29, Caja 19, Item 1, and Caja 10, Item 13f, and Caja 25, "Teoría del Pueblo," 1954. Details about her work with the Nationalist Party in Puerto Rico and her sojourn in New York City were reported by the local Internal Security division and the FBI office in San Juan, which can be found at the Puerto Rico Capitol Library, "Carpetas del FBI," Sub-Serie 32, vol. 39, Doc. 100-3-4951. See also the testimonies offered by undercover agents during her trial about her attendance of various Nationalist activities, in AGPR, Serie: Nacionalistas, Tarea 90-29, Caja 8, Item 15b (a series of police accounts about her and other Nationalists). The charges brought against her appear in AGPR, ibid. Caja 25, "Teoría del Pueblo ..."

2. AGPR, ibid. Conclusion based on my review of the Vega Alta prison logs.

3. AGPR, Ibid. Also an FBI report filed by the SAC San Juan on March 5, 1954, offers great details about a meeting he attended at the governor's office where the impending arrests of the Nationalists the following day were discussed. Though Juana Mills is not listed by Ché Paralitici, his book is a great resource for anyone looking for brief accounts of the Puerto Ricans who were imprisoned for their political beliefs during the twentieth century. For details, see *Sentencia impuesta: 100 años de encarcelamientos por la independencia de Puerto Rico* (San Juan: Ediciones Puerto, 2004), pp. 101-81.

4. AGPR, ibid. Also Tarea 90-29, see Caja 19, Item 1, "Report" by police officer Manuel G. Urrutia.

5. AGPR, Ibid. Also Tarea 90-29, see Caja 24, Item 11. According to a letter from the Secretary of the District Court of Arecibo, Alejandro Quirós, three men had posted bail on Mills' behalf in June 1954. They were: Isabelo Díaz Maldonado, barrio Monacillos, Río Piedras; Narciso López González, Calle Pesante #222, Santurce; and Nicolás Torres Díaz, a resident of Puerto Nuevo, Hato Rey.

6. For details about the sentencing of Mills and others in Arecibo, May 31, 1955, see the report by Alejandro Quirós in AGPR, ibid. Tarea 90-29, Caja 20, Item 13f; also Caja 21, Item 24.

7. The reports of Mills, activities during the 1960s appear in Ruth M. Reynolds' dossier #1340, Doc. 000129, located in Box 48 of "The Ruth Reynolds Papers," Centro de Estudios Puertorriqueños Archives, Hunter College, Manhattan. The 1962 report is included in Emily Vélez de Vando's dossier #2220, archived also at the Centro Archives, Box 1, Folder 18, Doc. 00018.

8. Details about Ojeda's Nationalist activities and arrests were located in AGPR, Nacionalistas, Tarea 90-29, Caja 8, Items 14 and 15b; also in Caja 19, Item 11, and Caja 24, Item 14.
9. For details of the sentencing of May 31, 1955, see AGPR, ibid. Caja 19, Item 11.
10. Details of her 1954 arrest are also found in AGPR, ibid. Caja 25, Items 14, 15.
11. According to Pedro Albizu Campos' FBI file #105-11898, Section 14, p. 31, Ojeda "was convicted on February 8, 1955, for one violation count of Puerto Rico's Sedition Act, Law #53 and freed on bond in August 1955, pending appeal." Another note in the same FBI file reported that in January 1956 she was seen delivering packages to the state penitentiary for Albizu and others. An FBI message of April 26, 1956 (p. 72), reported that Ojeda and Albizu's half-sister, Ana María Campos, had visited Albizu at the Presbyterian Hospital in Condado, Santurce.
12. The information about Ramona Padilla and her son Ernesto Negrón was published by reporter Peggy Ann Bliss in the *San Juan Star*: "Naranjito Mother, Son Tell the True Story," Oct. 30, 2000, pp. 4, 6. For a detailed discussion of the role played by Ñin Negrón in the Naranjito events during the Nationalist uprising, see Miñi Seijo's book, *La insurrección Nacionalista en Puerto Rico, 1950* (Río Piedras: Editorial Edil, 1989), chap. 13.
13. Bliss, "Naranjito, Mother, Son Tell the True Story."
14. Ibid.
15. Ibid.
16. Angelina Torresola's age was reported by Heriberto Marín's death notice placed on Facebook on September 7, 2015. The information about her siblings was uncovered during the research process for the various biographical essays included in this book.
17. The surveillance accounts about Angelina Torresola were reported by Puerto Rican undercover agents and FBI men stationed in San Juan. Other information was filed by FBI censors in Pittsburgh, Pennsylvania, where Angelina's letters to Blanca Canales were read and translated into English. Copies of those letters were then sent to FBI headquarters in Washington, D.C., and to three regional offices: San Juan, New York, and Chicago. The reference of Angelina's letters is cited in the section devoted to Blanca Canales in this book.
18. Copies of Angelina's arrest orders can be reviewed in AGPR, Fondo: Departamento de Justicia, Serie: Nacionalistas, Tarea 90-29, Caja 21, Item 11a-g; also in Caja 8, Item 15b, which contains a photograph of her arrest.
19. The 1954 trial in Arecibo has been documented at length in other sections of this book. For details about Angelina Torresola's sentencing and transfer to the prison in Vega Alta, see AGPR, ibid., Tarea 90-29, Caja 25, Items 5, 14, 15. For details about her one-day stay in Vega Alta prison, see AGPR, Fondo: Departamento de Justicia: Serie: Escuela Industrial Para Mujeres, Tarea 60-A-19, Caja 9.
20. Reports of her activities were filed by the Internal Division of Puerto Rico's Police Department and the FBI agents stationed in San Juan. Comments about her devotion to her sister Doris and Pedro Albizu Campos were made by Heriberto Marín.
21. Internal Security and FBI reports cited. Comments made by former cell mates: Isabel Rosado, Interview, 1998; Ruth M. Reynolds, Interviews with Blanca Vázquez, and by Heriberto Marín.
22. According to a death notice placed on Facebook by Heriberto Marín Torres, September 7, 2015.
23. Information about Monserrate Valle and her imprisonment in Arecibo was provided by Isabel Rosado, Interview, April 1998.
24. Housing details of Leonides Díaz, Juanita Ojeda, and Monserrate Valle in the Arecibo prison were discussed by Ruth M. Reynolds during one of her interviews.
25. Reynolds, Interview, ibid.

About the Author

Dr. Olga Jiménez de Wagenheim is Professor Emerita in History, Rutgers University, Newark Campus, where she taught 27 years and where she received the Outstanding Teacher of the Year Award (1991), the Humanitarian Award (1998) and many others.

She has a Ph. D in Latin American and Caribbean History from Rutgers University (1981), an M.A. in Latin American History from the State University of New York at Buffalo (1971), and a B.A. in History and Education from Inter American University, San Juan, Puerto Rico (1970), where she graduated Magna Cum Laude and won the Salvador Brau History Prize.

Dr. Jiménez de Wagenheim has published several books and numerous articles on Puerto Rico and Puerto Ricans. Among her books are: *Puerto Rico: An Interpretive History From Pre-Columbian Times to 1900* (Markus Wiener Pub., 1998), *Puerto Rico's Revolt for Independence: El Grito de Lares* (Westview Press, 1984), *El Grito de Lares: sus causas y sus hombres* (Huracan, 1984), and co-edited with Kal Wagenheim, *The Puerto Ricans: A Documentary History* (Praeger, 1973, Markus Wiener, 2013).

She has received several fellowships, including a Fulbright Fellowship to Argentina (1991); Honored Member of Phi Beta Kappa (2001); a Ford Foundation Fellowship (1973–76); two grants from the National Endowment for the Humanities (NEH) and several others from state and local agencies for her Oral History Project on the Latino community of NJ.

Since 1999 she has been actively volunteering at the Newark Public Library, where she co-founded the New Jersey Hispanic Research and Information Center (NJHRIC). The Center consists of three components: the Sala Hispanoamericana, the Hispanic Research Center, and the Puerto Rican Community Archives. The Center's mission is to rescue, document and preserve the legacy of the Latino community of New Jersey, a mission that often requires, among other tasks, tape-recording the stories of members of the various communities. To support the Center's work she founded in 2001 a community group, Friends of the HRIC. In addition to her years of work at the Newark Public Library in the creation and development of NJHRIC she collaborates with various community-based groups as advisor to historical rescue projects. She has also appeared on several radio and television programs over the years.

Dr. Jiménez de Wagenheim was born in Camuy, Puerto Rico, is married to Kal Wagenheim and has two grown children: David Roberto and María Dolores.

Related Books by Markus Wiener Publishers

American Colonialism in Puerto Rico
by Efrén Rivera Ramos
"Provocative, extremely well documented, and innovative."
—*El Nuevo Día*
PB ISBN 978-1-55876-410-1

Battleship Vieques: Puerto Rico from World War II to the Korean War
by César J. Ayala and José L. Bolívar
"The authors masterfully weave together the political, economic, military,
and personal historical dimensions that have entwined the U.S. and Puerto
Rico in the small island of Veiques."—*Choice*
HC ISBN 978-1-55876-537-5   PB ISBN 978-1-55876-538-2

Clemente! The Enduring Legacy
by Kal Wagenheim
"Wagenheim, . . . an ex-ballplayer and sports writer, is the right man to
perform the essentially serious task of bringing the real Roberto Clemente
closer to many fans."—*Publishers Weekly*
PB ISBN 978-1-55876-527-6

Cuentos: Stories from Puerto Rico
compiled and edited by Kal Wagenheim
A bilingual anthology of "stories . . . told by writers of acute perception
and strong powers of invention."—*Library Journal*
PB ISBN 978-1-55876-478-1

History of Puerto Rico: A Panorama of Its People
by Fernando Picó
Outstanding Academic Title of the Year. "Excellent . . . inordinately rich."
—*Choice*
"Picó is the leading historian of the island."
—*Hispanic American Historical Review*
HC ISBN 978-1-55876-370-8   PB ISBN 978-1-55876-371-5

**A New Deal for the Tropics: Puerto Rico during the Depression Era,
1932-1935**
by Manuel R. Rodríguez
HC ISBN 978-1-55876-517-7   PB ISBN 978-1-55876-518-4

The Pond [La Charca: Puerto Rico's 19th-Century Masterpiece]
by Manuel Zeno-Gandía
"The first English translation of a classic of Latin American fiction . . .
depicting life in [19th-century] Puerto Rico."—*The Nation*
PB ISBN 978-1-55876-092-9

Puerto Rico 1898: The War after the War
by Fernando *Picó*
"[The publisher is] to be congratulated for making available this important work, along with other first-rate works in Puerto Rican and Caribbean history."—*Hispanic American Historical Review*
HC ISBN 978-1-55876-326-5   PB ISBN 978-1-55876-327-2

Puerto Rico: An Interpretive History from Pre-Columbian Times to 1900
by Olga Jiménez de Wagenheim
"A work of substantive scholarship and meticulous research."
—*Midwest Book Review*
HC ISBN 978-1-55876-121-6   PB ISBN 978-1-55876-122-3

Puerto Rico Inside and Out: Changes and Continuities
by Fernando *Picó*
"An unforgettable glimpse into the extraordinary diversity of cultures that compose Puerto Rico."—*Midwest Book Review*
HC ISBN 978-1-55876-481-1   PB ISBN 978-1-55876-482-8

The Puerto Ricans: A Documentary History
edited by Kal Wagenheim and Olga Jiménez de Wagenheim
"An essential source book for a better understanding of the Puerto Ricans."
—*The New York Times*
HC ISBN 978-1-55876-563-4   PB ISBN 978-1-55876-564-1

Slave Revolts in Puerto Rico
by Guillermo A. Baralt
"Fascinating reading that makes us witnesses of an episode in our history that was both great and tragic."—*El Nuevo Día*
HC ISBN 978-1-55876-462-0   PB ISBN 978-1-55876-463-7

Taíno Revival: Critical Perspectives on Puerto Rican Identity and Cultural Politics
edited by Gabriel Haslip-Viera
"An exciting and unique contribution to Caribbean Studies."
—*Hispanic American Historical Review*
HC ISBN 978-1-55876-258-9   PB ISBN 978-1-55876-259-6

Women in San Juan: 1820-1868
by Félix V. Matos Rodríguez
"Meticulous research . . . based on extensive archival work."
—*Hispanic American Historical Review*
PB ISBN 978-1-55876-283-1

CPSIA information can be obtained
at www.ICGtesting.com
Printed in the USA
LVHW051136050523
746045LV00001B/1